THE ECONOMIC DEVELOPMENT OF *Libya*

*Report of a Mission Organized by the
International Bank for Reconstruction and Development
at the Request of
the Government of Libya*

THE ECONOMIC DEVELOPMENT
OF LIBYA

PUBLISHED FOR The International Bank for Reconstruction and Development
BY The Johns Hopkins Press, Baltimore

THE MISSION

P. S. Narayan Prasad,	Chief of Mission
T. D. Ahmad,	Adviser on Public Health
D. S. Ferguson,	Adviser on Water Resources
Kurt Krapf,	Adviser on Tourism
Habib A. Kurani,	Adviser on Education
Warren H. Leonard,	Adviser on Agricultural Production
Franz Lütolf,	Economist
W. Sidney McCann,	Mineralogist
G. M. McKelvie,	Adviser on Transport and Public Utilities
Zuhayr Mikdashi,	Research Assistant and Interpreter
G. C. W. Chr. Tergast,	Agricultural Economist
Wybold van Warmelo,	Adviser on Industry and Handicrafts
E. Peter Wright,	Chief Economist
Mrs. Liselotte Boesch,	Secretary
Miss Mary Sfeir,	Secretary

PREFACE

This is the report of an economic survey mission to Libya, which was organized by the International Bank for Reconstruction and Development at the request of the Libyan Government, and with the help of other international agencies. The main task assigned to the mission was to appraise the progress of Libya's economic development since Independence and to propose, in a form as specific and as practical as possible, appropriate targets for further development over the next five to ten years.

The mission consisted of thirteen members representing nine different nationalities. The Mission Chief and the Chief Economist, both members of the Bank's regular staff, paid a preliminary visit to Libya in November-December 1958, and the main mission arrived in the country in January 1959, remaining there until early in April. After leaving Libya the mission reassembled at the Bank's headquarters in Washington to prepare its report.

During their stay in Libya the members traveled extensively in the three provinces, visited all the important development projects and had many discussions with ministers and officials of the federal and provincial governments, with the National Bank of Libya, with private bankers, businessmen and farmers, and with representatives of the foreign aid agencies. The Mission Chief had the honor of being received by His Majesty the King on two occasions.

The present report, after reviewing the progress made in recent years and discussing the new long-term possibilities opened up by the discovery of oil, puts forward specific recommendations for a development program to be undertaken during the next five years and discusses the steps which will have to be taken if this and subsequent programs are to be carried through successfully.

In drawing up this program the mission proceeded on the assumption that, while the discovery of oil, a potentially rich new natural resource, holds out the long-term prospect of establishing a prosperous economy, the petroleum industry is unlikely in itself, either directly or indirectly, to provide employment and wages for more than a small fraction of the Libyan people. The majority must therefore look to other occupations for their livelihood.

At present, agriculture and the processing of agricultural products appear to be the activities for which Libya is best adapted, given the small size of the population, the location of the country, the comparative underutilization of available land and the lack of industrial resources. Fisheries and tourism also hold out potentialities for development and, over the longer period, probably some petrochemical industries. To build up this more prosperous and balanced economy it is necessary during the next five years to advance the abilities and skills of the Libyan people; to secure to the agriculturists individual rights in land; to provide improved government services to agriculture; to extend water and soil conservation work; to use the available water resources wisely; to provide better facilities for credit, marketing, cold storage and transport. If these promising possibilities are to become a reality, education and technical training have to be accorded a high priority and government must be better organized.

The mission has felt it necessary to say a good deal in the report about the problems involved in adapting the present organization of government in Libya to the requirements of efficient and rapid economic growth. The suggestions made for strengthening the authority of the federal government and for securing better coordination between the center and the provinces in the planning and execution of development programs spring from the conviction that major changes in government organization are absolutely vital if Libya is to take full advantage of the great opportunities opened up by the discovery of oil.

The main report contains all the mission's principal conclusions and recommendations. Supplementary information is included in a series of annexes.

In transmitting the report to the Government of Libya, the President of the Bank noted that since the Executive Directors and management customarily do not review the recommendations of missions in detail, the report as transmitted represented the views of the mission rather than positive recommendations of the Bank. The letter added, however, that the Bank believed that the findings of the report deserved the most careful consideration and discussion. Similarly, while other international agencies were given an opportunity to comment on the portions of the report of particular interest to them, responsibility for the recommendations of the report is to be regarded as that of the mission alone.

ACKNOWLEDGEMENT

The mission wishes to acknowledge the generous cooperation extended to it in all aspects of its work by officials of the federal and provincial governments, by members of the various foreign missions in Libya, in particular by the Resident Representative of the United Nations, and by the many private citizens with whom the mission had occasion to consult. Among the officials, the mission wishes specifically to acknowledge the assistance of Dr. A. N. Aneizi, and of Mr. R. J. Cunnell, Governor and Deputy Governor respectively of the National Bank of Libya, who together with their staffs acted as liaison officers with unfailing effort.

POLITICAL TERMS

A provincial governor in Libya, who is the direct representative of His Majesty the King, is known as the *Wali*. The federal Cabinet is known as the Council of Ministers, and the equivalent in the provincial government is the Executive Council. Provincial Ministers are known as *Nazirs* and their departments as *Nazirates*.

CURRENCY EQUIVALENT

The currency unit in Libya is the Libyan pound which is exchangeable at par with the pound sterling and is thus equivalent to 2.80 U. S. dollars. All conversions have been made at this rate in the report. The Libyan pound is divided into piasters (100 piasters $=$ £L 1) and milliemes (1,000 milliemes $=$ £L 1).

UNITS OF MEASUREMENT

The metric system is in use in Libya and has generally been used in this report for measuring weights, distances and dimensions. All references to tons are to metric tons, except where otherwise stated. The Libyan financial year runs from April to March, the agricultural year from October to September.

PRICES

All figures of past expenditures in this report are in terms of the actual prices that prevailed at the time. Estimates and projections of future expenditures are notionally in terms of constant 1958/59 prices, i.e., no allowance has been made for possible increases in Libyan or world prices above the levels ruling at the time of the mission's visit.

x

TABLE OF CONTENTS

STATISTICAL APPENDIX

ANNEXES

LIST OF MAPS

ANNUAS

LIST OF MAPS

THE MAIN REPORT

The Mission's Task

The main task assigned to the mission was to appraise the progress achieved in Libya's economic development since Independence and to propose, in a form as specific and practical as possible, appropriate targets for Libyan economic development over the next five to ten years. In carrying out this task the mission was asked to indicate not merely the investments needed to achieve the targets suggested, but also the legal and institutional changes required.

A Dual Economy

Libya is a good example of what is sometimes called a "dual economy." Most Libyans still lead a very simple life, their diet is plain, their wants are limited, they have little knowledge of twentieth-century technology, tribal traditions are strong. This section of the Libyan population has been little touched by all the development that has taken place in the past fifty years. The majority (perhaps 200,000 workers) till the land or graze their livestock on the fringes of the desert, largely consuming what they produce, supplying most of their own needs. For shelter they have a low one or two-roomed house, a tent, a tin-shack or a cave; for clothes home-spun woollen barracanes; for transport a camel, horse or donkey. The property of a family or a *kabila* may be considerable, but their living standards generally remain austere. Such amenities as electricity and running water are practically unknown.

Increasingly men from the country are drifting to towns, sometimes taking their families with them, sometimes leaving them behind. Here they earn money and buy more goods, but they do not necessarily eat better, and housing conditions are frequently worse than in the country, particularly in the shanty towns of Tripoli and Benghazi. There is much underemployment on the land and in the towns, where many occupations are seasonal. But there is little involuntary unemployment, and for many jobs labor is hard to get.

The other face of the economy is to be seen in the city of Tripoli,

3

and to a lesser extent in Benghazi, Sebha and some of the other towns, with their modern villas, brightly lit streets, shops, cinemas, restaurants and gas stations. It is to be seen in the large and prosperous farms in Tripolitania owned and managed mostly by Italians and by a few foreign firms, but some also by Libyans, who are usually merchants as well. It is to be seen in the large number of government offices and other public buildings, fine new schools and hospitals, modern roads and other public works.

This modern sector of the economy is not a new thing. It was developed by the Italians before World War II and since the war it has been revived and supported by foreign aid and foreign military expenditures, which are presently equal to over one-third of the Libyan national product. A relatively large number of foreigners are still to be seen in Libya, some of them permanent residents like the 40,000 Italians in Tripolitania, others living there on a more temporary basis—foreign troops, technical assistance personnel working under the United Nations and United States aid programs, oil company employees and so forth. These people enjoy a much higher standard of living than the average Libyan, and a sizeable part of the Libyan economy is geared to serving their needs. An estimated 20,000-25,000 Libyans are directly employed by foreign governments (working mainly at the military bases) and oil companies. Many others work in industries and service trades which depend largely on foreign demand, or on demand financed by foreign aid—building and construction, for example, road haulage, the catering trade, car hire firms and important segments of wholesale and retail distribution.

The growth of a comparatively advanced and prosperous element on the edges of what is still predominantly a primitive rural community has inevitably created difficult problems of adjustment. Opportunities have been provided for a minority, albeit a rapidly increasing minority, of Libyans to enjoy a much higher standard of consumption. By no means all who have had the opportunity have wanted to take it—a fact which helps to explain the apparently high level of domestic savings in Libya today. But some have, and the results are to be seen in the rising Libyan demand for imported foods, western-style clothes, wrist watches, cameras, bicycles, radio sets, factory-made furniture, motor cars, modern houses and apartments and so forth. Quite a number of Libyans are now earning salaries and wages comparable with those earned by their counterparts in European countries, and more and more people are dissatisfied with the jobs they have got and are looking for something better. Many are leaving the countryside in search of work in the towns or in the desert with the oil companies, and land is going out of cultivation for lack of labor (particularly in the Fezzan). A new middle class is growing up in the cities of Tripoli and Benghazi composed of office workers, government officials, teachers and the like; and an increasing number of young people are going to secondary schools and universities. There is a restlessness amongst this younger generation of Libyans and a need to canalize their energies into constructive work.

The process of change is being hastened by the discovery of oil. Plans are already being made for the exploitation of the oilfields located in the Sirte desert both in Cyrenaica and in Tripolitania. A pipeline has been ordered, surveys are being conducted to determine the best points for the shipment of the oil, and one company has undertaken to construct a refinery in Libya. Meanwhile large sums continue to be spent on exploration by the 16 companies which have secured concessions in the country, and barely a month passes without news of fresh discoveries. Clearly big new developments lie ahead. The mission is keenly aware of what this can mean to a nation which has hitherto participated only on a small scale in the material benefits resulting from modern technology, and which is naturally anxious to free itself from its present dependence on foreign support.

Many of the changes that are taking place are healthy. More Libyans are traveling about inside and outside the country than ever before. New tastes are being developed and new wants are being discovered, particularly by those who work in close contact with people from other countries and those who have been abroad to study. All this is good for economic growth. Up to a point it may also be good that people are drifting away from unremunerative rural occupations to better paid jobs in oil development, industry and the service trades. But there are great disadvantages in too uneven a distribution of income and wealth; in a minority of Libyans getting rich while the mass of the population remains very poor; in too sharp a division between the modern and the traditional sectors of the economy; in more people leaving the land than there is any hope of finding jobs for in the towns; in the sense of frustration that will be engendered if the results of development fail to match up to expectations.

Impact of Oil Discoveries

These considerations have weighed heavily with the mission in drawing up the recommendations for economic development that are set out in this report. Oil revenues may now enable Libya to become economically self-supporting within the foreseeable future and at the same time to enjoy a steadily increasing income. Nevertheless, as the experience of other countries has shown, the discovery of oil does not provide an easy or a complete solution to the problem of economic development. It is particularly important that the wave of optimism which naturally accompanies an oil boom should not be allowed to divert attention from the pressing need to improve the lot of the rural population, who will not necessarily share in the new prosperity any more than they have shared in the rise in national income which has taken place during the past five years.

It is much too early yet to say exactly what the eventual impact of oil development on the Libyan economy will be. Clearly it will mean more money for the government, although it is likely to be several years yet before there is any *large* increase in oil revenues. It will also mean new jobs for Libyans, some of them with high salaries, on the payrolls of oil companies or in other operations associated with oil. But for the reasons given in Chapter 4 we doubt whether, even allowing for the construction of a refinery and possibly the establishment later on of new industries based on oil, the direct employment given by the companies and their contractors will be equal to more than about 5 percent of Libya's total labor force. As for indirect employment, the expenditures of the oil companies in Libya will have a "multiplier" effect in stimulating demand and creating jobs in industries and trades which can cater to the needs of the companies and their employees (the construction and transport industries and the hotel trade, for example). This effect is being felt already, and it is likely to be most pronounced during the next few years when exploration and development are proceeding simultaneously. Thereafter both the direct and indirect employment created by the oil industry could well decline somewhat, creating difficult problems of adjustment. The scale of any such adjustment would depend in part on the level of foreign military expenditures in Libya, which in recent years have contributed a great deal to the expansion of the economy.

Human Resources for Development

This report is concerned primarily with the next five years—the period, that is, before we expect any big flow of oil revenues to the government. During this period, as the mission sees it, attention should be concentrated on the problems that have to be tackled in developing the other sectors of the economy—problems which existed prior to the discovery of oil, and which may not be any easier to solve now than they were before. These problems can be grouped under two main headings. First, there are the problems connected with the physical character of the country—the sparse and irregular rainfall, the shortage of water and soils impoverished by centuries of neglect; the paucity of known mineral resources apart from oil; and the dispersal of a small population over a very large area, which calls for exceptionally heavy per capita expenditure on transport and communications and greatly complicates the business of distribution and marketing. Second, and more difficult to resolve quickly, there are the human problems arising out of Libya's past history and the lack of opportunities given to the Libyan people to acquire education and experience in self-government and in modern techniques of production.

It cannot be too strongly emphasized that economic development does not depend simply on how much money is invested in farms, factories, roads, harbors, schools, hospitals, public buildings and so forth. It depends also on the kind of social and political institutions a country has, on the aims and policies of the government, on the education and training of the people and on the value attached by all classes of society to the benefits accruing from increased production. That is why we have felt it necessary to comment at some length on the human, institutional and administrative problems involved before entering into a detailed discussion of economic programs and policies.

Already, as the mission sees it, Libya's capacity to invest money fruitfully in productive schemes is being limited by lack of experience in administration and planning, by weaknesses in government organization and by shortages of trained personnel. Very few Libyans have yet had time to acquire advanced technical and professional skills or training in administration; there is an acute shortage of skilled craftsmen, artisans and intermediate technicians; and Libyan farmers are generally without the knowledge and experience needed to make good use of the capital placed at their disposal. The immediate need is therefore to accord the highest priority to a well-conceived program of education and training at all levels, while at the same time creating a more effective organization for the planning and execution of economic projects and policies. Much will be said in this report on both these subjects.

Education and Training

At the time of Independence, more than 90 percent of the population were illiterate and only a handful of Libyans had been given an opportunity to study at a university or to qualify for a recognized profession. Although facilities for education in Libya have since been greatly expanded, and in addition some hundreds of young Libyans have been sent abroad for training, there has not yet been sufficient time to produce more than a tiny fraction of the skills required. Education must therefore occupy a prominent place in any plans for the future development of the country's resources. The justification for giving the highest priority now to this aspect of development is greatly strengthened by the prospect of large oil revenues materializing within five to ten years.

An educational program cannot, however, be contained within a period of five or ten years, and its full results will not be seen for decades. A long-term assessment has to be made of the prospective demand for different types of trained manpower and definite goals set, to be reached in stages. A proper balance has to be maintained between primary, secondary and higher education, between the education of children and the education of adults and between general education and vocational training. The mission has some comments to offer on priorities in Chapter 13. Generally speaking, now that a fairly broad base has been created by the rapid expansion of primary school enrollment in the past few years, we feel that the emphasis should be increasingly shifted to vocational training and adult education, including agricultural extension services.

Learning comes with experience and responsibility, and more and more Libyans are picking up knowledge on the job, whether it be in government or in private employment. Indeed, the mission was greatly impressed with the keenness and administrative ability displayed by a number of the senior officials it met. There are certain types of skill, however, which can only be acquired after long study and practice. Doctors, lawyers, economists, accountants, engineers, architects, agronomists, foresters, veterinarians, chemists—professions such as these demand many years of general education and specialized training before a person is qualified to practice, and he requires further years of practice before he is able to assume high responsibility. The mission has no doubts about the capacity of Libyans eventually to acquire these and other skills. But it will inevitably be a long time before enough Libyans have been trained to replace the foreigners who at present occupy all but a very few of the posts requiring higher technical qualifications.

The mission strongly urges that Libya should continue in the meantime to take full advantage of the technical assistance provided by the United Nations and its specialized agencies, by the United States and by other friendly countries. The need for these programs will remain for many years to come, as will also the need for the Libyan Government to employ a considerable number of expatriate officials in key posts in the government service. In saying this we are well aware of the disadvantages of Libya having to depend on foreign experts for advice and we are strongly in favor of Libyans progressively taking over more posts of responsibility as and when they are suitably qualified to do so. But much harm can be done to Libya's interests by too rapid a displacement of foreigners, and it is hoped that the United Nations and its specialized agencies in particular will be ready to maintain, and in some cases extend, their technical assistance programs. At the same time, when a post in the Libyan Government service has to be filled by an expatriate, the salary and terms of service offered should be such as will attract a good man and encourage him to remain in Libya for a reasonable period of time. Short-term assignments (e.g., for one year or less) are seldom satisfactory.

Popular Attitudes and Institutions

Certain attitudes and institutions are naturally more conducive to economic growth than others. Libya is no different from other countries in having a number of traditions and customs which stand in the way of such growth, and which will have to be changed if a rapid rate of development is to be achieved. A conspicuous example is the system of tribal ownership of land and water rights, which does not allow the individual cultivator the security or incentive he needs to improve his land and increase his output. This system was developed in response to the needs of a nomadic people dependent for their livelihood on animal husbandry and shifting cultivation. With its emphasis on collective rights and obligations, it is unsuited to the requirements of settled farming. Many of the Libyans and foreign experts with whom the mission discussed the question claimed that tribal ownership of land and water rights was the biggest single obstacle to the development of agricultural production and forestry in Cyrenaica, as well as in parts of Tripolitania, and that until the system was changed there was little hope of real progress. We find it difficult to dispute this view, and we have accordingly recommended that urgent consideration should be given to the enactment of land and water laws securing individual rights of ownership or tenure (see Chapters 7 and 8).

Another factor retarding economic progress in Libya is the prevailing attitude towards appointments to government jobs, which are frequently made on the basis of personal friendship or family connections rather than merit. Political patronage of this kind is by no means confined to Libya; indeed, it is a conspicuous feature of some highly developed countries. Nevertheless, it is a practice which is incompatible with efficient public administration, not only because it is wasteful of money and manpower, but also because it is extremely bad for the morale of the regular officials, who are trying conscientiously to do an honest job of work.

Manual labor is commonly regarded in Libya as undignified, and most boys who go to secondary school or university consider it beneath them to work with their hands. This attitude accords ill with the tremendous need for more skilled workers in agriculture and industry and for people capable of giving practical demonstrations to farmers of modern techniques of cultivation.

The status of women in society also has an important bearing on economic development. As one of the best known authorities on the subject has said, "Restrictions on the work women may do are also everywhere a barrier to economic growth . . ."[1] There are a number of reasons why this should be so. If women are allowed to work outside the home, the supply of labor is increased, and there are more opportunities for specialization, which tends to raise both the quantity and quality of output. At the same time the money the women earn stimulates demand and helps to enlarge the market for consumer goods. One of the most serious handicaps to economic and social development in Libya is the difficulty of finding people for jobs which in most other countries are filled mainly or in part by women—for example, nurses, teachers and stenographers. The mission found many Libyans who were anxious to see women play a more prominent role in the life of the country, and the fact that a number of secondary schools for girls have been opened in the past few years is an indication that attitudes are changing.

These points are mentioned as an illustration of the kind of changes which must take place in any country that is seeking economic development. Some Libyans may well feel that the price of development is too high and that it would be better to stick to traditional ways of life,

[1] W. Lewis, *The Theory of Economic Growth*, George Allen and Unwin, 1955, page 116.

at whatever sacrifice in terms of material progress. Such feelings are fully entitled to respect, but they may not be very realistic. Great changes are bound to come now that oil has been found, and the mission noted many signs in Libya of an awakening interest in the possibilities of economic growth, coupled sometimes with a sense of frustration among the younger generation at the maintenance of what they considered to be out-moded customs.

Government Organization

Economic development demands unity of purpose and action. No development program can succeed in Libya unless the federal and provincial governments are ready to put their full weight behind it and join together in a common endeavor to raise the standard of living of the nation as a whole. The discovery of oil presents the Libyan people with great opportunities. It can also help to weld the three provinces together and to create a new sense of national unity.

While recognizing that each of the three provinces has its own distinctive traditions, characteristics and problems, the mission has tried throughout its work to think in terms of Libya as a whole and to produce a program for economic development that is truly national in scope. The present organization of government, for quite understandable reasons, places much emphasis on the rights and powers of the provinces, and though it was apparently the intention of the Constitution (Articles 36-38) that the federal government should be responsible for making economic policy and supervising its execution, the federal authorities have been hesitant and irresolute in asserting their rights, and the provinces have been jealous of surrendering their privileges. The mission is convinced that, if the economic development of Libya is to be carried out with speed and efficiency, it is necessary to avoid the confusion caused by having three or four different policies or procedures in respect of such vital matters as trade, income tax, banking and audit arrangements. The confusion of functions and responsibilities, particularly in respect of the subjects listed in Article 38 of the Constitution, and the delays that take place because the center and the provinces are unable to agree on action are not conducive to rapid economic progress.

There were good reasons for the creation of a federal system of government for Libya at the time it gained its Independence. This does not, however, alter the fact that from a strictly economic point of view there are serious drawbacks in so poor a country with a population of little over one million having to maintain four separate governments, each with its own head of state, its own parliament, its own cabinet and an extensive range of departments. Quite apart from anything else, it is an extremely costly system for the Libyan taxpayer to support—and it is he who in the last resort must foot the bill. The mission recommends therefore that everything practicable should be done, within the framework of the Constitution, to streamline the organization of government and to eliminate unnecessary duplication of functions as between the center and the provinces.

We also believe that the authority of the federal government should be strengthened in certain directions. Our specific recommendations are set out in Chapter 6. They include an extension of the powers of the federal government in respect of taxation (notably income tax and excise duties), the creation of better coordinating machinery at the center for the preparation and execution of development programs, the establishment of a Federal Ministry of Agriculture and Natural Resources, arrangements for securing a more rational distribution of federal grants-in-aid to the provinces and the gradual unification of the federal and provincial civil services.

Various changes and innovations in the machinery of government are suggested in this report with a view to improving the administration of economic affairs and tackling some of the institutional obstacles which stand in the way of more rapid development, particularly in agriculture. We have recommended, for example, stricter controls over government expenditure, the separation of the accounts of revenue-earning public enterprises from those of general government, the creation of an independent authority to run the port of Tripoli, new institutions for the provision of credit to agriculture and industry and more positive government action to assist in the marketing of agricultural produce.

Economic and Financial Policies

We have also discussed in Chapter 15 the general economic and financial policies that should be followed in mobilizing Libya's resources for development and guarding against some of the dangers that every country encounters in a phase of rapid economic growth. One of the most pressing problems is how to deal with the shortages and price increases resulting from the rapid expansion of demand for many types of goods and services which is associated with the operation of the oil companies. Office space, houses and apartments in the main towns are hard to get, and rents have soared. Prices of many imported goods have risen sharply—furniture, for example, office equipment, electric gadgets and other household goods. In some cases the higher prices are attributable in part to increases in customs duties, but traders and contractors have also taken advantage of the buoyant state of the market to increase their profits. Nor have price rises been confined to goods purchased mainly by the foreign community. The cost of living of the ordinary Libyan family in Tripoli or Benghazi is undoubtedly higher now than it was a year ago; meat prices in particular are much higher, though this may be partly due to special factors affecting meat supplies.

A conspicuous effect of the oil boom has been to aggravate the scarcity of skilled and semi-skilled labor and to give a sharp upward push to wages and salaries. This in turn adds to the costs and prices of locally produced goods and services and gives a fresh twist to the inflationary spiral. At the same time it creates serious difficulties for the federal and provincial governments, which are losing some of their best employees to the oil companies and which will sooner or later be forced to raise civil service pay scales. Moreover, building costs have risen steeply, and government is having to pay more for its own capital works—roads, schools, hospitals and so forth.

There is no simple or complete solution to this problem, but there are various things which the Libyan Government could do to moderate the inflationary impact of oil development. The obvious answer to shortages and rising prices is an increase in supplies, and government action could help in a number of ways to bring this about. Imports should be permitted to come in freely. Encouragement should be given to the immigration of skilled workers from abroad, including particularly Libyans who left the country under the Italian occupation and settled in Tunisia, Egypt and other neighboring countries. All major building and construction projects should be open to tender from foreign firms so as to encourage competition, and these firms should be encouraged to establish branches in Libya, possibly in conjunction with private Libyan capital.

While the main accent in the present situation should be laid on measures to increase supplies of goods and services, restraint must also be exercised over demand, especially over consumption. Here government fiscal policy has an important role to play. Private savings should be encouraged, and those who benefit from the oil boom, including traders and the higher paid workers, should be required to pay more in taxes. The mission attaches great importance in this connection to the institution of a federal income tax and to improvements in the machinery for assessment and collection of tax. So far as the government's own expenditures are concerned, it may be desirable to defer certain capital projects for a time until the present upsurge of private demand has slackened off and until pressures on the building industry have been eased.

Taxation can be used to restrict private demand and thereby combat inflationary pressures; it can be used to mobilize resources for private development; and it can be used as a means of redistributing income in favor of the poorer sections of the community. All three aspects are considered in Chapter 15, where we have more to say about fiscal policy. In recent years, when the funds for public investment have mainly been provided from abroad, no serious efforts have been made to mobilize Libya's own resources for development, nor does there appear to have been any real appreciation of the true cost of capital. A different approach is needed now that Libya has a good prospect of soon becoming financially independent. The mission has therefore recommended that the government should in future raise more money through taxation and internal borrowing, and that a number of changes should be made in the present system of taxation. We have also recommended that increased charges should be levied for public utility services and water provided for irrigation at public expense, so that the costs of supplying these services can be recovered from the beneficiaries.

Investment Priorities

One of the main purposes of this report is to put forward a five-year program of public investment for the consideration of the Libyan Government. The outline of such a program is contained in Chapter 5, and the details are elaborated in the chapters that follow. It is not, of course, a matter of starting with a clean slate. Development is a continuous process. Many projects are already in progress, and others are planned. The pattern of investment cannot be suddenly altered overnight, and much of the expenditure to be carried out during the next year or two is already committed. The mission's program thus in large part represents a continuation of existing lines of development rather than any radically new departure. We have, however, suggested that in places the emphasis should be shifted, that less should be spent on some things, more on others; and where we have felt that there are mistakes and omissions to be rectified, we have recommended changes in policies and the manner of their execution.

Libya has made real progress since Independence in developing its resources, and the national income has risen considerably. This progress has been facilitated by the financial and technical assistance received from the United Nations, the United Kingdom, the United States and other friendly countries.

Altogether, from the beginning of 1952 to the end of 1958, about £L 30 million was allocated for expenditure by the foreign aid agencies on schemes of economic development and social betterment.[2] Much of this effort was directed to repairing the physical damage caused by the war to roads, harbors and other installations and to providing some of the basic economic and social services which had been neglected under previous administrations, most notably in the fields of education and health. Considerable amounts were invested in long overdue measures of soil and water conservation, which are made necessary by the sparsity and irregularity of the rainfall. The country has also been equipped with many new roads, public buildings and other capital assets.

The results of this development have not always been spectacular, and in certain respects they have been disappointing, especially in agriculture, upon which well over half the population directly depend for their livelihood. Dissatisfaction with what has so far been achieved has understandably led to criticism of the foreign experts and the foreign aid agencies who have been largely responsible for the preparation and execution of development projects. While some of this criticism may be justified (see Chapter 3), the mission feels that the critics often tend to underestimate the time it takes to build up an economy from such modest beginnings, and in the face of the obstacles to which we have referred earlier.

A broad distinction can be made between investment in economic projects and investment in social projects. The first is aimed directly at increasing production through the provision of more capital for agriculture, industry, mining, fisheries, tourism and supporting facilities such as power, transport and communications. The second is aimed at improving the condition of the people through the provision of better facilities for education, health, housing, sanitation and so forth. The maintenance of a reasonable balance between these two types of investment is one of the major problems facing the government of every

[2] The term "foreign aid agencies," as used in this report, refers to the Libyan Public Development and Stabilization Agency (LPDSA), the Libyan-American Reconstruction Commission (LARC), the Libyan-American Joint Services (LAJS) and the United Nations Technical Assistance Mission. The origins and activities of these agencies are described in Chapter 3.

underdeveloped country. The value of good social services is obvious. But if too much emphasis is placed on social investment at the expense of economic investment, a country may find itself unable to produce enough to pay for the social services it has created. The danger of this happening in Libya has been much reduced by the prospect of oil revenues accruing in the not too distant future, and the mission believes that there is ample justification in these circumstances for considerable further investment in education, health and community services. We attach particular importance both to education and training and to better housing for workers in the towns, where we recommend that the government should give high priority to schemes for the construction of low-cost housing (see Chapter 14).

Oil production now clearly offers the best prospect for the long-term expansion of Libya's national income. But, as indicated above, it is hardly likely to offer employment for more than a small proportion of the present population, still less for the additional numbers to be expected as the population grows.[3] Libya's other principal natural resource is in agriculture and the raising of livestock. The mission believes that there is considerable scope for developing settled agriculture. Moreover, it can see no other way of providing a satisfactory way of life for the majority of the people who now depend on the land for their livelihood, particularly since agriculture provides the basis for much of Libya's manufacturing industry and trade.

The paramount need to concentrate on improving farming conditions and raising agricultural output remains unaffected by the discovery of oil, and the mission regards this as the most important of all the tasks to be undertaken in the field of economic development. We have also given special attention in the report to the exploitation of two other natural resources which have been neglected in the past, namely fisheries and tourism. Clearly neither is of comparable importance to agriculture, but we believe that both could be developed as valuable supplementary sources of income and employment (see Chapters 9 and 10). The prospects for tourism have been considerably brightened by the discovery of oil which should result in increased demand from oil company employees for holidays and recreational facilities in Libya.

Oil apart, present conditions in Libya do not favor the development of industry on a large scale. The home market is small and scattered, most industrial materials have to be imported (apart from

[3] It is generally supposed that the Libyan population is growing at the rate of about $1\frac{1}{4}$ percent a year, but this could well be an underestimate (see Chapter 2).

agricultural processing), and industrial skills have still to be cultivated. However, the operations of the oil companies may open up some new opportunities for investment in manufacturing industries. Various possibilities are mentioned in Chapter 9, among them cement. It is understood that two private projects to establish cement factories, one in Tripolitania and one in Cyrenaica, have been put forward since the mission's visit, but the mission does not have enough detailed information to judge their merits.

In present conditions Libya should rely mainly on private initiative and private capital to promote the development of manufacturing industries. Considerable interest in such development is now being displayed by foreign firms, some of which are seeking the collaboration of Libyan businessmen in establishing joint ventures. Provided the government is not expected to assist either by putting up money itself or by giving promises of protection against imports, private investment in industry should be given every encouragement. On the other hand if assurances of government assistance or participation are sought, the proposals should be scrutinized very carefully, and the government should insist on a thorough investigation being made by independent consultants into the technical and economic aspects of the project before giving any commitment to support it. Firms which are primarily interested in selling plant and machinery for a new factory are seldom to be relied upon to offer impartial advice in such matters.

Minerals other than oil appear to hold out little immediate prospect for development, although the potash deposits at Marada might be suitable for commercial exploitation now that natural gas has been discovered in the vicinity. The possibility of new discoveries of minerals should not, of course, be entirely ruled out, and the mission is recommending the establishment of a federal department of hydrology and geology, which among other things would be responsible for carrying on the work of minerals investigation.

The mission recognizes that at the present stage of Libya's development there are comparatively few projects in the public sector where one can count with any assurance on much immediate and tangible return on the capital invested. Some economic projects, therefore, have to be justified as much by social and political considerations as by any assessment of their capacity to pay their way. The construction of new roads to outlying desert oases is an example. This is not to say, however, that economic criteria should be disregarded, or that Libya should squander the money it receives on extravagant public works which can neither pay for themselves nor contribute to the long-term improvement of the social environment. On the contrary, the prospective economic benefits to be obtained from every project should be carefully assessed and compared with the costs to make sure that the return will be adequate to justify the investment.

All investments in government buildings, schools, hospitals and roads involve continuing costs for their upkeep, and too little regard has been paid in the past to this aspect of investment. The mission cannot emphasize too strongly that maintenance of existing assets should, as a general rule, receive priority over new construction—that is, sufficient funds should be set aside for the upkeep of existing roads, schools, hospitals and so forth before anything is allotted for building new ones. Before additional investments are undertaken their maintenance costs should be carefully assessed to make sure that the country can afford to support them. Traveling around Libya the mission found many roads and public buildings that were not being properly maintained, or not being maintained at all, while large sums were being spent on new works, often in the same districts. In future, much larger provision should be made for maintenance in the revenue budgets of the federal and provincial governments, and we have allowed for this in our program.

Agriculture and Forestry

Agricultural development in Libya presents a number of challenging problems. Given the sparsity and irregularity of the rainfall and the impoverishment of the soil through many centuries of neglect, large investments are needed in measures of soil and water conservation simply to preserve the existing assets and to prevent a further deterioration in farming conditions. Much of the money allotted to agriculture by the foreign aid agencies has in fact been spent, and rightly spent, on schemes of afforestation and dune fixation, flood control, surface water conservation, ground water investigations and so forth, which cannot be expected to yield a quick return on the capital invested. Indeed, even in the long run the return is often incalculable. One can only say that, if the investment had not been undertaken, the state of agriculture would be considerably worse than it is. The Libyans themselves have little tradition of settled farming, and this alone makes it difficult to achieve rapid progress in agriculture. The problem is further complicated by the fact that in present circumstances small farming is one of the least remunerative of occupations, and that earnings in trade, manufacturing, building and construction, service industries and government employment are generally higher.

The over-all rate of return on capital invested in Libyan agriculture is likely in present circumstances to be small by comparison with most other countries. But in the absence of alternative opportunities for creating enough employment in the other sectors of the economy, every effort must be made to improve the lot of the farmer and pastoralist and to help him to make better use of the resources at his disposal. At present the small farmer labors under a number of serious handicaps. His methods are primitive and his knowledge of modern farming techniques almost non-existent. He has great difficulty in obtaining credit, except at exorbitant rates of interest. He has no organization for marketing. He has little or no protection against imports.

Unless and until the agricultural community is better rewarded for its efforts, it will be extremely difficult to stimulate the growth of agricultural production. The mission believes that a combination of measures will be needed to produce this result, including changes in the present system of land ownership, the restriction of certain imports, improvements in the marketing of domestic agricultural produce, direct financial assistance to the farmer and the dissemination of knowledge through the agricultural training and extension services. The problem is discussed at greater length in Chapter 8.

Afforestation deserves more attention than it has received in the past. More trees are badly needed in Libya for soil and water conservation, and as a source of timber supplies. The main difficulties in the way of forestry development lie in the grazing practices of the nomads, the uncontrolled ravages of the goat, unrestricted collection of firewood, tribal ownership of land and inadequately staffed forestry services. Until a really determined effort is made to tackle these problems, little is to be gained by stepping up the programs of planting. But if the necessary conditions can be created for successful afforestation, the mission recommends that this should be accorded a high priority in the allocation of the additional funds that will become available for development out of oil revenues.

Special Needs of the Fezzan

The mission has tried throughout its work to think in terms of Libya as a whole and to view the claims of each of the three provinces with complete impartiality. The economic characteristics of the Fezzan, however, are so distinct from those of the other provinces that a rather special approach to its problems is called for. Detailed proposals for dealing with these problems will be included in the appropriate chapters, but we would like to say something first about the thinking behind them.

The Fezzan has always been predominantly a subsistence economy. In past centuries it used to derive a subsidiary income from the caravan trade, and when the caravan trade declined around the end of the nineteenth century, foreign garrisons moved in and provided the desert oases with a new source of income and employment. Now the caravan trade is dead and the foreign garrisons have left. But two new sources of external income have appeared in the form of federal subsidies and oil exploration. Total government expenditures in the Fezzan, including the expenditures of the aid agencies, have risen from little over £L 400,000 in 1954/55 to about £L 750,000 in 1957/58, while the revenue collected in the Fezzan was only £L 40,000 in 1954/55 and less than £L 100,000 in 1957/58. A completely new town has been built in Sebha, complete with a royal rest-house, parliament buildings, government offices and a residential section for Nazirs and officials. Many Fezzanese have been employed on construction work or taken onto the regular government payroll as officials, clerks, drivers, mechanics, post office workers, workshop employees, watchmen or the like. Others have left the land to work for the oil companies, either in the Fezzan itself or in other parts of Libya.

These developments have brought about important changes in the economic life and social structure of the province. The traditional feudal system is being undermined. An acute shortage of agricultural labor has resulted in large tracts of land going out of cultivation, and an increasing proportion of the food consumed in the Fezzan is being imported from outside. The use of money is being extended as more and more of the people work for wages. Meanwhile, the population is gradually declining as young people go away to live and work in Tripoli. The population recorded in the 1954 census (just under 60,000) was smaller than in Turkish times, and it may have decreased further since.

The mission believes that, isolated though it is, the Fezzan constitutes a unique and valuable element in the life of the country, not least because of the rare quality of its people, who have shown themselves more than usually capable of mastering new skills and adapting themselves to changing conditions. Those who wish to look for employment outside the Fezzan should not be discouraged from doing so.

But life is likely to continue in the desert oases for decades to come and it might be reinvigorated by the discovery of new sources of oil or other minerals or even by unforeseen technological changes (e.g., in surface transportation). The right line of development in the meantime, as we see it, should be to make the Fezzan more self-reliant and to provide better economic opportunities for the people who remain there.

In more concrete terms, this means concentrating on making better use of the dates which constitute the province's most important agricultural resource; stimulating production of cereals, vegetables and fruit for local consumption, and in the case of early vegetables possibly also for export; experimenting with new crops such as linseed and castor beans that might be grown in the oases for export; improving the quality of livestock and livestock products; continuing a program of geological research; and developing the handicrafts industries, which have already achieved a modest reputation for products of distinction. The mission has considerable doubts about the feasibility of growing cotton on a large scale in the Fezzan for export.

We attach the highest priority in the Fezzan to the construction of more public wells for the supply of water to small farmers and village cooperatives (see Chapter 7). Agriculture cannot be expected to make much progress so long as the control over water is vested in the hands of a minority of wealthy well-owners. On the other hand, we do not favor large investments in new roads, apart from the main Fezzan road, which is already under construction. Distances in the Fezzan are too great, and the potential traffic at present in sight too small, to justify the construction of additional hardtop highways. There appears to be scope, however, for more use to be made of air transport for administrative and other purposes, and we have recommended the establishment of a regular service of light aircraft based on Sebha (see Chapter 12). Such a service would, of course, have to be subsidized by the federal government, but this is the kind of subsidy which we feel can be justified by the special circumstances of the Fezzan, especially insofar as it helps to facilitate communication and consultation between the provincial and federal governments.

The Italian Community

The Italian community occupies a rather special position in the Libyan economy. According to the 1954 census, there were then 38,000 Italians still living in the country, practically all in Tripolitania. These Italians retain their right of Italian citizenship. Two-thirds of them live in and around the city of Tripoli and most of the rest in the "demographic" colonies established by the Italian Government before the war at the places then known as Bianchi, Preveglieri, Garibaldi, Oliveti, Micca, Crispi, Gioda and elsewhere. One-third of the farms in these colonies have been returned to the Libyan Government, but about 1,400 remain in Italian hands, and their future is governed by a Libyan-Italian agreement signed in October 1956. Under this agreement the Italian Government is continuing to provide the present occupants of the farms with financial assistance until 1960, and thereafter the occupants obtain full rights of ownership. There are also a number of private Italian farms in Tripolitania, some of them large and prosperous.

Italian farms are on the average considerably more developed than farms owned by Libyans and make a major contribution to Libyan exports. The management of industry in Tripolitania is almost entirely in Italian hands, and Italians play an important role in the operation of public utilities, the staffing of the medical services, agricultural research, banking and commerce, the management of hotels and many other branches of economic activity. The skills which the Italians can offer, and their experience of modern farming techniques, are valuable assets for the Libyan economy.

It is only natural, in the light of past history, that there should be difficulties on both sides in establishing a satisfactory and enduring basis for Libyan-Italian relations in Libya. The mission believes, nevertheless, that it is very much in the economic interests of both communities that such a basis should be found, and that the Italian community should be more closely integrated into the social and economic life of the country.

Conclusions

The present rate of gross investment in Libya (excluding oil investment) is perhaps equal to about 15-20 percent of the national product —a much higher proportion than in most other underdeveloped countries.[4] There does not, however, appear to be any close relationship between this investment and the growth of national income. Income has certainly risen substantially in the past five years, but the rise is attributable more to increased expenditures by foreign governments and oil companies than to domestic capital formation. There are in any case

[4] For the basis of this calculation see Annex I.

a number of reasons why the ratio of the increase in income to the increase in capital in Libya might be expected in present conditions to be unusually low (except, of course, in the oil industry). Shortage of skills; the heavy concentration on social investment which takes a long time to yield fruit; the need in agriculture to make good heavy arrears of investment in measures of soil and water conservation; the high costs of government and investment in government buildings; the dispersal of a small population over a huge area necessitating abnormal investment in transport and communications—all these factors, and particularly the first, help to explain why economic development programs have so far yielded only limited dividends in terms of increased output.

Oil production appears likely to result in further large increases in national income over the next five to ten years. Most of the additional income will consist of revenues accruing directly to the federal and provincial governments, and it has been decided in advance that 70 percent of the revenues left after payment of concession fees, royalties and income tax should be earmarked for financing economic development. This is a wise decision. The main problem of development in the circumstances will be how best to use the large sums of money available to promote the well-being of the nation as a whole. Only a minority of the population can expect to earn their living by working in the oil industry or in the other industries and trades that will be most immediately affected by the impact of oil operations. Other sources of livelihood must be developed to provide employment and income for the majority, whose needs will not automatically be taken care of by the growth of oil production.

Apart from oil, Libya's principal natural resource is in agriculture and the raising of livestock, and the mission believes that, with good administration, better education and training and an adequate supply of capital, much larger production can be obtained from the land than is being obtained at present. It also believes that good opportunities exist for the development of fisheries and tourism. However, two prior conditions must be fulfilled before all these opportunities can be properly exploited. The supply of human skills must be greatly augmented and enriched; and important changes must be effected in popular attitudes and institutions.

The Libyan Government is about to take into its own hands the administration of economic development, which has hitherto been largely planned and executed by various foreign aid agencies. This change is to be welcomed in that it will place the responsibility for development where it belongs and will provide an opportunity for better coordination of development activities within the framework of a single over-all program—instead of the separate and rather disjointed programs which have existed hitherto. At the same time the impeding changeover adds urgency to the need for strengthening the authority of the federal government, streamlining the machinery of federal and provincial administration and securing closer day-to-day cooperation between the center and the provinces.

The mission recommends that the size of the public development program should be increased gradually, rather than in one big jump, and that the main emphasis during the next three or four years should be placed on improving education and training, strengthening the organization of government and bringing about the institutional changes that are needed, particularly in agriculture, to ensure that capital can be used more fruitfully. This is because we believe that a fairly modest program, well conceived and well executed, will be of greater benefit to Libya *at this stage* than a larger program which cannot be carried out effectively because of shortage of skills and lack of experience in administration. The groundwork will then have been laid for a more rapid advance to be undertaken later on when large oil revenues begin to flow in.

The longer-term outlook for the economy is promising. Libya is more fortunate than some oil-producing countries in that it has other natural resources to exploit and no problem of over-population to contend with. Shortage of water for agriculture and soil erosion are the main physical obstacles to economic development, and these can in time be overcome by the application of more capital to the land, particularly if means can eventually be found for desalting sea water for irrigation at a reasonable cost—a possibility that may well be brought within reach of a country with abundant supplies of cheap power in the course of the next ten or twenty years. Great opportunities lie ahead. Wisdom, energy and enterprise will be needed to take full advantage of them.

CHAPTER 2 CHARACTERISTICS OF THE LIBYAN ECONOMY

Historical Background

The United Kingdom of Libya came into being on December 24, 1951 following a decision taken by the United Nations in November 1949 that the three territories of Tripolitania, Cyrenaica and the Fezzan should be constituted a fully sovereign and independent country. Before the war these territories had been under Italian rule, and after Italy's defeat they were occupied by the Allied powers—Cyrenaica and Tripolitania by Britain and the Fezzan by France. The present state is a constitutional monarchy with a federal system of government, under which each of the three provinces enjoys a large measure of autonomy.

Although Libya is the third or fourth largest country in Africa with an area well over half the size of India, its present population is only about 1.2 million. Approximately 95 percent of these are Moslems of Arabian and North African descent. The principal minority community consists of Italians, of whom some 30,000-40,000 are still living in Tripolitania and retain their Italian citizenship. There are also several thousand Jews who are Libyan citizens, together with small minorities of Maltese, Greeks and other nationalities. The population is heavily concentrated near the Mediterranean coast, two-thirds living within a radius of 200 kilometers from Tripoli and one-quarter in the coastal zone of Cyrenaica between Agedabia and Tobruk. The rest of Libya consists almost entirely of desert, and habitation is confined to widely scattered oases, which support a population of about 100,000 in all.

The settled areas of Tripolitania and Cyrenaica are divided by hundreds of miles of desert, and in early times the two provinces had very different histories. Tripolitania was first colonized by the Phoenicians, Cyrenaica by the Greeks, and though both subsequently became part of the Roman Empire during the first century B.C., they continued to live separate existences throughout the Roman period, which lasted until the middle of the fifth century A.D. During this period the coastal areas of Libya are believed to have supported two or three times as many people as they do today—thanks in the main to a highly developed system of settled agriculture, which was made possible by the careful organization of water resources.

The collapse of the Roman Empire in North Africa was marked, first, by repeated incursions of Berber tribes from the south and later by the invasion of the Vandals from Spain. Roman influence was briefly reasserted by the Emperor Justinian, and Libya was ruled for a time from Byzantium. The Arabs first invaded the country in the middle of the seventh century, and a more permanent Arab settlement took place 400 years later. As time went on, settled agriculture dwindled in importance, and the country was increasingly given over to a nomadic way of life. However, the coastal towns and the caravan centers in the Sahara retained commercial links with Europe and other parts of Africa and the Middle East. Tripoli itself was occupied at different times by the Arabs, the Sicilians, the Spaniards, the Knights of Malta and the Turks, and under the Karamanli dynasty, who ruled the city from 1711 to 1835, it became a stronghold of the Barbary pirates.

It was not until the middle of the nineteenth century that the Turkish Government in Constantinople made a serious attempt to bring the whole of Libya, including the Fezzan, under its administration. The latter years of Turkish rule were marked by a general improvement in the economic condition of the country and by the establishment of a more orderly system of government. The country appears to have been more or less self-supporting in cereals, importing in bad years and exporting in good ones; trade was developed with foreign countries through the export of livestock, hides and skins, wool, esparto grass, sponges, citrus fruit, dates and other products; a fairly flourishing handloom industry existed in the coastal towns; and Tripoli remained an important terminus of the caravan routes from the Sudan and West Africa, although the caravan trade began to decline from about 1880 onwards.

Italy began her occupation of the country in 1911-12. The Italians met with strong resistance from the Libyans in their efforts to colonize the country and to develop it as a military base, and the first 20 years of the Italian occupation were marked by continuous unrest, particularly in Cyrenaica and the Fezzan. As a result Italian settlement proceeded slowly, only getting under way in Tripolitania in the 1920's and in Cyrenaica in the 1930's. Initially Tripolitania (with the Fezzan) and Cyrenaica were separately administered, but they were formally unified at the beginning of 1934 as the Italian colony of Libya.

The Italian Government is estimated to have spent 1.8 billion lire (possibly equivalent to around $150 million in pre-war dollars at pre-war rates of exchange) on public works, utilities and agricultural development during the 30 years of its administration. Most of the investment up to 1936 was directed to the construction of railways, roads, ports and public buildings, but in the latter phase (1936-42) two-thirds of the expenditure was on agricultural development and land reclamation. About 4,000 Italian families had settled on the land in Tripolitania by 1940 and more than 2,000 in Cyrenaica, partly in private concessions and partly in large public settlements, and approximately 225,000 hectares of land were being developed by the settlers in the two provinces. By 1941 the Italian population of Libya numbered 110,000, of whom 70,000 were in Tripolitania. The whole of the Italian colony in Cyrenaica was evacuated by the Italian Government in 1942, and many other Italians left the country during and after the war.

The Italian administration left Libya a valuable legacy of buildings, roads, ports and other public installations, together with the results of fairly extensive research work relating particularly to agriculture and mineral resources. At the same time the substantial Italian investments in agriculture and industry have contributed to the growth of the Libyan economy as a whole and provide a useful base for future expansion. It must be recognized, however, that the Libyans paid heavily for what the Italians achieved. They were pushed off some of the best farming land in the country, large numbers of their livestock were lost in the fighting (especially in Cyrenaica), and their traditional industries suffered severely from competition from Italian products. Moreover, the Italians did little or nothing to prepare the Libyan people for self-government. Education and technical training were neglected, and Libyans were virtually excluded from the administration. As a result, through no fault of its own, Libya has remained heavily dependent on foreign administrative and technical personnel, and the training of Libyans to replace them is still the most difficult of all the problems associated with economic development.

Cyrenaica was the province of Libya which fared worst under Italian rule, and it sustained much the most serious damage in the World War II, when its territory was fought over for two years. The pre-war Italian investments in Cyrenaica were never given time to bear fruit, and the Cyrenaican economy today is in almost every sense much less developed than that of Tripolitania. The Fezzan economy is less developed still.

Population

A census taken in 1954 with the help of the United Nations gave a total population of just under 1.1 million, of whom 738,000 were living in Tripolitania, 291,000 in Cyrenaica and 59,000 in the Fezzan. About 74 percent of the population were classified as "settled," 18 percent as "semi-nomads" and 8 percent as "nomads." One-quarter of the settled population, or 18 percent of the whole, was concentrated in the two main cities of Tripoli (130,000) and Benghazi (70,000). The populations of the smaller towns cannot be precisely defined, but it would probably be true to say that roughly 25-30 percent of the total population in 1954 were town-dwellers and that 45-50 percent were settled in rural areas; the remaining 25 percent were nomads or semi-nomads earning a living from livestock and shifting cultivation. The proportion of nomads and semi-nomads is highest in Cyrenaica (about 45 percent in 1954) and lowest in the Fezzan (less than 10 percent). There appears to be a gradual but fairly steady shift away from nomadic life to the towns and settled farming, and the proportion of semi-nomads and nomads to the total population is very likely rather smaller now than it was five years ago, while the proportion of town-dwellers has almost certainly increased.

Reliable statistics of births and deaths are hard to come by, but it is generally supposed that the population is growing at about $1\frac{1}{4}$ percent a year. This is a very low figure compared with most other countries in North Africa and the Middle East. In Morocco and Tunisia, for instance, the population is believed to be growing at the rate of about 2 percent a year, and in Jordan at 3 percent. The birth rate in Libya appears to be at least as high as in other Arab countries, possibly higher. If the rate of population growth is indeed as low as $1\frac{1}{4}$ percent, the explanation can only be found in the exceptionally high infant mortality rate, which is apparently due in large part to lack of domestic hygiene and mistaken feeding practices (see Chapter 14). Improved health measures and better education of women could rapidly change this situation and result in a higher rate of population growth more in line with trends elsewhere in North Africa and the Middle East. The mission has meanwhile assumed for want of better information that the Libyan population is growing at a rate of between $1\frac{1}{4}$ to $1\frac{1}{2}$ percent a year, and that the total population of Libya in 1959 is in the region of 1.2 million. This could well be an underestimate.

Land and Water

Libya has a land area of 1,760,000 square kilometers, but owing to lack of water no more than 5-10 percent of this can be put to economic use, and possibly not more than about 1 percent is suitable for settled cultivation. Even so, on the basis of the existing population this would provide nearly 1½ hectares of cultivable land per inhabitant, which is a good deal more than is at present being cultivated in most Middle Eastern countries. Agriculture and animal husbandry always have been, and must clearly continue to be, one of the mainstays of the Libyan economy, and there is enough land and water, if properly conserved, to support a considerably larger farming population than at present at a higher standard of living.

Only about 0.4 percent of the country is at present under static farming, while a further indeterminate proportion is used for shifting cultivation, grazing and forest land. Apart from the desert oases the present pattern of land use is largely dictated by the rainfall and most of the cultivated land is located in four areas—(i) the coast of Tripolitania from the Tunisian border in the west to Misurata in the east, together with the plain behind it, which is known as the Gefara; (ii) the edge of the plateau surrounding this plain (the Gebel); (iii) the Barce Plain, which is a limestone outcrop close to the Cyrenaican coast between 300 and 400 meters above sea level; and (iv) the Cyrenaican highlands (the Gebel Akhdar or "Green Mountain"), which are situated between Barce and Derna mostly at levels between 450 and 800 meters.

Even in these areas rainfall is sparse and highly irregular. Less than half the settled area of Tripolitania can normally expect an annual rainfall of more than 300 mm., and the whole of this may occur in a few days in the winter, while in some years there may be practically no rain at all. To add to the hazards of cultivation, northern Tripolitania is frequently swept by violent, hot, sand-bearing winds from the desert (*ghiblis*) and is occasionally plagued by locusts. Rainfall in the coastal areas of Cyrenaica is generally in the region of 200-250 mm. a year, but the Barce Plain and the Gebel Akhdar are better favored, with an average of more than 400 mm. a year over the area as a whole and as much as 500 to 650 mm. a year in the extreme north. Here, too, however, practically all the rain falls in the winter, the climate is extremely irregular, and partial or total droughts are frequently experienced. Practically no rain falls in the Fezzan.

The data required for a full assessment of the water resources are not yet completely available (see Chapter 7). The first water table in the coastal zone of Tripoli varies from 5 to 25 meters in depth below the surface, and the second water table is 20 to 25 meters below the first, while there is an artesian aquifer at a greater depth. A considerable number of small springs are found in the Gebel, and underground water has been located there in a few places, generally at depths of 50 to 70 meters. On the coastal plain near Misurata the water table is 5 to 20 meters below ground level, and below that there is an artesian aquifer generally about 300 meters down; the water from both these sources is brackish. A number of good springs issue from the foot of the eastern Cyrenaican escarpments, and underground sources are to be found on the coastal plain near Benghazi, though the water there is frequently brackish. In the Fezzan the water table is generally found in the oases at depths of 5 to 10 meters below ground level, while near Brak and Traghen artesian aquifers have been tapped at depths of 65 to 100 meters, resulting in flowing wells with sweet water. The oil companies have recently discovered water at many places in the desert at varying depths, but the supplies have not been of much use from an agricultural standpoint since there is seldom any settled population in the vicinity, and few of the places are easily accessible.

Considerable progress in the exploration of ground water has been made in Tripolitania, where about 100,000 hectares (one-fifth of the regularly cultivated area in the province) are now under full or part-time irrigation. This has assisted in the development of a variety of commercial crops in addition to barley, wheat and dates which traditionally have been the staple products of Libyan agriculture. Olives are grown extensively along the coast and in parts of the Gebel, so are groundnuts, citrus fruit, grapes, castor seed, tomatoes, potatoes and other fruit and vegetables. Tobacco is grown around Tripoli and in the Gebel. Esparto grass, which grows wild in the Gebel, was first collected in Turkish times for export to Britain where it is used to make bank notes and high quality paper. This trade still continues, but its volume is diminishing as the reserves of esparto grass are becoming exhausted, and as esparto grass is being displaced by other materials in the manufacture of paper. Indeed, the overexploitation of these reserves by careless methods of picking has been a major cause of soil erosion in the Gebel, and indirectly of floods which in recent years have harassed Tripoli (see Chapter 7). Livestock have never played such an important role in the economy of Tripolitania as they have in Cyrenaica, but they are the chief means of livelihood for at least one-fifth of the population. The main grazing areas are in the Gefara and the Gebel. Sheep and goats predominate and are bred primarily for meat and milk, with wool, skins and hair as by-products. Cattle and camels are used primarily as draft animals, but also give some meat and milk.

In Cyrenaica the Barce Plain and the northern part of the Gebel Akhdar contain some of the best soil for cereal cultivation in Libya. The scope for irrigation is much less even than in Tripolitania, but the rainfall is higher, and conditions are more favorable for dry farming than in most other parts of Libya. The agricultural potential of this area, however, has not yet been fully exploited, and the general standard of farming in Cyrenaica is lower than in Tripolitania. Barley and wheat are the main crops, supplemented by fruit and vegetables, which are mostly grown in market gardens close to the towns. The majority of the local population of Cyrenaica look to livestock rather than to settled agriculture as their principal source of income, and large numbers of sheep, goats, camels and other animals are raised in the Gebel Akhdar and on the fringe of the desert. Many of these animals are driven on the hoof across the border into Egypt to be fattened and slaughtered there; a few are shipped to Greece, Malta and other Mediterranean countries. Livestock constitute Cyrenaica's largest export, and the total value of livestock production in the province is probably greater than the value of all its agricultural produce.

The oases of the Fezzan, together with Jalo and Kufra in Cyrenaica and Gadames in Tripolitania, have a combined population of about 75,000. Some of them were once important points on the caravan routes from the interior of Africa to the Mediterranean, while more recently their economies were geared to meeting the needs of occupying forces—first the Turks, then the Italians and finally the French. With the virtual disappearance of the caravan trade and the withdrawal of foreign garrisons from the desert, the oases have been left with extremely limited means of livelihood. Separated by great distances from each other and from the coast, they are very largely self-contained communities except to the extent that they are supported, as some of them increasingly are, by subsidies from the federal government and the foreign aid agencies. Water they mostly have in abundance, but its use is limited by shortages of the labor and capital required to bring it to the surface and distribute it to the gardens. Dates, wheat and barley are the staple crops. Most of the oases also produce small quantities of fruit and vegetables, Jalo being noted for the excellence of its tomatoes. Livestock are raised in small numbers.

Oil and Other Minerals

Oil exploration in Libya started in 1955, and by the beginning of 1960 16 foreign companies were engaged in prospecting. Oil has so far been struck in more than twenty places, and occurrences of natural gas have been noted in several others. A number of the oil strikes have been described as highly promising, and there appears to be a very good chance that commercial production will begin within the next two or three years. It is too early yet, however, to form any reliable assessment of the prospects, which are discussed in more detail in Chapter 4.

Known resources of other valuable minerals are few. Libya has ample supplies of marine salt along the coast and good deposits of gypsum in the Gefara. Recent investigations have revealed the existence of large deposits of iron ore in the Shatti Valley in the Fezzan. The ferrous content averages about 45 percent, but the deposits are too far from the coast to offer much hope of economic exploitation. Small deposits of natron are being worked in the Fezzan, and there are fairly large deposits of potash at Marada in the Sirte Desert which might offer some possibilities of development now that petroleum has been discovered in the vicinity (see Annex IV). There are also minor occurrences of sulfur, manganese, lignite, alum and sodium carbonate in different parts of the country. None of these, however, appears to be of much commercial value. Deposits of limestone and clay are known to exist together at one or two places, notably near Homs in Tripolitania, but insufficient information was available at the time of the mission's visit to determine whether these would be suitable for the manufacture of cement.

Fisheries and Tourism

Libya possesses two other natural assets which have hitherto been little exploited, but which the mission believes could be further developed. The first is fishing. The Libyan coast is well endowed with sponge beds, and the off-shore fishing grounds contain considerable quantities of reputedly excellent fish. At present the fishing is mostly done by Italians, Greeks and Maltese. It is unlikely that the Libyans could compete successfully in the near future in the highly specialized business of collecting sponges, but they should be able to obtain a larger share of the ordinary fishing.

Another of Libya's valuable assets is the Mediterranean climate, which is especially attractive in winter, spring and autumn. Combined with the remarkable Greek and Roman antiquities at Cyrene, Leptis Magna and other ancient sites, the sun should provide a good foundation on which to build up a tourist trade.

Industry

The Libyan market is much too small and widely dispersed for the development of manufacturing on a large scale. The lack of indigenous supplies of raw materials and fuel has been an additional factor inhibiting the growth of industry. Quite a wide range of small factory industries has nevertheless been established during the past 25 years, based mainly on the processing of local agricultural products. The majority of these industries are located in and around the city of Tripoli and are managed by Italians. They include flour milling, olive oil refining, tobacco and salt manufacture (both state monopolies), textiles, footwear and clothing, vehicle repairs, printing, fish processing, the manufacture of soap, the canning of fruits and vegetables and the manufacture of beer, wine and soft drinks. Altogether factory industries in Libya probably employ 15,000-20,000 people and contribute about one-tenth of the national output. In addition, considerable numbers of men and women are engaged on a part-time basis in handicrafts such as handloom weaving, the manufacture of mats and carpets, basketwork, shoemaking and carpentry.

Existing Pattern of Economic Activity

One of the most striking features of the present-day Libyan economy is the extent of foreign activities in the country. The United States and the United Kingdom both maintain air bases in the country, and British troops are stationed there. The treaties under which the Libyan Government has granted rights to these bases provide for financial and economic assistance to be given to Libya by the United States and the United Kingdom for a period of years (see Chapter 3). The United Arab Republic and the predecessor Government of Egypt, together with France, Italy, and a number of other countries have also given financial assistance to Libya, and the United Nations has accepted special responsibilities in the field of technical assistance. The total value of all grants and loans made to Libya by foreign countries and the United Nations has averaged rather over £L 13 million a year from 1957/58 through 1959/60 (see Table 1 on page 48). In addition, military, diplomatic and other expenditures by foreign countries in

Libya have been officially estimated at about £L 10 million in 1957 and £L 7 million in 1958. The local expenditures of foreign oil companies came to over £L 4 million in 1957 and nearly £L 9 million in 1958 (excluding the value of goods directly imported from abroad).

The value of Libya's gross domestic product in 1958 has been officially estimated at about £L 52 million (equivalent to about £L 43 or just over $120 per head), and some rough calculations made independently by the mission tend to support this figure as being of the right order of magnitude (see Annex I). It must be emphasized, however, that both calculations are subject to a considerable margin of error. It would appear that only about one-quarter of the total product is derived from agriculture, forestry and fishing and about one-tenth from industry and mining (excluding petroleum prospecting). Most of the rest (say 60 percent of the gross domestic product) is attributable to wholesale and retail trading, banking and insurance, building and construction, petroleum prospecting, transport and communications, the renting of houses, personal services, public administration and defense. This varied group of activities, which between them probably provide a living for nearly 100,000 Libyans, are closely linked either with foreign aid or with the expenditures of foreign governments and oil companies in Libya. These external sources of income make possible a high level of imports, which is the basis of most of the profits earned in wholesale and retail trading, commerce and banking; they provide more than half the revenues of the federal and provincial governments; and they create a big demand for offices and houses (especially in Tripoli and Benghazi), transport and personal services.

Since 1958 the domestic product has undoubtedly increased further as the operations of the oil companies have stimulated activity in various sectors of the economy, particularly building, transport, wholesaling and retailing and other service trades. Not enough information is available, however, for any meaningful estimate to be made of the rate of growth in output.

The sectors of the economy in which incomes have risen fastest since Independence are for the most part those which have been financed either by foreign aid and foreign military expenditures in Libya or, more recently, by the oil companies. The classes which have benefited most in this situation are the merchants and shopkeepers, building contractors, employees of foreign governments and oil companies, hotel proprietors, taxi and truck drivers, waiters, domestic servants and Libyan government employees. Industry has also expanded in response to the general increase in demand, and the average industrial worker is undoubtedly better off now than he was ten years ago. By contrast, except for a few large farms run mainly by non-Libyans, the farmers, pastoralists and agricultural workers have benefited comparatively little. The difficulties of finding markets for their produce have been aggravated by the large flow of imports financed out of foreign aid (including gift wheat and subsidized flour). Today, although well over half the Libyan people still depend on agriculture and animal husbandry for their living, they probably receive only about one-quarter of the national income. It is hardly surprising in these circumstances that labor is steadily drifting away from the land in search of more remunerative employment elsewhere, and that the government's efforts to stimulate agricultural development have met with little apparent success (see Chapter 3).

The value of Libya's imports of goods and services is roughly equal to 50 percent of the value of its own production—an extraordinarily high proportion matched by few other countries in the world. A large part of these imports is absorbed by the modern sector of the economy. Merchandise imports amounted to about £L 23 million in 1957 and rather over £L 24 million in 1958—that is, before payment of customs duties and excluding equipment and supplies directly imported by foreign governments and oil companies. Less than one-fifth of the foreign exchange required to pay for these imports was obtained from the proceeds of Libya's merchandise exports; the rest came from invisible exports in the form of the expenditures of foreign governments and oil companies and from foreign aid. Total receipts of foreign exchange from these three sources both in 1957 and 1958 were more than sufficient to cover expenditure on imports, and Libya was able to add approximately £L 9 million to its external reserves during the two years. These reserves increased further in 1959.[1] In addition, there are indications that there has been some export of private capital.

Libya's imports more than doubled in value between 1954 and 1958, even after excluding goods imported directly by the oil companies (Statistical Appendix, Tables S.15-S.17). Roughly 25 percent of the goods imported in 1957 and 1958 consisted of cereals, tea, sugar, fruit and

---

[1] The net foreign assets of all official and banking institutions rose by £L 4.6 million in the calendar year 1957 and by £L 5.1 million in 1958 (see Statistical Appendix, Table S.11). Most of this rise was apparently accounted for by government institutions. Gross foreign exchange holdings of the National Bank of Libya increased from £L 11.5 million at the end of March 1957 to £L 19.7 million at the end of March 1959 and £L 25.4 million at the end of January 1960 (see Statistical Appendix, Table S.12).

vegetables, dairy products and other foods, while nearly another 20 percent was made up of textiles, clothing, pharmaceuticals and miscellaneous consumer goods. The remaining 55-60 percent consisted of coal and coke, petroleum, machinery, trucks, cars, iron and steel, nonferrous metals, cement, asphalt, timber, fertilizers, chemicals, rubber tires and a large variety of miscellaneous raw materials and manufactures. Italy and the United Kingdom were much the largest suppliers, followed by Germany, the United States, France, Holland, Ceylon and Egypt.

During the five years 1952 to 1956 Libya's earnings from exports and re-exports fluctuated around a mean of about £L 4 million a year, (see Statistical Appendix, Tables S.11, S.13 and S.14). Exports of sponges are not included in this figure because, although they appear in the customs returns, they are not a Libyan product, and Libya obtains only a very small part of the proceeds. Record export earnings of £L 5.2 million were achieved in 1957, thanks to exceptionally large shipments of olive oil; in 1958, when olive oil exports declined again, earnings were £L 4.8 million. Apart from olive oil, supplies of which are subject to wide variation from year to year, the principal exports are groundnuts, livestock and livestock products, castor seed, scrap metal (a wartime legacy) and esparto grass. About two-fifths of Libya's exports go to Italy (three-fifths in 1957) and one-sixth to the United Kingdom, with Egypt, Germany, Malta and Greece as the other main customers. Total earnings from exports and re-exports are equivalent to about 10 percent of Libya's gross domestic product.

Use of Resources

Libya's production and imports have to provide the real resources not only for the country's own needs, but also for its exports and for the expenditures in Libya of foreign governments and oil companies. After these last three items have been deducted[2] resources amounting probably to something like £L 55 million were left for Libya's domestic use in 1958. The mission has estimated (on the basis of some very rough calculations) that about 55-60 percent of these resources were absorbed by private consumption, 20-25 percent by the current expenditures of the federal and provincial governments, the municipalities and the

---

[2] The expenditures of foreign governments in Libya and the exploration expenditures of the oil companies have both been treated throughout this report as "invisible exports." On these definitions, Libya's import surplus was about £L 4 million in 1957 and rather over £L 3 million in 1958.

foreign aid agencies and 15-20 percent by gross capital formation, public and private (see Annex I).

The proportion of resources absorbed by public expenditures in Libya is extraordinarily high by comparison with most other countries. If current and capital expenditures are combined, it works out at about one-third. The mission analyzed the accounts of the federal and provincial governments, the LARC and the LPDSA in some detail and found that, out of total public expenditures of £L 17 million in 1957/58, approximately £L 6.6 million was spent on general administration, the police forces and the army, £L 4.7 million on health, education and other social services and £L 5.7 million on economic services, mainly agriculture, public utilities, transport and communications (see Statistical Appendix, Tables S.3-S.10). Total public expenditures in 1957/58 were almost twice as large as in 1954/55, and they appear to have risen by at least another £L 2 million (12 percent) in 1958/59.

It is difficult to draw a clear line between current and capital items, but out of the total of £L 17 million spent in 1957/58 it would appear that about £L 5 million represented capital expenditures of one sort or another. The average annual level of public capital expenditures over the three years 1955/56 to 1957/58 appears to have been a little over £L 4 million divided approximately as follows: agriculture, irrigation and soil and water conservation 29 percent; electric power and water supplies 18 percent; roads, ports and civil aviation 18 percent; communications and broadcasting 8 percent; education, health and housing 11 percent; the construction of the new summer capital at Beida and other public buildings 14 percent; industry, minerals and miscellaneous 2 percent. The proportion of public investment directed into immediately productive channels was rather low.

The mission was unable to obtain any reliable estimates of private investment. A considerable amount of private building has been taking place in Tripoli, and to a lesser extent in Benghazi, mainly for the purpose of providing houses for the foreign community. Some private investment has been taking place in agriculture, particularly on the larger farms in Tripoli which are owned by Italians and foreign companies. Private manufacturing industries have also been expanding and so has private road transport. In the light of all these developments the mission would suggest £L 3-4 million as a rather conservative estimate of gross private investment in 1958.

The rapid increase in Libya's income during the past three or four years has by no means been fully reflected in the living standards of the

Libyan people. As already noted, the additional income has been very unevenly distributed, and only a comparatively small part of it has reached the mass of small farmers and pastoralists who comprise more than half the population. Average figures of per capita income are therefore a rather misleading guide to the standards of living of the people.

If the mission's calculations are approximately correct, private consumption per head of population in 1958 (including resident aliens) was still only about £L 25-30 ($70-84) a year—a figure that compares unfavorably with most other countries in North Africa and the Middle East. Nevertheless, there are indications that consumption levels are considerably higher on average than they were even five years ago. For example, per capita consumption of both cereals and sugar appears to have risen by about 50 percent during the past five years, and there has simultaneously been a marked shift in the Libyan diet away from the cheaper foods such as barley and dates toward more expensive foods like wheat bread and pasta. It is by no means uncommon nowadays to see wireless sets in the poorest Libyan homes, and purchases of bicycles, wrist watches, ball-point pens and many other comparative luxuries have undoubtedly been on the increase. Moreover, in assessing living standards account must be taken of the extensive social services now provided free or at a minimal charge to large sections of the population. These include free medical services for most of those within reach of a hospital or dispensary and free schooling, usually including a daily meal, for about 60 percent of the children between the ages of 6 and 12 and for 15 percent of those aged 12 and over.

Public Finance

Roughly half of all public expenditures in Libya are financed out of domestic revenues and the other half out of foreign grants and loans. The United Kingdom is contributing £L 3.25 million a year directly in support of the Libyan budget, while grants and loans from the United States have been running during the past three years at the rate of $25-30 million a year. Most of the United States money is earmarked for the financing of specific development projects, but in 1958/59, for the first time, the United States agreed to allocate $2.8 million for budget support, as well as $5.2 million in the form of non-project assistance to be spent by the foreign aid agencies.

Customs duties are the main source of domestic revenues, contributing just under £L 5 million to the federal exchequer in 1957/58 and £L 6.4 million in 1958/59. The federal government also derives small sums from miscellaneous fees and duties (see Statistical Appendix, Table S.2). Until recently there was a profit on the operations of the Posts and Telecommunications Department, but this has been turned into a substantial loss by the high cost of operating the new telecommunications system.

Personal income tax and business profits tax are at present levied only by the provinces. The rates are low (10 percent for businesses, 8 percent or 4 percent for individuals, according to income), and there is no regular system of progression. Tripolitania obtains rather over one-third of its revenue from these sources (£L 1,138,000 in 1957/58 and £L 1,468,000 in 1958/59); the rest comes mainly from the profits of the tobacco and salt monopolies (£L 714,000 in 1958/59), government trading in sugar (£L 350,000), the profit on the operation of Tripoli port (£L 241,000) and miscellaneous indirect taxes (£L 406,000). Cyrenaica raises its revenue in broadly similar ways, but on a smaller scale—£L 1,189,000 in 1958/59 as compared with £L 3,709,000 for Tripolitania. The revenues of the Fezzan are much smaller still, adding up to only about £L 100,000.

The federal government is directly responsible for less than one-third of total public expenditures in Libya, although its expenditures have been growing more rapidly than those of the provinces. In 1958/59, for instance, it spent about £L 5 million, while the Tripolitanian Government also spent £L 5 million, the Cyrenaican Government £L 3.2 million, the Fezzan Government rather under £L 1 million and the LARC and LPDSA together £L 4.6 million. All three provinces are heavily dependent on grants-in-aid from the center. The amount of these grants are determined annually on an ad hoc basis.

Partly as a result of the increase in foreign aid during the last few years, government revenues have regularly exceeded expenditures, and both the federal and provincial governments have been able to accumulate cash reserves, which have mostly been deposited with the National Bank of Libya and invested in foreign securities. The total of federal and provincial government balances with the National Bank at the end of March 1958 was about £L 4½ million. In addition, the foreign aid agencies had unspent balances of about £L 5½ million, most of which were already earmarked for particular projects. The balances of the federal and provincial governments with the National Bank rose by a further £L 4 million between the end of March 1958 and the end of December 1959.

Libya has no internal public debt. Its external public debt at the beginning of 1960 was limited to two United States Government loans for the expansion of electric power in Tripoli; the first, in the amount of $3.5 million, was extended under the Mutual Security Act in 1957, the second, in the amount of $5 million, was made by the Development Loan Fund in 1959.

Currency and Banking

The Libyan pound is maintained at parity with sterling, and the law requires 100 percent foreign exchange backing for all currency issued. A central bank, the National Bank of Libya, was established in 1956 in place of the former Currency Board (see Annex II). The National Bank has the sole right to issue currency; it holds the deposits of the federal and provincial governments; it administers a system of exchange control and it also conducts a small commercial banking business of its own. As of the beginning of 1960, there were eight regular commercial banks in Libya, all of them controlled from outside the country.

The volume of currency in circulation outside the banks rose from £L 5 million at the end of 1956 to just under £L 9 million at the end of 1959. During the same period, sight deposits rose from £L 8.8 million to £L 10.5 million. Sight deposits have thus regularly exceeded the currency in circulation. This is a rather unusual situation in an underdeveloped country and reflects the large amount of business conducted with and by foreigners in the two main commercial centers of Tripoli and Benghazi. When Libyans transact business with one another, payment is usually in cash, and few Libyans make regular use of banking facilities, although the banking habit appears to be growing slowly.

Commercial banking in Libya is at present very largely tied up with the financing of imports and exports, but there is a certain amount of lending to industry and agriculture, as well as occasional credits for private house-building and increasing provision of installment credit for the purchase of cars and other durable consumer goods. Advances are usually limited to 3-12 months with interest rates in the range of 7-10 percent. The interest offered on deposits ranges between 1 percent and 4½ percent. The commercial banks are required by law to hold liquid assets equivalent to at least 20 percent of their deposits, and in the absence of local interest-bearing securities the bulk of these assets are held abroad. Most, though not all the banks maintain a fairly high degree of liquidity, which reflects the lack of secure investment opportunities in Libya.

Only the larger and more prosperous farmers in Libya are in a position to obtain credit from the commercial banks. The mass of small farmers look to local merchants for finance and are charged exorbitant rates of interest, which are often concealed in the high prices the farmer has to pay for his supplies and the low prices he receives for his crop. A National Agricultural Bank was founded in 1955 with an initial capital of £L 500,000, and this has since been raised to £L 1 million. The Bank has so far mainly concentrated on seasonal crop loans and other short-term financing (see Chapter 8).

Libya has no institution for financing medium-term or long-term private investment, it has no organized capital market, nor are there any specialized savings institutions. The commercial banks, most of which are able to draw on funds outside the country if they need to, have little incentive to recruit additional savings. Libyans in any case generally prefer to invest their savings in tangible assets such as gold and silver ornaments, houses, real estate and stocks of merchandise. These traditional preferences have been reinforced in recent years by the high returns to be obtained on building offices and houses for foreigners and catering to their needs in other ways.

Costs and Prices

There is an almost total lack of reliable data about prices in Libya. An official cost of living index was instituted some years ago in Tripoli, but it is widely held to be unrepresentative. The price level as a whole has unquestionably risen during the past five years, and particularly during the last two, as a result of the rapid expansion of demand associated with the large inflow of income from abroad. The fairly free availability of imports has acted as a check on general inflation, but some prices have nevertheless shot up, especially the prices of goods and services consumed mainly by foreigners and by the upper Libyan income groups—for example, housing rents in Tripoli and Benghazi, hotel and restaurant charges, cars and luxury imports. Tariff increases have also added to the prices of most imported consumer goods. On the other hand, prices of certain staple commodities have been held down or even reduced as a result of official price controls or economies made possible by expansion of the market; examples are bread, salt and cigarettes.

It is difficult to say how far these price increases have added to the cost of living of Libyans in the middle and lower income groups. Those living near the subsistence level in rural areas are, of course, little affected, since they buy very little in the market, and the prices of most of the things they do buy (e.g., tea, sugar and cigarettes) have not changed very much as a result of the oil boom. On the other hand, most Libyans living in the towns will in varying degrees have felt the impact of rising prices. For example, a survey of retail prices in Tripoli shows the price of mutton rising by 9 percent between December 1958 and December 1959, the price of beef by 10 percent and of lamb by 46 percent. It would also appear that rents paid by some people in the middle and lower income groups have risen considerably during the past year. The evidence in fact tends to support the view that it is seldom possible to have sharp price increases in one sector of the economy without the effects spreading to some extent to other sectors.

One price has certainly increased in response to the upsurge of demand, and that is the price of labor. The relatively high wages and salaries offered by the oil companies and by other foreign employers have set standards which are entirely out of line with the previous pattern of incomes in government service, industry and agriculture. The present statutory minimum wage for government employment, industry and trade is 25 piasters (70 US cents) a day, and the minimum for oil workers is 35 piasters (98 US cents) a day. But actual wages paid by foreign employers are frequently well in excess of the minima, and oil company employees normally receive substantial additional payments in kind (e.g., free food and accommodation). It has become more and more difficult in these circumstances to retain workers on the land; the rate of labor turnover in trade and industry has increased, while standards of discipline are deteriorating; and government is liable to find its best men drifting away to more remunerative jobs elsewhere.

Summary

To sum up, Libya's economy has received considerable support since Independence from foreign financial and technical assistance, foreign military expenditures and oil exploration. Growth has been mainly concentrated in the sectors which cater directly to the needs of the foreigner or which are financed by income from abroad; these are wholesale and retail trading, personal services, building and construction, transport and government. At the same time public investment has been heavily concentrated in transport and communications, public utilities, government buildings and social services. There is need now for speeding up the development of Libya's own productive resources which has so far made relatively little progress. This is necessary in order to improve the economic position of the small farmers, agricultural laborers and pastoralists who comprise a majority of the working population. The pattern of economic growth, which remains lopsided at present, is reflected in the distortion of wage and price relationships and in the uneven distribution of income and wealth. Although such imbalances are perhaps inevitable in countries like Libya which have received a sudden rapid increase in external income, it is nevertheless important that they should be redressed as soon as possible.

CHAPTER 3   *FOREIGN AID AND*
ECONOMIC DEVELOPMENT

Libya and the United Nations

Since the United Kingdom of Libya came into being in accordance with the decision taken by the General Assembly of the United Nations in 1949, the Assembly has maintained a continuing interest in the country's progress. Shortly after Independence, in February 1952, the Assembly requested the Economic and Social Council "to study, in consultation with the Government of the United Kingdom of Libya, ways and means by which the United Nations, with the cooperation of all governments and the competent specialized agencies, and upon the request of the Government of Libya, could furnish additional assistance to the United Kingdom of Libya with a view to financing its fundamental and urgent programs of economic and social development, giving consideration to the possibility of opening a special account of voluntary contributions to that end."

The United Nations and its specialized agencies have in fact undertaken an expanded program of technical assistance in Libya, and both financial and technical assistance have been provided by a number of member countries, including Egypt (subsequently, the United Arab Republic), France, Italy, Pakistan, Turkey, the United Kingdom and the United States. The last two countries have played a particularly important role in helping to finance Libya's economic and social development because of their special relationships with Libya and because of the fact that they have both been granted rights to maintain military bases in the country.

It can be argued, and is so argued in Libya, that the money made available to the Libyan economy by the United Kingdom and the United States is not strictly foreign aid at all, but payments for services rendered to these countries by the Libyan Government in affording them special facilities, including the use of public land and buildings, airports and public highways. According to this view, the payments in question should be regarded for purposes of economic analysis as invisible exports rather than as official grants and loans. While not

44

disputing that there may be some force in this argument, the mission has followed the definitions set out in the relevant treaties with the United Kingdom and the United States, which provide specifically for financial and economic "assistance" to be extended to Libya by these two countries (see below).

Special Treaties with United Kingdom and United States

Assistance from the United Kingdom is granted under the Treaty of Friendship and Alliance concluded between the two countries in 1953, which gives the United Kingdom the right to important military facilities in Libya, including the "exclusive and uninterrupted use for military purposes" of certain specified lands and buildings and permission for United Kingdom public aircraft "to fly over and, in any emergency, land on and take off from any of the territory of Libya, including territorial waters."[1] Under the original financial agreement attached to this Treaty the United Kingdom undertook during the five financial years 1953/54-1957/58 to pay £L 1 million a year to Libyan development organizations and £L 2.75 million a year to the Libyan budget. A new agreement was negotiated in 1958, under which the United Kingdom is providing £L 3.25 million a year in the form of budgetary aid for a further five years, but with no additional contribution to development.

American assistance stems from two agreements concluded in 1954, which among other things give the United States the right to occupy and use certain areas in Libya for military purposes, including the important Wheelus Air Base on the outskirts of Tripoli.[2] Under the economic agreement Libya was to receive an initial sum of $7 million (together with some grain) followed by grants of $4 million annually during the six fiscal years beginning July 1954 and $1 million annually during the eleven years beginning July 1960. Actual assistance from the United States has substantially exceeded the amounts envisaged in the 1954 agreement. Loans have been made as well as grants, together

[1] *Treaty of Friendship and Alliance between Her Majesty in respect of the United Kingdom of Great Britain and Northern Ireland and His Majesty the King of the United Kingdom of Libya,* Treaty Series No. 3 (1954), H.M.S.O. London, Cmd. 9043 (in English and Arabic).

[2] *Mutual Defense Assistance: Agreement and Memorandum of Understanding between the United States of America and Libya,* U. S. Department of State Publication 5743 (in English and Arabic). *Economic Assistance to Libya: Agreement between the United States of America and Libya,* U. S. Department of State Publication 5740 (in English and Arabic).

with special shipments of gift wheat and other cereals to meet shortages in drought years. The greater part of American financial assistance to Libya has been earmarked for specific development projects, but recently, at the request of the Libyan Government, an increasing proportion has taken the form of budgetary grants-in-aid.

Organization of Foreign Aid

Two special agencies of the Libyan Government were created to handle funds granted by foreign countries for development purposes. The first of these is the Libyan Public Development and Stabilization Agency (LPDSA), which was set up in 1952 to program development funds received from the United Kingdom and other countries. The second is the Libyan-American Reconstruction Commission (LARC), which was set up in 1955 and has been entirely concerned with the programing of American money. As an adjunct to LARC, a separate organization, the Libyan-American Joint Services (LAJS), was created in 1955 to assist in the implementation of programs financed by American funds in the fields of agriculture and natural resources, health and education.

In addition, the United States and the United Nations have both been providing technical assistance to Libya on a wide scale. The U. S. technical assistance program has been operated through the United States Operations Mission in Libya (USOM), and many of the personnel recruited under this program have been assigned to service with the LAJS. Private American consultants have been employed by the U. S. Government to advise on particular aspects of development such as road construction and the expansion of electric power facilities. The UN technical assistance has been organized for the most part through FAO, ILO, WHO, UNESCO and other specialized agencies and has been coordinated by the UN Technical Assistance Mission in Libya.

The picture of technical and financial assistance provided to Libya since 1952 is summarized in Table 1. It should be noted that the table shows allocations and not actual transfers.

The organization and working of the foreign aid agencies have been described in the 1958 report of the Libyan Development Council[3] and in a memorandum transmitted to the Secretary-General of the United

[3] *Financing of Development Programs: A Report on Development Expenditures Planned and Made in the Years 1952-3 to 1957-8*, Development Council, United Kingdom of Libya, 1958.

Nations by the Libyan Prime Minister in 1958.[4] In the present report we shall confine ourselves to a broad review of the development activities carried out by the agencies since Independence. We should mention in passing that the expenditures of the LARC and LPDSA have not been confined exclusively to economic development in the sense in which this term is normally used. The LARC, for example, has spent considerable sums on the continued maintenance of existing highways and on meeting the recurrent costs of education and health services. Again, the LPDSA has been required by law to allocate one-quarter of its funds (after the deduction of management expenses) to a Stabilization Fund, which was created for the purpose of providing relief in time of natural calamity from famine and floods.

It may be added that, while some of the funds of the LARC, and to a lesser extent of the LPDSA, have been used to meet recurrent expenditures, the federal and provincial governments have been spending part of their own budgetary funds on capital projects. The most important instance is the Exceptional Budget instituted by the federal government in 1955, which has been used to finance the construction of the new administrative center at Beida, along with minor works for the development of agriculture, water resources and tourism. The construction of the new capital at Sebha in the Fezzan has been mainly financed out of federal grants-in-aid to the province, although the aid agencies have also made an important contribution. It is still true, of course, that all public capital expenditure has in effect been financed out of foreign aid, since the domestic revenues of the federal and provincial governments fall a long way short of covering their current expenditures.

Previous Development Programs

The first postwar development program for Libya was based on the report of a UN economic survey mission led by Mr. Benjamin Higgins, which visited the country in 1951-52.[5] An earlier report on the Libyan economy was submitted to the United Nations by Mr. John Lindberg.[6] The Higgins report, which was prepared at a time when only very limited financial resources were in sight, recommended development

[4] *Memorandum on the Technical Assistance Received by the Government of Libya from the United Nations for Transmittal to the Secretary-General.*

[5] *The Economic and Social Development of Libya*, United Nations, New York, October 1953.

[6] *A General Economic Appraisal of Libya*, United Nations, New York, 1952.

TABLE 1   Foreign Economic Aid Allocated to Libya

(Libyan fiscal years: £L '000 equivalent)

	1952-53	1953-54	1954-55	1955-56	1956-57	1957-58	1958-59	1959-60
United States								
Technical co-operation	554	490	530	580	689	943	939	945
Project assistance	—	—	—	1,071	1,786	5,921	3,929	3,929
Non-project assistance[a]	—	—	1,786	1,428	1,428	1,428	2,856	2,856
DLF loan	—	—	—	—	—	—	—	1,786
PL 480, Title II, famine relief[b]	—	—	70	939	742	425	87	1,391
PL 480, Title III, relief[c]	—	—	—	37	94	419	638	477
Total	554	490	2,386	4,055	4,739	9,136	8,449	11,384
United Kingdom								
Budgetary grants	2,360	2,750	2,750	2,750	3,000	3,250	3,250	3,250
Development assistance	380	1,000	1,000	1,000	1,000	1,000	—	—
Total	2,740	3,750	3,750	3,750	4,000	4,250	3,250	3,250
Other Countries								
France	218	100	100	100	235	10	130	—
Italy[d]	10	10	10	10	10	10	1,010	—
United Arab Republic[e]	—	—	10	10	10	10	10	—
Turkey[e]	—	—	10	10	10	10	10	—
Pakistan	—	—	—	—	—	—	10	—
Total	228	110	130	130	265	40	1,170	—
United Nations[f]								
Technical assistance	233	275	208	215	261	262	260	250
Grand Total	3,755	4,625	6,474	8,150	9,265	13,688	13,129	14,884

[a] Includes the $4 million a year Special Purpose payments granted out of Department of Defense funds.

[b] Estimated world market value based on $63 a metric ton for wheat and $50 a metric ton for feed grains plus shipping costs.

[c] Commodity Credit Corporation reimbursement prices, which are above world

expenditures of £L 2.3 million in 1952/53 and an annual average of £L 2.8 million for the following five years. A five-year development program was prepared along the lines recommended and was adopted as the basis of LPDSA's activities. However, it was never fully carried out. Initially, the LPDSA took over a number of projects started under the British administration, including the building of a new waterworks and power station in Benghazi and the reconstruction of the quays in Tripoli harbor, and the agency did not have enough funds to launch out into an entirely new program.

Later on, when the LARC came onto the scene and American aid was greatly increased, the original five-year plan was felt to be out of date, and a new program was put forward early in 1956 by an "International Committee" composed of representatives of the Libyan Government, the USOM and the UNTAM. This program amounted in effect to a statement of estimated development requirements for the five-year period 1956/57-1960/61. These were assessed at about £L 42 million. A large number of individual projects were included, but the program lacked balance and cohesion. It was suggested for adoption by the LARC as a basis for the allocation of U. S. project assistance funds, but although many of the projects have in fact been taken on by the LARC and the LPDSA, the program as such has never been carried out.

A number of development programs have been drawn up from time to time by the provincial governments. Each province at one point prepared a long-term program covering a period of ten to twenty years,

---

levels, plus shipping costs.

d Not all the annual allocations of £L 10,000 have actually been received. The figure for 1958-59 includes a sum of £L 1 million equivalent transferred by Italy to Libya in cash under the Libyan-Italian Agreement of 1956; this agreement provides for the transfer of an additional £L 1,750,000 in the form of equipment and services, but this transfer has not yet been made. The figures in the table exclude financial assistance given by the Italian Government to Italian farmers in Libya. The amounts of such assistance in recent years have been substantial.

e United Arab Republic aid was allocated by the Predecessor Government of Egypt until union with Syria was declared on February 22, 1958. Only part of the aid shown as allocated by the United Arab Republic and Turkey has actually been received by Libya. The above figures, however, exclude the substantial payments made by the Egyptian Government, and subsequently the UAR Government, toward the salaries of Egyptian teachers in Libya.

f The UN figures are on a calendar year basis and show the amounts obligated by the United Nations and its specialized agencies under the expanded program of technical assistance to Libya.

and the Cyrenaican Government prepared a five-year program for the province for the period beginning April 1958. None of these programs was based on a realistic study of economic needs and resources, and none has been adopted for action.

The Development Council

A Development Council was set up in June 1956 to assist in co-ordinating the work of economic development. The Permanent Under-Secretary of the Ministry of Finance originally served as chairman of the council, and its first director was the Deputy Resident Representative of the United Nations Technical Assistance Board. The council now has a full-time Libyan chairman and a small staff of Libyan and expatriate officials. The council's functions have been purely advisory, and it has had no responsibility either for the allocation of funds or for the execution of projects. Its secretariat has initiated a number of economic studies and produced two reports on development activities, but the council has never had sufficient staff to undertake a comprehensive survey of the economy or to play its proper role in the formulation of development policy.

The Libyan Public Development and Stabilization Agency

The LPDSA started operations in April 1952. The chairman of its board is a Libyan official (the Permanent Under-Secretary of the Ministry of Finance), and the Libyan Government has majority voting rights. The general manager is British and his deputy a Libyan. The staff of the organization is small, and its management expenses have averaged about £L 37,000 a year. Total contributions to the agency's funds from the time of its inception to the end of 1959 amounted to about £L 7½ million, of which £L 5,720,000 had been earmarked for development and £L 1,375,500 had been allocated to the Stabilization Fund, the remainder being accounted for by management expenses. Since the beginning of April 1958, when the British ceased to contribute directly to development funds, the LPDSA has been mainly financed out of U. S. aid, a sum of £L 1 million being allocated to the agency from this source in 1958/59.

The activities of the LPDSA have been heavily concentrated in transport and public utilities, which between them accounted for over half the funds allocated to development by the agency during the first seven years of its existence. Important projects carried out in these two sectors include the reconstruction and re-equipment of Tripoli harbor (about £L 545,000 spent up to the end of September 1959), maintenance and improvement of the Fezzan road (£L 590,000), resurfacing of the road between Susa and Derna in Cyrenaica (£L 67,000), improvements to urban water supplies in Tripolitania and Cyrenaica (£L 507,000), the expansion of the electric power system in Cyrenaica (£L 522,000) and construction of new runways and lighting at the civil airports of Idris (£L 282,000) and Benina (£L 273,000). Among the major projects in other sectors are the construction of water-spreading works in the Wadi Megenin in Tripolitania, the provision of equipment for the Zorda experimental farm in Cyrenaica, the construction of a new hospital at Jefren, a TB sanatorium at Cyreme and a nurses' training center in Tripoli, popular housing in Cyrenaica, the equipment of the technical and clerical training center in Tripoli, a training college for men in Benghazi and a boarding school in Agedabia.

An important function of the agency has been to act as technical advisor to the federal government on public works and engineering problems. For example, it has financed an investigation into the reconstruction of Benghazi harbor and a study of the future development of electric power in the Tripoli area, and it was largely responsible for the arrangements made with a foreign contractor to construct the main buildings at Beida.

More than half the expenditure out of the Stabilization Fund of the LPDSA has been for the purchase of emergency supplies of barley for Cyrenaica and wheat for the Fezzan (mainly in 1952/53 and 1953/54), for expenses incurred in the distribution of American gift wheat, for which the agency has been largely responsible, and for purchases of wheat and barley seed. In addition, extensive relief works have been carried out in Tripolitania and Cyrenaica at a cost of £L 424,000 (mainly in 1955/56), and several villages in the Fezzan have been partly reconstructed at a total cost of £L 33,500; another £L 65,000 has been spent on repairing flood damage in Cyrenaica (mostly in 1954/55 and 1955/56). Relief works have included measures of soil and water conservation in Tripolitania and the construction of a new road from Barce to Tolmeta in Cyrenaica.

The Libyan-American Reconstruction Commission

The LARC, like the LPDSA, has the Permanent Under-Secretary of the Ministry of Finance as chairman of its board, and the Libyan Government has majority voting rights. The present director of the agency is a Libyan, and until recently a U. S. government official acted as advisor. The LARC itself operates mainly as a programing agency, working closely with the U. S. Embassy and USOM in matters concerning the allocation of funds and the execution of major projects and with the LAJS in the implementation of continuing programs in agriculture and natural resources, health and education. The staff of the LARC is small, but the LAJS has approximately 2,000 Libyan and expatriate employees, about 50 technical advisors from the United States and an administrative budget presently in excess of £L 200,000 a year.

A total of over £L 19.6 million ($55 million) had been allocated by the U. S. Government to the LARC up to the end of March 1959. Of this, £L 14.3 million ($40 million) had actually been received by the agency. No further allocations are being made to LARC, and since the beginning of April 1959, with minor exceptions, all U. S. aid funds have been channeled through the Libyan Ministry of Finance. Steps are also being taken to wind up the central administrative unit of the LAJS.

All the U. S. contributions to the LARC have been in the form of grants except for one ICA loan of $3.5 million for the expansion of the Tripoli power undertaking. More recently, in June 1959, a second loan of $5 million for this project was made by the U. S. Development Loan Fund, but this has not been included in the LARC program.

Reported expenditures of the LARC at the end of March 1959 were £L 14.4 million, out of a total of £L 19.6 million allotted to projects. Allotments were divided between the main sectors as follows:

	£L '000	Percent of total
Agriculture, forestry and fisheries	1,580	8
Water resources and minerals	1,556	8
Electric power	4,030	21
Telecommunications	1,851	9
Broadcasting	1,013	5
Roads (including workshop equipment)	2,471	13
Education	2,639	14
Health (including domestic water supplies)	1,584	8
Capitalization of National Bank	700	4
Capitalization of National Agricultural Bank	1,000	5
Administration and miscellaneous	1,135	5
Total allotted	19,559	100

Much the largest single project financed by the LARC is the expansion of the Tripoli power undertaking. Including the money provided for the purchase of a 70 percent interest in the undertaking by the Libyan Government, more than £L 4 million has already been allotted by the U. S. Government to this project, and a further £L 1.8 million has been earmarked for it in the form of the DLF loan mentioned above. Other major projects in the LARC program include the creation of a telecommunications system linking the main centers of population and designed ultimately to provide an important new link in the international network; the establishment of a Libyan broadcasting system; the settlement of 120 families on newly irrigated land by the Wadi Caam on the coast of Tripolitania; flood prevention work in the Wadi Megenin; the improvement and maintenance of the coast road and the Fezzan road; the setting up of the National Bank of Libya and the National Agricultural Bank; and the foundation of a Libyan university. Apart from these big schemes, expenditures on the development of agriculture and water resources have been spread over a wide range of smaller projects for soil and water conservation, ground water investigations, irrigation, livestock improvement, experimental stations, agricultural training and extension work, assistance to co-operatives and so forth. The educational program embraces, in addition to the university, the construction of school buildings, the payment of school teachers' salaries, a program of audio-visual education, the provision of overseas scholarships and a number of projects for technical and vocational training. In health the main expenditures have been on the rehabilitation of Libyan hospitals, basic public health schemes, health training facilities and improvements in rural sanitation and domestic water supplies.

The United Nations

"The technical assistance provided by the United Nations to Libya covers a very wide field and experts from the several UN agencies are giving invaluable aid in almost every aspect of the country's development. For the most part these experts serve in an advisory capacity, but in several cases they have also been required to assume executive responsibilities within the Libyan Government where this is made necessary by the non-availability of appropriately qualified Libyan personnel. A number of UN experts have also been assigned to Libya to carry out specialist investigations in some of the fields where basic information is most urgently required. Financial assistance for the country's development needs is not, of course, provided by the United Nations, although in a few instances the UN agencies do provide limited amounts of equipment and supplies; many UN technical assistance projects in Libya are therefore supported by funds provided by the government and received under bilateral agreements for economic aid."[7]

United Nations technical assistance has supplemented Libya's meager resources of professional and administrative skills in many ways. For example, two experts in public administration carried out a survey of the federal and provincial governments and made recommendations for increasing efficiency in the public service; one of these experts has remained in Libya to assist in carrying out the recommendations approved by the government. A school of public administration was opened by the United Nations in Tripoli in January 1957 with an initial enrollment of 35 students. One UN statistician has been serving since 1953 as director of the Government's Central Statistics Office, and two others have been responsible for taking a population census, the results of which have recently been published. For a number of years the United Nations has provided the services of an economist who has acted as Economic Advisor to the Libyan Government; in one instance the expert concerned also served as Director of the Development Council.

FAO has been particularly active in Libya, and more than 35 FAO experts have served in the country since Independence, in addition to a number of consultants called in to advise on special problems. The regular FAO mission includes forestry advisors, agronomists, horticulturists, livestock experts, a date specialist and an advisor on cooperatives. A broad division of functions has been worked out in practice between FAO and USOM under which the former has concentrated mainly on agricultural research, policy matters and advisory services, and the latter on the execution of agricultural development projects involving training, extension and soil and water conservation works. One of FAO's primary objectives in Libya has been to train Libyan counterparts to replace its own experts, but while some progress has been made in this direction, it has inevitably been slow because most agricultural skills can only be acquired through long training on the job.

UNESCO and WHO also maintain permanent missions in Libya.

[7] *Memorandum on the Technical Assistance Received by the Government of Libya from the United Nations for Transmittal to the Secretary-General,* page 16, paragraph 42.

The WHO program has been mainly concentrated on public health training, tuberculosis control (BCG campaign), nurse education and medical and child health; the United Nations Children's Fund has cooperated in a number of WHO projects by providing equipment and supplies. A school of nursing has been established by WHO in Tripoli and an institute for medical assistants and sanitarians in Benghazi. UNESCO has laid particular stress on adult and fundamental education, both rural and urban, including such diverse activities as the production of educational films, assistance in the drafting of a broadcasting law, the training of kindergarten teachers and teaching in rural handicrafts. Finally ILO has cooperated with the Libyan Government in three projects—the drafting and implementation of a social insurance law; the establishment of a handicrafts center in the Fezzan; and the operation of a technical and clerical training center in Tripoli. This last project was started as a joint venture of the Libyan Government and UNESCO.

An important feature of the UN technical assistance in Libya has been the award of fellowships and scholarships to Libyans for overseas study. Approximately 100 such awards have been made since Independence, the majority of them in the field of public administration.

The Results Achieved

Reference was made earlier in the report (pages 33-38) to the broad impact of foreign aid on the Libyan economy, and it was pointed out that only a comparatively small proportion of investment had been directed into immediately productive channels. In the absence of reliable statistics of agricultural output, it is impossible to say with any degree of certainty what the trend has been, especially as output fluctuates violently from year to year for climatic reasons. Undoubtedly real progress has been made in some fields—for instance, in the cultivation of groundnuts, which were almost unknown in Libya ten years ago and are now the country's largest single export; in the growth of olive oil production resulting in part from the maturing of trees planted under the Italian administration; and in the cultivation of new potatoes and other winter vegetables for export. On the other hand, the mass of small Libyan farmers and pastoralists remain desperately poor, and rural conditions, except on some of the larger farms owned and managed by Libyans, Italians and foreign merchants, contrast unfavorably with the flourishing state of trade and service industries and with the fairly rapid growth of manufacturing production.

These observations are not to be taken as a criticism of what the Libyan Government and the foreign aid agencies have been trying to do. They reflect rather the inherent difficulties of promoting balanced economic development in the circumstances in which Libya found itself at the time of Independence. Much of the initial effort had to be directed toward making good the neglect of education and training under the pre-war administration and to repairing the physical damage to harbors, roads and other installations caused by the war and by lack of proper maintenance during and after the war. On top of this, the very size of the country in relation to the paucity of its population and the poverty of its natural resources (oil apart) makes heavy expenditure on internal transport and communications a political and administrative necessity. The federal coast road and the proposed new road to the Fezzan, for example, cannot come anywhere near to paying for themselves in a narrow economic or financial sense. But if these roads were not built, it might prove extremely difficult to hold the three provinces together. Finally, as already noted, there are the peculiar difficulties associated with agricultural development.

The tendency for economic development to be held back more by administrative and institutional factors than by any shortage of money is evidenced by the fact that, out of a total of £L 19.6 million allotted by the U. S. Government to the LARC up to the end of March 1959, only £L 14.4 million had been spent at that date—and in earlier years the lag was relatively larger. An accumulation of funds in the "pipeline" is a normal phenomenon in a country receiving U. S. project assistance. In Libya, however, it has been combined with the building up of cash balances by the federal and provincial governments.

The UN technical assistance program has been of the greatest value to Libya in helping to fill the gap in technical and administrative skills left on the termination of foreign rule. Although the experts assigned to Libya under this program are supposed to act only as advisors, many of them have out of sheer necessity come to fill executive roles. Technical assistance has also been provided to Libya on a large scale by the United States and, in the educational field, by Egypt. It is further relevant in this context to mention the considerable number of senior technical and administrative posts in the Libyan government service which are occupied by expatriate officials drawn mainly from Middle Eastern countries and the United Kingdom.

The mission heard many criticisms of foreign experts during its stay in Libya, but it found the more responsible Libyans deeply appreciative of the technical assistance received, particularly from the United Nations. Certainly, without this assistance, Libya could have made very little economic progress in the period since Independence, and it would have much more insecure foundations to build on for the future. Inevitably, some of the technical assistance given has suffered from defects in organization, from the choice of the wrong individuals and from the fact that many of the experts assigned to Libya stay there for too short a time to make their contributions really effective or to ensure continuity in the execution of projects. On the whole, the mission obtained the impression that assistance given on an international basis through the United Nations and its specialized agencies had been more highly valued by Libyans than assistance given bilaterally by individual countries. The expert working in Libya under the auspices of an international agency is less likely to be faced with a problem of divided loyalties than one who is directly employed by a foreign government, and there are advantages in having a program of technical assistance organized and executed by a multi-national group, which is usually able to draw on a wider variety of experience than a purely national one.

Perhaps the most serious shortcoming of foreign aid to Libya from the economic point of view has been the poor coordination between the work of the different foreign aid agencies and the failure to integrate this work into a properly thought-out program for the development of Libya's resources as a whole. The agencies have been handicapped by the lack of an economic staff. Only in exceptional cases has detailed consideration been given to the economic justification of a project before it has been undertaken or to an assessment of its benefits after it has been completed. There has been much overlapping of technical investigations and research, a quite unnecessary profusion of experts' reports dealing with almost every conceivable aspect of social and economic development and conspicuous lack of central libraries or record offices where the results of the research work done in various fields before and since the war are available for reference. As a result, development has proceeded in a rather piecemeal and haphazard fashion.

There has been a noticeable tendency for countries giving aid to seek special preferences for their own nationals in the award of contracts instead of opening them to competitive international bidding. While this practice is quite understandable, the mission feels that it has sometimes worked out to Libya's disadvantage. In certain cases the fees paid to foreign consultants have rightly come in for a good deal of criticism by Libyans.

It is hardly surprising in the circumstances that the Libyans should have become rather impatient at the apparent lack of progress made and openly critical of the foreign aid agencies. In fact, no project can be executed by the agencies without the formal approval of the Libyan Government, and some of the projects which have come in for the severest criticism have been initiated at the government's special request. Nevertheless, the mission got the impression that the foreign aid agencies have not always taken the Libyan authorities fully into their confidence, and that consultation has sometimes been little more than a formality. As a result, the Libyans do not feel that the program is really theirs, and if a project fails, or is exposed to public criticism, it is too easy for the Libyan Government to disown responsibility and leave the foreigner to get the blame. More important, the Libyan authorities are not given enough opportunity to make their own mistakes and learn from them; to put it another way, they are denied the experience that comes with responsibility.

Certainly more might have been done to give the Libyan people a sense of identity with the activities of the agencies and to encourage local initiative. Maximum public participation and voluntary effort are vital ingredients in any successful program of economic development. The difficulties of securing such participation and effort in Libya are certainly considerable, but better results might have been achieved if the work of the foreign aid agencies had been more closely integrated at all levels with the organization of the Libyan Government.

American aid procedures pose a special problem in a country such as Libya where the greater part of public investment is being financed out of U. S. funds, in that the Libyan Government does not know from year to year how much aid it can count on. Indeed, the final decision on the amount of aid that will be made available during any given Libyan financial year is not taken until several months after the year has begun. This encourages lax budgeting and makes it difficult to make proper plans for economic development.

The disadvantages of having economic development planned, financed and executed through separate agencies have long been recognized both by the Libyan Government and by the other governments concerned. A proposal was accordingly put forward some time ago for the establishment of a new Development Council to formulate and supervise the execution of public investment programs, and a draft law authorizing such a body has been under discussion for more than a year. The delay in reaching any final decision on the proposal reflects the many conflicting interests involved and the differences of opinion as to what the functions of the council should be, and how it should be composed. We have more to say on this subject in Chapter 6.

Prospects for Oil Production

When the mission arrived in Libya in January 1959, oil had already been discovered in several places, and the prevailing atmosphere in oil circles appeared to be one of cautious optimism. This optimism has since been greatly reinforced by a number of exciting finds. The most sensational strike to date was made in June by Esso Standard (Libya) Incorporated, when a well at Zelten in Cyrenaica in a 12-hour test produced 37° API oil from a depth of 5,500 feet at a rate of 17,500 barrels a day. A second strike was made by the same company in August at a point a few miles from the first, a one-hour test producing oil at the rate of 15,000 barrels a day from a depth of 5,770-5,915 feet. The Zelten field lies about 150 kilometers from the Mediterranean coast and just under 400 kilometers south of Benghazi.

By the beginning of February 1960 oil had been struck in over 20 places, although not all of these wells can be expected to be commercial producers. The map facing page 60 shows the concessions granted up to this time and the places where oil had been found. A list of the discoveries is set out in Table 2. Apart from Zelten, the most promising area so far located lies in the eastern part of Tripolitania approximately 150 kilometers south of the Gulf of Sirte. Thus there is every prospect that both coastal provinces will have producing fields.

Orders have already been placed for a 30-inch pipeline to connect Zelten with the coast, and delivery is expected in 1961. Meanwhile, surveys are being made of the coasts of Tripolitania and Cyrenaica to determine the best points for the shipment of the oil. Although the Gulf of Sirte is occasionally exposed to severe winter storms, no major difficulties are apparently contemplated in constructing suitable terminal facilities which could be used both for the export of the oil and for the import of equipment and supplies.

So far as the mission is able to judge, commercial production of oil is likely to start in both Cyrenaica and Tripolitania within the next two or three years. It is not yet possible, however, to make a reliable assessment of the longer-term outlook for oil production in Libya as a whole, or to say exactly what arrangements will be made for the development of the oilfields already discovered.

59

Exploration meanwhile is being carried on with renewed vigor, and almost every month brings news of further discoveries. The companies have a special incentive to press on as fast as they can because, under the terms of the Libyan Petroleum Law of 1955, they are required to surrender 25 percent of their concession areas within a period of five years from the date of the concession and a further 25 percent within eight years. About half the present concessions were granted at the end of 1955 and a majority of the remainder during 1956, so that the years 1959-61 are likely to be peak periods for exploration activity.

TABLE 2   Oil Discoveries in Libya

(Position on February 9, 1960)

Company	Well and Concession Numbers	Production (bbls./day at time of test)	Gravity API
Oasis	A1–32	500	39
"	B1–32	500	36
"	B3–32	500	36
"	F1–32	750	41
"	F2–32	8,000	41
"	A1–26	450	40
"	B2–59	testing	
Esso	B2–1	500	46
"	C1–6	17,500	37
"	C2–6	15,000	39
"	C3–6	1,600	39
Libyan American	A1–17	500	40
" "	B1–17	900	35
" "	C1–17	1,200	37
Gulf	A1–66	900	38
"	E1–66	175	39
Amoseas	B1–47	3,650	36
"	B2–47	500	37
Libya Shell	A1–70	700	44
Mobil Oil	B1–12	850	34
CPTL	B1–49	100	45

SOURCE: Libyan Petroleum Commission

Many factors have to be taken into account in assessing the outlook for production. These concern not only the physical conditions on

the supply side, but also the marketing of the oil. At present, there is a world-wide surplus of supply over demand and production is being held down below capacity in many areas. This does not mean that Libyan oil cannot find a market, but it may affect the rate at which supplies of Libyan crude can be worked into the existing pattern of supply and demand, as well as the prices at which the oil is sold.

Much will depend on the individual positions of the companies producing oil in Libya. The fact that a large number of companies are operating is to Libya's advantage because it ensures that a wide range of markets will be open to Libyan oil. Moreover, there appear to be good reasons for expecting Libya to have a competitive advantage over some other important producing areas on account of lower production and transport costs. The natural market for Libyan oil is Western Europe, where demand for petroleum products has been rising very rapidly—at the rate of about 15 percent per year. Libya's own consumption of oil is too small to have much effect on the position.

Impact on the Economy

The mission is not, of course, in a position to forecast exactly when, or in what amounts, the Libyan Government will obtain revenues from oil. Small sums have already accrued from concession fees, and royalties are payable at the rate of 12½ percent of well-head value from the moment production begins—very likely within two or three years from now. It might be a further two or three years, however, before the Libyan Government starts to share in profits, since the oil companies are entitled under their existing agreements to write off the cost of previous exploration and development expenditures against profits at a rate not exceeding 20 percent a year. The mission has accordingly assumed for the purposes of this report that there will be no *large* increase in government oil revenues before 1965. This is purely an assumption, not a forecast, and in presenting our program in the next chapter we have allowed for the possibility that larger revenues may be forthcoming earlier.

The Libyan economy has already felt the impact of oil operations through the large expenditures incurred by the companies on exploration. Local expenditures by the companies in Libyan pounds were reported at over £L 4 million in 1957 and nearly £L 9 million in 1958. Out of these sums approximately £L 500,000 and £L 1,250,000, respectively, were paid in wages and salaries to Libyans directly employed by the companies, and most of the remaining expenditures represented purchases of (mainly imported) supplies through local contractors. In addition, the companies have brought large quantities of supplies and equipment into Libya on their own account. Exploration expenditures will have risen a good deal further during 1959, and the upward trend may be expected to continue for a year or two. Moreover, from 1960 onwards some companies will be spending increasing sums on developing facilities for producing and transporting the oil that has been discovered. Pipeline and pumping stations will have to be built, power supplied, shipping terminals established, houses and other amenities provided for the workers and so forth.

Employment of local labor may reach a peak during the next few years, when exploration and development are proceeding rapidly side by side. The mission was informed that about 6,000 Libyans were on the companies' payrolls at the beginning of 1959, and the number has no doubt increased since. Later on, however, as production gets under way, demand for labor may subside somewhat unless the tempo of exploration is maintained. The actual business of producing and transporting oil is never likely to be a major source of local employment, since oil operations are highly capital-intensive. This applies also to oil refining. In Saudi Arabia, for example, where 49 million tons of oil were produced in 1958 and 8 million tons were refined locally, only about 12,000 nationals were employed in the oil industry. Even in Venezuela or Iran, where oil operations are highly developed, the number of workers employed in production and refining is less than 50,000. These figures suggest that Libya should not expect the oil industry to provide direct employment for more than a small proportion of its labor force in the foreseeable future—say, about 5 percent as an outside figure.

The indirect impact of oil company operations on the economy is to be observed, particularly in Tripoli, in the sharp rise in prices of housing rents, hotel accommodation and other services bought mainly by foreigners, in the almost equally sharp rise in wages and salaries paid to skilled and semi-skilled Libyan workers, in the establishment of many new Libyan and foreign trading and construction enterprises catering to oil company requirements, in the acceleration of the drift of labor from the land (most conspicuously in the Fezzan) and in the general boom in trading and servicing activities of all kinds. There is already an acute shortage of skilled and semi-skilled workers which makes it extremely difficult for other employers, including government, to obtain the men they need. One department of the Tripolitanian Government has alone lost over 20 of its best men in the space of twelve months, and other branches of the administration have no doubt had similar experiences.

These developments carry with them serious dangers for the stability of the economy and pose difficult problems which call for the careful attention of the Libyan authorities. One of the most challenging of all problems in such a situation is how to ensure that the increased income generated by oil production is invested in such a way as to secure the well balanced development of the economy as a whole. In some countries which have been drawing large revenues from oil over many years, the masses are still desperately poor, agriculture remains backward, and there is widespread unemployment and underemployment. This is not necessarily because the governments concerned have been indifferent to the welfare of their peoples. In part at least, it is because they have not known how to use oil revenues to the best advantage. For example, too much money has sometimes been spent on massive construction projects which take a long time to bear fruit, while smaller investments that yield a quick return have been neglected. Again, too little attention is apt to be given to social welfare expenditures in such fields as health, education and popular housing, which are of immediate benefit to ordinary people.

These considerations have been borne in mind by the mission in framing its recommendations for public expenditures during the next five years. We shall return to them in more detail in the next chapter. Later on, in Chapter 15, we discuss the economic and financial problems arising out of the oil boom.

Industrial Implications of Oil

Oil discoveries have led to speculation about the possibilities of developing new oil-based industries in Libya. It is far too early yet to assess these possibilities with any precision, but the Libyan Government is rightly concerned that no worthwhile opportunities should be overlooked, and it may therefore be helpful to refer briefly to some of the relevant factors.

Libya should certainly have a refinery to supply the bulk of its own requirements of petroleum products. Present civilian consumption is in the region of 100,000 tons a year, consisting mainly of motor spirit, diesel, fuel oil and kerosene. There will also be a substantial demand for these products from the foreign military and air forces stationed in the country. A local refinery with a capacity in the region of 200,000-250,000 tons a year would thus appear to be a sound initial investment—with the possibility of expanding its capacity later on. It is understood that one company has in fact undertaken to construct a refinery of about this size, the stated capacity being 1½ million barrels a year.

In addition to an oil refinery, and possibly related to it, there might eventually be opportunities for establishing in Libya small plants for the manufacture of such products as fertilizers and carbon black, based either on the waste products of a refinery or on natural gas. At the moment, this must be regarded as a rather uncertain prospect, but every encouragement short of direct government assistance should be given to enterprises which may be interested in putting up capital for ventures of this kind. Petroleum industries, it should be added, are generally very small employers of labor, and the gains to the economy from the establishment of such industries are liable to be overestimated.

Libya is at present receiving many enquiries from foreign businessmen who are interested in the possibilities of setting up factories in the country. In general, genuine private foreign investment should be welcomed so long as no direct assistance is required from government either in the form of capital participation or of protection against imports. On the other hand, offers from foreign firms which are primarily interested in selling plant and machinery, and which are not prepared to put their own capital into enterprise, should be scrutinized very carefully. Some of the proposals of which the mission has heard sound extremely suspect. The discovery of oil may well open up opportunities for the establishment of some new industries in Libya which were not previously economic, and private enterprise should be encouraged to take advantage of these opportunities. But the government should beware of supporting uneconomic ventures for the local manufacture of goods which can be obtained much more cheaply from abroad.

Probably the most important aspect of oil production from the point of view of the development of Libyan industry is that it will provide a new and presumably cheaper fuel, whether consumed directly by industry or indirectly through its use in the generation of electricity. The new Tripoli power plant in particular, which is designed to run on fuel oil, may be able to effect substantial economies in cost by using domestically produced oil instead of imports.

Cheap and abundant supplies of kerosene will be of particular value to the Libyan economy if they can take the place of charcoal as a household fuel and as a fuel for bakeries and other commercial establishments. Charcoal burning is one of the main causes of the denudation of forest areas in Libya and the resulting soil erosion. It might well be a sound policy for the government to subsidize the distribution of simple kerosene lamps and stoves in order to accelerate the process of substitution. We would also suggest that kerosene sold for domestic consumption should be exempt from excise duties. In the meantime, import duties on kerosene could with advantage be reduced.

Natural gas is another potential source of fuel for local consumption. Demand in Libya for space heating and cooking would probably not be large enough to justify the installation of a piped supply, even in the capital cities, unless sources of supply could be found in the vicinity, but the economics of bottling natural gas for distribution to the Fezzan and other outlying areas might be worth investigation. If experiments at present being carried out in the United Kingdom in the large-scale use of natural gas imported in liquefied form prove successful, Libya might be a possible source of supply.

The Petroleum Commission

The day-to-day conduct of business with the oil companies is handled by the Petroleum Commission, which is a semi-autonomous public authority consisting of four persons appointed by the federal and provincial governments. The Commission has two full-time advisers, one dealing with general policy and legal matters, including negotiations with the companies, and the other with technical problems.

It is remarkable that so small a staff should have been able to cope so well with the many and varied problems that have arisen. The growing volume of work, however, makes it, in the mission's view, imperative that the permanent professional staff of the Commission should be strengthened. In view of the importance of oil to the Libyan economy, it is essential that the Commission should be staffed by men of the highest integrity and ability, and that its work should be handled in a thoroughly businesslike way. To assist the Petroleum Commission the mission recommends that the Libyan Government should try to secure the part-time services of a high-level consultant versed in the intricacies of the oil business, who could advise on future dealings with the oil companies.

CHAPTER 5 *OUTLINE OF A FIVE-YEAR DEVELOPMENT PROGRAM*

Guiding Principles

The mission, in drawing up a development program to be carried out during the next five years, has been guided by three principal considerations:

1. that the governing factor in Libyan economic development at the present time is a shortage of trained men, which limits the country's capacity to absorb capital and which is reflected in deficiencies in the organization of government, in extensive dependence on expatriate officials and experts and in the low productivity of Libyan agriculture and industry;
2. that, in view of the many uncertainties surrounding the future of oil production, no major increase should be assumed for the next few years in total government revenues from foreign aid and oil combined; but
3. that, looking beyond the next four or five years, Libya might reasonably expect a substantial and rising income from oil revenues, and that plans for development in the meantime should be based on the assumption that such revenues will be forthcoming, even though their magnitude cannot be at present foreseen.

Consistently with this approach, the specific recommendations for public development expenditures set out in this report relate to the five years from April 1, 1960, to March 31, 1965. No attempt has been made to give a year-by-year breakdown of the program, in part because most of the decisions affecting the level and pattern of public expenditures for the first year of the period (i.e., the Libyan fiscal year 1960/61) will have already been taken by the time the report is presented, and the mission has no detailed knowledge of the expenditures proposed. However, we do not anticipate any serious difficulties in accommodating these expenditures within the totals suggested for the various sectors for the five years as a whole.

The program is restricted in size to what the mission believes the federal and provincial governments have a good chance of being able to carry out effectively during the five-year period. Even within these limits, the mission considers that there is urgent need for important changes in government organization and policy, and special attention is given to these matters elsewhere in the report, particularly in Chapters 6 and 15.

Many countries embarking on large-scale programs of capital investment have found the capacity of the building trades to be a major bottleneck. This consideration has been borne in mind by the mission in making recommendations for capital investment in such fields as transport, education, health, housing and public buildings. At present the resources of the Libyan building and civil engineering industry are heavily engaged in carrying out public works (e.g., the Fezzan road) and work for the oil companies. It is important therefore, that, before major new construction programs are undertaken by government, a careful assessment should be made of available resources of materials, personnel and organization.

It is especially desirable to avoid leaving projects half completed and locking up valuable capital to no purpose. So far as major projects are concerned, the danger of this happening can be much reduced by putting contracts out to international tender and by encouraging constructional firms from overseas to set up branches in Libya. At the same time a liberal policy should be followed in issuing immigration permits for skilled labor, supervisory personnel and professional staff such as architects and surveyors. This will not only expedite the work, but will also help to keep building costs down.

The mission has not ruled out the possibilities either that larger revenues will materialize within the next five years, or that the technical and administrative limitations on the planning and execution of development programs will be more quickly overcome. Should both these possibilities be realized, there would be room for larger expenditures than allowed for in our main program, and we have accordingly put forward a Supplementary Program indicating the directions in which we consider that expenditures during the next five years might most usefully be increased if the necessary resources of finance and personnel are available. In any case, we suggest that a fresh review of development plans and prospects should be carried out in three or four years' time when the outlook for oil revenues will be much clearer.

The favorable assumption we have made about the longer-term prospect for oil revenues has a number of implications for development during the next few years. It means, first, that Libya can safely devote a larger proportion of its resources than might otherwise be prudent to long-term schemes for improving its human and physical assets, even though these may not yield an immediate economic return —for example, afforestation and other measures of soil and water conservation, education and training, health services, sanitation and housing. Second, since oil revenues will be received in foreign exchange, alternative measures for closing the gap in the balance of payments by increasing exports and saving imports, while still important, need no longer be accorded such high priority in determining the pattern of development. Third, measures to develop agriculture can be justified by the need to provide a better way of life for those engaged in it, even where, as may sometimes be the case, they cannot be justified simply by economic considerations. Agricultural and animal husbandry are certain to remain for many years ahead the principal occupations of the mass of the Libyan people. The agricultural population, unlike those employed in government service, trade and industry, will not derive much benefit automatically from the growth of oil production, and special efforts are required to ensure that they have the opportunity of obtaining a reasonable share of the resulting increase in national income.

The program described in this report is essentially a program of government action designed to assist and encourage private enterprise. It is the farmer and manufacturer who must produce the goods. Government policies should be directed toward creating a favorable climate for private effort and investment, and we discuss in Chapter 15 various things which should and should not be done if healthy and balanced economic growth is to be achieved. The Libyan Government, in the mission's view very wisely, has left a wide field of investment open to private initiative, particularly in such sectors as industry and tourism. The chapters on these sectors are largely devoted to consideration of ways in which private enterprise can be helped to take full advantage of the opportunities for development, and the mission's recommendations on industry and tourism have been framed primarily with this objective in mind rather than with the idea of promoting large-scale public investment.

The Main Program

The public capital expenditures recommended for the five-year period starting April 1, 1960, add up to £L 25 million—that is, an average of £L 5 million a year. They are summarized in Table 3. These expenditures are expressed in terms of the prices prevailing at the time of the mission's visit early in 1959. Building costs in Libya have risen since then and both wages and profits have increased in response to the sudden upsurge of demand. The actual sums of money that will be required to carry out the physical investment recommended by the mission will therefore in some cases be rather larger than indicated in Table 3.

The mission's proposals entail substantial net increases in recurrent expenditures related to development, particularly in respect of road maintenance, telecommunications, education and health services and agricultural administration. Since the mission does not have up-to-date figures of actual government expenditures, it can indicate only very approximately what the trend of "above-the-line" expenditures might be if the mission's recommendations are adopted. Some illustrative figures are set out in Table 4. It must be emphasized that these figures make no claim to precision.

In addition to new projects recommended by the mission, the program includes provision for expenditures likely to be incurred after April 1, 1960, on the major continuing programs and projects which have already been started by the Libyan Government, and for some of which finance has been earmarked from U. S. aid funds or other sources.[1] For example, the LARC has substantial funds still unspent out of its allocations for well construction and irrigation projects, forestry, school building, health services and so forth. There are also certain major engineering projects under way which will not be completed for two or three years: examples are the Tripoli power expansion scheme, the LARC telecommunications project and the construction of the Fezzan road, for which a contract has been let by the federal government. All these schemes are included in our five-year investment program. For lack of detailed information we have omitted a few of the smaller capital projects being financed by LARC (e.g., the development of municipal slaughter houses). However, the sums involved, are so small that their exclusion will not make very much difference to the totals. The mission's estimates of actual investment in 1955/56-1957/58 are given in Table 3 for purposes of comparison. These are approximate only, since the way the government accounts are prepared makes it impossible to distinguish at all clearly between current and capital expenditures.

---

[1] Substantial U. S. aid funds have also been allocated for the financing of recurrent development expenditures (e.g., the payment of teachers' salaries). These are not included here, but are subsumed in the mission's program of additional recurrent expenditures set out in Table 4.

TABLE 3   Five-Year Program of Public Expenditures

(£L '000)

	Five-year program	Annual average	Per-cent of total	Estimated 1955/56– 1957/58 average	Per-cent of total
Water resources	3,050	610	12	628	15
Forestry and dune fixation	1,520	304	6	126	3
Agriculture	3,600	720	14	404	9
Total	8,170	1,634	32	1,158	27
Roads	2,650	530	11	536	12
Benghazi harbor	1,500	300	6⎱	105	2
Other ports	355	71	1⎰		
Civil airports	800	160	3	78	2
Telecommunications	500	100	2	333	8
Total	5,805	1,161	23	1,052	24
Electric power	3,400	680	14	485	11
Town and village water	700	140	3	261	6
Total	4,100	820	17	746	17
Education	2,250	450	9	218	5
Health	1,175	235	5	233	5
Housing	1,000	200	4⎱	43	1
Sanitation	800	160	3⎰		
Total	5,225	1,045	21	494	11
Industry, handicrafts and fisheries	750	150	3	82	2
Capitalization of National Bank	300	60	1	233	5
Antiquities and tourism	150	30	1	10	—
Public buildings[a]	500	100	2	579	13
Grand total	25,000	5,000	100	4,354	100

[a] The provision for public buildings is intended to cover additional office accommodation and other buildings required to carry out the mission's development proposals. It does not include any allowance for possible further extensions to the administrative center at Beida or for other building not directly connected with economic development.

TABLE 4 Five-Year Program of Additional Recurrent Expenditures on Development

(£L '000)

	(1) Approximate expenditure in 1959/60	(2) Projected expenditure in 1964/65	(3) Projected annual average 1960/61–1964/65	(4) Increase of col. 3 over col. 1	(5) Total additional expenditures proposed for five-year period
Geology and water resources ⎱ ᵃ Agriculture and forestry ⎰	900	1,400	1,215	315	1,575
Industry, handicrafts and fisheriesᵇ	—	70	70	70	350
Antiquities and tourism	50	125	100	50	250
Transport and communicationsᶜ	1,200	2,000	1,850	650	3,250
Educationᵈ	3,000	4,850	4,030	1,030	5,150
Healthᵉ	1,500	1,915	1,740	240	1,200
Development Council	15	35	35	20	100
Total	6,665	10,395	9,040	2,375	11,875

ᵃ The additional expenditures recommended by the mission are for the establishment and upkeep of a Federal Ministry of Agriculture and Natural Resources, an Agricultural Development Board for Cyrenaica, a Land Survey Department, a Federal Department of Geology and Hydrology and various provincial services.

ᵇ Minor items of expenditure relating to the administration of industry, handicrafts and fisheries are included in the present budgets of the federal and provincial governments. In the analysis of public expenditures given in the Statistical Appendix these have been treated as part of the costs of general administration, as it is difficult to identify them separately. The additional expenditures recommended by the mission are for the creation of new machinery for the administration of industrial policy, the provision of technical advice to private industry, management training, workers' education, engagement of foreign instructors and specialists, training of Libyans abroad in selected industrial techniques and the administration of a fisheries development project.

ᶜ For a detailed explanation of this item see Chapter 12, page 251.

ᵈ Assumes an increase of 10 percent per annum in recurrent expenditures on education (see Chapter 13, pages 274–275).

ᵉ Assumes an increase of 5 percent per annum in recurrent expenditures on public health (see Chapter 14, pages 298–299).

The estimates of net additional recurrent expenditures given in Table 4 take account of various proposals made in this report for securing economies in government expenditures. The mission is proposing, for example, that substantial reductions should be made in the staffs of the provincial governments, that the two provincial railways should be closed down (involving a saving of about £L 75,000 a year), and that medical supplies for the health services be centrally purchased. Present costs of general administration in Libya are extremely high, and the mission believes that the extension of government activities in certain fields, along the lines recommended in this report, should be accompanied by strenuous efforts to promote greater efficiency in public administration. The mission also considers that there is urgent need for stricter controls over public expenditure (see Chapter 6).

The mission has no exact information about what the government spent in 1959/60. In the previous year (1958/59) it appears that total public expenditures in Libya amounted to about £L 19 million (see Statistical Appendix, Table S.1), and we assume that expenditures in 1959/60 have been rather higher—say, £L 20-21 million, of which about £L 5 million may have been on capital account and £L 15-16 million on current account.

Our investment program does not envisage the level of capital expenditures rising above the present level of £L 5 million a year, except to the extent that cost increases add to the figures set out in Table 3. On the other hand, our program of recurrent expenditures on development allows for these expenditures to rise by nearly £L 4 million between 1959/60 and 1964/65 (i.e., the difference between columns 1 and 2 of Table 4). The implication of our recommendations therefore is that total public expenditures, recurrent and capital, will rise from an estimated £L 20-21 million in 1959/60 to at least £L 24-25 million by 1964/65. If, over and above the items of expenditure listed in Tables 3 and 4, allowance is made (a) for the increases in civil service pay that will be needed to keep pace with the growth of wages and salaries in the private sector and (b) for possible increases in nondevelopmental expenditure (e.g., on defense), total public expenditures in 1964/65 will be even higher—say, about £L 26-27 million.

Such a high level of public expenditure (equivalent to over 50 percent of the estimated gross domestic product for 1958) can only be justified on the assumption that large oil revenues will eventually be forthcoming to sustain it. If anything were to happen to invalidate this assumption, the shape and size of the development program would have to be reconsidered.

Sources of Finance

Libya's domestic public revenues, including the revenues of the municipalities, amounted to £L 9.6 million in 1957/58 and to about £L 12 million in 1958/59. The yield of existing taxes, particularly import and excise duties, income tax and business profits tax, should grow with the continued expansion of activity associated with oil development. So also should the revenues obtained from the tobacco monopoly and government trading in sugar.

The mission has put forward a number of proposals for changes in taxation in Chapter 15, and if adopted, these should yield some further increase in tax revenues towards the end of the five-year period. More important, they should result in a more equitable distribution of the tax burden. The mission has also recommended that consideration be given to the introduction of a post office savings scheme and to the creation of a local market for Libyan government securities. There appears to be little justification for Libya to borrow abroad in foreign exchange to cover local currency expenditures when there are possibilities of mobilizing resources through internal borrowing, and it is important in the mission's judgment that the necessary institutional framework for such borrowing should be created during the next five years against the time when technical and organizational limitations on development expenditures are less restrictive than they are now.

Foreign aid allocated to Libya in the three years 1957/58-1959/60 have averaged rather under £L 12 million a year, excluding U. S. and UN technical assistance and relief food shipments. If government receipts from foreign aid and oil revenues combined continue over the next five years at the current level (as the mission has assumed), adequate funds should be available for financing total public expenditures within the range of, say, £L 22-27 million a year, especially in view of the fact that there will be a substantial carry-over of unspent government funds at the beginning of the period (see page 39). We would like to stress, however, there will be no room during the next few years for extravagant expenditures on public works outside the fields covered by our program. Nor will government be able to afford the necessary increases in civil service pay unless vigorous steps are taken to reduce the present excessive numbers on the public payroll.

Supplementary Program

If, contrary to the assumption made above, really substantial oil revenues should be forthcoming before 1965, and if in the meantime some of the administrative and technical obstacles to the execution of a larger development program have been overcome, the mission suggests that a Supplementary Program of development expenditures might be undertaken in the latter part of the five-year period. Five main areas for such additional public expenditures are indicated in the report. These are (a) education and training, (b) development of water resources for irrigation, (c) afforestation and other measures of soil and water conservation, (d) agricultural credit and (e) low-cost housing, town and village water supplies, sanitation and other welfare expenditures.

Education and training is the area in which technical and organizational limitations are probably most easily managed, provided that no limit is set to the recruitment of foreign teachers and instructors. In the case of water resources, there is no technical limit to the drilling of wells in areas where water is known to exist, since this can be carried out with imported equipment under the supervision of foreign technicians. The same is true of town and village water supplies and improvements in sanitation. On the other hand, programs for flood control and afforestation involving controlled grazing, the resettlement of nomads and similar measures are much more difficult to organize. It will also take time to set up adequate machinery to handle housing and community development programs. Agricultural credit raises complex and difficult problems of management and supervision, and the mission would like to stress the importance of proceeding cautiously with the expansion of credit facilities until an adequate institutional framework has been established.

Specific recommendations for increased expenditures are included in the chapters dealing with individual sectors. No attempt has been made to total up these expenditures, since it is inherent in the conception of the Supplementary Program that it should be elastic. Progress in dealing with the organizational problems of development is likely to vary a great deal from one sector to another. Consequently, while it may prove feasible to adopt some parts of the Supplementary Program before 1965, others may have to be deferred. In any case, as already mentioned, the mission recommends that the whole development program should be reviewed in three or four years' time.

CHAPTER 6   *GOVERNMENT ORGANIZATION*

The problem of government organization was briefly stated in Chapter 1, together with the mission's conclusion that, if a program of coordinated economic development is to be carried through efficiently and expeditiously, the existing system of administration in Libya needs to be streamlined and the position of the federal government strengthened. The present chapter deals more fully with this subject and considers in some detail the machinery that should be set up to administer a program of economic development, and how that machinery should be staffed and operated.

THE STRUCTURE OF GOVERNMENT

The Present System

Libya's system of government is a very elaborate one for a country with such a small population. In addition to nine or ten Ministries at the center there are no fewer than 23 Nazirates in the three provinces, making a total of between 30 and 35 government departments in all. At the time of the mission's visit total numbers on the payrolls of the federal and provincial governments together ran as high as 35,000-40,000 (excluding the Libyan Army, but including the federal and provincial police forces, teaching and medical staff, post office workers and daily paid labor). Within this total the Tripolitanian and Cyrenaican Administrations each employed several times as many officials as the federal government. Total personal emoluments paid to government workers in 1957/58 were about £L 6-7 million a year, or more than 12 percent of the gross domestic product. This is a very high proportion by comparison with other underdeveloped countries; for instance, it is about double that for India, Lebanon or Nigeria. There are also the heavy additional expenditures incurred on the building and maintenance of government offices, official transport and other administrative overheads.

A further costly feature of the Libyan system of government is the maintenance of two separate federal capitals. It is understandable why this arrangement was made at the time of Independence, but there appears to be much less justification for it now that the kingdom is more firmly established. More than £L 100,000 was spent in 1957/58 on moving the federal government from Tripoli to Benghazi, and substantial extra costs had to be incurred in providing offices and other accommodation in Benghazi while accommodation in Tripoli was left practically unused. At the end of 1959 the government moved back to Tripoli, and another large bill for the move will have to be presented to the Libyan taxpayer. The construction of a federal administrative center at Beida in Cyrenaica at an initial cost of £L 2.5 million has added further to the expenses of administration and made the system still more unwieldy. The frequent moves of the government have had an unsettling effect on all concerned and have inevitably resulted in loss of efficiency, completely disrupting the work of some departments for weeks on end.

The present high cost of government makes heavy demands on the Libyan citizen, who in the final analysis has to pay for it. It also involves the unproductive use of manpower, for which more useful employment should be found in developing the country's resources. Furthermore, the multiplication of government departments and agencies results in much confusion of functions and responsibilities, which has slowed down the process of administration and often made it very difficult to get decisions taken at all. This confusion has centered particularly around the interpretation of Articles 36-39 of the Libyan Constitution, which define the respective functions of the federal and provincial governments. Article 36 specifies certain matters such as defense and foreign affairs in which legislative and executive powers shall be exercised by the federal government, subject to the proviso in Article 37 that the executive power may in certain circumstances be delegated to a province. Article 38 lists a further 27 matters in which "the legislative power . . . shall be within the competence of the federal government, while the executive power in connection with the implementation of that legislation shall be within the competence of the provinces acting under the supervision of the federal government." All residual powers are assigned in Article 39 to the provinces.

Article 38 covers a number of subjects which are of central importance in relation to economic development. Examples are the organization of imports and exports, control of companies and banks, income tax, monopolies and concessions, prospecting and mining, shipping and navigation, major ports, civil aviation, public health, labor and social security. It appears to be the intention of the Constitution that the federal government should have the sole responsibility for determining policy in these matters, and that the provincial governments should carry this policy out. Unfortunately, the dividing line between the making of policy and its execution is not an easy one to draw, and there has been a tendency for the Constitution to be interpreted in such a way that the effective power of policy-making rests with the provinces and not with the center. Many important issues of policy arising in connection with subjects listed under Article 38 have in practice been decided by the provinces, sometimes without even consulting the federal government, and policies have frequently differed from one province to another. A number of instances are cited in the subsequent chapters of this report. Each of the two coastal provinces has its own system of income tax, and its own rules for the registration and licensing of industry. One set of import restrictions is applied in Tripolitania, another in Cyrenaica, and controls have actually been imposed on the movement of goods between the two provinces. At one time even the administration of exchange control was a provincial responsibility. Health regulations vary from province to province, and the different provinces follow entirely different practices in such matters as the registration and procurement of drugs and the recruitment and pay of doctors.

One source of difficulty is that the distinction made in Article 38 between "legislative power" and "executive power" does not always correspond in practice with the distinction between making policy and implementing it. Policy is often made without legislation at all, and even where there is a law, policy may find its effective expression in the regulations issued under the law rather than in the law itself. Moreover, Article 38 tends to be too rigid in its provision that laws relating to the subjects listed under it should be implemented by the provinces. In some cases this has turned out to be quite impracticable.

Quite apart from these difficulties, it is open to question whether some of the subjects listed in Article 38 ought to be handled by the provincial governments at all, except purely as agents of the federal power. Control of imports and exports, for example, regulation of banking and control of civil aviation are exercised by the central authority in most federations. Income tax likewise is usually a federal subject. There may be provincial income taxes as well, but these are separate from and additional to the federal tax. Certainly in the Libyan context the mission would strongly advise in favor of the transfer of income tax from the provinces to the center. As a first step in this direction, we would urge that immediate action be taken on the present draft income tax law, which provides for a number of important improvements in the tax system (see Chapter 15).

The mission has not considered in any detail what amendments might be needed to the Libyan Constitution to give effect to its recommendations on government organization. Such a task would in any case be beyond its competence. For the most part, however, we believe that our proposals for strengthening the authority of the federal government are consistent with the letter and spirit of the Constitution. We put them forward in the conviction that important administrative changes will be needed if Libya is to take full advantage of the great opportunities for development that now lie ahead.

Strengthening the Federal Government

The ministries of the federal government primarily concerned with economic development are the Ministry of Finance and the Ministry of National Economy. There is at present no Ministry of Agriculture. The Ministry of National Economy has a general responsibility for agricultural policy at the federal level (and also for grain storage), but the Directorate of Agriculture within the ministry is quite inadequately staffed, consisting at the time of the mission's visit of a single expatriate official. There are separate Ministries of Health and Education. There is no Ministry of Works, but the Libyan Public Development and Stabilization Agency and the Libyan-American Reconstruction Commission have undertaken the planning and execution of public works on behalf of the federal government. It has already been decided by the government that both these foreign aid agencies should shortly be wound up.

Ministry of Agriculture. The mission's first proposal for strengthening the federal government is that a Ministry of Agriculture and Natural Resources should be set up at the federal level with responsibility for the formulation and coordination of national agricultural programs and policies, including the direction of agricultural research. The main task of this ministry would be to promote the development of settled agriculture in Libya along the lines suggested in Chapter 8. We cannot see how this development can be effectively organized without a central staff and without a minister of high standing to support the claims of agriculture in the Council of Ministers. The ministry should have separate departments for agricultural production, marketing, research, training, animal husbandry, forestry and fisheries and should take over part of the staffs of the provincial Nazirates of Agriculture, which should be reduced in size. The ministry should also absorb the grain storage organization and the geological department of the Ministry of National Economy, and the geological department should be enlarged and converted into a Department of Geology and Hydrology, which would supervise the further exploration and development of Libya's mineral and water resources on the lines suggested in Chapter 7. All technical assistance in the agricultural field should be channeled through, and coordinated by, the Ministry of Agriculture, and the chiefs of the FAO and USOM agricultural missions in Libya should be attached to the ministry as advisors. Consultation between the center and the provinces should be secured through regular meetings between the Minister and the three Nazirs and through the establishment of an official committee on agricultural development, over which the Permanent Under Secretary of the Ministry would preside.

Ministry of Finance and Economics. Second, the mission recommends that the remaining functions of the Ministry of National Economy (notably trade, industry and tourism) should be transferred to the Ministry of Finance, which would then become a Ministry of Finance and Economics. Given the acute shortage in Libya of trained administrators, we do not believe that there is any justification for having separate departments to deal with finance and economic affairs. However, we would suggest that, while taking over responsibility for trade and industry, the Ministry of Finance should be relieved of certain functions which do not properly belong to it (e.g., cooperatives and labor affairs).

The Ministry of Finance and Economics should be charged with sole responsibility for the regulation of imports and exports and the formulation of industrial policy, including measures for the protection of local industries and the promotion of industrial expansion. In all such matters it should maintain the closest relations with the Development Council (see page 86) and it should look to the council and to the National Bank for advice on broad questions of economic policy.

The present staffing of the Ministry of Finance is quite inadequate to discharge even its traditional functions in the fiscal sphere, let alone the additional functions which we are proposing it should take over. The department should therefore be strengthened by the recruitment of additional staff, including expatriate officers where necessary, and the organization of the department should be thoroughly overhauled.

Grants-in-Aid to the Provinces. Although the provincial governments depend on grants-in-aid from the center to cover nearly half their expenditures, no conditions are attached to the grants, no set principles are followed in determining the amounts, and the federal government exercises no control over the way in which the money is spent. The need to legislate for the allocation and expenditure of federal grants-in-aid has long since been accepted in other federations, and it is explicitly recognized in Article 174 of the Libyan Constitution, which requires that "the method and amount of such allocation shall be determined by federal law in a manner that will guarantee to the provinces an increase in the amounts to be allocated to them by the federal government, such increases to be proportionate to the growth of the federal revenue and such as will guarantee to them a constant economic progress."

It seems very doubtful whether the rules laid down in Article 174 for the determination of grants-in-aid could be applied in practice. No government can guarantee to the provinces "a constant economic progress" because their economic progress depends on many factors which are quite outside the control of the federal government. Furthermore, it is difficult to justify the concepts that grants-in-aid should be constantly increased in proportion to the growth of federal revenues. The federal government may have to raise additional revenues to meet new and important tasks laid upon it (e.g., in the sphere of defense), and there appears to be no reason why the provinces should be entitled on this account to receive more money. As the mission sees it, the only sensible criterion for fixing federal grants-in-aid is the financial needs of the provinces concerned, and experience shows that these needs may vary considerably from time to time and from province to province.

The mission adheres very strongly to the view that the allocation of federal grants-in-aid to the provinces should be governed by recognizable principles based on considerations of economy and equity, and that, as in other countries, some system should be devised under which the apportionment of funds can be initially decided and periodically reviewed in accordance with these principles. Proposals for a law on federal grants-in-aid were put forward for the consideration of the federal government some years ago, but no action has yet been taken. We recommend therefore that the government should give immediate attention to this problem with a view to presenting a bill to Parliament at the earliest opportunity. The law should confine itself to laying down general principles, and the interpretation of these principles should be entrusted to an impartial tribunal specifically appointed for this purpose. The proposal for such a tribunal or Finance Commission is examined in more detail in Annex III, which discusses its possible composition and methods of operation.

Federal grants-in-aid may take the form either of general grants in support of ordinary provincial expenditures or of specific grants tied to particular purposes. Specific grants in their turn may be for ordinary recurrent expenditures (e.g., on the maintenance of education and health services, roads and so forth) or for capital projects. The task of a Finance Commission would be to allocate funds from current revenues (import duties, federal income tax, budgetary grants from abroad, etc.) to meet recurrent expenditures. The practice of earmarking a proportion of federal grants-in-aid for specific purposes is followed in most other federal states, and the mission believes that it would be in the interests of Libya as a whole that the greater part of future allocations of money to the provinces should be made on this basis.

The allocation of funds for capital expenditures would be a separate matter to be determined in accordance with the requirements of a national development program, and as such it would fall within the sphere of the Development Council rather than of the Finance Commission. The latter would, of course, have to take into account development needs in apportioning revenues to meet recurrent expenditures, and it would be an advantage to have the economic adviser to the Development Council as an ex officio member of the Finance Commission. The functions of the Development Council, and the whole question of the organization required for the preparation and execution of development programs, are discussed on pages 86-89.

Unification of the Civil Service. The mission considers it of the greatest importance that steps should be taken to bring about gradually the unification of the federal and provincial civil services and the establishment of a single system of civil service recruitment for Libya as a whole, together with the regular interchange of officials between the center and the provinces. In India, for example, recruitment to the higher administrative service is centrally controlled by the Public Service Commission, which sets the examinations, selects the successful candidates and allocates them initially either to the federal government or to one of the provincial cadres. An official may then be seconded for some part of his career from one of the provinces to the center or vice versa. This helps to promote cooperation between the federal and provincial governments and to give each a better understanding of the problems of the other. The adoption of a similar practice in Libya would in our view prove in the long run to be very much to the country's advantage. We have suggested that a start should be made with the interchange of officials by the transfer of selected Libyan staff from the provincial Nazirates of Agriculture to help in establishing a federal Ministry of Agriculture.

Federal-Provincial Relationships. As a corollary to the strengthening of the authority of the federal government in the direction of economic policy, better machinery should be created for regular consultation between the federal and provincial administrations. On a number of occasions in the past there has been a feeling in the provinces that they have not been properly consulted by the federal government about decisions vitally affecting their interests—for example, changes in customs duties, nationalization of the Tripoli power undertaking, or the choice of route for the Fezzan road. The mission was not in a position to judge how far these feelings were justified. But it cannot be emphasized too strongly that an atmosphere of mutual confidence and day-to-day cooperation must prevail between the provinces and the center if the federal system of government is to function efficiently, and everything should be done by both federal and provincial governments to create such an atmosphere.

Federal and provincial officials should be permitted, and indeed encouraged, to exchange information freely in the process of policymaking. At present communications between federal and provincial officials are supposed to pass up to the top of each government, across at the highest level and then down again. For example, if an official of one of the Nazirates wishes to write to his opposite member in the federal government, his letter may have to be approved first by his Nazir and then submitted to the President of the Executive Council who in turn passes it to the Wali; the Wali then communicates with the Prime Minister who passes the letter down to the responsible minister who in turn passes it to the official concerned. Such cumbersome and circuitous procedures cannot be reconciled with the needs of efficient administration, and the mission strongly recommends that practice in Libya should be brought into line with that usually found in other countries.

One way of ensuring adequate consultation between the center and the provinces is by having regular interdepartmental committees of officials to coordinate policies in particular fields. The members of these committees should be drawn from the departments of the federal and provincial governments and the National Bank. However, it must be recognized that, while some such committees are essential, it is easy to have too many, since excessive proliferation of committees is liable to take up so much of the time of the officials concerned that they are unable to give proper attention to their departmental duties. This appears to be a very real danger in Libya, especially in view of the distances between the provincial capitals. The number of committees must therefore be strictly limited, meetings should only be held when there are important matters to discuss, agenda and papers should be carefully prepared and circulated well in advance of the meetings, and adequate secretarial arrangements should be made.

At one time there used to be formal arrangements for periodic meetings of a supreme administrative council consisting of the Prime Minister and the Walis of the three provinces, which would review important matters of common concern to the federal and provincial governments. The possibility of reviving a council of this kind might well be considered now that a new chapter in Libya's development has been opened up by the discovery of oil. The council should meet every three or six months, and a committee of federal and provincial officials might be formed to prepare the ground for the meetings and to advise on the subjects under discussion.

Management of Public Enterprises

It is at present the normal practice in Libya for revenue-earning public enterprises such as railways, ports, civil airports, electricity and water undertakings to be run by ordinary departments of the provincial governments. Experience in other countries has shown that this arrangement has many disadvantages. The management is subjected to constant political interference, and day-to-day decisions, which should be taken promptly, are frequently delayed because they must be referred to the Nazir or even to the Executive Council. Departmental control of expenditures and the subordination of the staff to civil service rules make for excessive rigidity, hamper the conduct of business and complicate the problem of recruiting and retaining competent technical staff. Lack of proper commercial accounting frequently makes it difficult to discover whether the undertaking is operating at a profit or a loss, and the fact that the undertaking has no control over the disposal of its own revenues removes one of the main spurs to efficiency and sometimes results in needed development being held back. For these and other reasons it has usually been found that public enterprises are better run by autonomous corporations which are free to operate according to strictly business principles, the minister or nazir exercising only general control over policy.

An independent corporation has recently been established to take over the Tripoli power undertaking. The mission welcomes this move and has suggested in Chapter 11 that the responsibilities of the corporation should eventually be widened to include electricity supply in the other two provinces. We have also recommended the creation of an additional authority of this kind to administer the affairs of Tripoli port (see Chapter 12). In principle, there might be advantages in placing the Cyrenaican ports, the civil airports and urban water supply under similar management, but we have felt that this would impose too heavy a burden of reorganization on the Libyan administration, and we have accordingly proposed that the existing arrangements should be continued for the time being—subject, however, to the important proviso that the accounts of all revenue-earning undertakings, including posts and telecommunications, should be kept entirely separate from those of general government. We have made no recommendations for the reorganization of the management of the two provincial railway systems because we believe it to be in Libya's interests that the railways should be closed down within the next few years. Both are running at a considerable loss, and their traffic could easily be taken over by the roads.

Provincial Administration

The assumption by the federal government of larger responsibilities for policy-making and coordination should be accompanied by the transfer to the provincial governments of certain executive functions at present carried out at the center. In particular, we recommend that the Federal Department of Roads should be relieved of its executive responsibilities, and that all road works, including work on the federal roads, should in future be carried out by the provincial administrations under federal direction, with the federal government retaining control over funds (see Chapter 12). This will involve some transfer of technical and administrative personnel from the center to the provinces. The development of water resources is another field in which we envisage new tasks being imposed on the provincial administrations, and we have recommended in Chapter 7 that the provincial governments should establish Water Resources Branches to handle work hitherto done mainly by the Libyan-American Joint Services. American technicians now working with the LAJS could be attached to the Water Resources Branches as advisers.

The changes which we have suggested, taken as a whole, should enable the provincial governments to reduce the number of their departments and generally to streamline their organization. As one example, there is no need for separate Nazirates of Communications and Public Works in the provinces, and we suggest that these two departments should be amalgamated. At the same time the Nazirates of Finance should be relieved of some of their executive responsibilities such as the management of the salt monopoly and left free to concentrate on their proper functions of budgetary control. Again, the Departments of State Property in the provinces could be handed over to the provincial Public Works Departments in conformity with the practice in many other countries. The process of simplifying administration in the provinces and cutting down the number of staff employed would be further assisted by a rigorous pruning of government controls. Controls which in our view should be abolished or simplified include those over industrial licensing, imports and exports and inter-provincial trade and migration (see Chapter 15).

The mission is in no doubt that the total numbers of staff employed by the provincial governments could, and should, be reduced. At the beginning of 1959 there was an administrative establishment (classified and unclassified) of nearly 6,000 civil servants in Tripolitania and well over 4,000 in Cyrenaica, as compared with 1,200 employed by the federal government. The mission heard of many provincial officials who had little real work to do, and a study of departmental establishments confirms the impression that there is ample room for economy. Another area in which economies might be made is the district administration in Tripolitania, which appears to be unnecessarily complicated and costly.

Consultative Bodies

It is frequently desirable that government should consult with outside interests in the making and administration of economic policies. This will usually be done informally through day-to-day contacts between ministers, Nazirs and officials on the one hand and private individuals on the other. In the course of its travels in Libya, the mission was surprised to find how seldom most of the ministers, Nazirs and senior officials apparently visited the smaller towns and villages to study conditions for themselves and to talk with the people. The success of a development program in a democratic country must depend to a large extent on how far it expresses the wishes and aspirations of ordinary people and on how far they feel themselves identified with it and with the government which is responsible for carrying it out. From this point of view, much is to be gained by senior representatives of the government getting around the country as often as they can instead of remaining tied to their offices in the capital.

Apart, however, from informal contacts between members of the government and the public, there are advantages in having one or two regular consultative bodies, through which outside advice can be obtained and information exchanged. We suggest therefore that consideration might be given to establishing national advisory councils on agriculture, industry and transport in which representatives of the federal and provincial governments could meet periodically (say, every three months) with farmers, merchants, bankers and businessmen to discuss problems of mutual interest. The non-official members of these councils should be drawn from all three provinces. Other such councils (e.g., on tourism) might be created in due course if the initial experiment is successful.

MACHINERY FOR ECONOMIC PLANNING

A Central Planning Staff

It has been agreed in principle that the LPDSA, LARC and LAJS should be wound up, and that the Development Council should be reorganized to take charge of the planning and coordination of economic development programs. Opinions in Libya, however, have been divided on the new setup of the Development Council, and a draft law authorizing the reorganization is understood to have been under discussion for over a year without any final decision having yet been taken. The foreign aid agencies have meanwhile continued to function more or less as before, though U. S. aid funds are no longer being channeled through the LARC, and the central administrative unit of the LAJS is being disbanded (see Chapter 3).

The latest proposal, as the mission understands it, is that the Development Council itself should be composed of three ministers of the federal government, including the Prime Minister who would be chairman, and three Nazirs representing the provincial governments. The Governor of the National Bank would not be a member, but might be invited to attend meetings of the council and participate in its deliberations. The council's main responsibility would be to prepare a long-term development program and supervise its implementation, but the actual execution of projects would be entrusted to the ordinary departments of the federal and provincial governments. The council would prepare an annual development budget for approval by the Council of Ministers and subsequent submission to Parliament. The funds necessary to finance this budget would come mainly from foreign grants and loans and from oil revenues, 70 percent of oil revenues being specifically earmarked for this purpose under existing legislation.

A Development Council organized along these lines would be primarily a planning and not an executive body. As such, it would represent a compromise between those who favor an autonomous planning board with executive powers functioning outside the ordinary machinery of government (on the lines of the Iraq Development Board) and those who believe that development projects should be planned and administered by the individual departments of the federal and provincial governments with a minimum of central coordination or control.

The mission is in agreement with the view that the machinery for economic planning should be organized within the existing government structure, and not outside it. On the other hand, as will be apparent from what has been said earlier in this report, we see the need for much stronger central direction and coordination of economic development activities than has existed in the past. Hitherto the final responsibility for making economic policy and initiating development projects has been divided between the various organs of the federal and provincial governments and the foreign aid agencies, and the result has been that key decisions have often been taken not by the Libyan Government, but by foreigners. Alternatively, matters have been allowed to drift along without any decision being taken at all. Evidence of this drift and indecision is to be found in the numerous draft laws which have been formulated for consideration by ministers, but on which no action has ever been taken—for example, the draft law for the introduction of federal income tax, the draft law for implementing Article 174 of the Constitution, the draft law on the reorganization of the Development Council and so forth.

The mission therefore strongly urges that action be taken to reorganize the Development Council without further delay. There is still apparently some difference of opinion in Libya as to whether the council should be composed of ministers and nazirs or whether its membership should be limited to senior officials. Judging by the experience of other countries, the mission considers that a ministerial council would be distinctly preferable. A development program has to be guided by political as well as economic considerations, and a ministerial council will carry more weight with Parliament and public opinion than one composed simply of senior officials. Moreover, the fact that ministers and nazirs have participated in drawing up the program will help in steering it through the Council of Ministers and the provincial Executive Councils. A further general argument in favor of a council composed of ministers rather than officials is that the latter tend to be too deeply involved in their own departmental affairs and interests to bring an independent and detached outlook to bear on the task of planning.

However, if in spite of these objections it is felt that an official body would be better suited to Libyan conditions, the mission would rather that the council be established on this basis than that further precious time should be lost in too-prolonged a debate on the merits and demerits of one type of machinery or another. Whatever its membership, the council should be equipped with a strong permanent staff of administrators and economists, who should be responsible for giving general advice on economic policy, studying financial and economic trends and drawing up specific and detailed development programs. The council should also have a technical wing headed by a qualified engineer to assist ministries and nazirates in preparing engineering and constructional projects, hiring foreign consultants, putting out contracts to tender and supervising their execution.

While the Development Council should be responsible for advising on the allocation of the funds which are available for development from oil revenues and other sources, the council itself should not handle the money. This is essentially the function of the Ministry of Finance, which should be in charge of disbursements and the control of expenditure. All development funds in fact should be channeled through the accounts of the Ministry of Finance in the same way as other budgetary appropriations.

The new Development Council will require a considerably larger annual budget than the present council. We have tentatively suggested a figure of £L 35,000 a year (see Table 4), but this may not be enough. It is most important that the council should not be bound by civil service rules in matters of recruitment, and that it should be able to offer high enough salaries to attract and retain men of first-rate ability, both Libyans and expatriates. For some years at least it will be necessary for the council to rely mainly on expatriates to fill the senior economic and technical posts, but promising young Libyans should be recruited at the outset to work under them, so that in due course they will be qualified to take over.

The staff of the council, which might be attached to the Prime

Minister's office, should make regular reports to the Council of Ministers on the progress of economic development, working in close consultation with the Ministry of Finance, the Central Statistics Office and the National Bank. In view of the great shortage of economists and statisticians in Libya and the limited number of good men who can be attracted from abroad, it is most important that economic and statistical research should be properly coordinated, and that the responsibilities of the different agencies and departments should be clearly defined. The Development Council would appear to be the right body to undertake this coordination.

Statistical and Economic Services

The preparation of sensible plans for economic development is made difficult in Libya, as in many other underdeveloped countries, by the lack of reliable and up-to-date information about what is going on in the economy. In agriculture, for example, no soil survey has yet been undertaken, records of land ownership are fragmentary, and very little is known about the present pattern of land use. Statistics of agricultural production and livestock numbers are collected both in Tripolitania and Cyrenaica, and the two statisticians primarily responsible for this work are entitled to credit for achieving the results they have in the face of considerable obstacles. It is admitted, however, that many of the estimates will not stand up to examination, nor is there any valid basis for comparing the figures for the two provinces or even the figures for different years in the same province. Plans are now in hand for an agricultural census to be carried out with the assistance of FAO, and this should be given every encouragement by the responsible authorities. It should not, however, be undertaken until adequate preparations have been made and the field staff have been properly instructed in their work.

Information about production in other sectors of the economy is even more scanty. There is no regular compilation of statistics of industrial production, records of road traffic are maintained only on the most haphazard basis, and very little is known about the movements of trade within the country. A census of urban production and employment, which was carried out in four towns by the Central Statistics Office at the beginning of 1959, marks a useful beginning to the more systematic assembly of data, but considerable doubts must be expressed about the accuracy of some of the returns.

A population census was conducted under the supervision of a UN expert in 1954, preliminary results were announced in 1955 and the final report was due to be published in the early part of 1960. While the long delay in publication is regrettable, the census is a most valuable contribution to knowledge of the Libyan economy and reflects well on the statisticians responsible for its organization and execution. It includes an occupational breakdown of the population, but important shifts have taken place in the past few years with the rapid expansion of government expenditures and the arrival of the oil companies, so that the 1954 figures can no longer be taken as a very reliable guide to employment. No regular employment statistics are kept, and there is urgent need for a comprehensive survey of skilled manpower.

Another conspicuous gap in the collection of basic economic information exists in respect of wholesale and retail prices. Official cost-of-living indexes are prepared for Tripoli town, one for the Libyan and one for the non-Libyan population, but the weighting of the indexes is now generally recognized as being completely unrepresentative. An effort to put the indexes on a more realistic basis is long overdue.

Trade statistics are published by the Central Statistics Office on the basis of returns supplied by the Customs Department, and the statistics are used in conjunction with data obtained from the commercial banks, foreign governments and other sources for compiling official balance of payments estimates. The National Bank of Libya also collects information on the balance of payments through its Exchange Control Department, which started operations early in 1958, but at the time of the mission's visit no attempt had been made to coordinate this information with that obtained by the Central Statistics Office. Very considerable discrepancies appeared to exist in respect of certain important items. The Central Statistics Office has experienced considerable difficulty in extracting information from other departments and agencies and this has led to unfortunate delays in the publication of the balance of payments estimates. The estimates for the calendar year 1957 were only completed in the autumn of 1959.

The National Bank of Libya assembles and publishes statistics of money and banking, including, of course, statistics of its own operations. These provide useful information about an important sector of the economy, but there is considerable scope for improvement in the collection, analysis and presentation of the material. A number of steps have recently been taken to bring this about.

Far too little is known at present of the financial operations of the federal and provincial governments. It was only with considerable difficulty that the mission was able to piece together the rough picture of public expenditures by main categories which is reproduced in the Statistical Appendix. To do this we had to examine in great detail the ordinary budgets and accounts of the four governments, the "exceptional budget" of the federal government, the reports of the Auditor General and the provincial auditors, the accounts of certain departmental enterprises and municipalities, the annual reports of the LPDSA and the financial statements of LARC. Nowhere in Libya are all the government accounts kept together, nor, so far as we could discover, was there anyone familiar with the total picture. We found that it was frequently impossible to determine from the budgets the purposes for which funds had been voted, nor was there any recognition of the distinction between current and capital items.

Against this background the mission attaches high priority to the improvement of government statistical and economic services in Libya. The main obstacle to be overcome is a lack of awareness of the importance of these services at all levels of the government service. As a first step we recommend that the Central Statistics Office should be transferred from the Ministry of National Economy to the Prime Minister's Office. We also recommend the unification of government statistical services on an all-Libya basis, with branches of the Central Statistics Office attached to the offices of the provincial Governors. This would be in place of the present arrangement under which each of the provinces has its own statistical organization. We envisage that all the government statisticians should be on the CSO establishment, but that they should be seconded on occasion to posts in other departments of the federal and provincial governments.

The country's present statistical resources should be considerably expanded by the recruitment of additional foreign personnel, pending the training of Libyans to replace them; we suggest an initial target of six qualified statisticians from abroad. A few promising Libyan graduates should be selected for training abroad with the statistical services of other governments and international institutions. At the same time Libyans with secondary school education should be recruited for statistical work and trained on the job under the supervision of the Director of the Central Statistics Office.

The National Bank of Libya should continue its efforts to build up a statistical and research staff of its own. As a broad division of responsibility we suggest that the assembly of monetary and banking statistics, statistics on the balance of payments and data on industrial finance and agricultural credit should be in the hands of the National

Bank, and that all other statistics should be in charge of the CSO. Liaison between the two statistical agencies should be maintained through regular contacts between their directors. In addition, we suggest that an interdepartmental statistical committee should be formed to provide a forum for the discussion of problems of general interest. It should include representatives of the Development Council, the Central Statistics Office, the National Bank, the Ministry of Finance and Economics, the Customs Department and the provincial Nazirates of Finance and Trade.

Improvements in the statistical services should be accompanied by a marked strengthening of the organization for economic planning and the analysis of economic information. As already noted, we envisage the primary responsibility in this field as resting with the Development Council. In addition, the National Bank should maintain an economic research staff as at present. First priority in recruitment of economists, whether expatriate or Libyan, should be given to finding staff for these two institutions. It may also be desirable for certain ministries and nazirates to have their own economic advisers, but insofar as there is an over-all shortage of suitable personnel we recommend that the claims of these departments should be accorded a lower priority.

FINANCIAL CONTROL

The mission cannot emphasize too strongly that proper financial control is essential to efficient public administration, especially in a country such as Libya where government disposes of a high proportion of the national income. Control should operate at a number of different levels. The Ministry of Finance should control the expenditures of the federal government, including grants-in-aid to the provinces; the Nazirates of Finance in each province should control the expenditures of the provincial government; and each spending department, federal and provincial, should have its own internal machinery for keeping a constant check on its financial operations.

All government accounts should be subjected to independent audit. The Auditor General and the provincial auditors should be responsible for scrutinizing the accounts of the finance departments, as well as of all ministers and nazirs, and their observations should be embodied in formal annual reports and placed before Parliament. Eventually, we believe that Libya should aim at establishing a single system of audit for the whole country, with the Auditor General having responsibility for auditing the accounts of the provincial governments as well as those of the federal government. This would require prior agreement between the Federal Parliament and the Legislative Councils of the provinces.

At present the Federal Parliament and the Legislative Councils in the provinces exercise only the most perfunctory control over the spending of public money. Annual budgets are presented, but there is seldom any serious parliamentary debate on financial matters, and the budgets receive little publicity. The budgets have to be prepared before the amount of foreign aid is known, and the expenditures of the aid agencies are separately determined without reference to Parliament. We have referred already in Chapter 3 to the difficulties of reconciling American aid procedures with the principles of sound fiscal management in Libya and we would urge that the Libyan Government consult with the U. S. authorities on possible ways of overcoming these difficulties. No such problem arises at present in the case of British aid, which has been negotiated on a five-year basis.

Some guiding principles relating to audit are set out in the UN report on public administration in Libya.[1] The mission urges that these principles be rigidly observed in practice, and that efforts be made to avoid laxity in the control of public expenditures. The sections of the federal Ministry of Finance dealing with budgets and estimates and with the control of accounts are seriously understaffed, and though the situation in this respect appears to be rather better in Tripolitania, it is still far from satisfactory. There are long delays in closing government accounts, and there is need for information to be made more readily available about how much money is being spent and what it is being spent on.

This is one of the branches of public administration where the need for improvement is urgent. It is all the greater now that there is a prospect of substantial oil revenues accruing to Libya in the not very distant future. A satisfactory solution requires both the recruitment of additional personnel, including a number of qualified accountants from abroad, and an acceptance on the part of Ministers and Parliament of their constitutional responsibility for the expenditure of public money. An important aspect of financial control is the control of civil service establishments. At present this control, insofar as it exists at all, is exercised by the Civil Service Committee. In the mission's view, a more satisfactory arrangement would be one which linked budgetary

[1] *Administrative Survey of Departments of Central Government and Provincial Administration of Libya*, H. C. Elvins and F. A. Hynes, 1955.

control and the control of civil service establishments, and we recommend that the latter function should be transferred from the Civil Service Committee to the Ministry of Finance in the case of the federal government and to the Nazirates of Finance in the provinces. Within the limits of the authorized establishment the permanent head of each department should be responsible for internal office organization, including such matters as discipline and promotions. The Civil Service Committee should continue to be responsible for recruitment and for general conditions of service.

THE CIVIL SERVICE

Libya has a civil service law which is applied with minor variations in all three provinces. The law was soundly conceived with the objective of building up a strong civil service tradition and it embodies well-tested principles of public administration, including recruitment of civil servants by competitive examination. As is inevitable in a country with so brief an experience of modern government, difficulties have been encountered in applying the law in practice and in gaining acceptance of the ideas underlying it—the idea, for example, that civil servants should be independent of politics, and that there should be checks on the exercise of arbitrary power by ministers and nazirs.

Moreover, the way in which the civil service law has been administered has not always been conducive to good government. In particular, a rather inflexible and unimaginative interpretation of the rules relating to pay and promotion has sometimes acted as a barrier to efficient organization. Article 9 of the law provides that "where necessary Libyans or foreigners may be appointed under special contracts, to be agreed by the [Civil Service] Committee, governing the terms of service including remuneration." But full use has not been made of this provision. The mission was told, for example, of a number of government departments which were unable to recruit specialists for key posts because they were not allowed to offer salaries in line with the going market rates. Again, it was our general impression that promotion within the service is liable to be governed too much by seniority and too little by merit. These are matters which will doubtless be put right in time as more experience is gained of civil service problems; and it may be added that no civil service anywhere in the world has ever found perfect answers to all its problems.

One of the main defects of the present system of civil service administration in Libya, as the mission saw it, was the tendency for senior officials to be shifted around with great frequency from one post to another, often without regard to their special experience or qualifications. This is not calculated to promote efficiency or morale, and if the practice continues, it will become increasingly difficult to retain good men in the public service.

It is also essential that civil service pay scales, particularly in the higher grades, should keep in step with the general rise in salaries in other occupations. Civil servants, of course, enjoy certain advantages and fringe benefits (e.g., low rents and free medical treatment) which are not always available to those in private employment, and due allowance must be made for this in comparing salaries. Nevertheless, the earnings of senior officials are tending increasingly to lag behind those of people with comparable qualifications outside the civil service, particularly since the arrival of the oil companies in Libya, and an upward revision of civil service pay scales is already overdue. We suggest therefore that the matter of civil service pay should be referred to an independent tribunal for early decision.[2]

Increases in pay should be accompanied by an extension of hours of work. Although a few of the top Libyan civil servants work very hard, the basic work week in the Libyan civil service averages only 33 hours, which is much less than is usual in other countries or in private employment in Libya. The shortage of trained administrators in Libya, combined with the heavy responsibilities of government, would suggest that longer hours should be worked. A 40-hour week would seem to be an appropriate minimum, and a strong case can be made out for rearranging the working day into morning and afternoon sessions, with a break for lunch in between.

The traditional practice of working six hours in the morning without a break (normally 8 a.m. to 2 p.m.) is plainly not conducive to efficiency. It was defended to the mission on the grounds that many officials had to travel a long way to work and could not get home to lunch; nor could they afford to pay for a meal in a cafe or canteen. This is not a convincing argument. There are many other countries (India and Pakistan, for example) where junior officials are no better paid than in Libya, and where the average journey to work is as long or longer, and yet office hours provide for a midday break.

The mission is in no doubt that civil servants in Libya, and particularly senior civil servants, should be paid more. But the country

[2] A study of civil service pay scales was made by two foreign experts in 1957. No action was taken on it, however, and it is now rather out of date.

can only afford to pay them more if their productivity (i.e., output per man) is increased and their number reduced. Longer hours of work, and a rearrangement of the working day, should be considered from this point of view.

It is readily accepted by all concerned that Libya should proceed as fast as is consistent with administrative efficiency in reducing its dependence on expatriate officials (as distinct from technical experts). Some progress has already been made in this direction, though it would appear that the standards of administration have been lowered in the process. The mission therefore attaches the highest priority to training schemes for Libyan civil servants.

As we see it, there are three lines of approach which should be pursued simultaneously. The first is to attract to Libya a small number of really first-class people with experience of administration in other underdeveloped countries and to assign these men to senior posts in the civil service with specific responsibilities for putting the organization of their departments on a sound footing and giving practical training on the job to Libyan officials working under them. Normal salary limits should be waived if necessary to attract and to retain the right people.

The second line of approach to the problem of civil service training is to send Libyan officials abroad to gain experience of administration by working with other governments and international institutions or by participating in courses at schools of public administration such as the administrative staff colleges which have been set up in India, the United Kingdom and some other countries. However, the art of administration cannot generally be taught in schools; it has to be picked up on the job, and training in one's own country is usually better than training abroad. For this reason, we would suggest that training abroad should be reserved for a few of the younger Libyan officials of not less than 25 years of age who have had a broad enough general education to profit from it, and who have had not less than five years experience of government work in Libya.

A third approach is to look to some foreign university (e.g., in the United States), which might be ready to send out to Libya for a period of a few years a team of specialists to work alongside Libyans in organizing a particular branch of government activity (e.g., the statistical services or agricultural extension work). Valuable results have been achieved by this method of training in a number of other underdeveloped countries, and the direct association of a particular university with a training scheme of this kind has the advantage of ensuring a continuing relationship which is lacking when foreign experts are recruited on an individual basis from different countries.

The above suggestions refer particularly to the higher levels of administration. For the training of intermediate and lower grades there is already a School of Public Administration staffed by the United Nations. In addition, the UN Adviser on Public Administration has proposed a program of in-service training, and we recommend that this should be implemented as rapidly as possible now that boys from secondary schools are beginning to enter the civil service in increasing numbers. Our observations on general education and technical training are set out separately in Chapter 13.

While every effort should be made to expedite the training of Libyans, there is no alternative at present to the employment of a considerable number of expatriate officials in key posts in the federal and provincial administrations. These officials by and large carry a heavy load of responsibility and need full support and encouragement. In order to attract the best qualified personnel, it is necessary to reward them on scales which would compensate them suitably in relation to their domestic levels of income and the inconvenience and loss of income involved in leaving their home countries. It is thus inevitable that they should be paid more than most Libyans, as indeed they are, and if the Libyan Government wishes to attract and retain suitably qualified foreign personnel, it must be ready to accept such costs. Failure to do this has sometimes resulted in an important vacancy remaining unfilled for a long time, much to Libya's disadvantage. Another defect in the present system of recruiting foreign personnel is that contracts are usually extended only for one year at a time. The Government should be prepared to offer the assurance of longer-term employment, subject to reasonable notice of termination applicable on both sides.

The salaries paid to foreign technicians in the regular employment of the Libyan Government are by international standards comparatively low, but lavish fees are frequently paid to consultants engaged to advise on particular aspects of economic development (e.g., roads and telecommunications). The marked disparity in the treatment accorded to the two groups of foreign technicians is hard to justify, and the mission believes that the payment of higher salaries to regular officials might sometimes prove to be an economy by reducing the need for hiring more highly paid consultants.

We have already discussed in Chapter 3 the technical assistance provided under the UN and U. S. programs. Now that LARC, LPDSA and LAJS are to be disbanded, the personnel employed by these agencies will have to be reassigned. Jobs will presumably be found for most of the Libyans concerned in the regular departments of the federal and provincial governments. At the same time we believe it would be in Libya's interests if some of the American, British and other foreign staff of the agencies could serve as technical advisers to government departments, particularly to the federal Ministry of Agriculture and National Resources, which we have proposed should be set up.

GOVERNMENT CONTRACTS

The mission had an opportunity to examine some of the contracts entered into by the Libyan Government with Libyan and foreign firms and found only one which appeared to conform to the basic requirements normally laid down in other countries. The most important of these contracts, together involving sums of nearly £L 10 million, had to do with the creation of a telecommunications system, the expansion of the Tripoli power plant, the construction of the main buildings at Beida and the Fezzan road. There were also a number of smaller contracts entered into by the provincial governments.

The present regulations with regard to contracts appear to be in need of review, and the mission recommends that in future the Ministry of Justice and the Auditor General should always be consulted by the government in drawing up rules and regulations governing calls for tenders and the acceptance of contracts. Four vital principles are involved:

1. Tenders should be invited only after surveys or technical appraisals have been carried out, drawings prepared, specifications drafted and bills of quantities listed by competent technical staff.
2. Responsibility at every stage must be squarely placed on the technical head of the department concerned.
3. There must be no secrecy in the technical work of preparing bills of quantities or specifications or in revealing the names of tenderers and prices tendered. Nor should the advice of the consulting engineer or consultant be regarded as secret; it should in fact be made available to prospective tenderers. For important works the name of the successful tenderer and the amount of his contract should be made public, as in most other countries. Not only must everything connected with contracts be open and above board, but it must be seen to be open and above board.

4. No adviser of government on contracts, including the consulting engineer or consultant, should have any financial interest in the contract or execute any contract work except as provided in the penalty clauses of the printed "Conditions" of the contract.

It is particularly undesirable that a prospective contractor or concessionaire should be allowed to suggest the terms of his own contract, as has happened in some cases in the past. No contractor or concessionaire should allow himself to be placed in this position unless he is prepared to suggest terms not less favorable than the most favorable terms granted in similar circumstances elsewhere.

CHAPTER 7 *WATER RESOURCES*

The soil of Libya is known to be potentially fertile over large areas including the desert regions, but rainfall is low and erratic and droughts are frequent, so that water or its absence is the critical factor in Libyan agriculture. In order to stabilize the agricultural economy of the country, and to increase the income of those engaged in agriculture, the provision of irrigation water wherever possible is of primary importance. The mission recommends that the development of water resources for agriculture should be accorded high priority in the economic development of Libya.

The Romans demonstrated what could be done by a careful husbanding of the limited available water resources of Libya. By an energetic application of capital works—the construction of numerous cisterns, dikes, dams and the like—the Romans were able to establish a thriving agricultural society which supported a population two or three times the size of the present population; and there is no conclusive evidence that the rainfall in the coastal zone was any heavier in those days than now. Down the centuries, the Roman water works have been allowed to fall into disrepair and disuse—although, such was the durability of their construction and the effectiveness of their design, that many of the Roman underground cisterns are now being rebuilt for present-day use. The achievements of the Romans serve as an indication of what might still be done in this respect.

Geology and Hydrology

Desert conditions prevail over much of Libya and the climate is typical of hot and arid countries. The influence of the Mediterranean, however, differentiates the zones of settled agriculture and continuous occupation in Tripolitania and Cyrenaica from the desert. In these zones the weather is variable and there is a winter season which can generally be depended on to bring rain and coolness.

In Tripolitania, the rainfall is greatest in the vicinity of Tripoli itself, where the mean annual precipitation over 78 years was 371.3 mm., and in the central and eastern part of the Gebel, where the mean

100

is over 300 mm. annually. But the main characteristic of the Tripolitania climate is its instability, due to the contrary effects of the Sahara
and the sea. The total rainfall may occur within a few days, while
severe droughts, affecting sometimes the whole of the province and
sometimes only part of it, occur frequently, and may result in almost
total crop failures, two successive years of drought being not infrequent.

In Cyrenaica, the Gebel Akhdar plateaus have comparatively high
winter rains and humidity, westerly and north westerly winds bringing
rainfall averaging more than 300 mm. annually to an area 8,200 square
kilometers in extent. The central plateaus, 3,800 square kilometers in
extent, have more than 400 mm. rainfall, while in the extreme north
1,300 square kilometers receive more than 500 mm. The rainfall drops
off on all sides of the Gebel and only a small portion of the coastal
belt gets more than 200 mm., while the desert to the south of the Gebel
rarely has any rainfall. The irregularity of the climate is as great as in
Tripolitania, and while the rainfall is generally less torrential and the
run-off slower and proportionately smaller, partial and total droughts
occur with almost similar frequency.

In the Fezzan the climate is arid and rain falls only at rare intervals,
varying both as to location and time of year. Recent records of rainfall
at Sebha over five successive years varied from a 101 mm. maximum to
a 15 mm. minimum, and the average was 68 mm., while in some places
no rain has fallen over several consecutive years.

In Tripolitania and Cyrenaica the temperature is normally high,
but is moderated near the coast by the sea and on the Gebels by alti-
tude. However, at Azizia, situated in the Gefara of Tripolitania and
only 30 kilometers from the sea, it has been reported that a shade
temperature of 136° was recorded in 1932, and this is one of the highest recorded anywhere in the world. The winds are an important factor
in agriculture in these two provinces, bringing rain and coolness from
the sea and sand and heat from the desert. The most important wind
from the standpoint of agriculture is the hot, violent and very dry
wind which blows from the desert, carrying sand and dust with it. This
wind is the *ghibli*. It dries the soil, parches the vegetation and may
have a disastrous effect on fruit trees and grain crops, sometimes making the difference between a good crop and a bad one. In the Fezzan
the differences between day and night temperatures are extreme and
temperature changes, together with the strong desert winds, can cause
extreme discomfort. The winds blowing from the Sahara are intensely
hot during the summer months and often cold in the winter.

There have been extensive studies of the geology and hydrology of Libya, done during the Italian colonial period and by the aid agencies and oil prospecting companies after World War II, but there is still much work required in the field and laboratory before the details required for an adequate understanding of these subjects are obtained. A brief description of what is already known is given in Annex V.

Water Sources and Conservation

The often propounded theory that underground rivers bring significant supplies of water from the Nile or from Central Africa to Libya's coastal areas has little geological support or hydrological substance. The rain, scarce and erratic though it be, brings Libya's water supply and provides the ground water recharge required to keep the springs flowing and the wells supplied. Most of Libya's settled agriculture is possible only where there are accessible underground water resources, and the absence of an accessible supply, or a limited recharge rate where accessible supplies exist, have been basic factors in restricting the extension of cultivation. Only in the most intensively cultivated part of the country, around Tripoli and along the Tripolitanian coast, is the ground water recharge rate insufficient to meet the present agricultural irrigation demands, and this local over-exploitation is a danger signal indicating that irrigated agricultural development must be controlled without delay, so that the demands on the ground water supplies do not exceed the recharge rate. This means that any future extension of cultivation in Tripolitania will generally have to take place in areas away from the coast and from Tripoli.

The ground water supplies in the coastal belt are recharged by percolation and by subsequent ground water movement. Consequently, in order to achieve maximum percolation and to reduce run-off and evaporation losses, grazing and range management practices preserving perennial grasses and shrubs, afforestation of wadi catchments, terracing, construction of dikes and water spreading must all be made to contribute to soil and water conservancy and help increase the amount of water available for ground water recharge. It is therefore a primary duty of government, as well as of the agricultural and pastoral landowners, to promote all the soil and water conservancy techniques that are economic.

Flood run-off spreads out delta-wise where the wadis debouch onto the plains supplying soil moisture there and augmenting ground water supplies. No matter what large conservancy works government undertakes, it is the agriculturalist and the pastoralist who must do the bulk of the soil and water conservancy with their numerous small-scale individual efforts. These efforts cannot be undertaken on the scale required unless "self-help" procedures under government guidance are adopted. The mission stresses the need for government to support such self-help measures as soil and water conservancy works, terracing, diking, grazing control, flood spreading and cistern repairing; it also stresses, here and elsewhere in the report, the basic need for the introduction of a land tenure law.

There are perhaps two potential future methods of augmenting Libya's water resources: by salt water conversion and by cloud seeding. A great deal of research is presently going into developing a cheap method of salt water conversion, and the progress made with this research should be followed closely by the Libyan Government. By means of evaporation and distillation plants, fresh water can be produced from salt or saline water, but at present only at costs which make its use for agriculture absolutely prohibitive (about 20-25 piasters per 1,000 gallons). Recently, however, there have been significant developments in the technique of water desalination at low cost using the electrodialysis method. Treatment of brackish water is already possible at costs which are appreciably lower than the cost of treatment of sea water, and research is now being done to discover cheap and efficient techniques for large output units. As comparatively large quantities of water are always involved in irrigation of agricultural and horticultural crops, over-all costs in the neighborhood of 2.5 piasters per 1,000 gallons would have to be achieved to make the use of desalinated water an economic proposition for most crops in Libya. While methods of achieving this will no doubt ultimately be found, it does not appear that it will be a practical proposition in the near future, and we are therefore unable to recommend schemes for the desalination of salt or brackish water for agricultural or horticultural use in the program we have outlined for the development of Libya's water resources.

The mission has studied the research data available on cloud seeding with some care and recommends that the Libyan Government follow with close attention the practical application of this research in Australia and America. It appears at the moment that several more years of research and practice will be necessary before sure and economical methods of augmenting rainfall by cloud seeding are available. As soon as it appears likely that successful methods of cloud seeding are possible in countries with similar cloud and climatic conditions to Libya's, the Meteorological Department should anticipate the demand for basic data on the subject by selecting control areas in the Benghazi coastal plain and the Gefara of Tripolitania and establishing rain gauges there. Airline operators using Libyan airports could be asked to supply information about cloud elevations, depths and temperatures. This information would make possible an assessment of the cloud seeding potential of the two areas and, if favorable, would justify making full-scale experiments when techniques developed elsewhere are judged to be practical and potentially effective.

Federal Department of Geology and Hydrology

At present in Libya there is no one department or office in which the great mass of information about the geology of the country and its mineral and water resources can be lodged, nor is there the technical staff available to continue the search for more information and offer to the federal and provincial governments the expert advice required on these matters. There is a Geological Department in the federal Ministry of National Economy, but it is lacking in technical staff, equipment and basic data and it can at best supply opinions, not advice. This assessment of the value of the department implies no criticism of its present staff who have to work within the limits of the data and means available to them.

The mission recommends that the existing federal Department of Geology be reorganized as the federal Department of Geology and Hydrology and equipped to study and extend the knowledge of the geological, mineral and ground water resources of Libya, in order that more use may be made of, and fuller value obtained from, the work done in prewar years by the Italian geologists, and in postwar years by various aid agencies. The new department should be part of the proposed Ministry of Agriculture and Natural Resources and should be provided with a laboratory and a library. It should also do exploratory work in the field. Although a federal department, the mission strongly recommends that its offices and laboratory should not be required to move when the federal government changes its headquarters, but that it should be based permanently in either Benghazi or Tripoli.

An important duty of this department will be to collect all the available records of the work done previously on these subjects to form the nucleus of the departmental library. The department should receive the data collected by every department of government and agency in this field in order to correlate them and add to the detailed information shown on the geological and hydrological maps.

Previous geological surveys have indicated that, apart from oil, there is little apparent prospect of valuable minerals being found which can be exploited commercially. Accordingly, in considering the proposed duties of the department, emphasis has been placed by the mission on the need for proving the location and dimensions of the ground water resources and on advising government on the application of a water law. The mission recommends that the department, in addition to gathering and interpreting data, sponsor a program of exploratory drilling, the field work of which should be carried out by provincial Water Resources Branches. These branches would be staffed and equipped to undertake this program, and the expense and delays consequent on moving drilling rigs and personnel between the provinces would be avoided. The provincial branches would recover the cost of this work from the federal department, and financial provision has been allowed for this in the federal estimates. The federal department should integrate its field work with the provincial Water Resources Branches, and the executive work required for the development of mineral and water resources should actually be carried out by provincial organizations or by private enterprise.

The mission recommends that steps be taken to recruit expatriate staff to occupy the senior appointments in the department and Libyan personnel to take over the technician posts. Now that LARC and LAJS are being disbanded, appropriate USOM experts might be attached to the department as technical advisers. Suitably educated Libyans should be chosen for overseas training as geologists to assume in due course the senior appointments. The mission also recommends that the financial provision required to meet the cost of the department and to supply and equip suitable office and laboratory accommodations should be made available as required from April 1960 onwards. The mission estimates the total cost of the department at £L 385,000 for the five years from April 1960 to March 1965.

Provincial Water Resources Branches

The development and improvement of the use of the water resources of Libya for agriculture is now almost entirely the responsibility of the LAJS in respect of both technical staffing and financing. In the five years from 1954/55-1958/59 the total expenditure by the provincial governments and the aid agencies on soil and water conservation, on irrigation and wells and on water investigations was approximately £L 2,350,000, averaging £L 470,000 annually. In Tripolitania, there are well-drilling and irrigation branches of the Nazirate of Agriculture, financed by the provincial government to the extent of £L 75,000 in 1959, which are working in liaison with the LAJS engineers and geologists. In Cyrenaica, the Public Works Department undertakes on request the design and construction of small works for the use of water for agriculture, but does not initiate action. In the Fezzan, the provincial government assisted the agencies' programs to the extent of promising to supply office and yard accommodation for the agencies' staff and personnel engaged on well drilling.

The mission recommends that each province should set up a Water Resources Branch to undertake and extend the work now done by the agencies. The nucleus of an organization of this kind already exists in the Nazirate of Agriculture in Tripolitania. In the other two provinces it may be better if the Water Resources Branches are set up in the Nazirates of Public Works to avoid duplication of workshops, drawing offices and other engineering facilities.

The foreign experts now employed by the agencies should be attached to the new Water Resources Branches as advisers, the subordinate technical staff and the equipment used by LAJS should be taken over, and Libyans should be sent abroad for training in hydraulic engineering. Meantime, as it will take five years for Libyans to qualify professionally and as it will be advisable for them to have at least five years' subsequent experience on hydrology before taking over the senior appointments, the mission recommends that certain appointments be filled for ten years by qualified and experienced expatriates.

In connection with water laws to be proposed, enforcement officers should be included on the staffs of the Water Resources Branches. The services of these officers are required immediately in Tripolitania, where overexploitation of the ground water resources has led to serious lowering of the water table level around Tripoli and to salt water intrusion along the coast, and also in the Shatti Valley of the Fezzan, where indiscriminate artesian well-boring has caused wastage of water and deterioration of soil. As the country's water resources become more fully developed elsewhere in Libya, it will be desirable to appoint more of these officers to enforce such additional controls as may be necessary to ensure full use without overexploitation.

A Water Law

Because water is Libya's most precious resource, its control and conservation should be recognized as a primary duty of government. Water is nowhere plentiful in Libya, but the mission observed that much of the available supply is used wastefully, or is unused, or is lost through lack of conservancy measures. The use of water (but not its conservancy) has long been controlled in Libya by law: Moslem law, customary law and the Ottoman Civil Code. Each law held sway in one or more parts of the country until they were all superseded by the water law introduced during the Italian colonial period. Though the Italian law is still the valid water law of the country, it is nowhere enforced, and the laws of the earlier administrations, though officially superseded, are still accepted in varying degrees in the desert oases and in places where the nomadic way of life prevails.

In the more developed parts of the country there is now no legal control exercised over the use of water. Because of this lack of control by law and because conditions vary so much in the three provinces, there is serious overexploitation of water resources in Tripolitania, some underexploitation in Cyrenaica, and waste in the Fezzan. Elsewhere in this report the mission has discussed the consequences of these abuses and neglects and has advised that, to correct them, the use of water for agriculture, industry, municipal and domestic purposes should be controlled and regulated by a newly enacted Libyan law. Suggestions on the drafting and administration of such a law are set out in Annex VI.

The mission is fully aware of the difficulties which both the federal and provincial authorities will have to overcome in drafting a law with such comprehensive rules and regulations as will reconcile the many existing and conflicting claims of ownership and usage with the government's control and development proposals. The mission therefore recommends that the federal law should confine itself to asserting the state's ownership of water; to insisting that the use of water be subject to control and license; to providing for that control and licensing to be done by the legally constituted Control Boards of the provincial authorities under rules and regulations approved by the federal government; and to ensuring that the decisions of the provincial Control Boards shall always be subject to a right of appeal. Control of water resources currently varies between the three provinces; water use has been developed in Tripolitania by individuals for individual use, in Cyrenaica on a tribal basis, and we are recommending the development of artesian wells in the Fezzan on a cooperative use basis, subject to public ownership (see page 118). Thus the provincial authorities will be left the task of making and operating, with federal sanctions, their own rules and regulations in such a manner as will accord with their particular customs, conditions and stages of development.

Development Proposals

Libyan climate and geological factors are such that the possibilities for large-scale irrigation works are remote, at least until technical long-range investigations have been completed. There are no rivers with a perennial flow, there are no continuous periods of wet-weather flow in the rivers, there are no great possibilities of constructing storage reservoirs to retain flood flows and there are no known underground rivers which can be tapped for irrigation supplies. Therefore such water resources as are available should be developed for agricultural use in the following ways: by water conservancy to prevent run-off and evaporation losses, by making full use of spring supplies, by planned use of the ground water supplies and by improving irrigation practices to conserve water.

The mission thus recommends that government assistance in achieving maximum possible development of the use of water for agriculture be planned along the following lines:

1. Investigations and studies, carried out by the federal Department of Geology and Hydrology, to discover fully the country's accessible underground water resources and to make the information obtained generally available to the government and to commercial enterprises.
2. Administration of the Water Law by the provincial Water Resources Branches to ensure that full and reasonable use is made of the resources available and to ensure that the ground water supplies are not overdrawn.
3. Construction of specific development works through the agency of the Water Resources Branches to provide facilities for the use of water where private enterprise cannot, for technical and social reasons, provide these facilities.
4. Planned self-help and credit programs to encourage water conservancy and irrigation to the limit of the water resources available.
5. Engineering surveys and investigations to explore and develop, wherever practicable, any possibility for large-scale water storage and flood spreading schemes.
6. Agricultural research to achieve better irrigation techniques which will lead to economies in the use of water, together with the rigorous application of techniques already well known and tested.

The mission's proposals for the organizing and financing of the federal and provincial water development agencies of government are based on the foregoing recommendations being implemented. Finally, the mission recommends that a water rate be charged to users of water for irrigation in every case where the maintenance and running costs of the irrigation works is done by government agency.

The nature of the works proposed are so diverse and are individually of such small extent that it is not possible to assess directly the total economic benefit that will accrue from them. Moreover, much will depend on the progress made in overcoming the present obstacles to the development of agricultural production which are discussed in the following chapter. The better organization of water resources along the lines we recommend will undoubtedly create opportunities for achieving substantial crop increases, possibly amounting in total to as much as £L 500,000 a year (and considerably more in drought years). But these increases will not be fully realized unless many other things are done at the same time to promote greater efficiency in agriculture.

There will, of course, be other direct advantages accruing from the controls and works proposed, notably the prevention of loss of the more fertile topsoil and the lessening of flood damage. While the full social and commercial value of the water conservancy works cannot be estimated with any precision, there is no doubt that they will make for a general improvement in the standard of living of the Libyan agriculturalist, rich and poor alike.

Development Works in Cyrenaica

In Cyrenaica, there are over 200,000 hectares of land where settled agriculture is practiced and some 5,000,000 hectares of grazing land. The more plentiful rainfall on the Gebel plateaus is sufficient to ensure good crops in most years, but even there, if water could be found in sufficient quantity, its use for irrigated agriculture would be justified by the higher crop yields resulting and as an insurance against drought years. At present, there are only 2,000 hectares of irrigated land in Cyrenaica, situated chiefly on the coastal plain around Benghazi and on the narrow strip of flat land along the coast from Susa to Derna. This is only one percent of the area of settled agriculture and emphasizes the small extent to which the water resources in the province have so far been developed.

On the southern slopes of the Gebel Akhdar there are extensive grazing ranges, where better use could in time be made of the rainfall and of the underground water supplies to provide the facilities that the nomad tribesmen, now using the ranges, require for a more settled way of life. To this end, the hydrologic and geologic surveys should be extended there to give a more complete picture of the resources and accessibility of the underground water.

If the results of these investigations are encouraging, an endeavor might be made later on to locate more wells for domestic and stock supplies on the southern slopes before the water, by percolation, reaches unexploitable depths. Also, more water conservancy dikes should be constructed in the wadis to improve conditions for settled farming. By these methods, a more settled way of life can be gradually encouraged and villages may grow up around the wells. It must be recognized, however, that until more progress has been made with measures to control grazing the immediate effect of drilling more wells is likely to be merely to encourage the multiplication of livestock and to aggravate the problem of overgrazing. More effective control of grazing should therefore be regarded as a prerequisite to the development of water resources in this region.

In the absence of reliable information about the availability of ground water in Cyrenaica, the mission has had difficulty in suggesting a concrete program for well drilling. This is the region of Libya where the need for preliminary ground water investigations is greatest, and where the main exploratory effort of the federal Department of Geology and Hydrology should initially be concentrated, following up the valuable work already done in the province by the LAJS. If the water can be found in the right places, a program for the construction of 80 wells in Cyrenaica over five years at an estimated average cost of £L 8,000 per well would seem a reasonable goal, and a sum of £L 640,000 has accordingly been included for this purpose in our table of proposed capital expenditures. We have some doubts, however, whether so large a program will prove practicable. Investigations must come first.

There are 40 listed springs, and many unlisted small springs, issuing from the faults and fractures of the limestones in the Gebel terrain, and it is unfortunate that, in such a riverless country, many of them are so situated that their waters are inaccessible for agricultural use and that the land suitable for irrigation which others command is so limited in extent that the water available cannot be fully utilized. Nevertheless, there are other springs which are accessible and which command enough land to require their full flow, where improvement of irrigation practices and facilities could be carried out. LAJS is improving the irrigation works at some of these springs, sometimes on a self-help basis, and the mission has made provision in the program for Cyrenaica for this work to continue. However, to get the potentiality of these Gebel springs into perspective, it should be realized that their total flow, even if accessible and fully exploited, would provide sufficient water to give full irrigation supply for only 4,000 hectares of land, or partial irrigation for 10,000 hectares; and it is doubtful if even 50 percent of the total flow can be utilized for agriculture.

There are springs at two places where preliminary surveys are required to determine whether the water can be used for irrigation. These springs are Ain Mara, situated just off the main road from Beida to Derna about 70 kilometers from Beida, and the Ain Zeiana-el Coefia complex, situated close to the sea 14 kilometers northeast of Benghazi. Further details of the proposed surveys at these two locations will be found in Annex VIII. The mission recommends that they should be given high priority in the investigation program of the provincial Water Resources Branch. If the surveys indicate that the springs can be used economically for irrigation, we further recommend that suitable provision should be made in the Supplementary Program for their development. It will probably be several years before the preparatory work is completed and before legal rights to the land and water are satisfactorily determined. No capital works should be undertaken until this is done.

On the first escarpment of the Gebel Akhdar, at its western end, there is a wide, flat, saucer-shaped plain known as the Barce Plain, where there is an area of settled agriculture extending to 28,000 hectares of land with a heavy clay (*terra rossa*) soil. The annual rainfall varies between 300 mm. and 500 mm., and the plain has no gullies allowing run-off to the sea. The rainfall not lost in evaporation percolates down through the *terra rossa* soil and the limestone rock underlying the basin and thus becomes lost to agriculture through its inaccessibility. The ground water supplies available on the Barce Plain are limited to a few perched water tables which can be easily overdrawn; so far, no extensive artesian aquifer has been discovered there. Farming on the Barce Plain is therefore not irrigated farming. The rain is generally adequate for grain and fruit crops, and vegetables can be grown on the moist soil which is exposed when the lake (left in the center of the plain by winter rainfall) recedes.

If a plentiful supply of ground water could be found at a depth at which it could be economically used for agriculture, the value of the Barce Plain to agriculture would be greatly enhanced. The mission considers that, while it may not have a great chance of success, a detailed survey should be carried out in the Barce Plain to determine whether the ground water is lost through relatively concentrated flow channels or through general seepage into a porous limestone saucer floor. If the former, some method of exploiting it for agriculture may be possible. The search for artesian aquifers should also be continued by the Department of Geology and Hydrology.

Many underground cisterns have been excavated throughout northern Cyrenaica from the time of the Roman occupation onwards, but over the years many of these have become useless through neglect. A cistern repair program was started on a self-help basis in 1957 by LAJS, and up to March 1959 nearly 200 had been repaired at an average cost of £L 500 each. This seems to be a high figure, but the cisterns in Cyrenaica have generally a capacity of 1,000 cubic meters or more, compared with the 100 cubic meters' average capacity of cisterns in Tripolitania, and also, due to the inaccessibility of the cisterns, the cost of bringing such materials as sand, cement and water is high. Nevertheless, the mission is of the opinion that, if cistern repairs were to some extent mechanized by using light mechanical plant such as bucket conveyors for excavating silt and sand, grouting machines for closing leaks and cement guns for sealing walls, all operated by a mobile power unit, the repair cost could be reduced to an average of £L 300 per cistern. In Cyrenaica, cisterns have an immediate value to agriculture, livestock and domestic life. It is therefore desirable that cistern repair work should be carried on to the fullest extent that staff and equipment resources allow, and the mission has therefore made provision of £L 300,000 in the five-year program for repairing and renovating 1,000 cisterns at an average cost of £L 300 per cistern. The demand for assistance for cistern repairs is likely to fall off after this program has been completed.

Development Works in Tripolitania

The wedge-shaped coastal plain in Tripolitania, just over a million hectares in extent, which lies between the mountain escarpment and the sea and stretches eastwards from the Tunisian border to where the mountains reach the sea near Homs, has a fertile and intensively cultivated belt along the coast where much of the land is irrigated. Behind this belt lies the Gefara, semi-arid flat land interspaced with sand dunes, which is used mainly for pasturing livestock, although some shifting cultivation is carried on. Certain parts of the Gefara not only enjoy a comparatively good rainfall, but have underground water resources of high yielding capacities and at such depths that irrigated agriculture is possible and economical for certain crops. The soil is generally a fertile light sandy clay which is unfortunately easily turned into sand dunes by bad cultivating methods and by wind erosion. The geology and hydrology of the Gefara have been studied extensively and reported on in the past by Italian and United Nations experts,[1] and its ground water resources are presently being investigated and assessed by the U. S. government geologists working with LAJS. These reports and surveys supply the background material against which our proposals and recommendations are set.

The coastal plain, including the Gefara, has been classified by the agricultural department as follows (in thousands of hectares):

Irrigated and potentially irrigable land	322
Land suitable for dry farming and grazing	470
Sand dunes	203
Coastal salt marshes	75
Total	1,070

The potentially irrigable land is land where unused ground water resources are known to exist. According to official estimates, the total area actually under irrigation in the whole of Tripolitania is only about 100,000 hectares, and this could well be an overestimate. There is no doubt therefore that considerable room exists for expansion of irrigated farming.

Tripoli is situated on the coast where the rainfall of the province is highest and the ground water resources most accessible; consequently, the countryside surrounding the city is agriculturally the most highly developed part of the coastal plain and indeed of all Libya. However, in the neighborhood of Tripoli, on the landward side, the agricultural demand for irrigation water has resulted in overexploitation of the ground water resources and progressive lowering of the water table level to such an extent that, unless water use is controlled, the cost of irrigation may before long exceed the economic limit. There is also the very real danger that, near the coast, the demands being made on

[1] "Artesian Water in Libya," Salvatore Laurenti, *Annali Africani Italiani,* Vol. III-IV, Rome, 1938. On the geological position and origin of the artesian water tables of the Tripoli Gefara and the Mesurate region and *Subterranean Waters in Libya and their Importance in Agriculture,* Ardito Desio, Milan, 1940. *Water Resources and Development in Libya,* R. Pioger, FAO Adviser to Libya, 1952.

114 THE MAIN REPORT

the ground water resources may create cones of depression extensive enough to induce salt water intrusion from the sea and make irrigated farming impossible. There is, therefore, the paradox that the ground water resources of the coastal plain are both overexploited and under-exploited.

The area of the overexploitation which is taking place around Tripoli has become known as the "Tripoli Quadrangle" (see map facing page 120). In the Funduk bin Gascir-Suani ben Adem area at the inland or southern side of the Quadrangle, the level of the ground water has declined as much as 15 meters since 1930. Adjacent to the coast the average drop has been about two meters since 1940, and this has been accompanied by a rise in the chlorine-salt content of the water.

The irrigated area in the Quadrangle is now probably 16,000 hectares. The irrigation water usage is estimated at over 90 million cubic meters annually, and the domestic and industrial requirements of Tripoli city bring total consumption to something in excess of 100 million cubic meters annually. Estimates of the recharge flow to the ground water reservoir of the Quadrangle are necessarily speculative, but for a year of average rainfall an optimistic figure for the annual local recharge of the water resources in the Quadrangle is 20 million cubic meters, some of which is undoubtedly lost because of its inaccessibility. The difference between the consumption and the recharge figures is met by an induced flow of ground water from adjacent areas and by the unreplaced water from storage, released by lowering water levels in and around the Quadrangle. The present demand on the water resources in the Quadrangle may be more than 50 percent in excess of its accessible recharge potential. Consequently, this situation, not unusual elsewhere in the world where the use of ground water is not rigidly controlled, calls for urgent measures to restrict the use of water within the Quadrangle, coupled with the controlled expansion of the use of water in suitable areas *outside* the Quadrangle.

Within the Quadrangle, however, even greater demands than in the past are likely to be made on the ground water resources when the installation of a 20,000 kw. generating plant at the Tripoli power station is completed and additional power for pumping becomes available. It is estimated that demands for power will be made which will double the area of irrigated land there. In 1958 the electric and diesel pumps sold in Tripoli totaled more than 900 in number, with a power potential of more than 5,000 hp. The combined lifting capacity of these pumps, if the average lift of water is 20 meters, is over 90 million cubic meters annually, compared with a capacity of perhaps six million cubic meters which could be lifted in *dalus* (bags or buckets usually made of goatskins) by animal power in the same time from the same number of wells. Faced with this situation, government must exercise control over the use of water along the lines indicated on pages 106-107.

The mission foresees, however, that ultimately the overexploitation of ground water resources within the Quadrangle will be stopped by the economics of pumping. If water levels drop much further, it will no longer pay to pump water for most crops, and other forms of agriculture using less water will be developed.

In anticipation of possible private demand for land elsewhere in the vicinity of Tripoli, we recommend that ground water and soil surveys should be made in the Bir Ghnem area south-west of the town, and that these should be followed by an economic survey of irrigation resources, agricultural cropping patterns and marketing potentials. Plans should be prepared for well-spacing, farm lots, community centers, roads and electric power lines, together with detailed estimates of development costs. An outline of the mission's proposals in this respect is set out in Annex VIII. Financial provision for the survey should be made in the ordinary budgets of the Nazirates of Agriculture and Public Works.

Elsewhere in the Gefara, because of topography, rainfall and ground water deficiencies, there appears to be little immediate possibility for extension of irrigated farming, but the mission's proposals for investigating water conservancy measures in the Gebel (see page 116) might make possible more intensive agriculture on the flatlands at the bottom of the escarpment. The sand dunes of the Gefara provide valuable recharge areas for ground water replenishment, and there may be good reasons for retaining certain of the sand dunes within and around the Tripoli Quadrangle for this purpose, and confining dune reclamation there to minimum perimeter fixation in places where encroachment on agricultural land occurs. There is reason to believe that the large dune area known as the Sand Sea (see map facing page 120) provides a significant amount of the water recharging the ground water supplies near Tripoli itself, and until more study has been given to this possibility, reafforestation of the dunes should be restricted to the absolute minimum required for fixation.

An ever-present danger of salt water intrusion exists along the whole coast of Tripolitania, where there are already extensive areas of salt-impregnated soil (known locally as *sebcha*) which have gone out of cultivation. This overexploitation of water on the coast is more serious than the overexploitation of the inland water resources, as salt water intrusion has resulted in the permanent loss to agriculture of the land affected. The mission was informed that, when more power becomes available in Tripoli, there will be an immediate demand for electric pumps to replace the *dalu* buckets in the intensively cultivated vegetable gardens around Tripoli, even though the ground water resources along the coast are already subject to excessive demands. The danger is one only government control can avert. Sentinel wells should be established along the coast, and any rapid increase of salinity of the water in these wells should be a signal for closing down all power pumping in the locality affected, only the use of *dalu* buckets being permitted for lifting water. The mission appreciates that such a drastic measure will be unpopular and will be resisted by the farmers affected, but the penalty of a laissez-faire policy will be the loss to agriculture of the valuable and populous coastal strip. The foregoing observations apply equally to the coastal areas near Misurata which are now irrigated by *dalu* buckets and where also the demands for power pumps are increasing yearly.

Geological and geophysical surveys at the Taorga springs could well be a prelude to further developmental activities, the details of which are described in Annex VIII. A place should be found for these surveys in the programs of the provincial Departments of Agriculture and Public Works. If the results of the surveys are satisfactory, additional works could be undertaken as part of the Supplementary Program.

On the southern slopes of the Gebel Nefusa the rainfall decreases rapidly to the south until the true desert is reached. Where the mean annual rainfall is more than 200 mm., these southern slopes provide land on which grain and fruit trees can be grown and livestock grazed. Below the 200 mm. rainfall zone fixed agriculture is possible only on the flat land in the bottom of the wadis. The ground water is inaccessible throughout this area, except at some small springs and from wells offering only meager flows. Consequently, all such water conservancy measures as dike building, contour plowing, terracing and cistern storing should be encouraged, and the mission has included items for these in the proposed capital works program of the Water Resources Branch. The mission particularly stresses the necessity of extending the hydrological investigation survey into these regions, so that the full potential of water resources will be known and it will be possible, should the resources justify it, to plan for their development.

The Wadi Tareglat, which lies half way between Beni Ulid and Homs, is one of the large wadis draining the southern slopes of the Gebel, and a special study of the whole of its catchment should be carried out to discover its hydrological and agricultural potential. Details will be found in Annex VIII.

The mission has recommended in the development program for Tripolitania for the next five years that, excluding the Wadi Megenin scheme, £L 830,000 should be allocated for providing wells and irrigation works, terraces and dikes and repairing cisterns, and considers that this work will be within the scope of the Water Resources Branch of the Nazirate of Agriculture. The mission recommends that the reconstruction of the irrigation facilities on the farms now in Arab ownership at Crispi and Gioda should be included in this program. This work will involve recasing (and lining with concrete) the artesian wells and reconstructing the irrigation canals. These wells and their irrigation channels will have to be maintained by government, and we recommend that the farmers should be required to pay an irrigation water rate.

The Nazirate of Agriculture has estimated the irrigated land in Tripolitania at 100,000 hectares. The mission suggests that the government's policy for the next ten years should be to use the resources of the Geological and Hydrological Department and the provincial Water Resources Branch to obtain data and prepare schemes aimed at doubling this irrigated area by development of the proven water resources (chiefly by private enterprise), and that the government's supporting program be prepared and executed as its financial, technical and administrative resources permit.

Development Works in the Fezzan

The Fezzan covers over half a million square kilometers of land which is mostly desert. The inhabitants number about 60,000, and the bulk of this population lives in the Jofra oases and the three strings of oases lying in the Shatti Valley and in the areas between Sebha and Ubari and Murzuk and Tmessa.

There are two basic factors which control agriculture in the Fezzan: first, crops cannot be grown without irrigation water and, second, agricultural land has no value without associated water rights. Until recently agriculture was practiced only in the oases, and these oases had developed where the water table lies near the surface. The usual method of lifting the water was to bring it to the surface in *dalu* buckets by human and animal power. The owner of a well usually owned the land irrigated by it and could lease the land, with the supply of water required to irrigate it, to non-well-owning farmers on a crop-sharing basis.

In postwar years the artesian aquifer at Brak in the Shatti Valley has been extensively exploited. About 50 artesian wells have been bored there; generally, they are unlined and uncapped and mostly privately owned. The owner of an artesian well can control the cultivation of a much bigger area of land than can the owner of a *dalu* well, and if it is a flowing well, he is not dependent on labor to get the water raised. However, in the absence of farmers willing to cultivate the land, the water from an unlined and uncapped well will run to waste, and this is what has been happening in the Shatti Valley. Furthermore, flowing artesian wells occur only on the low ground around, or in, the oases, and it is there that drainage is always difficult. The soil in the oases of the Fezzan naturally tends to be saline, and the unchecked flow from the artesian wells, or the overexploitation of irrigation water from the few capped wells, combined with the high water table in the oases and the lack of efficient drainage, has resulted in the precipitation of salts on the surface and the conversion of good fertile land to saline land.

The artesian aquifer is less exploited around Sebha and in the string of oases to the south, from Murzuk to Tmessa, because water pressure is such that pumping is generally necessary. There is naturally an insistent demand in this area for the government to supply pumps and motors so that the comparatively plentiful supply of artesian water can be used for agriculture. This demand is particularly strong in those villages where the younger men have left to work for the oil companies.

A program for the development of the water resources should be prepared and executed in conjunction with the drafting and implementation of land tenure and water laws. This would ensure that new wells were drilled, cased and capped, or provided with pumps and motors, that lined irrigation channels and drains were made and, if necessary, storage reservoirs provided—all to serve cooperative communities of small-holding farmers. These wells and their irrigation systems would have to be operated and maintained by the provincial Water Resources Branch, and the mission suggests a five-year program involving the drilling of 40 wells and the development of irrigation schemes around them. The wells should be sited where the land served by them can be owned by the farmers using the well water, but with the government retaining the ownership of the water, the wells and the irrigation systems, maintaining them and charging a water rate to cover maintenance costs.

The mission suggests that the owners be required to case and line the existing uncapped artesian wells in the Shatti Valley with concrete and cap them to control their flow. If this is not done, either the wells should be compulsorily acquired by the government and brought under efficient control or they should be plugged. The waste of water and the consequent permanent damage being done to agricultural land can be stopped only in this way.

The mission also recommends that a self-help program be inaugurated for improving the existing *dalu* wells. The yield of these wells could be increased by cleaning and deepening, while casing with local rock or concrete would prevent contamination of the water. Provision has been made for a modest program on these lines which, if it becomes popular, can readily be expanded.

The mission was impressed by the successful way in which the spring water resources in Ghat and Gadames are controlled and distributed in a manner decreed by customary law and suggests that they provide a model for the development of the communities using the artesian wells in other oases. The farmers using the artesian well water should participate in a cooperative way in water control and distribution so that the proposed new water law will eventually come to be accepted in place of customary law.

Flood Prevention in the Wadi Megenin

Periodically flood waters sweep down the channel of the Wadi Megenin to Tripoli, causing interruptions to communications, damaging town property and inundating agricultural lands and crops in the vicinity. The inconveniences and the financial losses suffered have led to a great deal of attention being given by the provincial government to schemes for mitigating the severity of these floods. The Wadi Megenin catchment is 650 square kilometers in extent and is situated in the Gebel Nefusa south of Tripoli, country where the terrain is very broken and where the valleys cut deeply into the hills. Formerly, the catchment was uninhabited and had a thick cover of esparto grass, but over the last 30 years pastoralists have occupied the land. Constant overgrazing has tended not only to remove the esparto grass cover, but also the sparse annual grasses and vegetation which have been growing in its place. This has resulted in soil erosion which is intensive in certain parts of the catchment. Consequently, less water than formerly now percolates down to feed the ground water table, while the floods are of greater frequency and intensity.

There have been two previous attempts to mitigate the floods coming from the Wadi Megenin catchment. The first, which was started in 1952, involved the construction of diversion structures, irrigation canals and controls. A major flood in 1955 destroyed much of the work already done, and subsequently a modified diversion project was carried out. The latter, using the diversion structures built for the previous scheme, is concerned only with the diversion of flood water into reservoir storage areas, where the flood water is trapped and the silt load dropped. This project will have a limited life because, until erosion upstream has been checked, flood water will deposit large quantities of solid material in the traps so that, after about ten years, they will no longer be effective.

A government committee, which reported on aspects of flood prevention, has recommended that a law should be enacted to give the government power to control grazing and agriculture over the whole of the catchment. It has also recommended that funds totaling £L 1 million be made available to implement the full scheme of soil and water conservancy, including afforestation, outlined in its report. It was realized that the remedial measures necessary to reduce or stop erosion in the whole of the catchment would unavoidably cause serious disturbance to the lives of the people now living there.

The mission has studied these recommendations and the many reports and proposals concerning flood relief measures for the Wadi Megenin and has formed the opinion that no permanent control of erosion can be achieved while the catchment is farmed and grazed. We therefore recommend that a part of the catchment where erosion is most intensive should be declared a Government Forest Reserve, in which soil and water conservancy works would be carried out in conjunction with selective afforestation. The proposed area, in and around the Wadi Huelfa, covers 180 square kilometers (see map facing this page). The mission envisages that the conservancy works and the afforestation required to stop erosion and reduce the flood run-off intensity from that part of the catchment will require five years to effect, at an estimated cost of £L 160,000 (for details, see Annex VII).

The proposals will necessitate moving all the inhabitants out of the Wadi Huelfa area, excepting only those required for work with the Forest Department, and this will be the first and most difficult part of the scheme. Probably 200 families will have to be moved to the Gefara and given facilities to practice settled agriculture on the land lying below the high banks recently constructed to trap the flood waters. An irrigation and land development scheme in the new area should be prepared as an integral part of the project. The water held behind the banks recently constructed for the flood water diversion scheme could be used for supplying water for semi-irrigation of 2,000 hectares of land. Each family moved from the catchment should then be settled with ten hectares of land and a house. Resettlement should be carried out by a committee composed of officials from the Nazirates concerned and under the chairmanship of a government officer experienced in this type of work; the irrigation works should be executed by the Water Resources Branch. The capital cost of this resettlement program is estimated at £L 175,000 over the five years.

After resettlement of the present inhabitants, the Forest Reserve would be demarcated and animals would be prevented from grazing there. The reserve would be developed by the Forest Department and controlled by that department under the Forest Law. In addition, such dikes, dams and terraces as are considered necessary to control erosion would be constructed under the supervision of the Water Resources Branch. Finally, trees would be planted in suitable locations designated by the Forest Department. It may be added that trees are at present being distributed for planting in the catchment area, but the mission has considerable doubt about the value of such planting so long as the area is occupied by nomads.

The mission also proposes certain channel improvements and road protection works in the vicinity of Tripoli (costing £L 50,000) designed to ensure a quick run-off for any flood water reaching the neighborhood of the city and to reduce interruption to road traffic. This will bring the total capital cost of the first stage of the Wadi Megenin flood relief scheme to £L 400,000 (including an allowance for contingencies). Of this £L 100,000 would be for establishing the forest reserve and has been included in the forestry program in Chapter 8. Annual recurrent expenditures on maintaining the proposed flood control works are estimated at £L 20,000.

The adjacent Wadi Hamman area is also in the high rainfall belt and erosion is active there, though not yet of the intensity reached in the Wadi Huelfa area. After the Wadi Huelfa Forest Reserve area has been established, the mission recommends that erosion in the Wadi Hamman area (115 square kilometers) be tackled in a similar way by the removal of the inhabitants and the establishment of the Wadi Hamman Forest Reserve. In this case the mission suggests that the inhabitants of the Wadi Hamman area (probably under 200 families) should be moved out and resettled in the Bir Ghnem area, and that this should be the responsibility of the committee already established to deal with the earlier resettlement. While it may not be possible to extend active work to the Wadi Hamman area during the first five years (and therefore financial provision for such work is not included here), the mission urges that the Wadi Hamman proposal be regarded as an integral part of the total Wadi Megenin project, and that early plans be laid for its implementation.

After the Wadi Huelfa and Wadi Hamman Forest Reserves have both been established and the conservancy and grazing improvements in other parts of the catchment take effect, the possibility of construction of water storage dams in the wadi can be reconsidered. This possibility has been investigated in the past by Italian engineers and by the LPDSA, but the uncertainty of the incidence of floods and their annual volume in drought years and the increasingly heavy silt loads being brought down from the areas of rapid erosion were held to rule out such a possibility, at least until erosion in the catchment had been controlled.

Flood Prevention at Wadi Gattara

The Wadi Gattara drains the western end of the Gebel Akhdar and its flood waters have been known to cause damage at Berca on the outskirts of Benghazi. This is reported to have happened in 1938, and again in 1954, but only slight damage and minor inconvenience were caused. A flood prevention scheme for the Wadi Gattara seems therefore to be of doubtful necessity, and while the mission does not wish to anticipate the findings of the committee now investigating this flood problem, it has not included in the program for water conservancy any specific provision for it. However, the mission suggests that some conservancy works are desirable in the middle reaches of the wadi in the Gebel country and suggests that this can be done as part of the water conservancy works outlined on pages 109-112.

In 1954 the flood flow was estimated at 135 cubic meters per second at the Wadi Rugbuleh Naga (halfway down the main wadi) and 200 cubic meters per second at the delta where the wadi debouches onto the coastal plain. It appears that the upper half of the wadi produces two-thirds of the flood flow and that, by construction of dikes and terraces and by tree planting there, the flood intensity can be greatly reduced. The LARC has already built dikes in some of the wadi branches, and these have stopped the flood flows from them. The committee will no doubt consider the possibility of continuing this work, and as there is no silt problem associated with the floods in this wadi, of building a low flood flow retention reservoir at Raghut el Naga.

Flood Water Storage

There are several wadis in Tripolitania which on occasion discharge some of their flood waters into the sea. The mission recommends that these wadis be the subject of hydrologic and geologic investigation with a view to ascertaining the possibilities of flood retention dams and water spreading diversions. The importance of retaining the Gebel rainfall water for agriculture by all economically feasible means is so great that the possibility of preventing flood losses to the sea must be fully explored. The mission's development program for water resources therefore includes provision for expert investigation of this subject.

However, the mission stresses the unlikelihood of there being any economic scheme for the storage of flood water behind high dams constructed in the Gebel wadis. Once irrigated agriculture is established below a high dam, the water supply *must* be guaranteed. A three years' supply is generally considered the desirable amount of storage required to ensure the supply over drought and rainfall deficiency years: in Libya it is a minimum amount. The mission therefore does no more than recommend the investigation of any site in the Tripolitania Gebel where the geology, run-off and soil conditions indicate the likelihood of there being economic high dam project with an associated agricultural development scheme. The less costly water-spreading projects are a possibility on the Gefara below the Gebel, where the wadis discharge flood water to the sea, and should be investigated.

Irrigation Practice and Research

The traditional system of irrigation in Libya is to lead the water from the wells to small plots called gedula, generally about two meters by three meters in size. Each plot is surrounded by a low earth bank to hold the water in it until it disappears by both infiltration into the soil and evaporation losses. When the ground water table is high, as in most coastal fringe areas, this method of irrigation has the disadvantage of inducing the precipitation and concentration of any salts present in the water in the upper soil, with the result that increasing amounts of water are lost through evaporation and so proportionately greater amounts of salts are precipitated. The development of a more efficient method of irrigation and the provision of drainage systems in the coastal areas is a subject for investigation by the departments concerned.

The water requirements of the various crops have received some attention in the research station at Sidi Mesri, but the farmers have little knowledge of the subject of water application to crops beyond the thought that, the more water applied, the better the crops. The mission noted that, when water was raised by mechanical means, it was often used more lavishly than when it was raised by human and animal power. The agricultural departments have a duty to disseminate more knowledge to smallholders about the water requirements of the various crops grown. In this connection the mission suggests that more use could be made of related research information from other Mediterranean countries. The agricultural extension services could organize an intensive campaign in the Tripoli Quadrangle to educate the farmers there in the water economies they can practice. This service could be extended to all the coastal areas. Not only are the farmers in the Quadrangle faced with increased charges for the electrical power they use, but they must, as the water table drops, use more power to lift the water they require.

Another economy in the use of water can be achieved by lining the canals leading water from the wells to the crops. Field trials should be carried out by the departments concerned, with the object of evolving a cheap method of manufacturing canal lining. In the meantime, the extension services in each of these provinces should develop a self-help program for lining canals with a clay-cement mix and so reduce seepage losses, which are often 50 percent or more of the water raised. Spray irrigation is practiced extensively in Tripolitania by large-scale farmers, but the capital cost of the fittings required is high and some technical ability is required for its operation; it does not seem therefore to be a suitable method for smallholders.

The level of the ground water table is generally low enough in Libya to prevent drainage troubles leading to soil alkalinity, but this is not so in the coastal fringe areas and in the Fezzan oases. Agricultural experimentation should be carried out to establish good drainage practices for these areas with regard to both depth and lining of ditches. If some low-cost technique can be devised for restoring the fertility of the alkaline soils in the coastal strip of higher rainfall, much valuable land might be available adjacent to populous areas where agricultural land is in demand. Drainage experiments should be started which, in conjunction with the flushing action of the periodic rainfall and plowing, might make reclamation possible at reasonable cost.

Summary of Proposed Expenditures

The recommendations which we have made in this chapter would entail total expenditures, by both federal and provincial authorities, of £L 4,325,000 over the five years 1960/61—1964/65. This total would be distributed as follows:

(£L '000)

	Staff	Mainte- nance	Plant and equipment	Capital works	Totals
Federal Department of Geology and Hydrology	100	270	15	—	385
Cyrenaica	125	225	100	1,330	1,780
Tripolitania					
(i) Works excluding Wadi Megenin	125	175	60	830	1,190
(ii) Wadi Megenin scheme	—	100	—	300	400
Fezzan	55	100	5	410	570
Totals	405	870	180	2,870	4,325

As can be seen from the above table, capital outlays in the public sector would amount to £L 3,050,000 over the five years 1960/61— 1964/65. Expenditure on constructional works would be allocated as follows:

(£L '000)

Cyrenaica

Constructing 80 wells with lining, pumps and motors, pump-houses or windmills, well heads and storage tanks at £L 8,000 per well	640
Construction of new and reconstruction of existing irrigation systems with headworks, storage reservoirs, lined canals, etc. Fifteen in number at average cost of £L 10,000 per system	150
Repairs and renovation of 1,000 cisterns at £L 300 per cistern	300
Self-help program for terracing and diking for soil and water conservancy	240
Total	1,330

Tripolitania

Wells and well fittings for public purposes	200
Irrigation schemes (number and details not specified)	300
Repairs and renovation of 1,500 cisterns on a self-help basis at £L 100 per cistern	150
Self-help program for terracing and diking for soil and water conservancy	180
Wadi Megenin flood relief scheme	300[a]
Total	1,130

Fezzan

Well fittings, including well lining, caps, aprons, windmills, pumps, motors, pump-houses, tanks and canal lining. Forty wells at £L 10,000 per well	400
Self-help program of well repairs and improvements	10
Total	410

ᵃ An additional £L 100,000 for establishing the Wadi Huelfa Forest Reserve, which is connected with this scheme, is provided in the forestry program set out in Chapter 8.

No estimates can be given of the costs of additional works that might be undertaken as part of the Supplementary Program, since these costs can only be assessed after further detailed investigations. As it is, our minimum proposals for development will make heavy demands upon the administrative and technical resources available and will call for important institutional, legislative and organizational changes. We consider therefore that, until these proposals have been implemented, little is to be gained by attempting to define the scope of possible supplementary projects.

The mission has no detailed information about the sums at present being spent on staff and maintenance by the government departments and agencies concerned with geology and water resources. We have estimated that the recurrent expenditures on staff and maintenance required to carry out the program outlined in this chapter would amount to £L 1,275,000 over the five years or an average of £L 255,000 a year. Perhaps about 40 percent of this (say £L 500,000 or £L 100,000 a year) might be additional to what it being spent at present on comparable work by the Ministry of National Economy, the Nazirate of Agriculture in Tripolitania, the LARC and the other foreign aid agencies.

CHAPTER **8** *AGRICULTURE, LIVESTOCK AND FORESTRY*

Traditionally the Bedouin of Libya have been pastoralists first, cultivators second. For centuries the nomadic way of life has prevailed over most of the country away from the coastal towns, and it has been argued that this manner of living is well adapted to the physical conditions.[1] But while the Bedouin society has shown a great capacity for survival, neither its values nor its organization equip it to take advantage of the opportunities for economic growth opened up by the revolution in technology which has taken place during the last 150 years. There are already signs that nomadism in Libya is gradually giving way to settled farming, and it is the mission's belief that this trend must be encouraged if there is to be any hope of major progress in agriculture.

For all the drawbacks of arid soil and uncertain rainfall, the mission believes that Libya has the physical resources needed to develop a moderately prosperous settled agriculture. Moreover, these appear to be the only natural resources in Libya at present capable of providing a livelihood for the majority of the existing population, and for the additional members to be expected as the population grows. Oil production may soon become more important as a source of income, but hardly as a means of employment. Indeed, we consider it would be unwise to rely on the oil industry providing direct employment for more than 15,000-20,000 workers, as against the 200,000 or so who are now engaged in agriculture and animal husbandry.

The physical potentialities of Libyan agriculture are demonstrated by what was achieved in Roman times through the methodical organization of the country's limited supplies of water. There is evidence that settled farming was then well established on the coasts of Tripolitania and Cyrenaica, supporting a population between two and three times as large as does Libya today. Olives and cereals appear to have been the principal crops, and many farms kept livestock as well, including cattle. Soil erosion in the intervening centuries has resulted in the destruction

[1] For a statement of this view see E. E. Evans-Pritchard, *The Sanusi of Cyrenaica*, Oxford University Press, 1949, pages 34-39.

127

of much good agricultural land, and the desert has encroached in many places. But where capital, organizing ability and technical know-how are available, it has been shown that farming in Libya can still be made to pay well today.

In Tripolitania particularly, but also in Cyrenaica, there are a number of large commercial farms and plantations employing hired labor, equipped with tractors and other machinery and irrigated from wells, sometimes with their own powerhouses to supply electricity for pumping. Many of these farms are owned and managed by Italians, a few by foreign businesses and some by Libyans. Crops include groundnuts, castor seed, olives, tomatoes, citrus fruit, vines, new potatoes, asparagus and other winter vegetables. There are also hundreds of smaller family farms and gardens run by Libyans and Italians which have wells for irrigation, animals for plowing and drawing water and facilities for marketing their produce in the towns. Some of the products of these family holdings are of excellent quality and command a ready market at home and abroad—for example, olives, groundnuts, and citrus fruit in Tripolitania, grapes in the Gebel Akhdar in Cyrenaica, bananas in Derna, tomatoes in the Jalo oasis and certain types of dates in the Fezzan.

The excellent results achieved by the main agricultural experimental stations (e.g., in growing citrus fruit at Sidi Mesri) leave no doubt that physical conditions in Libya are well suited to the production of a wide variety of crops, and that in some of these crops Libya has special advantages over most other countries catering to the European market. Many vegetables can be grown in Libya during the winter months when they are scarce in Europe. A British firm, for example, which recently acquired a large farm near Tripoli, has had great success with the cultivation of new potatoes for sale in the United Kingdom; and it has started production of asparagus, which is marketed by air. Libya also appears to be particularly well suited for the cultivation of groundnuts, which have been introduced into the country since the war and are now the largest single export (over £L 1 million in 1958). The Libyan product is of the edible variety and is mainly consumed as nuts rather than used for the extraction of oil.

The success of some of the larger commercial farms is in striking contrast to the picture of poverty, waste and frustration presented by the typical small farmer who uses primitive tools and methods to scratch a miserable living from the land. Ignorant as he is of modern farming techniques, and with little capital at his disposal, his fate is in the hands of the landowner and merchant on the one hand and the weather on the other. He usually cultivates his land on a share-cropping basis, or on a communal basis with other members of his tribe. The quality of his produce (mainly cereals, fruit and vegetables) is generally poor. He is seldom able to obtain credit, except what the merchant extends him (usually on exorbitant terms), and a bad drought or a *ghibli* can practically wipe out his whole crop. When he has a surplus, he must take it to the local market himself or accept what the middleman offers; either way the price he gets is uncertain, and he may get no price at all. In many places the mission observed perishable commodities going to waste for lack of a buyer.

The most serious physical difficulties that have to be overcome in the development of Libyan agriculture are the shortage of water and the erosion of the soil. The scope for the better organization of water resources has been discussed already, and the problem of soil erosion is examined later in this chapter. But, as a broad judgment, the mission is convinced that the limitations on the expansion of agricultural production derive more from human than from physical factors. Five major problems have to be tackled:

1. land ownership and tenure, with particular reference to the system of tribal ownership which still prevails over much of Cyrenaica and parts of Tripolitania;
2. the supply of adequate credit to small farmers;
3. the wider dissemination of knowledge of modern farming and livestock practices—essentially a matter of agricultural training and extension services;
4. marketing facilities and the related questions of agricultural prices and protection against imports; and
5. government organization for the administration of agriculture.

The mission believes that a concerted effort by the government to tackle these problems is an essential condition of satisfactory agricultural progress in Libya, and each is discussed in the following section. Thereafter the report goes on to consider the pattern which agricultural development should follow, the prospects for particular crops, technical support for agriculture and the special problems arising in connection with animal husbandry and forestry.[2]

2 General references to "agriculture" in this report should be assumed to include animal husbandry. Likewise, for the sake of brevity, the term "farmer" is frequently used to denote the pastoralist as well as the cultivator.

CONDITIONS OF DEVELOPMENT

Land Rights

"There can be no doubt as to the superiority of individual over communal tenure. This shows itself in its effects both on investment and on innovation. If large numbers of people are free to use the same piece of land, each for his own purposes, each has an incentive to take what he can out of the land without putting anything back. In these conditions, as soon as land begins to be scarce, it begins also to deteriorate through overcropping, or excessive pasturage, or failure to take appropriate measures for soil conservation. It pays no individual to invest in improving the land, in fertilizers, in drainage, or in improved grasses. Trees will be planted if the right of individuals to their fruit is recognized, as it usually is, but trees will not be planted for general purposes, such as for shade or for afforestation. Communal tenures worked passably in Africa so long as populations were very small in relation to land, but population pressure everywhere causes such tenures to destroy the land. Investment apart, communal tenure is a handicap to innovation. Livestock cannot be bred selectively unless they are segregated and their mating controlled; neither is it convenient to experiment with new agricultural methods in circumstances where communal activity imposes its own routines. These are the reasons why communal tenures are disappearing rapidly in places where they flourished fifty years ago. Many people regret their passing for sentimental reasons, but there is no reason to doubt their incompatibility with economic development." [3]

These observations, made in the context of a general discussion of the organization of agricultural development, are very relevant to the system of tribal ownership of land which prevails over much of Cyrenaica and parts of the Gefara and Gebel in Tripolitania. Under this system the different members of a tribe or *kabila* use the same piece of land for grazing their animals or cutting firewood, and though the individual may be allowed to cultivate part of the land for his own use, he is not free to sell it or to mortgage it for credit, and he may always be asked to vacate it by the head of the tribe.

The tribal lands in Libya manifest all the weaknesses inherent in communal ownership. Large tracts in zones of high rainfall, which are

[3] W. Arthur Lewis, *The Theory of Economic Growth*, George Allen and Unwin, 1959, page 121.

well suited to the cultivation of crops, are used instead for grazing and
have often been overgrazed to the point where the most palatable
grasses have been replaced by unpalatable shrubs or bare ground. Little
or nothing is invested in productive improvements. Where crops are
cultivated, yields are low. Afforestation and soil conservation practices
are neglected. Overexploitation of the soil leads to denudation of vegetable cover, which causes soil erosion and loss of fertility until finally
the land is abandoned and its occupants move elsewhere.

In the mission's judgment, the first and most essential reform needed
to promote the extension of settled agriculture in Libya is the enactment of a land law securing permanent individual rights in land. Such
laws exist in most other parts of the world, including the more progressive Arab countries. In Libya land tenure is in theory still regulated by
a former Italian law (Royal Decree No. 1207 of 1921), which has never
been repealed and is therefore still supposed to be in operation (in
accordance with Article 210 of the Constitution). In actual practice,
however, this law seems to be applied only where individual rights
were already established and registered at the time of Independence.

The mission is aware that tribal customs and conventions are deep
rooted, and that any proposals for changing the present situation will
inevitably meet with considerable resistance. We are convinced, however, that changes must be made, and made soon, if the Libyan people
wish to establish a reasonably prosperous instead of a languishing agriculture. We propose therefore that a commission should be established
without delay by royal decree to examine the whole question of land
rights, to formulate a land policy promoting the permanent settlement
of the tribal population and to prepare a draft land law for the government's consideration. The chairman of the commission should be an
eminent Libyan with wide experience of public affairs, and the members should include at least one lawyer and one economist or administrator with experience of systems of land ownership and tenure in
other countries.

The new land law should be designed to promote security of individual tenure in all areas of Libya suitable for settled cultivation—say,
those with average annual rainfall of 250 mm., or more, or with ground
water available for irrigation. In other areas, the law might recognize
the existing rights of tribes to use the land for grazing and shifting
cultivation. All forests not individually owned should be designated
as government domain, and provision should be made for the extension
of state forests on land not suitable for settled cultivation.

At present, many of the small holdings in the coastal areas of Libya, as well as in the Fezzan, are cultivated, on a share-cropping basis. Often the tenant has little or no protection against eviction, and he receives no special compensation for any improvements he undertakes. One of the principal objectives of a land law should be to give reasonable security of tenure to existing tenants on privately-owned land and to ensure that rents are fixed in such a way that the farmer has an incentive to invest in long-term improvements.

There are no proper land records in Libya, and it is most important that a cadastral survey of all agricultural land should be started as soon as possible. The mission therefore recommends that a federal Land Survey Department be established to undertake this task, as part either of the Ministry of Justice or of the proposed Ministry of Agriculture. The initial capital expenditure required for the purchase of vehicles and equipment might be about £L 35,000, and we estimate recurrent expenditures on the operations of the department at about £L 75,000 a year.

A cadastral survey usually takes many years to complete, but there are various ways in which the work can be speeded up. Aerial photographs, for example, can sometimes be used in place of ground surveys for demarcating properties, and the resources of the Land Survey Department can be supplemented by engaging private firms to carry out some of the ground survey work. The mission believes that the need for a land survey in Libya is so urgent that extra costs will frequently be justified if they enable the work to be completed more quickly. We have therefore included an additional sum of £L 25,000 a year in our program of recurrent expenditures to provide for some of the work to be contracted out by the department.

Agricultural Credit

Present facilities for agricultural credit in Libya appear to be quite inadequate to the need. The big farms with established titles of ownership can obtain advances from the commercial banks, and over one-tenth of all commercial bank lending in 1958 was to the agricultural sector (see Annex II). But the only source from which the average small farmer can get credit is usually from the local merchant, through whom he buys his occasional supplies of consumer goods, seeds, implements and other requisites, and to whom he sells part of his crop. The odds in transactions of this kind are heavily weighted against a farmer. He usually pays a good deal more than the regular price for what he buys and he receives a poor price for what he sells.

There is a National Agricultural Bank, with headquarters in Tripoli, which started operations in 1957 for the purpose of developing and raising the standards of agriculture, pasture and forestry. The bank has a capital of £L 1 million, though its authorized capital was set at £L 5 million. Its lending to date has been entirely on a short seasonal basis with interest at 6½ percent. The enlargement of the bank's capital by another £L 2 million is contemplated at an early date, and it has so far been envisaged that the additional funds will be obtained by borrowing abroad.

Located in Tripoli, with one or two branches in other places, the institution as now constituted is not in the mission's view able to cater adequately to the needs of the widely scattered farming community and its procedures for credit assessment are too slow to be effective. The bank's record in providing credit facilities for the newly formed cooperative movement has been particularly disappointing. Further, in a community with a little over a million people, it is open to question whether it is necessary to maintain two or three major national banking institutions with high overhead costs of organization and management. Considerable economies would be achieved if the functions of central banking, agricultural credit and industrial finance could be combined in a single institution, as they used to be, for example, in Australia.

The mission therefore recommends that the National Agricultural Bank should be wound up and merged with the National Bank of Libya and be designated as its Agricultural Credit Department. There would also be established, as proposed in Chapter 9, an Industrial Finance Department for the provision of credit to industrial establishments. Such a step should promote both economy in manpower and organizational efficiency. The Agricultural Credit Department should be separate from other departments of the National Bank and headed by a director with considerable experience in the operation of agricultural credit, preferably in an underdeveloped country. This director would report directly to the Governor, and the accounts of the department should be kept separate from the rest of the bank's operations, so that the department's activities as such would be open to public scrutiny.

An advisory council should be set up to keep the operations of the Agricultural Credit Department under review and make suggestions for policy. This council should include representatives of the government departments concerned, together with farmers and traders, and it should meet at least twice a year. The Board of the National Bank might be suitably enlarged to include a member with special knowledge of agricultural problems. Apart from having branches at each of the places where the National Bank is already established, the Agricultural

Credit Department should establish its own separate branches in areas where conditions call for such a step.

Capital for the Agricultural Credit Department should initially be provided by the government, together, of course, with the assets that would be taken over from the National Agricultural Bank. Later on it might be possible for the National Bank to raise additional funds for agricultural credit by floating its own bonds on the market with a guarantee from the government. We suggest that the Agricultural Credit Department should be started with a capital of £L 2½ million, including the £L 1 million taken over from the Agricultural Bank, and that this should be augmented by a further £L 1 million in the course of the next five years. We have therefore included provisions of £L 2½ million for agricultural credit in our five-year program. We would not, however, rule out the possibility of further funds being provided under the Supplementary Program if the activities of the department progress satisfactorily.

The mission advises against the Agricultural Credit Department being given the privilege of borrowing from the Central Banking Department, at any rate for the time being. Its initial capital should provide the limit of operations, and any profits arising from its operations should be carried into separate earmarked reserves and should not be merged with those of the National Bank of Libya. Likewise any losses should be shown separately and written off against capital or should be reimbursed by government. At a later stage, when agricultural credit operations take a firm root, limited provision for discounting the paper of the Agricultural Credit Department by the Central Banking Department might be considered.

While seasonal crop finance would inevitably constitute the largest section of the work of the Agricultural Credit Department, it would also have to develop facilities for medium-term and long-term lending for such purposes as the construction of wells and irrigation channels, the planting of orchards, the leveling or terracing of lands and the purchase of machinery and equipment. The mission feels that, having regard to the backward conditions of the Libyan agricultural economy and the need for offering a stimulus in as many different ways as are consistent with prudent management, the agricultural credit agency should consider making loans at rates of interest somewhat lower than 6½ percent, at least in the initial stages. Lending policies must, of course, be related to the cost at which the department itself is able to borrow.

The department will have to frame its policies with a fair measure of flexibility. It should adhere to principles of prudent financial management in such matters as wide distribution of credit risks and careful selection of persons and projects, and it should also seek to establish in its relations with its borrowers respect for careful and sound financial attitudes, especially with respect to repayment of debts. Nevertheless, agricultural credit in Libya is surrounded by many factors of risk, including those which arise from the vagaries of climate, and no agricultural credit institution can cater adequately to the needs of the small farmer unless it is prepared to insist on somewhat less rigorous security requirements than may be appropriate in other countries.

Provision of credit must be closely linked with the work of the agricultural extension services and the development of rural cooperative societies. The mission is well aware that very little progress has yet been made in either of these two fields and recognizes that for the time being the agricultural credit agency will itself have to assume more widespread and onerous responsibilities with respect to the distribution and supervision of credit than would normally be desirable. At the same time we consider it to be of the utmost importance that a concerted effort should be made by the federal and provincial governments, with the help of foreign advisers, to overcome the present deficiences in agricultural education and to encourage cooperation amongst the farmers. To say, as some do, that Libyan farmers cannot be persuaded to enter into cooperative credit and marketing arrangements is a counsel of despair, which the mission feels unable to accept. It will no doubt be a slow process, and there are strong resistances to be overcome. But much will depend on the quality of leadership offered by government and on the energy and single-mindedness with which the objective of agricultural development is pursued.

Cooperative Societies

Rural cooperative societies have a key role to play in any program for raising agricultural production in Libya. We do not think that it would be advisable to try to organize cooperative production societies, in which the members jointly own and cultivate the land and share the proceeds. Such societies have seldom proved successful elsewhere. But cooperation in the distribution of credit and marketing, in the purchase of seeds and implements, and possibly in the operation of farm machinery, is an essential element in any scheme for developing the small farming sector.

A Cooperative Law was enacted in Libya in 1956, and regulations for the registration of cooperative societies were published in 1958. The FAO has been playing an active part in this work and maintains an agricultural credit and cooperatives expert on its field staff in Libya. By November 1959 over thirty general agricultural cooperative societies were established, eighteen in Tripolitania, nine in Cyrenaica and six in the Fezzan; their total membership was about 6,000 and their share capital £L 21,000. These cooperatives have so far functioned mainly as thrift and credit societies, but some are beginning to branch out into wider activities such as the procurement of agricultural supplies for their members and the marketing of produce. Some cooperatives have already distributed improved seeds, fertilizers, insecticides, cement and small implements, while a few also own tractors.

The figures quoted show that the rural cooperative movement in Libya is still in its infancy. A major educational effort is required to create a wider understanding amongst farmers of the proper functions and methods of operation of cooperative societies, to train managerial staff of the cooperatives and to build up an adequate government supervisory service. Libya should learn from the experience of other countries in which cooperation has already made some progress, and we suggest that brief visits to such countries might be arranged for groups of tribal leaders and farmers from the three provinces. We also recommend that two or three of the senior officials concerned with cooperatives in the federal and provincial governments should be selected for courses of overseas training in cooperative methods. A few junior officials in the agricultural service should be given opportunities to gain experience abroad later on, after an initial period of work with the cooperative movement in Libya.

The primary responsibility for fostering the development of cooperatives should rest with the proposed federal Ministry of Agriculture and with the Nazirates of Agriculture in the provinces. These departments should work in close relationship with the Agricultural Credit Department of the National Bank, which should seek to channel as much of its credit as possible through cooperative societies, making the societies responsible for the supervision and collection of loans. Likewise, wherever marketing societies are set up and they have surplus produce for storage, credits against the warehouse receipts for such produce might be given either by the commercial banks or as a part of the agricultural credit system.

Marketing Arrangements

Between one-third and one-quarter (by value) of Libya's agricultural produce is exported and the remainder is consumed at home. The principal commodities exported are groundnuts, olive oil, livestock, hides and skins and other animal products, esparto grass, almonds and castor seed. Minor agricultural exports include citrus fruit, potatoes, tobacco and (in good crop years) cereals. All these exports are handled by private trade except for esparto grass and tobacco. Esparto grass is collected, baled and shipped by a government-owned corporation and tobacco exports are organized by the government monopoly in Tripolitania. Olive oil and livestock products have to go through various stages of processing before they are exported, but most of the other agricultural exports are shipped more or less in their raw state. Exports of livestock consist mainly of animals driven across the border for sale in Egypt; some are also shipped to Malta, Greece and other Mediterranean countries. Apart from livestock, livestock products and esparto grass, most agricultural exports are accounted for by the organized sector of Libyan agriculture, which is located mainly in Tripolitania, and in which the Italian farmers play a leading role.

Production for the home market consists predominantly of animal products (meat, milk, wool, hides, etc.), cereals, dates, olives, tobacco, citrus fruit, grapes, tomatoes and other fruits and vegetables. A large, but indeterminate proportion of animal products, cereals and dates is consumed by those who produce them and thus never enters the market at all. On the other hand, the greater part of the production of olives, citrus fruit, grapes, tomatoes and other fruit and vegetables is sold, in some cases directly by farmer to consumer (notably in the small town and village markets), but more often by farmer to merchant or manufacturer.

Many of the large farms in Tripolitania have their own marketing organizations. Some are run by merchants or trading firms; some have their own processing facilities (e.g., plants for the manufacture of olive oil). The *Consorzio Agrario della Tripolitania,* a multi-purpose association founded by Italian farmers in 1915 and now including more Libyan members than Italian, carries out certain marketing functions, but these do not appear to have been particularly successful, and the organization has never got down to the level of the small farmer. Tobacco growers in Tripolitania have an assured market in the monopoly, which is obliged to take all the tobacco for which licenses have been issued at prices fixed in advance. The marketing of esparto grass is also handled by a government organization which fixes prices and employs agents to take delivery of the grass at collecting points in the Tripolitanian Gebel.

None of these marketing arrangements really covers the needs of the mass of small farmers and market gardeners who have to take their chance in the local town or village markets or entrust the marketing of their surplus produce to local merchants and accept whatever prices the latter offer. These small producers usually know next to nothing about the market possibilities outside their own neighborhood; they have no transport of their own other than a camel or a donkey; they have few facilities for storage; their products are ungraded and often of poor quality; and no one seems particularly interested in helping them. One of the main troubles is that, with imports freely available, the domestic producer is almost invariably confronted with a buyers' market, and his chances of competing successfully with imports are limited not only by his own inefficiency, but by the high costs of internal transport and by the difficulties of preserving perishable produce in Libyan conditions.

Clearly, there is no simple solution to this marketing problem. No organization for marketing can overcome basic deficiencies in the product, and much effort has got to be devoted to raising standards of production and securing better quality goods—a subject on which we have more to say later on. Equally, however, steps to raise agricultural efficiency will fail in their object unless they are accompanied by adequate incentives and marketing facilities.

The mission considers it essential that the Libyan Government should play a more active role in assisting the unorganized section of the farming community to find markets for its produce. We recommend specific action along the following lines:

1. Creation of an Agricultural Marketing Department as part of a federal Ministry of Agriculture, headed by a director with practical experience of agricultural marketing problems and preferably also with specialized knowledge of markets in the Mediterranean area.
2. Fixing of minimum support prices for wheat, to be announced in advance of each season, coupled with an undertaking by the government to buy up at these prices wheat delivered to specified grain storage points.
3. Increases in tariffs on selected agricultural imports, combined with measures to restrict imports of wheat and flour.

The main functions of an Agricultural Marketing Department, as we see it, should be to give continuous study to the problems involved in marketing produce at home and abroad and to advise government, farmers and industry on measures for overcoming these problems; to give information and advice to farmers (through the extension service, and in other ways) about market possibilities and the conditions required to exploit them; to encourage better grading of agricultural produce and the adoption of measures designed to improve quality and raise sanitary standards (especially for livestock products); to assist in the organization of internal transport services and the timely procurement of shipping for exports; and more generally to establish closer links between the agricultural producer and potential buyers at home, including particularly domestic processing industries, the oil companies and foreign military establishments in Libya. This last function we consider to be of prime importance because the new oil centers in the desert will constitute a major concentration of purchasing power and a large potential market for such products as fresh fruit and vegetables, meat, eggs and poultry. In the past both the British and American forces have been ready to buy local agricultural produce,[4] subject to the limitations imposed by their health regulations, but they have only too often found their suppliers undependable and the quality of the goods sub-standard. So far as the mission is aware, little has been done to remedy these deficiencies, and we believe that a properly organized and energetic marketing department could make a valuable contribution in this field.

Since a substantial proportion of Libyan agricultural produce is sold to local factories (e.g., flour mills, tanneries, olive and sansa oil factories, the tomato paste factory, the government date-packing plant) close liaison must be established between the marketing department of the Ministry of Agriculture and the Ministry of Finance and Economics. The latter moreover, as the Ministry responsible for Libya's overseas trade, will be in a better position to seek out new markets abroad and generally to take care of export problems. The main initiative in the promotion of Libya's agricultural exports has hitherto been taken by the Tripolitanian Administration, and we would not wish to see this arrangement disturbed until the Ministry of Finance and Economics is properly equipped for the task. Eventually, however, it is our belief that export promotion should become a federal responsibility, and that the sector of the Ministry of Finance and Economics concerned with export problems should be suitably reinforced.

Issues arising in connection with the marketing of specific agricultural commodities are discussed separately on pages 147-156 and in Annex IX. Marketing problems are also discussed later in this chapter

---

[4] Purchases of Libyan produce by the U. S. Air Force at Wheelus Field amounted to about $220,000 (nearly £L 80,000) in 1958. Eggs were the main item, accounting for over half the total value. Also included were small quantities of potatoes, tomatoes and other vegetables and some non-agricultural items.

in connection with the mission's proposals for the development of former Italian farms in Cyrenaica (see pages 156-161).

Education and Extension Services

The education of boys for work on the land is discussed in Chapter 13, where proposals are made for imparting more of a rural bias to primary school education and for establishing new training schools for agricultural demonstrators. The two existing agricultural schools at el Aweila in Cyrenaica and Sidi Mesri in Tripolitania, and the new school being established at Sebha, will continue to be the main sources of Libyan staff for the government agricultural services, and the standards of entrance to these schools should be progressively raised as the general educational system is developed. Better training is needed at the schools, and the boys must be taught to work with their hands. For more advanced training in agriculture and forestry selected employees of the federal and provincial services should be sent to universities abroad, since the number of higher professional staff required would be too small to justify the establishment of a permanent agricultural college in Libya (see Chapter 13).

Programs for the training of extension workers have recently been started in each of the three provinces under the guidance of USOM personnel, and sums totalling £L 156,000 had been allocated for this purpose by LARC up to the end of March 1959. A further £L 137,500 has been provided in the U. S. aid program for the Libyan fiscal year 1959/60. Some progress has been made, but the development of extension work is being held back by the lack of Libyan supervisory staff. The programs are mainly concentrated at present on raising production of barley and wool through the use of better seeds and implements, improved shearing methods and other means.

Greater emphasis should in our view be placed on this branch of the agricultural service, and we believe that, at this stage of Libya's development, extension work should generally be accorded at least equal priority with experimentation or research in the allocation of funds and trained personnel. There is much knowledge available about techniques of farming in Libyan conditions which can be usefully passed on to the farmer without further trials, and the scope for raising agricultural production through the extension of existing knowledge, with little additional capital investment, is amply demonstrated by the great differences in efficiency between the best Libyan farms and the worst. Good salaries should be offered to attract the best graduates from the agricultural schools to the extension services, where the right sort of person can usually contribute more to the development of agriculture than by working in a headquarters office. It is no use, however, recruiting young men for extension work unless they are prepared to work with their hands and fully capable themselves of doing the things in which they are supposed to be instructing the farmer. An extension worker who is unable to plow a straight furrow, for example, is unlikely to command much respect.

Demonstrations should wherever possible be conducted on the farmer's own land or on tribal grazing areas rather than on model farms. However, courses of instruction should be held at the agricultural schools and research stations when there is a demand for them, and farmers should be given every encouragement to visit these schools and learn about what is going on there. In Tripolitania many of the Italian farmers offer practical demonstration of the value of improved cultural methods, and any steps which can be taken to foster closer relations between Italian and Libyan farmers would help in spreading knowledge.

Agricultural extension is as much a psychological as a technical problem, and the mission is not qualified to advise in any detail on the best ways of engaging the interest of the small cultivators and nomads in a campaign for the adoption of improved practices. Clearly, such a campaign will only succeed if it receives full support from the leaders of the farming community, tribal and religious authorities and local government officials. Anything that can be done in the ordinary schools to arouse the childrens' interest in farming, gardening and animals will contribute to the spread of knowledge. Agricultural shows, the offer of prizes and awards for outstanding achievements, the display of films and posters—all these have a role to play. Initially, the mission suggests that the main effort should be directed towards the former Italian farms in the Barce Plain and the Cyrenaican Gebel, since it is here, in our view, that both the need and the opportunities for fruitful extension work are greatest. We are proposing later in this chapter that a special organization should be set up to promote agricultural development in the area, and one of its main functions would be to help in building up an extension service.

Agricultural Administration

As pointed out earlier in this report, the mission believes that the absence of a federal Ministry of Agriculture is a serious weakness in the present system of public administration and recommends that such a ministry should be created as a matter of urgency. We also recommend regular consultation between the Minister and the three Nazirs and the establishment of an inter-departmental committee of officials to help in coordinating agricultural administration in the three provinces. Our proposals on this subject are outlined in Chapter 6 (page 78), and we suggest that the government's agricultural advisers in Libya should be invited to work out in detail the organization of the new ministry. Close working relationships should be established between the agricultural departments and the Development Council, and both the Development Council and the National Bank of Libya should be represented on the official committee on agricultural development.

Much of what is said in Chapter 6 about government organization in general applies to the administration of agricultural policy. We see considerable need for a fuller and speedier interchange of information on agricultural matters between the federal and provincial governments; for more regular tours around the country by ministers, nazirs and senior officials in order to keep in touch at the ground level with the problems of the ordinary farmer, who often has difficulty in obtaining access to the ear of authority; for the vigorous pruning of the headquarters staffs of the provincial Nazirates of Agriculture; and for the collection of better agricultural statistics. We also recommend the establishment of a national advisory council on agriculture, through which prominent farmers and tribal leaders can be associated with the formulation of agricultural policy and give the government the benefit of their special knowledge and advice.

PATTERN OF DEVELOPMENT

Existing Land Use

Only about one percent of the total land area of Libya is suitable for settled agriculture. Elsewhere there is too little rainfall, the ground is too rough or soil conditions are unfavorable. While large tracts of land are being overexploited as a result of uncontrolled grazing, much good agricultural land (from the standpoint of soil and water resources) has been abandoned or never exploited at all. In the Fezzan oases, for example, the area under cultivation is believed to have been reduced by about 50 percent within living memory. Many of the former Italian farms in Tripolitania and Cyrenaica have been abandoned (see Annex X). Some of the agricultural land that is used is used inefficiently.

Wheat and barley, for example, are sometimes planted on irrigated land which should be able to yield a higher return from fruit, vegetables or other crops. Marginal land in low rainfall areas is often planted to barley when it is suitable only for grazing. Rocky or eroded land in steep catchments with an annual rainfall of 300 mm. or more is inadequately developed as forest reserves.

The present patterns of land use in Tripolitania and Cyrenaica are illustrated in the maps facing pages 100 and 104. Settled agriculture in Tripolitania is largely concentrated in the coastal plain between Zuara and Misurata and in the region of the Gebel stretching from Giado through Jefren, Garian and Tarhuna to Cussabat. A high proportion of the largest and most prosperous farms are situated in the immediate vicinity of Tripoli which is far and away the largest market for agricultural produce in Libya and also the principal port of shipment for exports. Much of the land in the coastal area is irrigated from wells (see Chapter 7); only at the Wadi Caam between Homs and Zliten is there a perrenial flow of surface water suitable for irrigation. The farming colonies established by the Italian Government are located at various points close to the coast and in the Gebel around Tarhuna. Tripolitania has a few scattered areas of forest and scrub, and esparto grass grows wild over parts of the Gebel. Most of the Gefara and large areas of the Gebel are used for grazing livestock.

There is very little irrigated land in Cyrenaica apart from market gardens scattered along the coast, particularly in the vicinity of Benghazi and Derna; and the scope for the extension of irrigation is very limited (see Chapter 7). Some of the best land for cereal cultivation in Cyrenaica, and indeed in all Libya, is situated on the Barce Plain, where the Italians launched a wheat-growing scheme just before World War II. This scheme was abandoned during the war, and attempts made by the British military administration to revive it afterwards proved unsuccessful. Settled farming is also established in parts of the Gebel Akhdar lying near the main coast road from Barce to Derna. Altogether nearly 1,800 Italian farms with a combined area of about 65,000 hectares were established in Cyrenaica before the war by the *Ente per la Colonizzione della Libia;* of these about 1,100 were in the Barce district and the rest in districts of Beida and Derna. Much of the Gebel Akhdar is covered with forest and scrub, and the area is used extensively for shifting cultivation. The other main agricultural areas near the coast of Cyrenaica are south of Benghazi around Solluk and Agedabia where the principal crop is barley. The land in these areas is generally poor and the rainfall low.

The outlying desert oases in the Fezzan, at Jalo and Kufra in Cyrenaica and at Gadames in Tripolitania, used to grow practically all their own food, but they are coming to depend increasingly on supplies from outside, including flour, sugar, canned fish and other prepared foods. Dates are the principal crop in the desert oases. Cereals, fodder, tomatoes, vegetables and fruit are also grown, together with small quantities of tobacco and oilseeds. Livestock are reared in small numbers.

Guiding Principles for Development

One of the paradoxes of postwar economic development in Libya is that, while foreign aid has helped to finance schemes of agricultural development, it has at the same time made it more difficult for the small farmer to sell his produce because of the encouragement given to imports. Barley and dates, traditionally Libya's staple foods, have increasingly been displaced by imports of wheat and flour, including gift wheat from the United States and subsidized flour from Italy. The consumers' preference that has now been created for wheat bread and pasta will be difficult to change, and it may not be desirable to change it. But there is little point in trying to stimulate production of barley and dates for human consumption when the market for them is declining. Instead, the emphasis has to be shifted towards promoting greater use of barley and dates as a feed for livestock, concentrating production on the superior varieties for which there may be a market abroad and, whenever conditions are favorable, encouraging the cultivation of wheat in place of barley.

The adverse impact which the rapid growth of imports has had on the marketing of domestic foods is not confined to cereals and dates. Canned orange juice is consumed in the hotels of Benghazi while good oranges rot on the ground in Tripolitania. Considerable quantities of imported fruit and vegetables (fresh apples, onions and potatoes and various canned products) are sold in the coastal towns and reduce the incentive which the merchants have to buy from local producers. The quality of the imported foods is, of course, frequently better than that of the Libyan products which they replace; and some imports will always be needed when the corresponding Libyan products are out of season. But efforts to improve the domestic product are unlikely to succeed unless the Libyan farmer is afforded a greater measure of protection against imports.

It is not easy in these circumstances to prescribe a set pattern for the development of Libyan agriculture. There is little doubt that, where irrigation is possible, physical conditions in Libya tend to favor vegetables and tree crops rather than cereals—a conclusion supported by the good progress made in recent years by the larger capitalist farms in the cultivation of groundnuts, olives, castor seed, citrus fruit, almonds, carrots and new potatoes. Such crops as these, together with dates and vines, appear to offer the most promising possibilities for development on the production side. Not all of them look equally promising from the marketing standpoint. Certainly not dates, since there is already too much production for the home market to absorb, and the Libyan product is unlikely to be able to compete successfully on a large scale in foreign markets with dates from Iraq, Algeria and Tunisia—except possibly in Italy, where Libya enjoys a tariff preference (see pages 150-151). Prospects for increasing exports of citrus fruit must also be considered rather doubtful in view of the keen competition from other producing countries in the Mediterranean area. By and large, however, the mission believes that, where adequate capital, water and technical know-how are available, the most profitable lines of agricultural development in Libya will be found in specializing in production of oilseeds, vegetables, fruits and nuts for the foreign market and for the growing market that will be built up in Libya itself around the operations of the oil companies.

The more advanced farming sector is already developing on these lines, and it should be encouraged to do so. Government can help through its technical and marketing services (experimental work, pest control, enforcement of quality standards, etc.), through measures to secure the most advantageous use of scarce water resources (especially controlling the overexploitation of ground water in the Tripoli area), through general policies for encouraging private foreign investment in Libya and through the provision of public services such as approach roads, piped water and electricity, especially in opening up new areas for development, such as the Bir Ghnem area south-west of Tripoli (see Chapter 7).

There need be no immediate fear in Libya, as there is in overpopulated countries, that the extension of large-scale commercial farming will be at the expense of the small farmer. Land as such is not scarce, only the capital and technical know-how required for its development. When private enterprise, Libyan or foreign, is ready and able to supply these two factors of production, the economy as a whole will benefit from their being allowed to do so. The large-scale farming sectors should be regarded as mutually complementary, not antagonistic. As one example, a number of the larger farms in Tripolitania provide seasonal employment for small farmers and their families and thus enable them to supplement the incomes they obtain from their own holdings.

In short, and disregarding the human element, physical conditions in the agricultural areas of Libya appear to be well suited to capital-intensive farming and to favor fairly large holdings and a relatively high degree of mechanization, particularly where irrigation is not possible. It is worth noting in this connection that the typical size of the Ente farms established by the Italians in Cyrenaica was 25-30 hectares. Yields per hectare were expected to be low, and this has been the general experience where dry farming is practiced in Libya.

The development of the small farming sector presents different problems and calls for more active intervention by the government. The typical small cultivator has at present neither the capital nor the organizing ability nor the technical know-how to engage in specialized production for the export market. He must be able to grow something which produces a crop straight away and cannot plant all his land with olives, vines, citrus fruit or other tree crops, which take years to reach economic production. The crops chosen moreover must be such as require comparatively modest skills for their cultivation.

In these circumstances the mission considers that the balance of advantage lies in concentrating initially in the small farming sector on production for the home market. The acreage under wheat should be extended wherever possible, particularly in the Barce Plain, where the mission believes that conditions are suitable, notwithstanding the contrary views expressed by some experts. Production of barley should be encouraged in other areas with average rainfall of over 250 mm. with special emphasis on improving quality and ultimately re-establishing the export trade in this commodity which Libya once had. Cereal cultivation should, wherever possible, be integrated with the growing of pasture and fodder crops to meet the feed requirements of livestock. Provided that adequate credit is available, olive, almond and other fruit trees can also be cultivated in the Barce Plain, in the Gebel Akhdar and in some other dry farming areas in the coastal provinces. Citrus fruit may also have limited possibilities, but on the whole this is a crop which appears to require more care and skill in cultivation than the more inexperienced Libyan farmers can be expected to provide. Vegetables, oilseeds, poultry and livestock in our view constitute the other main lines of development for small-scale Libyan farming, and efforts should be directed towards developing a market for these commodities in the oil centers and to raising standards of production and marketing to the levels required to satisfy the demands of the foreign community. The cultivation of grapes for making wine might be extended in the Gebel Akhdar in Cyrenaica if an export market can be found for Libyan wine (e.g., in Germany).

At the same time something can be done to provide a better market for dates and the inferior qualities of barley—for example, through government purchases of dates for the school-feeding program and the creation of a livestock feed reserve. Tobacco cultivation, which is largely confined to Tripolitania, raises special problems of its own. The present system of permitting cultivation only under license and of guaranteeing a market for all the tobacco grown, regardless of type or quality, has had many undesirable results, and we recommend other arrangements should be made (see page 153).

Proposals have been put forward in Libya for the establishment of a sugar beet factory in Tripolitania and for growing cotton on a commercial basis in the Fezzan. The mission has considerable doubts about both these proposals and strongly advises against precipitate action. Complex problems are involved, and much further study is required before either line of development should be encouraged. Some of the factors to be considered are discussed on pages 154-155. Meanwhile, there may well be good opportunities for extending the cultivation of well-tried crops like groundnuts and castor seed, both of which might be found suited to small holdings in the Fezzan as well as in Tripolitania.

The mission recognized that no program for the development of the small farming sector of Libyan agriculture can be expected to achieve spectacular results in a matter of two or three years, or even five. Progress will inevitably be slow, particularly in the initial stages, and much patient effort will be called for on the part of the government. But we are convinced that this effort is worth making—indeed, that it must be made if the wealth that will come from oil is to be used wisely and well for the benefit of the Libyan population as a whole. We recommend that top priority in agricultural development should be given to the promotion of settled cultivation on the former Italian farms in the Barce-Beida area of Cyrenaica. We also have specific proposals to make for raising production in the small farming sector in Tripolitania and the Fezzan. First, however, some recommendations are offered with respect to particular crops. The present position and prospects of these and other crops are described in Annex IX.

Recommendations on Particular Crops

Cereals. Barley is the principal cereal crop in Libya; some wheat is also grown, and small quantities of millet. Production of cereals varies greatly from year to year according to the rainfall; during the five years ending in September 1958, for example, the range has extended from an estimated 60,000 tons in 1955/56 (crop year beginning in October) to over 150,000 tons in 1956/57. Average annual production during this period may be very roughly estimated at around 60,000-70,000 tons of barley and 20,000 tons of wheat.

Libya appears to have been more or less self-sufficient in foodgrains in late Turkish times, exporting in good years, importing in bad ones. In recent years, however, imports have regularly exceeded exports. This is partly because consumption has risen without any corresponding rise in production. But a more important factor has been the shift in the pattern of consumption in the towns from barley to wheat. Over the three years 1955/56–1957/58 apparent consumption of wheat and flour averaged about 100,000 tons a year (in terms of wheat equivalent). Little over one-quarter of this consumption was supplied from home production, and the remaining three-quarters were imported, mostly in the form of gift wheat from the U. S. and flour from Italy, which is sold at well below current world prices. Bags of Italian flour are nowadays a common sight in most Libyan towns, even in the Fezzan.

Thus, while Libya is still producing practically all the barley it requires for human consumption, there is a large and growing deficit in wheat. The expansion of domestic wheat production to cover at least part of this deficit should, in the mission's view, be adopted as one of the principal aims of agricultural policy. This can be done by extending the area under production, particularly in the Barce Plain, by better methods of cultivation and by improvements in handling and storage designed to reduce wastage (see Annex IX). Wheat can also be grown more extensively under irrigation in Tripolitania as a winter crop in rotation with various summer crops. Particular attention should be given to increasing production of *durum* (hard wheat used for making pasta) in the Barce Plain and other areas where soil and climate are favorable. This at present fetches a better price in world markets than softer wheats, and there is a substantial demand for it in Libya, particularly in Tripolitania. *Durum* grown in Cyrenaica is already transported in small quantities to Tripolitania and there should be room for the expansion of this trade. There may also be opportunities for Libya to export to other countries, as it did before the war to Italy.

In advocating the expansion of wheat production in Libya at a time when there is a world surplus, and wheat and flour can be obtained on advantageous terms from the United States and other countries, the mission has been strongly influenced by two considerations. First, wheat appears to be one of the crops best suited for cultivation by small farmers in many of the dry farming areas of Libya, particularly in Cyrenaica; it can also be grown in rotation with other crops on irrigated land in Tripolitania and the Fezzan. Second, an assured market can be found in Libya itself for all wheat that is produced locally, provided that the government is prepared to adapt its policies to this purpose. It seems to us advisable that plans for the development of the unorganized sector of Libyan agriculture should initially be based in large part on the cultivation of crops which do not involve a long period of waiting, which do not require irrigation, which make comparatively modest demands on the farmer's skill, which do not perish easily and which are not dependent on uncertain export markets. Wheat fulfills these requirements better than most other commodities. It might with advantage be rotated with mixtures of legumes and oats for fodder.

There will still be room for the expansion of barley production in areas where the rainfall is too low or soil conditions unfavorable for cultivation of wheat. More barley can be fed to livestock and used to build up an emergency feed reserve against drought years such as 1959, when large quantities of animal feedingstuffs were supplied to Libya by the United States as an emergency measure. At the same time, if quality can be improved through better methods of cultivation, more barley can be exported to Europe.[5] Belgium, Denmark, Western Germany and the United Kingdom all import substantial quantities of barley from the Middle East (notably from Iraq), and Libya should be able to compete in this trade, particularly in view of the fact that it is nearer than Middle Eastern countries to the markets in Northern Europe.

The mission recommends the adoption of the following policies to stimulate cereal production:

1. Institution of a wheat-growing scheme on the Barce Plain as part of a scheme for the development of that area (see pages 156-160), coupled with an intensive campaign to raise wheat yields all over Libya through better cultural practices (e.g., row planting with drills), the use of improved varieties of seed and the provision of better credit facilities.

2. Introduction of a price support scheme for wheat under which

[5] In pre-Italian times Libya exported substantial quantities of barley to the United Kingdom for use in the brewing industry. This trade was briefly revived during the period of British military administration after World War II, but has since almost entirely disappeared.

minimum prices for the various qualities would be announced
and widely publicized by the government in advance of each
season, and the government (or millers and merchants acting
as its agents) would purchase at these prices any wheat delivered
at specified collecting points in the growing areas. This scheme
should be operated by the proposed Marketing Department of
the Ministry of Agriculture, and use should be made, where
necessary, of the existing government-owned grain storage facilities, which include 15,000 tons of bulk storage capacity in modern silos at Tripoli, Suani ben Adem, Benghazi, Barce and Beida
(see Annex IX).

3. Continued regulation of wheat imports coupled with quantitative restrictions on imports of flour. Libya has milling capacity
sufficient to cover the bulk of its flour requirements (see Annex
XIII), and flour imports should be limited to special grades
which cannot be produced locally.

4. Maintenance of existing controls over the retail price of bread,
the price being fixed at a level which will allow reasonable margins for transport, storage, processing and distribution.

In effect, through its control over imports, the government can require the mills to accept all the locally produced wheat that is offered
for sale. Support prices have to be fixed high enough to offer an adequate incentive to the grower, but not so high as to make necessary
sharp increases in prices of flour and bread (or a large government subsidy in lieu). Information about present costs of wheat production in
Libya is sketchy and unreliable. The mission is, however, satisfied that,
if assistance is extended to the small farmer along the lines suggested
earlier in this chapter, it could be made profitable for him to take up
wheat cultivation in areas where conditions are suitable by fixing support prices not very much higher than the present prices at which imports of milling wheat can be landed in Libya (around £L 25-30 a ton).

An expert with experience of grain marketing problems in other
countries should be appointed to draw up a detailed scheme and subsequently to take charge of its operation as an official of the Agricultural Marketing Department. The department would take over the
existing grain storage organization of the Ministry of National Economy. Its main functions would be to set prices, supervise the operations
of private traders and to issue licenses for imports. It would only inter-
vene itself in the domestic market as a buyer of last resort.

Dates. Production of dates in Libya is variously estimated at between 30,000 and 70,000 tons a year. If a figure is taken midway between the two extremes, and if a price of one piaster per kilogram is imputed to the crop, the annual value of date production might be guessed at around £L 500,000 or one percent of the gross domestic product. Practically the whole crop is consumed at home, exports amounting to only 286 tons in 1958. Dates are mostly eaten by the poorer families in the growing areas; some are fed to livestock. The quality of Libyan dates is generally poor, though a few areas produce good commercial dates—notably Hon, Brak and Traghen in the Fezzan, Zliten in Tripolitania and Kufra in Cyrenaica. Cultural methods are mostly primitive, and the practice in many oases of throwing the dates on the ground when cut and then burying them results in their getting contaminated with sand.

Although date palms constitute one of Libya's principal natural resources, the mission is not very optimistic about the prospects of expanding date production, particularly as much of the existing crop goes to waste. We attach considerable importance, however, to making better use of the dates that are grown and to improving the quality of the product. With these objects in view the following recommendations are put forward for government action (see Annexes IX and XIII for further details):

1. The agricultural extension services should be used to propagate information about improved methods of cultivation and harvesting.

2. Research work should be concentrated mainly on developing by-products such as syrup, paste and alcohol. On the production side the government should rely mainly on research work done in other countries. Use of improved varieties of palm should be encouraged in the natural process of replanting, but no special replanting program should be undertaken.

3. Dates should continue to be bought and packed by the government for the school-feeding program (see Annex XIII). In addition, the use of dates as a concentrated livestock feed should be encouraged, and consideration should be given by the Ministry of Agriculture to building up reserve stocks for use as an emergency feed in periods of draught.

4. The possibilities should be investigated for developing a market for packaged Libyan dates in Italy, where up to 5,000 tons a year may be shipped free of duty. If the results of this investigation are negative, the effort should be abandoned (see Annex XIII).

Olives. Olive trees, mostly planted by Italians in Tripolitania before and since the war, are Libya's largest single agricultural asset. In 1957/58 the number of cultivated olive trees in Tripolitania was estimated at around 3½ million, of which approximately 750,000 had not yet reached the stage of production. The area in the province planted with olives was about 180,000 hectares, and output in the peak year 1957/58 amounted to about 70,000 tons of olives, from which 14,400 tons of oil were produced. In Cyrenaica the number of cultivated olive trees is much smaller (probably about half a million), though there are considerable numbers of wild olives scattered over the Gebel. As in other countries, production is subject to a two-year cycle. In good years substantial amounts of olive and sansa oil are exported (over £L 1.3 million in 1957), but when the crop is bad, exports decline sharply (e.g., only £L 61,000 in 1956 and £L 261,000 in 1954). On average during the last few years exports have accounted for just under one-fifth of total production.

The trees generally start to produce olives about ten years after planting, but they take something like thirty years to attain full production. One of the most serious problems in olive culture is the olive fly, which causes heavy losses in Libya where control measures are seldom applied. In view of the important role of olive cultivation in the Libyan economy the mission recommends that government research and extension services should give high priority in their programs to the adoption of improved methods of cultivation and harvesting, for which there is considerable scope, and to the control of the olive fly. At the same time new planting should be encouraged on dry land in Tripolitania and Cyrenaica where the average annual rainfall is between 200 mm. and 300 mm., seedlings being provided by government at nominal charge and credit extended in appropriate cases for the planting of new orchards, particularly in connection with the development of the Barce Plain and the Gebel Akhdar. Olives respond well to irrigation, but in Libyan conditions other crops such as winter vegetables may give a better return on newly irrigated land—a matter which calls for closer study on research stations in Libya.

The mission suggests the planting of 30,000 new olive trees a year for the next five years as a tentative goal for Tripolitania, and 10,000 trees a year for Cyrenaica. Larger plantings would be justified in Cyrenaica if good progress is made in extending individual land rights. The Nazirate of Agriculture in Cyrenaica has a program costing about £L 5,000 a year for rehabilitation of wild olives, so that these can be picked by nomads and provide them with additional cash income. The effort will be largely wasted unless steps are also taken to maintain the rehabilitated trees. It will be difficult to make satisfactory arrangements for this in the absence of a proper system of individual ownership and tenure. The mission recommends therefore that the project should be abandoned, except to the extent that the trees are established as belonging to particular tribes or individual farmers, who assume responsibility for maintaining them.

Tobacco. Cultivation of tobacco in Libya is supervised by the State Tobacco Monopoly in Tripolitania, which issues licenses to growers, fixes prices and is obliged to buy the entire crop of all grades, regardless of requirements. This system has resulted in overproduction of poor quality tobacco, and large stocks now held by the Monopoly, amounting in the case of the Perustitza type to ten years' supply. The crop is naturally popular with farmers because of the assured market and the good prices paid, and this has resulted in the overissue of licenses in Tripolitania. (Soil conditions in Cyrenaica are not generally suitable for tobacco cultivation, and no licenses have been issued there.) While the average quality of the tobacco grown has improved in recent years, much of it is still inferior, and about 20 percent of the tobacco used for the manufacture of cigarettes is now imported, particularly Oriental Turkish, flue-cured Indian and Italian Kentucky types. Small quantities of Libyan tobacco have been exported in recent years to Algeria.

The mission believes that perpetuation of the existing monopoly system, as applied to cultivation, would be contrary to sound principles of economics in that it encourages wasteful overproduction at the government's expense and results in the misuse of good land. Nor does there appear to be any justification for subsidizing a small privileged minority of tobacco growers at the expense of the rest of the community. We therefore recommend that:

1. Present subsidies on all types of tobacco should be reduced in stages, and should be granted only on leaf that meets reasonable quality standards.
2. A date should be announced two or three years ahead for the termination of the present licensing system, and with it of the Monopoly's obligation to buy all tobacco offered. No new areas should be licensed for tobacco cultivation in the meantime, and the areas licensed for production of the Perustitza type should be gradually reduced.
3. The Monopoly should continue its work of educating farmers in methods of improving cultivation and should explore possibilities of increasing exports, though these appear to be very doubtful.

Sugar Beets. Sugar beets have attracted much attention in Tripolitania as a possible base for a local sugar industry, and they have been grown for several years under irrigation as an experimental crop. The results of these experiments have not, in the mission's view, been very encouraging (see Annex IX), and on the basis of available information we would advise against trying to develop a sugar beet industry in Libya at this stage. This conclusion is founded on the following considerations:

1. Agronomic experiments on sugar beets in Libya to date indicate that the yields of roots and sugar per hectare would often be too low for economic production, especially when grown by small farmers. This is partly because the sandy soils in the coastal belt are unsuited to beet cultivation and partly because of the presence of nematodes (worms). It should be noted in this context that the yields to be expected from ordinary cultivation would be much below those achieved on experimental plots.

2. A minimum of about 4,000 hectares of sugar beets per year, in a rather compact block, is desirable to support a factory capable of producing about 10,000 tons of refined sugar a year (as compared with imports of nearly 18,000 tons in 1958). Since the presence of nematodes precludes sugar beets from being grown on the same field for more than one year in four, a block of about 16,000 hectares would be necessary. It would be difficult to find so large an area in Libya with suitable soils and water supplies. (The whole of the irrigated area in Tripolitania is estimated at around 100,000 hectares.)

3. A sugar factory with a capacity of approximately 10,000 tons of refined sugar would cost an estimated £L 2 to 2½ million to construct and equip. Sugar manufacture from beets involves highly technical and precise processes, and it would be necessary to employ foreign engineers, chemists and mechanics for many years to operate such a factory. Since it would operate only three or four months a year, labor costs would be high.

4. Sugar can be imported into Libya much cheaper than it can be produced in the country through a local sugar industry. The cost of imported sugar in April 1959 was £L 37½ per ton. Against this the mission reckons that the cost of producing sugar in Libya would be at least £L 60-65 per ton and possibly more. Replacement of imports by local production would either mean foregoing the revenue at present obtained by the federal and

provincial governments from sugar trading (about £L 1 million in 1958/59) or substantially raising the price to the consumer.

If the Government of Libya is still interested in the prospects for a beet sugar industry, in spite of the facts listed above, the mission suggests: (a) that experimental work on sugar beets be continued, with special emphasis on varieties, cultural methods, water requirements, fertilizers, diseases, insect pests and costs of production; (b) that more demonstration plots of sugar beets be grown by Libyan farmers; and (c) that the government obtain a consultant to advise on the production and economic aspects of sugar beets, as well as on factory requirements and costs. It is important that the consultant chosen should be independent, and not in any way connected with the business of selling machinery for a sugar beet factory.

Cotton. Proposals have been put forward in Libya for the commercial cultivation of cotton in the Fezzan. While the mission has not studied the problem in great detail, its preliminary conclusions are that such cultivation would not be anywhere near an economic proposition. The present market for raw cotton in Libya is a very small one, imports amounting in 1958 to only 56 tons; and although we see scope for the expansion of cloth manufacture in Libya through the development of the power loom industry (see Annex XIII), this will inevitably be a slow process. Even when the Fezzan road is completed, costs of transport from the Fezzan to the coast will be high (probably at least £L 8 per ton), and this alone would appear to rule out the possibility of Fezzanese cotton competing in export markets, especially at a time when neighboring countries are finding it difficult to dispose of their crops. According to rough calculations made by the mission, there might be enough water available in the Shatti Valley (apparently the most promising area for cultivation) for annual production of about 1,000 tons of cotton. But cotton is a labor-intensive crop, and a growing shortage of agricultural labor is one of the characteristics of the Fezzan economy. Indeed, some of the cotton grown there experimentally has not been picked for lack of labor. If there is considered to be scope for growing cotton for consumption in the Fezzan in conjunction with the development of the skills required to establish small spinning and weaving units to meet local requirements, experiments in cotton cultivation might be continued. Otherwise we suggest they should be abandoned.

Forage Crops. Supplementary forage crops to feed livestock during periods of drought, and to relieve the pressure of overgrazing on marginal lands, have so far received far too little attention from Libyan farmers. Alfalfa produces high fodder yields per hectare under irrigated conditions in Tripolitania and the Fezzan, while experiments in Cyrenaica indicate that oats or barley, harvested before maturity, are the most suitable feed crops for livestock in that province. Mixtures of fall-sown oats and vetch or field peas show promise as dry-land forage crops in the Barce Plain, and Sudan grass planted in March appears to have possibilities as a summer forage crop. The mission recommends therefore that supplementary forage production should be included in plans for the development of the small-scale farming sector, particularly in Cyrenaica, and that the Nazirate of Agriculture in Cyrenaica should conduct a pilot scheme to demonstrate methods of forage production to farmers on the lines already suggested by the FAO.

Other Crops. As already indicated, the mission sees a promising future in Libya for the cultivation of groundnuts, castor seed, almonds and winter vegetables such as new potatoes, carrots and asparagus for export. A few minor recommendations with regard to the production and marketing of these and other crops are set out in Annex IX. Export prospects for citrus fruit and other deciduous fruits are more uncertain, but every effort should be made to develop sales of fruit to the foreign community and the oil companies in Libya. The possibilities of producing high-grade canned fruit juices and canned fruits and vegetables should also be vigorously explored by the agricultural departments in conjunction with private industry (see Annex XIII). The cold storage facilities planned for Tripoli and Benghazi should help in the marketing of perishable commodities.

Search should meanwhile be continued for new crops, and every encouragement should be given to private firms, local or foreign, who may be interested in acquiring land in Libya for commercial farming. Judgments on the prospects for particular crops are notoriously fallible, particularly where, as in Libya, there is such a short and disconnected history of research and experimentation. But the success achieved within a few years in the cultivation of groundnuts is a hopeful augury for the discovery of other crops that can be profitably grown in Libya.

Regional Aspects

Gebel Akhdar Development Project. The mission recommends that first priority in the program for developing small-scale farming in Libya should be given to the former Italian farm settlements in Cyrenaica, and that a special Agricultural Development Board should be created to undertake this task. It might be called the Gebel Akhdar Development Board and should be set up as an autonomous public authority with its own funds. Its chairman should be a Cyrenaican with experience of farming problems in the province, and the other members (not more than four) should be selected from persons qualified in such fields as farm management, land settlement, agronomy, farm machinery operations and agricultural economics. At least one of the members should be an engineer. On broad policy matters the board would be guided by an advisory committee under the chairmanship of the Nazir of Agriculture for Cyrenaica and including representatives of the Ministry of Agriculture, the Ministry of Finance and Economics, tribal leaders, local farmers and cooperatives.

The mission's reasons for singling out the development of the Italian farms in Cyrenaica as a special project are threefold. First, this is a fairly compact area with good soil and better than average rainfall, which is at present seriously underutilized. Second, the small farmers in Cyrenaica are amongst the poorest and most backward sections of the Libyan population, and very little has so far been done to help them to improve their position. Third, considerable sums have already been invested by the Italians in clearing the fields, marking out farms, building houses and cisterns and providing access roads, and this investment is being allowed to go largely to waste. Many of the buildings and cisterns have fallen into disrepair and much of the land is overgrown with weeds or overrun with livestock. But a good part of the initial investment can still be salvaged and used as a basis for a new scheme of settlement and development. Additional investment in these farms is likely therefore, in the mission's view, to be more rapidly productive than investment in small-scale farming in other parts of Libya.

The mission's reasons for suggesting the creation of a special Development Board to handle the project are that an operation of this kind is unlikely to be carried out efficiently and energetically by an ordinary department of government, which is subject to direct political control and bound by civil service rules in matters of procedure, authorization of expenditure, wage and salary scales and so forth. An independent body, provided that the right people are chosen to run it, seems to us a better instrument for planning and executing what is in many ways a business venture.

The board should set up its headquarters at Barce, where it will be able to maintain close liaison with the research station at Zorda, the livestock center at Marzotti and the agricultural school at el Aweila. It should take over, extend and operate the farm machinery unit which has been established with UN assistance at Barce, and tractor services should be provided for farmers against payment of a fee. Those farmers in the area who are already being helped by the machinery unit should continue to receive the same service as at present. The board should cooperate with the Nazirate of Agriculture in building up extension services in the area and promoting farmers' credit and marketing cooperatives; and it should cooperate with the Water Resources Branch of the provincial government in planning the development of water resources. Initially the board itself should assume responsibility for the rehabilitation of farm buildings, the cost of which should be recovered from the tenants over a period of years. Credit should be extended to the farmers through the Agricultural Credit Department of the National Bank, which should open an office in the area, and the Development Board should act as a central supply agency for seeds, fruit trees, tools and other equipment. The board should instruct farmers in cropping patterns and methods of cultivation and should assist them in selling their produce by arranging the necessary facilities for storage and transport and by distributing market information.

Between one and two years will be required to set up the necessary organization and to plan the project in detail. We recommend therefore that the Cyrenaican Government, with the support and guidance of the federal government, the Development Council and the UN and U. S. technical assistance missions, should start the preparatory work without delay. Some suggestions as to how the project might be organized are set out in Annex XI. Resettlement and rehabilitation of the 1,772 Ente farms in Cyrenaica should be undertaken in stages and might be spread over five years, starting with 225 farms in the first year of the scheme (say 1962/63) and increasing to about 470 farms in the fifth year (1966/67). In selecting farmers for assistance under the scheme preference should be given in the first instance to those who are already in occupation and have demonstrated a capacity for settled agriculture. These farmers should be given the opportunity eventually to acquire full possession of the land, subject to satisfactory performance and subject to the fulfillment of their obligation to reimburse the board for the costs of rehabilitating the properties by means of annual payments spread over a reasonable period of years.

The mission, on the basis of some very tentative calculations, has estimated the average cost of repairing farm buildings at £L 300 per farm and the credits required for planting trees and providing initial.

working capital at about £L 320 per farm. For purposes of this calculation it has been assumed that the farms would average 25 hectares in extent, and that wheat, barley, grass and legumes would be the principal annual crops in the Barce Plain, supplemented by linseed, olives, almonds and other fruit trees. Perhaps one-quarter of each farm might be kept permanently under pasture. In the Gebel fewer cereals would be grown and more fruit, including pears, early varieties of apples and table grapes. Vines might be cultivated on a larger scale for making wine if overseas markets can be developed. Vegetables can be grown in the Gebel Akhdar—and in years when flood conditions prevail in the Barce Plain as well.

Total public investment in the project over the five years 1962/63 —1966/67 would work out on these figures at around £L 1,100,000. On the assumption that roughly half the farms are resettled during the first three years, investment in the period covered by the mission's program (1960/61–1964/65) would amount to £L 550,000, of which about £L 265,000 would have to be provided by the Development Board and £L 285,000 by the Agricultural Credit Department. In addition to the £L 265,000 required by the Board for the rehabilitation of farm buildings, it would need capital to establish its own offices, workshops and stores, to acquire more farm machinery and to purchase vehicles and other equipment. In all, we estimate its capital requirements over the five-year period at around £L 500,000 and its annual recurrent expenses at £L 35,000.

Small-Scale Farming in Tripolitania. Tripolitania has many advantages over the other two provinces in Libya from the point of view of agricultural production. It has a bigger and better organized local market, particularly in Tripoli itself; it has simpler internal transport problems and better facilities for export; and its supplies of ground water are more easily accessible than in most parts of Cyrenaica. A sizable sector in Tripolitanian agriculture has already been developed on more advanced lines by the Italian community, and a number of Libyans have also succeeded in establishing quite large and prosperous farms.

The condition of the majority of Libyan farmers in Tripolitania is nonetheless rather depressed, and they need full support from government along the lines suggested earlier in this chapter—through better credit and marketing facilities, training and extension services and so forth. The only land resettlement which we suggest should be undertaken by the Tripolitanian Government during the next five years is the movement of 200 families from the Gebel to the Gefara as part of the first stage of our scheme for flood prevention in the Wadi Megenin (see Chapter 7). In addition, we have recommended that preparatory surveys should be carried out by the government in the Bir Ghnem area and at the Taorga oasis with a view to the possible development of settled agriculture at a later stage (see Chapter 7).

Most of the Ente farms abandoned by Italians in Tripolitania are at present occupied by Libyan farmers; some are deserted. The Nazirate of Agriculture, in consultation with the agricultural credit agency, should give particular attention to providing farmers with the means to develop these properties, in which money has already been invested. One of the main obstacles to effective action in this matter apparently lies in the continued uncertainties surrounding ownership of the land in question. It has not even been clearly established whether it belongs in law to the federal or to the provincial government, and so long as this issue remains unresolved, no individual ownership or tenancy rights are being granted. A decision on the legal issues involved is long overdue, and the mission urges that both governments should collaborate in getting the present conflict of claims settled as quickly as possible.

The Desert Oases. The mission's proposals for the development of agriculture in the Fezzan were summarized in Chapter 1 (pages 19-21), and some of them have been elaborated in the present chapter with reference to particular crops. These proposals apply also to the outlying oases in Tripolitania and Cyrenaica. Stress has been laid in Chapter 7 on the importance of constructing more public wells in the desert oases so as to provide the small cultivator with access to water for irrigation and thereby reduce his dependence on the large proprietors of water and land.

The oases should clearly be able to meet their own requirements of cereals, fodder and livestock products. There appears to be something basically unsound from an economic point of view in substantial quantities of flour being imported over huge distances to remote centers of population which are adequately supplied both with water and soils suitable for cereal cultivation, and where small cultivators have difficulty in earning a living. The sight of an abandoned flour mill in one of the Fezzan oases, full of rusting equipment, served the mission as a further reminder of the strange distortions in patterns of production and trade which have occurred in Libya in recent years.

Conditions in a number of the oases are well suited to the cultivation of vegetables and oilseeds. It may even be economic to grow certain kinds of early vegetables for export—onions and carrots, for example.

Production of tomatoes in Jalo could be increased if demand is adequate, and the mission has suggested in Chapter 9 the possibility of establishing an additional tomato paste factory in Cyrenaica.

TECHNICAL SUPPORT FOR AGRICULTURE

Experimentation and Research

Considerable sums are being spent in Libya on agricultural experimentation and research (see Statistical Appendix, Table S.4), and valuable results have been achieved, particularly at the principal stations at Zorda in Cyrenaica and Sidi Mesri in Tripolitania where the programs have been in charge of FAO experts acting as advisers to the provincial governments. The highlights have been the research work on cereals and a seed multiplication program through which improved varieties of wheat and barley have been distributed to farmers; studies of cultural practices for various crops, including the use of commercial fertilizers; the first-class animal breeding work under way at the Marzotti livestock center in Cyrenaica; and investigations into crop diseases and pests, with particular reference to olives and groundnuts.

Notwithstanding these achievements, it is the mission's feeling that more could have been achieved for the money that has been spent. Too many experimental stations have been established, and there has been too little coordination between them. Many of the stations officially classified as experimental stations do not maintain recorded data on their work. There is a certain laxness in making findings freely available to government agencies, and in getting information down to the farmer through the extension services. Moreover, research has not been related closely enough to existing social and economic conditions, and too little attention has been given to the most important problem of establishing the sizes of holdings and the cropping patterns best adapted in present circumstances to the limitations of the small farmer. Other critical areas of research which have tended to be neglected include tillage practices, irrigation methods and costs and the comparative benefits to be obtained from irrigation of different crops.

The mission recommends the appointment in the proposed federal Ministry of Agriculture of a Director of Agricultural Research with broad responsibilities for the coordination of research work in the three provinces. One of his first tasks should be to make a survey of all agricultural experimental stations and farms, nurseries and laboratories to assess their effectiveness in solving Libya's practical problems in agriculture, animal husbandry and forestry. The survey should give special consideration to the enlargement, consolidation, relocation or abandonment of specific establishments in the interests of efficient work. Occasionally, a new station may be found necessary for studies under special conditions. The objective should be to reduce the number of stations to 10 or 12 well-located establishments. The survey should include an assessment of the needs for personnel, equipment, buildings and other facilities to carry out essential research projects. Special consideration should be given to the employment of college-trained Libyans, when they become available, for assignment to each foreign agricultural research specialist as a counterpart.

Each experimental station should be required to prepare an annual progress report of all experimental work done during the year. It should include pertinent summary data, together with conclusions drawn from the experiments to date. This information should be published and generally distributed both in Libya and in neighboring countries. Research workers in Libya should take full advantage of experimental results obtained in nearby countries in North Africa and the Near East in order to avoid unnecessary duplication of effort. The mission considers it particularly important that the results of past Italian research work for Libya should be systematically assembled in a central reference library; where necessary copies should be made available in translation.

Future agricultural research work in Tripolitania should be directed particularly towards crop rotations, water requirements of crops and their response to irrigation, plant protection (especially olives and citrus fruits) and agronomic work on wheat, barley, forage crops, groundnuts, potatoes and castor beans. An improvement in the quality of vegetables is most important, attention being given to the discovery of better varieties as well as to the control of diseases and insect pests. Forestry research should include experiments on simpler methods of dune fixation than those at present employed. Grazing experiments should feature prominently in the program of livestock research. Experimental work that should be stressed in Cyrenaica includes methods of cultivating cereals, forage crops, vegetables and vines, range vegetation, plant protection and livestock improvement.

In the Fezzan the mission recommends the establishment of a single experimental station to conduct all field experiments. The present demonstration farm at Traghen might be used for this purpose, with the farm at Brak retained as a sub-station. None of the other experimental stations or demonstration farms appear to serve any useful purpose. The research program should place special emphasis on improving cultural practices for dates and conducting experiments on proposed new crops such as cotton, linseed and castor beans to determine their suitability for conditions in the Fezzan. Work should also be done on irrigation practices and reclamation of alkaline land.

The level of public expenditure on research in recent years (about £L 125,000 in 1957/58, exclusive of personnel and equipment provided by FAO) is equivalent to about one percent of Libya's net agricultural output and appears to be reasonably adequate in the circumstances, given the shortage of trained personnel and the fairly extensive research work carried out under the Italian administration. Once again, however, the mission would like to stress the importance of making full use of the results obtained from relevant research work carried out previously in Libya or in other countries; of establishing better communications between the various research institutions themselves and between these institutions and the farmer; and of relating research work more closely to the practical use that can be made of it in present circumstances in Libya.

In this latter connection the mission suggests that investigations should be carried out on three or four small-holdings in an attempt to establish what size and layout of farm, cropping patterns and farm management procedures are best adapted to the needs of the typical family unit in present-day Libyan conditions. Three or four small-holdings might be selected, including at least one in the Barce Plain, and a family unit would be settled on each and equipped with the manual implements and work animals that the average small farmer might be expected to have. The families would be paid regular wages, with any profits or losses on operations being borne by government (subject to the payment of bonuses to the workers for good results). Cropping patterns would be laid down for the first year and changed from year to year to compare results obtained from different combinations of crops. Continuous study would be made of the labor requirements of each crop and the returns obtained. The experiments should continue over a period of five to ten years and should be extended to include the operation of tractor-drawn machinery.

The conduct of such research would require neither elaborate equipment nor highly specialized personnel. It could best be undertaken centrally under the supervision of the Ministry of Agriculture, working in close cooperation with the provincial Nazirates and with the Agricultural Development Board in Cyrenaica. One agricultural economist and two or three agricultural technicians should be sufficient to carry out the field work, and the accounting could be done by the ordinary departmental staff. Heavy outlays on a large number of specialized personnel and numerous different types of farms should be avoided. The research should help to throw light on problems of marketing, but this would not be the primary objective of the program. It should be possible to obtain significant results in three to four years, but the program should be set up on a longer-term basis.

Land Classification

There is urgent need for the systematic classification of agricultural land in Libya. The mission understands that such a classification has already been carried out for Tripolitania by USOM, and it is hoped that the results will be published shortly. A similar study in Cyrenaica would be of great value as a guide to agricultural development in the province.

As the next step, a general soil survey should be made of all agricultural land in Libya, using existing soil maps where these are available. The purpose of the survey should be to locate areas for possible new development and to serve as a guide for changes in patterns of land use in areas that are already cultivated—for example, a change from dry farming to irrigated agriculture. The survey should be supervised by the Director of Research in the new Ministry of Agriculture and might be carried out on a contract basis by a commercial firm. The soil analyses could be made at the chemical laboratory at Sidi Mesri. A detailed report should be published on conclusion of the survey, together with a general soil map. We estimate that the work might take three years to complete and cost about £L 25,000.

Soil Conservation

One of the main responsibilities of government in the field of agricultural development is to take proper measures for soil conservation. Soil erosion by wind and water is a major problem in Libya. It has been accelerated by widespread destruction of the vegetative cover by mismanagement of range lands, by the use of inappropriate techniques and tools in cultivation and by the lack of adequate windbreaks. The tractor-drawn, one-way disc plows and moldboard plows widely used on sandy soils in Tripolitania leave the land pulverized and exposed to wind action. Clean cultivation by such implements operated down slopes has already led to the formation of sand dunes in many orchards, particularly between Cussabat and Tarhuna, and south of Castel Benito. Unless drastic measures are taken, much of this land will return to sand dunes, possibly within five to ten years. A similar threat exists in the Fezzan where sand has started to drift on to abandoned farms for lack of adequate windbreaks.

Direct action by government to deal with this problem falls mainly under such headings as flood control, forestry and dune fixation, which are considered separately in another section of this report. But much also needs to be done to educate the farmer in the use of proper tillage methods and to encourage contouring and planting windbreaks, particularly on the Italian farms in Tripolitania.

Tillage on dryland farms, especially on sandy soils, should be practiced with implements that leave the crop residues on the soil surface (e.g., the blade or duckfoot type of plows that operate at a shallow depth). Crops like barley may be planted on alternate strips (rotating with fallow) between trees in olive or almond orchards to provide some vegetative cover for the land; this may reduce fruit yields, but the additional grain crop should largely compensate for the reduction. New orchards should be planted on the contour in order to reduce possible water erosion. Broad-base contour terraces might be considered on large farms. Finally, trees such as *acacia horrida* should be planted as windbreaks along the boundaries of orchards, about one meter apart, and tamarisks might be planted through orchards after every five to ten rows of olive trees in order to reduce the wind sweep. Where farmers are ready to undertake planting, the trees should be provided by the Forestry Department free of charge.

Plant Protection

The need for plant protection has been recognized by governmental agencies in recent years, and damage caused by insects and diseases is being tackled with the help of the FAO and the LAJS. Plant protection is one of the most important agricultural tasks in Libya because plant diseases and insect pests cause heavy losses in crop yields, reduce the quality of crops and jeopardize export markets. The ravages of the olive fly and the Mediterranean fruit fly are particularly devastating. In 1959 the federal government passed a phytosanitary law providing for the inspection of cultivated land and plants and for the necessary steps to be taken to prevent or control diseases and pests.

The new law is an important forward step. As further measures for plant protection, the mission offers the following suggestions:

1. Farmers and cooperatives should be provided with credit for the purchase of motor sprayers, atomizers or wheelbarrow sprayers.

An estimate given to the mission indicates a need for at least 60 additional motor sprayers for citrus trees, 140 more atomizers for olive trees and a large number of wheelbarrow sprayers for vegetable crops.

2. The current extension program in Tripolitania to demonstrate to farmers the use of chemicals for the control of plant diseases and insect pests is an important means for training farmers in the techniques involved and should be continued. A similar program should be initiated elsewhere in Libya. Farmers should pay for the chemicals used on their farms.

3. Plant protection cooperatives should be formed wherever feasible.

Farm Supplies

Farmers in Libya generally obtain their supplies of machinery, implements, fertilizers, seeds and so forth through the normal channels of private trade. Most of these goods are imported. In Tripolitania the *Consorzio Agrario* plays an important role in the acquisition and distribution of supplies, and some of the newly formed cooperatives in Tripolitania and Cyrenaica have been serving effectively as channels of distribution for improved seeds, motor pumps, small tools, fertilizers, insecticides and spare parts for farm machinery. Plants and seeds are provided on a limited scale by the research stations and experimental farms for distribution to farmers through the extension services and in other ways.

It should be the function of the government agricultural services to educate the farmer in the use of improved implements, seeds and fertilizers and to ensure that supplies of these things can readily be obtained on demand. This is mainly a question of providing adequate credit facilities and of encouraging the formation of farmers' cooperatives. Sometimes a government department or agency will need to take a direct hand in procurement and distribution, as we have suggested that the proposed Agricultural Development Board in Cyrenaica should do. Among improved hand tools or animal-drawn implements that the small farmer might be encouraged to use are the new breaker-ridged plow (Feist type), small cultivators and seed drills, and small threshers such as the Japanese treadle thresher. The hand sickle, scythe and cradle should be considered for the harvesting of wheat, barley and perhaps other crops.

Mechanization

Large tractor-drawn farm implements have become increasingly popular in Libya in recent years. An estimated 100,000 hectares of farm land are now mechanically cultivated, and there are over 1,000 farm tractors in the country, of which about 100 are owned and operated by the three provincial governments. Power-driven machinery is well suited for wheat and barley cultivation on heavy soils, and the Cyrenaican Government has subsidized the use of tractors in the Barce Plain as part of a project organized with the help of FAO. One of the main obstacles to farm mechanization has been shortage of Libyan personnel to operate and maintain the equipment, and wages paid by the provincial governments are too low to retain competent men in the work.

The mission believes that mechanization has an important role to play in the development of Libyan agriculture, and that while this is mainly a matter for private enterprise on the larger farms, the existing government farm machinery projects should be continued for the time being, tractor services being provided to small farmers on payment. As already suggested, the project in Cyrenaica should be taken over by the new Development Board, and particular attention should be given to proper maintenance of the equipment and to the training of drivers and mechanics. Higher wages should be offered to those who qualify in these trades, and they should be assured of regular employment. Eventually, the aim should be to hand over all heavy machinery operations to private contractors and farmers or to farmers' cooperatives organized for this purpose.

LIVESTOCK

Problems of Management

The raising of livestock is the most important rural occupation in Cyrenaica, as well as in the Gefara and parts of the Gebel in Tripolitania. In terms of output, annual sales of livestock and livestock products in Cyrenaica are probably worth more than sales of all other agricultural commodities combined. In Tripolitania, on the other hand, sales of agricultural commodities proper may be about three times as large as sales of livestock and livestock products. In total, there are rather more livestock in Cyrenaica than in Tripolitania. Sheep and goats predominate in both provinces. Camels, cattle, donkeys and horses are also important. Some rough estimates of output, and of livestock numbers, will be found in Annex I.

Most livestock in Libya are owned by nomadic or semi-nomadic tribesmen and are reared on communal grazing lands. Some wealthy townspeople also own large herds and hire nomads to graze them on tribal land. The range lands are mostly seriously mismanaged so that palatable perennial grasses have almost disappeared, and very little grazing feed is available between June and October. In some areas the numbers of animals may be as much as 50 percent larger than the grazing lands can support even in good years under present management conditions. Herds are relatively free from serious diseases, but they suffer badly from parasites and are extremely vulnerable to variations in rainfall. Losses in drought years have been estimated at between 30 percent and 60 percent of total numbers. There is a general lack of supplementary fodder crops or concentrated feeds, and mainly to meet an emergency created in Cyrenaica by lack of rainfall in the winter of 1958/59 some 40,000 tons of feed grains were given to Libya during 1959 by the United States.

The raising of livestock is an integral part of the nomadic way of life, and there are many deeply-rooted customs and attitudes associated with it which are very difficult to change. The pastoralist regards his herds not merely as a source of income, but as a store of wealth and a mark of social prestige. Traditionally, it is usually the numbers of animals a family has, and not their quality, that counts. As a result, herds increase far beyond the capacity of the land to support them in good condition, mortality rates are very high, and the commercial value of the animals brought to market is lowered. There is a danger in these circumstances that measures to provide the herdsmen with easier access to supplies of fodder and water will simply result in the multiplication of numbers without making any contribution to economic output.

In the mission's view, measures to encourage the development of settled agriculture in Libya will do more to reduce livestock numbers and raise the quality of the animals that remain than will any educational campaigns or range management schemes. There should be some place nevertheless in a Libyan development program for further modest experiments designed to secure better grazing practices. A number of small demonstration schemes are already being carried out by the LAJS, and a sum of just over £L 15,000 was allocated for this purpose out of U.S. aid for the Libyan fiscal year 1959/60. The mission recommends that these schemes should be continued.

Libya's natural pastures are an important economic asset, and ecological studies should be undertaken to provide the basic information required for a pasture improvement program. Teams of ecologists have been working in Morocco, Algeria and Tunisia, and similar work is in progress in Portugal and Turkey, with the object of obtaining essential data for determining the location and boundaries of pasture areas, their carrying capacity and the most suitable time and duration for stocking. A similar approach should be followed in Libya, and technical assistance should be sought from abroad for carrying out a study on these lines. When the study has been completed, the government will be in a better position to plan a long-range campaign for the gradual control of grazing. Meanwhile, the economic and social changes already in progress should tend of their own accord to create a more favorable environment for such a campaign.

Measures to improve supplies of forage should be associated with, and used to encourage, the conversion of nomads to settled farming and the adoption of better range management practices. The former Italian farms in Cyrenaica are mostly large enough to permit the grazing of small numbers of livestock in addition to the cultivation of crops, and the proposed Agricultural Development Board, with the assistance of the livestock experts, should take all possible steps to inculcate in the settlers a more commercial approach to livestock breeding. A campaign should be instituted to banish the goat from the settled farming areas and to concentrate resources on the raising of improved breeds of sheep.

The scope for growing more fodder crops in Libya has been outlined on page 156 above. The mission has also proposed that study should be given to the possibilties of making greater use of dates as a concentrated feed for livestock. If the results of such study are encouraging, a further study should be undertaken of the feasibility of storing at least 25,000 tons of dates at various points in Libya for use as an emergency feed reserve. Estimates should be made of the costs of buying the dates, transporting the dates to the storage points and keeping them in store. Both studies should be made jointly by the staff of the Marzotti livestock center and the FAO horticultural expert.

Livestock Improvement

Livestock improvement is under way at the Marzotti livestock center on the Barce Plain in Cyrenaica and at Garabulli in Tripolitania. Attempts are being made to improve the local fat-tail Barbary sheep through selection in order to improve the quality of the fleece. Crossbreeding has been tried between this and the Karaman breed imported from Turkey. An improved sire program for cattle and horses is also being conducted at the Marzotti center. The mission was impressed by what it saw of this work and recommends that it be continued.

There is urgent need in Libya for the enactment of a veterinary law to provide for (a) the prevention, control and eradication of animal diseases; (b) quarantine for imported animals to guard against the introduction of new diseases and parasites; (c) a proper system of meat inspection; (d) mobile veterinary units dealing with external and internal parasites; and (e) vaccination campaigns. Action along these lines is an essential prerequisite to developing an export trade in meat.

Processing and Marketing

The export of live animals to Egypt has traditionally been one of the principal means of livelihood for the Bedouin in Cyrenaica. Before the outbreak of the Italo-Sanusi war in 1923 this trade used to be considerably larger than it is now, and Cyrenaica also supplied Egypt with considerable quantities of clarified butter.[6] The value of the trade in 1958 (a fairly good year) was £L 636,000. Sheep, camels and cattle are the principal animals traded.

The continuance of this trade, and of the smaller export of live animals by sea to other Mediterranean countries, is clearly of great importance to the Cyrenaican economy. Government might help by establishing fodder stations on the Libyan side of the Egyptian border to enable animals to be fattened up before they are sold. At the same time more attention should be given to providing for the growing meat requirements of the foreign community in Libya, and to the possibilities of exporting meat. The institution of proper veterinary inspection and improvements in the quantity and quality of the meat produced are the essential first steps. Both will take time to bring about. But if these matters can be taken care of, there should be good prospects of developing sales of mutton and beef to countries in Southern Europe. The proposed cold storage plant in Benghazi could then make its full contribution to the growth of the Cyrenaican economy. Further comments on the cold storage project and on meat marketing will be found in Annex XIII.

Poultry farming should be encouraged in Libya with a view particularly to meeting the increased demands for eggs and poultry that will result from the expansion of oil operations. The experience of the Americans at Wheelus Air Base in buying Libyan eggs has not been encouraging. A special effort was made to help the local pro-

[6] E. E. Evans-Pritchard, *op. cit.*, page 37.

ducer, and eggs to the value of about £L 40,000 were purchased by the base in 1958. Generally, however, the quality was poor and packaging was defective, while the price paid was nearly 40 percent higher than the price of Danish eggs delivered to Italy. Efforts should be made to interest private firms in establishing poultry farms in Libya. As an example of what can be done to develop efficient poultry farming under difficult conditions, the mission suggests that the agricultural authorities in Libya might study the results achieved in Jordan at the Arab Development Society near Jericho. This is essentially a matter for private enterprise, but government could assist in various ways, including the provision of credit.

Considerable quantities of milk and milk products are consumed by those engaged in raising livestock in Libya. Most of this milk comes from sheep, goats and camels. Cows produce some milk, particularly on the Italian farms in Tripolitania, but most of the urban demand is met out of imports of processed milk (£L 156,000 in 1958) and milk products (£L 180,000 in 1958). A pilot dairy project has been started by the Nazirate of Agriculture in Benghazi to test the feasibility of producing economically for the local market, and the mission recommends that this project should be continued for another two years, with particular attention to costs. Possibilities of eventually developing a local dairy industry will depend on assurances of adequate fodder, enclosed pastures and concentrated feedingstuffs for dairy cows. Safeguards will be needed to ensure that the milk is produced under sanitary conditions.

The other principal livestock products in Libya are wool, hides and skins. Comments on the processing and marketing of hides and skins are included in Annex XIII. Improvements in the quality of wool production should be accorded a high priority in the work of the agricultural research and extension services, and demand for wool should be stimulated by the development of Libyan handicrafts and weaving on the lines suggested in the industrial sections of this report.

FORESTRY

Objectives and Priorities

Forestry presents great potential scope for fruitful long-term investment in Libya, and at a time when the opportunities for more immediately productive investment are limited by shortages of skills, afforestation should be accorded an important place in any program of economic development. The erosion of the land by wind and water poses a serious threat to agriculture in many parts of the Mediterranean area, and in no country is this threat more real than in Libya, where fierce desert winds blow frequently from the Sahara and sand dunes are steadily encroaching on farming land in the coastal provinces. The planting of more trees is essential for the conservation of soil resources, for the retention of water in the soil and in some cases for the control of flooding (notably in the Wadi Megenin—see Chapter 7). It is also needed to provide Libya with domestic supplies of timber. At present practically all the wood used in the building industry, furniture manufacture and other trades has to be obtained from abroad, imports in 1958 amounting to nearly £L 450,000 (including plywood and other semi-manufactures, but excluding furniture).

Libya is at present very poorly provided with forests, to some extent because of its unfavorable climate, but primarily because of the destruction of trees by men and animals which has continued unchecked for centuries. There are about 400,000 hectares of so-called forest land in the country, mostly in Cyrenaica, but much of it consists of low scrub and bushes. Much of the wood that is grown is cut prematurely for firewood or the manufacture of charcoal, scrub is uprooted for the same purposes, and goats wander more or less unchecked through most of the state forest areas. Some of the best trees are to be found on private farms.

Forestry programs have been initiated in both coastal provinces with the assistance of the foreign aid agencies, and there has been a steady increase in expenditure on afforestation and dune fixation from about £L 90,000 in 1954/55 to £L 229,000 in 1957/58 (see Statistical Appendix, Table S.5). These programs have helped to prevent the situation from getting worse, but little real progress will be possible until grazing and cutting of wood in forest areas is brought under proper control and until individual rights in land and state domain have been clearly established. In forestry, as in settled agriculture, the mission regards the enactment of a land law as a matter of great urgency (see page 131). In addition, the mission recommends that a federal forest law should be enacted, and that a federal Department of Forestry should be established under a technically qualified Chief Conservator of Forests as part of the proposed Ministry of Agriculture to lay down the policies to be followed in forestry development in Libya and to supervise their execution by the provincial governments.

The forestry departments in the coastal provinces are seriously understaffed, particularly in the higher grades, and the mission recommends that £L 10,000 a year should be added to the budgets of each department to provide for an increase in the number of senior posts (Assistant Conservators, Divisional Forest Officers, District Forest Officers) and the higher subordinate posts (Forest Rangers), and for overseas courses for Libyan forestry officers (e.g., in Cyprus and Syria).

Higher priority should be given to strengthening the forestry protection services in order to save the trees from despoliation and to guard against fire. We suggest an additional allocation of £L 5,000 a year for this purpose in the budgets of each of the provincial forestry departments. The existing forest guard training center, which is being operated by the Tripolitania Forestry Department at Hescian, is doing excellent work. The mission recommends that the standard of training at the center should be gradually raised and the period of training lengthened. The center should be used as a central forest training establishment for junior forest subordinates in all parts of Libya.

A single forestry experimental station should be established for all of Libya. Problems for investigation include costs of forestry operations, trials with indigenous and exotic tree species, spacing tests, experiments on various silvicultural operations, uses of local forest products and dune fixation. The cost of the facilities, equipment and staff might be in the region of £L 50,000 for the five-year period, and this should be accommodated within the existing budgets for agricultural experimentation and research (see page 163). The forestry station would come under the federal Ministry of Agriculture.

The mission recognizes that it will take time to create the institutional conditions necessary for the effective development of forestry and to build up staffs in the two provinces capable of executing greatly enlarged forestry programs. These appear to us to be the two main factors that must govern the rate of investment. Forests cannot be planted unless there is someone to plant them, and they should not be planted unless they have a good chance of growing to maturity. Subject, however, to these overriding limitations, the mission recommends that high priority be given to afforestation and dune fixation in the allocaton of funds available for investment in both coastal provinces.

A proper balance must be maintained in programs of planting between quick-yielding and slow-yielding varieties, the former (e.g., eucalyptus) providing a resource for commercial exploitation within nine to twelve years and the latter (e.g., pine) representing a long-term asset. The collection of firewood and the burning of charcoal in forest areas should be controlled by the forest departments. Now that oil has been discovered in Libya, cheap and plentiful supplies of kerosene should soon become available, and the mission has recommended elsewhere in this report (Chapter 4) that the use of kerosene should be actively encouraged as a substitute for firewood and charcoal in the towns.

A Program for Tripolitania

The forest area of Tripolitania in April 1959 was approximately 19,000 hectares. Most of this had been planted since 1952, government forest reserves accounting for 15,000 hectares and private plantings for about 4,000 hectares. The most successful results in afforestation have been achieved with various species of eucalyptus and acacia. About 6,000 hectares of eucalyptus are grown for lumber on the coastal plain. The remaining 13,000 hectares of forest land are mainly used to grow wood for fuel and other household uses.

The mission recommends that forest reserves in Tripolitania should be extended by planting an additional 16,000 hectares during the next five years. The main emphasis in this program should be placed on soil and water conservation, with production of commercial lumber as a secondary but nonetheless important objective. The most successful results have been obtained in the past with eucalyptus and acacia, but these species have their limitations, and other species, including pine, should be introduced wherever possible so as to secure diversification. Experiments with new species should be continued. Planting costs are estimated at £L 22-25 per hectare (excluding seedlings), and the total cost of the program might be about £L 380,000. This includes the establishment of a forest reserve in the Wadi Huelfa area as part of the scheme for flood control in the Wadi Megenin (see Chapter 7). As soon as the necessary steps have been taken to establish this reserve, it should receive priority in the planting of trees and might account for about one-quarter of the expenditures included in the five-year planting program.

The program of sand dune fixation should be continued in the coastal areas. The present practice of "dissing"[7] and planting trees in rows throughout the dunes should be continued for the time being in areas where dunes threaten to engulf adjacent agricultural land. However, this method is too slow and costly for the long-term rehabilitation of all the dune areas, and the provincial Forestry Department

---

[7] "Dissing" is the term applied to the planting of diss grass as a hedge to protect young trees in sand dune areas.

should investigate the possibilities of limiting dissing and planting to the perimeters of the dunes and to a few strips across them spaced at wide intervals. The present search for species of trees or shrubs that can be seeded from the air on dune areas should be continued. Under the system in use at present dissing is estimated to cost £L 30 per hectare and tree planting an additional £L 8 per hectare. As a tentative target for the five-year period, the mission suggests the fixation of 9,000 hectares at a total cost of around £L 340,000. If a cheaper method of fixation can be found, a larger area can be covered for the same expenditure.

The mission recommends that the Sand Sea south of Tripolitania should be dealt with as a special problem within the over-all program for dune fixation. This sea has an area of 60,000 hectares with a perimeter of approximately 176 kilometers, and there is some support for the belief that it collects a significant proportion of the ground water used by wells in the Tripoli area. It is accordingly suggested (a) that further evidence should be sought on the role of the Sand Sea as a ground water recharge area; (b) that estimates should be made of the amount of water transpired by different kinds of trees; and (c) that present dissing activities should be confined to the stabilization of the Sand Sea within its present perimeter. For this purpose perimeter planting with a continuous belt of forest, say one kilometer wide, might be supplemented with 250-meter wide strips across the dunes at intervals of one kilometer or more apart. Eucalyptus could be used on the perimeter, but the strips planted in the dunes should be confined to acacia.

Public programs of afforestation should be supported by encouraging private planting as much as possible. Trees should be supplied to farmers at a nominal cost, with credit where necessary. In particular, farmers should be required to plant windbreaks and shelter belts in order to reduce soil erosion. In addition to supplying seedlings, the Forestry Department should give advice on suitable species and cultural practices.

The present nurseries of the provincial Forestry Department can produce about 6 million trees a year, after allowance for seasonal losses. The average cost per seedling is about one piaster, excluding the cost of machinery and equipment. The cost of providing 30 million trees over the five years is thus estimated at about £L 300,000, with a further sum of £L 40,000 for the purchase and maintenance of equipment. This would bring the total investment recommended for Tripolitania to £L 1,060,000 over the five years.

A Program for Cyrenaica

The situation in Cyrenaica differs radically from that in Tripolitania in that there are approximately 385,000 hectares of indigenous *macchia* forests in the Gebel Akhdar, most of them in very poor condition. The main emphasis in forestry operations in the province should be placed for a number of years to come on the reservation, management and improvement of these indigenous forest areas. The mission suggests that, as a start, 40,000-50,000 hectares should be placed under irrevocable reservation by the government and converted by accepted silvicultural methods into high coniferous forests. Owing to the compact soils of much of the mountain area mechanized strip cultivation should be employed for reforestation. Pine should be the main species used, but consideration should also be given to the indigenous cypress and other coniferous species such as juniper, which, although of slower growth, may be more suitable for use on selected sites. Investigation should be continued into the possibilities of introducing exotic species. No livestock grazing or cutting of wood should be permitted in forest reserves, and every effort should be made to secure the cooperation of the tribes in enforcing the necessary controls.

The mission was unable to obtain any reliable estimates of the costs of forestry operations in Cyrenaica, but they appear to have been a good deal higher than in Tripolitania, in part because of heavier reliance on manual labor. Greater use of machinery should reduce the costs of planting. Bearing in mind the limitations of staff and the time that will be needed to establish suitable conditions for reforestation, the mission suggests that £L 400,000 should be provisionally allocated for capital expenditure over the five years on the conversion and improvement of the degraded *macchia* forests in the areas selected for reservation in the Gebel Akhdar.

Under existing conditions the skeletal soils of the coastal plain offer few possibilities for afforestation, but preliminary operations might be undertaken to stabilize and reclaim these almost barren areas, particularly between Benghazi and Tocra. The first step in such operations should consist of establishing long windbreaks of cactus, and the mission suggests that a sum of £L 35,000 (£L 7,000 a year) should be provisionally allocated for cactus windbreaks. Roadside planting of eucalyptus (in the lowland areas) and other suitable species (conifers in the upland areas) should continue, and we suggest a target of 3,500 kilometers for the next five years at an estimated cost of £L 10 per kilometer, of £L 35,000 in all. This would raise total capital expenditure on forestry operations in Cyrenaica over the five years to £L 470,000.

At the time of the mission's visit about 300 hectares in the Agedabia—el Ageila area had been dissed for dune fixation. The mission sees very little purpose in the continuation of dune fixation in this area since the dunes are not encroaching on agricultural land of any value. It should be the function of the Public Works Department to keep the coastal road clear of sand.

SUMMARY OF PROPOSED EXPENDITURES

We envisage that the recommendations made in this chapter in respect of agriculture, livestock and forestry might entail a total capital outlay in the public sector of the order of £L 5,130,000 over the five years 1960/61-1964/65. Details are as follows:

Capital Expenditures on Agriculture, Livestock and Forestry

(£L '000)

	Five-Year Total	Annual Average
Agriculture and Livestock		
Agricultural credit	2,500	500
Agricultural Development Board (Cyrenaica)	500	100
Commodity stocks[a]	500	100
Miscellaneous[b]	100	20
Sub-total	3,600	720
Forestry and Dune Fixation		
Program for Tripolitania	1,060	212
Program for Cyrenaica	470	94
Sub-total	1,530	306
Total agriculture, livestock and forestry	5,130	1,026

[a] National provision for acquisition of stocks by the Ministry of Agriculture in connection with the wheat marketing scheme and the scheme for creation of an emergency feed reserve.

[b] Including the initial capital cost of establishing a Land Survey Department, the total cost of conducting a soil survey, and provision of £L 40,000 for contingencies (e.g., for providing buildings and equipment for the agricultural services).

The following estimates are tentatively suggested for the additional recurrent expenditures that will be involved in setting up the new institutions which the mission has proposed for the administration of agriculture and in expanding the forestry services:

(£L '000)

	Five-Year Total	Annual Average
Federal Ministry of Agriculture	250	50
Agricultural Development Board	175	35
Land Survey Department	500	100
Provincial Forestry Services	150	30
	1,075	215

The provision indicated here for the Ministry of Agriculture would include the costs of staffing and operating the agricultural marketing services and also allow for some increases in other agricultural services (e.g., extension work and assistance to cooperatives). In such fields as research and experimentation and plant protection the mission does not envisage the need for increased recurrent expenditures in total, but there may have to be some shifts as between the budgets of the federal and provincial governments.

Schemes of afforestation and other measures of soil and water conservation are considered particularly suitable for inclusion in the Supplementary Program if the administrative and technical problems involved can be satisfactorily resolved. The need and the scope for such additional schemes appears to be rather greater in Tripolitania than in other parts of Libya. In Cyrenaica any Supplementary Program for agriculture should place main emphasis on additional credit and other facilities for developing settled agriculture in the Barce-Beida area. Marketing schemes and the creation of feed reserves may also merit larger allocations if the conditions necessary for their success are established more quickly than the mission has assumed.

CHAPTER 9 *INDUSTRY, HANDICRAFTS AND FISHERIES*

INDUSTRY

Present Position of Industry

The Italian occupation largely reserved entrepreneurship and management to its own nationals, with the result that up to the present day the great majority of the factory undertakings remain under foreign control. The only significant exception is Cyrenaica, where the evacuation of the Italian population in 1942 created industrial opportunities which Libyan entrepreneurs were quick to take advantage of. Further, Italian workers before the war supplied most of the skilled labor in Libya, and this situation has tended to perpetuate itself. With such labor relatively scarce and more costly, labor-saving techniques had been introduced on a rather more intensive scale than in many other countries in a similar stage of economic development. At the same time, wage rates have tended to be adjusted to Italian standards.

The backward state of agriculture, fisheries and animal husbandry, and the limited and extremely variable marketable surpluses, have restricted the development of agricultural processing industries, which are now mainly confined to olive oil and fish processing, the manufacture of tobacco and wine, the curing of hides and skins, and flour milling. Lack of known minerals, apart from oil, has been another factor inhibiting the growth of industry, and mineral-based industries are confined to the manufacture of building materials. A considerable part of Libyan industry accordingly consists of trades which convert imported materials into consumer goods; they include various food products, beverages, textiles, footwear, furniture, printing and light engineering (mainly maintenance and repair shops to service transport and agricultural equipment).

It is the size of the domestic market which has basically shaped the industrial structure. This market is small, not only because of Libya's limited population, but even more because of the uneven distribution of the people among the main settled regions, divided from

179

each other by large uninhabited areas. Social and economic differences between the nomadic, the settled rural and the urban populations and the considerable differences in their purchasing power and patterns of consumption have further split up the market, restricting the scope for large industrial units and narrowing down the range of products for which local manufacture is economic.

Estimates indicate that, in terms of the value of output, about 50 percent of industrial production refers to food, beverages and tobacco products, 10 percent to textiles, clothing and footwear, another 10 percent to housing materials and furniture and 30 percent to a variety of products and services which are largely based on imported materials. The average unit size of Libyan industry, as measured in terms of employment, is only five workers per establishment.[1] Of the 3,121 enterprises registered under the 1956 census of employment and production, 87 percent employed less than five workers per unit, whereas only 114 units employed more than 10 workers and 25 units more than 50 on an all-the-year-round basis. Recent developments have not changed this over-all picture, although it would appear that there are now more of the larger factory establishments.

Living standards in urban areas have improved considerably during the postwar years (see Chapter 2), and this, together with the large number of foreigners in the country, has resulted in an increase in domestic industrial output. It is extremely difficult to express this increase in statistical terms. Available statistics, which have only recently been collected, are limited in range, incomplete and not always reliable. By way of indication, and to place industrial growth in some perspective, an attempt has been made to present a broad picture in Table 5. These data should, however, be regarded with due reservation. In particular, it is important to remember that a substantial proportion of the increase in imports of consumer goods must be accounted for by the purchases of the growing foreign community, who tend to prefer foreign products to those manufactured locally.

As a rough guess, it might be said that Libyan industrial output has increased by something like 50 percent since 1952. Factory enterprises have contributed to increased output by expanding plant and equipment rather than through the establishment of new undertakings; on the other hand, the smaller enterprises, including craftshops, have responded to rising demand mainly by increasing in numbers rather than by growing into larger units. In general, it would appear

[1] Industry, as defined in this chapter, includes all manufacturing, processing and servicing activities, irrespective of the number of workers employed per establishment.

that, with a few exceptions and within the limits of the present social and economic structure, the strategic points in manufacture and processing are being covered by existing industries. However, few of these industries appear to have been altogether successful in standing up to foreign competition.

TABLE 5 Domestic Industrial Growth as Compared with Import Trends of Selected Commodities

(1954 = 100)

Commodity	Domestic output index (1957/58)	Import index (1957)
Tomato products	330[a]	240
Wrapping paper and cardboard	250[a]	300
Light engineering, repair and servicing shops	250[b]	—
Footwear of leather	250[b]	120
Printing	200[b]	—
Olive oil	175[c]	n.a.[d]
Soft drinks	170[a]	230
Fish products	160[b]	180
Salt	150[e]	—
Textile piece goods	150[b]	200
Tobacco products	150[a]	220
Leather	145[b]	180
Beer	110[a]	190
Alcohol	110[a]	—
Rugs and carpets	100[b]	490
Laundry soap	25[b]	230
Wooden and metal furniture	n.a.	400
Bakery products	n.a.	220
Ready-made clothing	nil[f]	185
Rubber footwear	nil	500
Cement	nil	260
Fruit juices	nil	240
Toilet soap	nil	220
Jams and fruit preserves	nil	200

[a] Based on statistical information collected from public and private sources.

[b] Based on certain growth indicators, derived from import statistics and other sources.

[c] Based on the average output during 1956–59 as compared with 1950–53.

[d] Not available for the comparable period.

[e] Based on actual sales of the Tripolitanian Salt Monopoly.

[f] A small semi-mechanized plant has recently started operation.

The Scope for Industrial Expansion

The future of industry in Libya will be greatly influenced by two factors—the progress of oil operations and the development of Libyan agriculture. Local oil and natural gas production will provide a cheaper source of fuel for industry as a whole and a potential source of raw materials for the manufacture of chemicals and fertilizers. The oil companies themselves moreover constitute an important new market in Libya for certain types of producer and consumer goods. Agricultural expansion likewise is important both because it is needed to supply raw materials for the processing industries and because increased farm income will provide a larger market for manufactured goods.

Apart from oil production itself and its derivatives the growth of Libyan industry must be directed mainly toward meeting the requirements of the domestic market, at any rate for the time being. The scope for developing exports of manufactured goods will be severely limited since, by and large, Libyan industry does not seem to possess the comparative cost advantages which would enable it to compete successfully in nearby foreign markets. Later on, there may be possibilities of producing petrochemical products for export to other parts of Africa and the Middle East, but this is probably a rather distant prospect.

Labor costs per unit of output in Libyan industry are rather high, and they are continuing to rise in response to the upward pull exerted on wages and salaries by the operations of the oil companies. This and the scarcity of traditional industrial skills in Libya are factors tending to favor the growth of capital-intensive rather than labor-intensive industries. The amount of capital per person employed in factory industries in Libya already looks high by comparison with most underdeveloped countries, and this tendency may well be accentuated in future.

The nature of the local market favors an industrial structure consisting mainly of small units. This has certain disadvantages. For example, it limits the scope for specialized management, it restricts industry's bargaining power in buying and selling and it narrows possibilities for government contracts. On the other hand, a small industry structure is well suited to the mobilization of small savings and makes less exacting demands on managerial skills. Faulty investment decisions resulting in loss of capital will have less serious repercussions on the economy as a whole if the undertakings are small. Further, small industry contributes to the growth of a business middle class which is a valuable element in society.

All in all, there appears to be no reason to expect any very striking change in the pattern of manufacturing industry in Libya as a result of the discovery of oil. It is quite illusory to suppose that Libya can suddenly be turned into a highly industrialized country, or that large-scale industrial undertakings can now be profitably established in the country. We have already mentioned the establishment of a small oil refinery as one of the more immediate possibilities. More significant from the employment point of view will be the boost given by oil exploration and development to the building and civil engineering trades and to the road transport industry. Servicing facilities for automotive equipment will have to be expanded, and it might eventually be economic to assemble certain types of such equipment locally. There may also be certain other types of producers goods for which demand will now be large enough to justify local assembly or manufacture—items of office equipment, for example, furniture and metal containers.

The manufacture of cement is one industry for which the prospects have certainly been improved by the discovery of oil, both because cheaper fuel will now be available and because there is likely to be a considerable demand for cement in connection with oil company operations. At least two private projects for establishing cement plants were being considered at the beginning of 1960, one in Tripolitania, the other in Cyrenaica, but it is not clear to the mission whether sufficiently detailed surveys have yet been made of local raw material supplies to enable firm plans to be drawn up. Deposits of limestone and clay are known to exist together at Homs in Tripolitania and near Benghazi in Cyrenaica, but at the time of the mission's visit in 1959 it was not known whether these would be suitable for the manufacture of quality cement at reasonable cost. Trial borings at Homs have shown the limestone there to be covered by a heavy overburden of clay which might make them extremely expensive to work. The problem of internal transport also requires careful investigation, since the cost of transporting cement from factory to consumer in Libya might well exceed the freight cost of imports.

As to the demand for cement, imports amounted to over 60,000 tons in 1958, and a fairly rapid increase can be expected over the next few years in connection with the development of oil production. Thereafter the higher level of consumption should be sustained for some time ahead. It is doubtful whether Libya can produce the special qualities of cement used in the construction of oil wells, but there will be large new requirements for shipping terminals, pumping stations, buildings and other installations.

Provided that other conditions are favorable, the prospective volume of demand would appear to be sufficient to justify the establishment of at least one small cement factory and possibly two. The central question therefore is whether cement could be produced and transported to the main points of consumption at costs comparable with imports. Preliminary cost calculations made by the mission cast some doubts on this, but the matter is one that needs careful and expert examination before a definite conclusion can be reached. Before supporting any private ventures the government should satisfy itself that such an examination has been carried out, and that the industry will be able to maintain itself without an excessive measure of protection. Government itself, as a major consumer of cement, has a direct interest in ensuring that domestic production does not result in a large increase in prices.

Study might also be given to the possibilities of making more extensive use of gypsum as a building material, particularly for construction of low-cost housing (see Chapter 14). Considerable deposits of gypsum are located in the Gefara between Azizia and Jefren, and this is a natural asset which might be worth exploiting in view of the shortage of other building materials in Libya. Crushing and processing are comparatively simple, and the initial investment required for the production of, say, 25 tons of gypsum a day would not be very large— possibly in the region of £L 50,000.

The mission believes that there is ample room in present circumstances for the further expansion of the agricultural processing and other light consumer goods industries, and various possibilities are discussed in Annex XIII. Among other things we have suggested continued research into the manufacture of date syrup, the expansion of vegetable canning and the establishment of a tomato paste factory in Cyrenaica. A good case can be made out for the construction of cold storage plants in Tripoli and Benghazi, though the mission has some reservations about the way in which the Benghazi project is being handled (see Annex XIII).

On the other hand, for reasons stated in Chapter 8, the mission strongly advises against establishment of a sugar beet factory and it has considerable doubts about the alternative proposal for setting up a factory simply to refine imported sugar. The scale of operations would almost certainly be too small to make such a factory economic, and it is doubtful if there would be any profitable outlets for the molasses, which would be left over as a by-product. The main uses of molasses are in the manufacture of cattle food, rum and industrial alcohol. Only small numbers of cattle are raised in Libya, there would be little demand for rum, and industrial alcohol can now be more cheaply manufactured from petroleum.

Both the leather and printing industries can be further expanded and we have recommended that they should receive special assistance from the government (pages 197-198). Opportunities for expansion also appear to exist in textiles, soap manufacture and the brewing of beer and soft drinks.

The comments made here and in Annex XII on the possibilities of industrial expansion are by no means exhaustive. They serve rather to indicate the mission's general line of thinking on industrial development and to substantiate its proposals regarding government policies to promote industrial growth, to which we now turn.

Government and Industry

The Libyan Government, in the mission's view very wisely, has left the development of industry almost entirely to private enterprise. Exceptions are the tobacco factory and salt monopoly in Tripolitania, the government printing presses in Tripoli, Benghazi and Sebha and a date-packing plant in Tripolitania, all of which belong to the provincial administrations. Much the largest of these government enterprises is the tobacco factory, which is operated under a management contract with a foreign company. It produces over 600 million cigarettes a year and at the time of the mission's visit employed about 450 workers.

The mission sees no reason to depart from the general policy of relying mainly on private initiative and capital to exploit the opportunities which exist for the further expansion of industry. Government has plenty of other things to do, and other uses for its money, without venturing into industrial operations for which it is seldom well equipped. It is true that in the past Libyan businessmen have usually preferred to invest their money in trade and real estate, which offer safe, quick and high earnings, rather than in agriculture or industry, where returns are slower and often lower. But so far as industry is concerned, the mission found little evidence that sound investment opportunities had been neglected, and the growth of industry under Libyan control in Cyrenaica (and to a lesser extent in Tripolitania) shows that Libyan capital stands ready to participate in industrial ventures if prospective profits are sufficiently attractive. Moreover, since the discovery of oil there has been a noticeable quickening of interest on the part of both Libyan and foreign businessmen in the establishment of new industries in the country.

The immediate danger is probably rather the other way—namely, that the oil boom will encourage hasty and ill-considered private ventures, which will find themselves unable to survive without government support. A number of these ventures are being promoted by foreign firms which are primarily interested in selling plant and machinery for new factories, and proposals from such firms should be viewed with a good deal of suspicion. The government should be extremely cautious about giving any sort of support to projects of this kind unless they are based on thorough investigations carried out by independent consultants. We suggest that it should be one of the functions of the Development Council to examine and advise the Ministry of Finance and the other appropriate authorities on all projects for private industrial investment on which government action is called for. It is in any case essential that the council should be kept fully informed about private investment if it is to draw up sensible development plans for the public sector.

This is not to say that government should play no part in promoting industrial expansion. On the contrary, the mission believes that the Libyan Government should be considerably more active in this field than it has been in the past. Libyan industry has in fact received very little special assistance from government since the war, and it is only lately that positive steps have been taken to improve the conditions under which industry operates.

The role of government in promoting industrial growth requires action on two broad and closely interrelated fronts: the creation of a favorable investment climate for existing and potential entrepreneurs so as to stimulate the exploitation of all available industrial resources; and the removal of physical and other obstacles which stand in the way of the establishment, enlargement and operation of industrial enterprises. Such action should take into account the need to encourage Libyan talent wherever possible with a view to reducing the present state of dependence on non-Libyan entrepreneurship, management and advanced technical skills.

More specifically, the mission recommends that the government should pay particular attention to the following matters:

1. improvements in the machinery for government administration and in the coordination of industrial policies at the federal and provincial levels;

2. simplification of procedures for licensing and registration;
3. more positive measures for industrial promotion, including the provision of technical and financial assistance to industry and the sponsoring of schemes for the training of labor and management; and
4. use of tariffs in place of import restrictions to afford limited protection to selected industries.

Administration of Industrial Policy

The administration of industry is largely vested in the provincial Nazirates of Finance and Economics. The Tripolitanian Administration, which had by and large displayed initiative in taking measures to assist industry, maintains a Department of Marketing and Industries, staffed by an expatriate director and three other officials. This department is also responsible for trade and export promotion, but with such a limited staff and such a variety of duties it is not easy to pursue a consistent and progressive industrial policy. The same applies more strongly to Cyrenaica and to the Fezzan. Moreover, no department of industry at present exists within the federal government, although a few officials are engaged in the administration of federal industrial legislation such as the 1956 law for the promotion of national industries. Consequently, public expenditure for industry (including minerals) during the period 1954/55 to 1957/58 has been extremely limited, amounting in total to only £L 273,000 or approximately 0.5 percent of all public expenditure during this period.

The mission considers it important to strengthen the government administration, both at the federal and at the provincial levels. This will be necessarily a slow process since it will take time to develop the experience required to administer industrial development. The hiring of such administrators from abroad is not a satisfactory substitute, and the mission therefore strongly recommends that a systematic training program be adopted to create a cadre of Libyan officials who will be able to assume in due time responsibility for guiding the industrial development of the country. The mission accordingly suggests that five young Libyan university graduates should be sent abroad for training during the next five years, preferably in an underdeveloped country like Turkey or India with considerable experience in industrial development measures. These trainees should spend at least two years abroad and should receive in-service training in agencies responsible for industrial development. Further, a high-level foreign industrial adviser should be engaged to assume for at least five years responsibility for the industrial development of Libya; he should be located in the Ministry of Finance and Economics and maintain close contacts with the provincial authorities. We have included £L 30,000 in our program of recurrent development expenditures to cover the cost of these two proposals.

The roles of the federal and provincial governments in the administration of industry should be clarified. The present situation in this respect is unsatisfactory insofar as the formulation of policies and their implementation, as well as the execution of specific projects, are carried out both on the federal and on the provincial levels without sufficient consultation or coordination between them. This results in a confusion of objectives, in excessive red tape and duplication of efforts. As a general principle of government administration in this field, the federal government should concern itself primarily with the formulation of policies and with the coordination of programs, including in certain cases the preparation of plans for specific projects. The federal government, in formulating policy, should act in continuous consultation with the provincial authorities, and to this end it is recommended that a consultative committee on industry should be established in conjunction with the new Development Council. This committee should consist of federal and provincial officials and of private citizens conversant with problems of Libyan industry, with UN experts and other foreign advisers included as necessary. It should meet regularly and should operate mainly as an advisory body and as a forum in which to reach agreement on the guiding principles affecting industrial development in the country.

The mission considers that all technical assistance (including the technical services to be provided by foreign specialists in specific trades) should be linked with measures to provide financial assistance to industry. Technical assistance supplied to industry without taking into account economic and financial requirements and repercussions is liable to be wasted whereas, conversely, financial assistance to industry is likely to be most fruitful if it is preceded by careful techno-economic investigations as to the soundness of a project. Further, since Libyan industry is too small to warrant the establishment of a separate industrial extension service, it would seem necessary to concentrate all technical assistance within the proposed industrial development agency as mentioned in the following paragraphs. In fact, this agency should function as the main technical arm of the federal and provincial authorities in their endeavor to promote industrial growth.

Registration and Licensing of Industry

Both in Tripolitania and Cyrenaica a businessman who wishes to establish a factory has to apply to the provincial government for a license, and the issue of licenses is governed in each province by a complicated set of rules and procedures. The federal government has for some time had under consideration a law for the registration and protection of industry which would replace the existing provincial licensing systems, and which would lay down uniform conditions for the granting of industrial licenses throughout Libya.

The mission considers neither the existing systems nor the proposed new licensing law to be well adapted to Libya's needs. As already stated, we believe that government industrial policy should be directed toward the creation of a favorable industrial investment climate, and that government controls and restrictions should be kept to a minimum, so as to give private initiative free scope to participate in the industrial process. It is extremely difficult to administer such controls effectively in a situation in which basic statistical information is as incomplete as it is in Libya, and in which there is such a scarcity of experienced government administrators. Moreover, controls always carry with them the danger that pressure groups may exert an unwholesome influence on government policy, which is detrimental to sound industrial development.

It is argued in support of the proposed law that private investors are inclined to overinvest in a certain trade when a pioneer has demonstrated its profitability, and the establishment of a second tomato paste factory in Tripoli is sometimes cited as an example. The mission, however, did not come across any conspicuous example in which private industry has made basically wrong investment decisions, and private enterprise will usually be in a better position than government to assess the viability of a project in which it has financial stake. Further, we are convinced that industry would strongly resent the power which government would assume under the proposed law to review all documents concerning the operation of the enterprise; such measures are decidedly not conducive to creating a favorable investment climate.

The mission therefore recommends that the licensing of industrial undertakings should be undertaken only when this is considered strictly necessary to implement an important area of government policy—for example, as a means of reserving for Libyan entrepreneurs a larger share in the ownership of industry. It would be sufficient for this purpose to enact an enabling law, which would give the government powers to institute a licensing system for a specific trade or trades if and when the occasion arose. At the same time a simple system of industrial registration should be introduced on a uniform basis for the whole country, with the main objective of assisting the official statisticians to collect, digest and publish statistical information for the use of both the government and private enterprise.

Law for the Development of National Industries

The Law for the Development of National Industries, which was enacted in 1956 and has been applied since 1957, enables the government to grant, under certain conditions, financial and other facilities to existing and to newly established industries with an installed power of not less than ten horsepower and employing at least ten workers. These facilities include (a) exemption from property tax for a period of ten years, (b) exemption from income tax for a period of five years, (c) exemption from customs duties on machinery, equipment and materials for a period not exceeding five years, and (d) payment in instalments over a period of ten years of the purchase price of government-owned land to be used as the site for the establishment of the factory.

The mission was informed that, up to the end of March 1959, eleven enterprises had been granted exemptions under the law; nine of these were controlled by Libyans and two by Italians. In principle, the law appears to be a suitable legal instrument to promote the establishment of new and the expansion of existing enterprises. We would suggest, however, that the administration of the law be simplified and liberalized in intent so as to provide for general instead of selective exemptions. This would cut out a lot of red tape and reduce the time taken between the filing of an application and the announcement of the government's decision—two matters on which the mission heard frequent complaint in Libya, both from the provincial authorities and from private businessmen.

We would also suggest that the law should be extended to cover the smallest enterprises. This could be achieved by interpreting Article 2 of the law in such a way that associations of small enterprises which together employ a certain minimum number of workers, and irrespective of the installation of power-driven equipment, are considered as an industrial enterprise within the terms of the law. Such an extension of the scope of the law would have the additional advantage of promoting the formation of industrial associations of small firms, which would extend their activities into joint raw material supply, collective marketing and other areas where small businesses may be able to benefit from common action.

Further, the mission questions the wisdom of regulating the employment ratio between Libyan and foreign (Italian) workers. It should be recognized that the Italian workers are making a useful contribution to Libyan industry, and that to limit their employment opportunities would be detrimental to the creation of a favorable investment climate. We fully appreciate the government's desire to increase the participation of Libyan workers in industry, but this should be achieved by increasing the relative productivity of Libyan as compared with Italian workers rather than through legislative action.

Foreign Capital Investment

A Law for the Investment of Foreign Capital was promulgated early in 1958. It does not apply to petroleum exploration and exploitation, which is covered by separate legislation. According to this law, a foreign enterprise is considered as such if not less than 51 percent of the total invested capital has been obtained from outside the country. Such enterprises may at the government's discretion be exempted from customs duties, income tax and other federal taxes for such period as the government may decide. Exemption from provincial taxes may also be granted subject to the approval of the provincial government concerned. The law provides further for the free repatriation to the country of origin of the invested foreign capital, of profits and of salaries of the foreign employees. In the event of expropriation, appropriate compensation is assured in accordance with the provisions of the Expropriation Law. An advisory committee consisting of representatives of the federal government, the relevant provincial government and the foreign aid agencies advises the government on the application of the law. The government may impose on an enterprise which benefits under the law various conditions relating to the employment and training of a certain proportion of Libyan personnel, to the participation of Libyan investors in the enterprise and their representation on the board of directors, and to the submission of reports regarding the development of the enterprise. Foreign enterprises established after January 1, 1952, but before the enactment of the law, may qualify for benefits, although not retroactively.

The mission was given to understand that at the time of its visit no foreign firms had been granted facilities under the law. In general, the provisions of the law appear to be soundly conceived, but everything depends on how they are applied, since the act confers wide discretionary powers upon the government. Fears of arbitrary action were expressed to the mission by a number of foreign businessmen, and while we have no reason to endorse these fears, we would strongly urge the government to do everything possible to clarify its intentions with regard to foreign investment and to clear up any prevailing doubts or misunderstanding. Nothing does more to discourage private investment than an atmosphere of uncertainty.

Protection of Industry

Important changes were made in the Libyan customs tariff in 1958 with a view to securing a greater diversification in the rates for various commodities and affording more protection to local industry. As a result, imports of finished products, which are being or can be produced in the country, are subject to rates (specific and ad valorem) varying between 20 percent and 40 percent, whereas imports of industrial raw materials are now free of duty or subjected to modest rates and imports of plant and machinery are taxed at a nominal rate of only 2 percent. The mission welcomes these changes and has no general recommendations to offer on the customs tariff except for a few instances mentioned elsewhere in this report where a further tariff adjustment should contribute to the development of specific trades.

Besides the modest measure of protection provided by the customs tariff, selected industries are shielded against foreign competition through a system of restrictions on imports. The provincial administrations are empowered to impose such restrictions on items listed by the federal government as subject to export and import licensing regulations. The Tripolitanian Administration has restricted imports of a few industrial products, including tomato paste, wrapping paper and, until recently, tiles; the import of shoes in both coastal provinces is subjected to a quota system; and the import of barracanes is prohibited so as to protect the handloom industry in Tripoli and the textile factory in Benghazi. There are no general restrictions on exports except for olive oil in years when the olive crop is insufficient to meet domestic demand.

Since each of the provincial administrations follows a different policy, special measures are required to restrict interprovincial trade in commodities which are subjected to import restrictions in one province, but not in the other. For example, the Tripolitanian Administration has prohibited the import of tomato paste from Cyrenaica where the import of this commodity from abroad is not restricted; on the other hand, the mission understands that the import of sweets from Tripolitania into Cyrenaica is controlled by license in order to protect candy manufacture in the latter province. Apparently there is no legal basis for such restrictions on interprovincial trade.

The mission shares with the government the view that in selected cases the protection of domestic industry against foreign competition is justified, particularly where infant industries require a "running-in period" before they are able to face up to foreign competition. On the other hand, all measures designed to insulate domestic industry from outside market forces are liable, sooner or later, to have an adverse effect on efficiency because incentives are lacking to raise productivity, increase quality, reduce costs and pursue an aggressive sales policy. Such measures are particularly dangerous under conditions such as in Libya where many industrial trades are represented by one or two factories only.[2] The consumer will suffer from higher prices and lower quality which in turn will restrict industrial growth, since domestic consumers will show an increasing preference for substitute foreign products. Moreover, it is extremely difficult to administer such a policy sensibly under Libyan conditions because of the lack of statistical information about the size of the local market and the prospects for its expansion. Finally, the present system of applying restrictions on a provincial instead of on a national basis is liable to be self-defeating since imports banned in one coastal province may be imported through the other (as has happened in the case of soap). This can be, and has been, prevented by restrictions on interprovincial trade, but such restrictions are undesirable in principle since they tend to delay the social and economic integration of the country.

The mission strongly recommends that sole responsibility for the regulation of imports should be vested in the Ministry of Finance and Economics in the federal government; in exercising this responsibility the Ministry should act in close consultation with the provinces. At the same time we suggest that, generally speaking, industries requiring special protection against foreign competition should be assisted by import duties rather than by quantitative restrictions. Tariffs should seldom reach prohibitive levels, and they should be reduced if and when it becomes evident that the protected industry can stand on its own feet.

[2] Examples are the beer, footwear, packing paper, power loom weaving, ready-made clothing and tomato paste industries.

Financial and Technical Assistance

Many Libyan industrialists have interests in trade, real estate and agriculture, and they usually find most of the capital they require for industrial investment out of their own resources, supplemented by funds put up by members of their families and friends. They may also turn to the commercial banks to finance working capital. The banks provide only short-term credit, but successive renewals of overdrafts in practice result in the extension of a limited amount of medium-term credit to industry at rates varying between 7 percent and 10 percent.

While the mission found no clear case in which lack of capital as such had prevented the establishment of an enterprise with reasonably good earning prospects, the lack of an organized capital market in Libya is something of a handicap to industrial development. Moreover, there is no institution to which the prospective entrepreneur can turn for technical advice in establishing a new industry. To remedy these deficiencies the mission recommends that the government should set up an agency to provide both credit and technical assistance for industry.

The mission has considered whether an industrial development bank could be successfully established in Libya. Eventually this might be possible, but we see no justification for such an agency at the moment, and we recommend instead a simpler organizational setup. As indicated earlier in this chapter, the prospects for the establishment of new factory undertakings appear to be rather limited, and industry will probably develop mainly through the expansion of existing industries, including the growth of small workshops into factories. Under these conditions an initial capital outlay of £L 500,000 should be sufficient to provide the financial assistance needed. This would be too small a sum to justify setting up a fully-fledged banking institution with its own independent management, and the mission feels that it would be better to start in a more modest way by establishing an Industrial Credit Department within the framework of the National Bank of Libya—with the proviso that later on, when it is firmly established, the department might be converted into an autonomous agency. The accounts and operations of the department should be kept entirely separate from the rest of the National Bank, and the manager of the department should report directly to the Governor.

The functions of the Industrial Credit Department would be to provide financial assistance to industry and at the same time to serve as the channel through which industrialists could obtain technical advice. The mission attaches great importance to the combination of these dual functions within a single agency. Two highly competent specialists should be employed to manage the department, one an industrial economist with experience in banking and industrial accounting practices, the other an industrial engineer capable of making a general appraisal of industrial projects from the technical angle. In addition, and according to the need for specialized technical services for particular industries, consulting specialists should from time to time be sought from the United Nations or USOM or be engaged directly by the department on a short-term basis to investigate new development possibilities and prepare well worked out projects for prospective entrepreneurs who want to interest themselves in industry. In this way the department would form the nucleus of, and assume prime responsibility for, all technical assistance to industry.

The department should approach its lending operations in a flexible manner and should make available short-, medium- and long-term credit, including underwriting and participation in equity capital if and when sound projects cannot be financed out of private sources or by private banks. In no circumstances should the department put up more than 50 percent of the total capital required. In its financial transactions it should place emphasis not so much on collateral as on the long-term growth prospects of a project, with particular reference to the initiative and technical and managerial skill of prospective borrowers and the capacity of the market to absorb the product. The granting of a loan should be only the beginning of an association between the department and the borrower. Continuous collaboration should be maintained between the two, so as to assist industry in improving the efficiency of its operations. The consulting services of the department should be available to enterprises which are not turning to it for financial assistance, fees being charged for these services when appropriate. In short, the department should in part operate as industrial consultants, who are at present entirely lacking in Libya.

The department should be advised by an investment committee under the chairmanship of the Governor of the National Bank, which would include representatives of the federal and provincial governments, the Development Council and a number of private individuals with industrial experience. Loan operations should be conducted on strict business lines, but the federal government should meet the cost of consulting services. A sum of £L 45,000, or £L 9,000 a year, has been included in the mission's program of recurrent development expenditures for the latter purpose.

Other Promotional Measures

Industrial Estates. The majority of existing factories in Libya are located in unsatisfactory premises, and few are housed in buildings specially designed for the purpose. The mission suggests that the government might consider the establishment of an industrial estate in Tripoli on lines similar to those tried out with success in many other countries. The main purpose of such estates is to provide suitable factory accommodation for small enterprises, sometimes at concessional rates. The estates are equipped with modern amenities, such as electricity, water, sewerage and storage facilities; they also offer a variety of services (e.g., for the maintenance and repair of equipment) which the individual enterprise cannot afford to provide for itself, but which can be profitably supplied to groups of small plants.

The creation of an industrial estate in Tripoli would encourage the transfer of existing plants from overcrowded areas in the center of the city, and this in itself would act as an inducement to the installation of new and modern equipment. At the same time management and labor would obtain a more suitable working environment. A possible site for the estate would be in the compound of the railway station and yards (assuming that the government adopts the mission's recommendation that the Tripolitanian railway should be closed down). This railway complex extends over an area of approximately 30 hectares and has ample accommodation which could in part be easily rebuilt into factory premises. The cost of establishing an industrial estate in this area with accommodation for 30 to 40 plants with a combined labor force of about 500 workers should not exceed £L 20,000. The cost might be increased to about £L 50,000 if the estate were to be located in the newly designated industrial zone in Tripoli. If the Tripoli experiment proves successful, a similar estate could be established later on in Benghazi, and possibly also in Misurata where the former Italian army barracks could provide suitable accommodation.

Management Training Programs. The mission has drawn attention to the low productivity of the Libyan worker. Raising productivity is primarily the responsibility of management, and the mission believes that there is urgent need for better-trained management, especially in the smaller undertakings. The government should help to provide suitable training facilities. At the present stage, it would be much too costly to provide such training in Libya itself, and the mission therefore recommends that funds be made available to enable government officials and small plant managers to receive such training abroad. A sum of £L 15,000 has been earmarked for this purpose in our program of recurrent expenditures. Among the centers providing the type of training required are the Technological University at Delft in the Netherlands, which runs an International Course on Small-Scale Industries, and Stanford University in California, where there is an International Program in Small Industry Management.

Workers Education. In addition to vocational training, attention should be paid to the education of workers in a more general sense. Improvements in labor productivity depend in large measure on the outlook of labor, its aspirations for social and economic progress and its interest in the enterprise in which it is engaged. In this respect there is considerable room for improvement in Libya. Workers often appear to be uninterested in their jobs, there is noticeable lack of pride in workmanship, and absenteeism rates are rather high. The labor movement, developed only since Independence, is still in its infancy. Because of the absence of well-trained and educated leadership and the lack of funds, the trade unions have no programs of education for their members. The Tripolitanian Government provided £L 5,000 in its budget for 1958/59 to support the labor movement, but this money had not been disbursed at the time the mission visited Libya. Considering that the future development of industry depends in large measure on the creation of an intelligent labor force, it is recommended that the government should increase and extend its aid to the movement so as to enable it to make its full contribution to the social and economic progress of the country. Such assistance might include grants to trade union leaders for study abroad and financial and organizational assistance in starting educational programs for the workers. We suggest an allocation of £L 30,000 for this purpose over the five years 1960/61 to 1964/65. The ILO may be able to help in providing advisory services on the planning and organization of workers' education programs, and on techniques of workers' education.

Leather and Printing Industries. The mission considers that there are two industries to which the government should give special assistance in improving skills and introducing modern techniques. These are the leather and printing industries. In respect of the former we recommend that £L 20,000 be spent on measures to promote better curing of hides and skins, £L 35,000 on establishing a pilot tannery in Tripolitania and £L 25,000 on operating the tannery as a production and training center (including the cost of sending two workers abroad for training). To assist the development of printing we recommend that £L 40,000 be spent on an apprentice training scheme in Libya and on a program of overseas training for young Libyan workers. These proposals are discussed more fully in Annex XIII.

Government Patronage of Industry. Considering the limited range of industrial products manufactured domestically, only very few of the government's requirements can be met by local industry. There are, however, two industries which could benefit to an appreciable extent from government patronage, namely textiles and footwear. Annual requirements of shoes and uniforms for the armed forces, including the police forces, are substantial, especially if projected against the limited domestic market. But so far this demand has been exclusively satisfied through import from abroad. There is no reason why the local shoe industry should not be able, with technical assistance, to manufacture boots and shoes for the government that are competitive with imported products, and the same applies to uniforms which could be supplied locally if measures are taken to develop the textile weaving and ready-made clothing industries. The mission therefore recommends that as a matter of policy both the federal and provincial governments should patronize domestic industry in preference to imports, provided that the quality of the local product is satisfactory and its price not more than 10 percent above that of comparable import products.

HANDICRAFTS

Handicrafts in Libya have received a good deal of encouragement from government. Late in the nineteenth century the Turkish administration established in Tripoli the Moslem Arts and Crafts School, which is still doing excellent work to train young boys in a variety of crafts. A few years ago the federal government, assisted by USOM, established a handicrafts center in Tripoli for graduates of primary schools, a small carpetry center for girls was recently set up in Benghazi, and a new project has just been launched (also with the help of USOM) for starting training centers for rug production in Cyrenaica. A crafts development project for the Fezzan was initiated in Sebha in 1957 with the assistance of the ILO, and this is progressing well. Some facilities have been made available by the Tripoli municipality for handicraft shops to be opened in the Suk el Mushir, which has become an attractive tourist shopping center. The Tripolitanian Administration is trying to promote the export of Libyan craft products by participating in various exhibitions abroad; it has also recently organized a handicrafts survey in the province, which should provide useful background information for the formulation of a consistent handicrafts policy.

Traditional handicrafts, as distinct from modern crafts which are the by-products of an advanced industrial economy, have in the past played a relatively minor role in Libya. One reason for this is that, under the Italian occupation, domestic production was unable to compete with cheap machine-made goods, and consumers' preference increasingly inclined toward the modern instead of the traditional product—a trend evidenced today in the sharp rise in imports of machine-made carpets from £L 19,000 in 1954 to £L 59,000 in 1957. A few handicrafts have nevertheless been developed in the coastal towns, including weaving and the working of copper, brass, silver and gold. At the same time the nomadic and semi-nomadic sections of the population have always supplied the bulk of their own simple needs by using wool, hides and skins, date palms and other local materials for the manufacture of clothing, footwear, tents, rugs, carpets, basketware and some pottery.

The large influx of foreigners before and since the war and the rise in local living standards have provided a fresh stimulus to the development of artistic crafts such as hand-woven rugs and carpets, fancy fabrics, leather goods, copper and brassware. It is to the improvement and expansion of handicrafts such as these that the government should now mainly direct its attention with a view to increasing sales to tourists and foreign residents in Libya and possibly exports as well.

A number of obstacles have to be overcome. Techniques are frequently obsolete, raw materials defective and marketing operations inefficient. The mission therefore recommends that, as a first step, the government should send two Libyans abroad for training in the development of artistic crafts, with particular reference to the introduction of improved techniques, design and marketing. Such training should be sought in an underdeveloped country with long-standing experience in this field. When the Libyans return home after completing their training, a specialist should be engaged for about two years to assist them in improving design and finishing and in adjusting Libyan handicraft products to the peculiar requirements of buyers at home and abroad.

The mission further recommends that handicraft emporia should be established in Tripoli, and possibly also in Benghazi, to serve as sales outlets. These emporia would have to be established and operated by the government, and it would be among their functions to fix standards, control quality and fix prices. They might also provide credit to the craftsman by supplying him with materials and tools against payment in kind. As the opening of such emporia is likely to meet with considerable opposition from local merchants, they should operate strictly as commercial undertakings, and their profits should be spent exclusively on measures for promoting handicrafts. They might be assisted by advisory boards consisting of merchants and others interested in the development of handicrafts. A sum of £L 25,000 has been included in the mission's program for the capitalization of the Tripoli emporium and £L 10,000 for the one in Benghazi, which should operate initially as a branch of the Tripoli establishment.

The Government of Tripolitania is planning to set up a center in Misurata to promote the development of carpet making and artistic leather work. This center would combine training with production, marketing and the provision of common facilities for local craftsmen. The eastern province of Tripolitania is the only area in Libya, apart from Tripoli itself, where there appears to be a good basis of traditional skill for building up artistic crafts production. The mission therefore supports this project and has included £L 50,000 in its investment program for its initial capitalization, with an additional £L 15,000 in the program of recurrent expenditures for the employment of a specialist in carpet making to take charge of the work for the first five years.[3] For technical assistance in leather work the center could draw upon the services of the specialist whom we have proposed should be recruited for the development of the leather industry. If the Misurata center could be accommodated in one of the former Italian barracks, initial capital costs could be substantially reduced.

Encouragement should be given to the formation of cooperative societies of craftsmen for the joint supply of raw materials and for the establishment of common production facilities. In this way groups of craftsmen could purchase their raw materials at lower prices and could also take advantage of the facilities available to larger industrial units under the law for the promotion of national industries. No industrial cooperatives have yet been established in Libya, and we suggest that a start might be made by organizing two such societies, possibly

---

[3] The mission is not familiar with the details of the scheme for starting training centers for rug production in Cyrenaica and has accordingly not made any provision for it in its program. The scheme has been launched since the mission's visit and is being financed by USOM. It is understood to include the use of new carpet designs, the supply of modern equipment (which it is hoped that the artisans will subsequently be able to purchase) and the creation of centralized marketing facilities.

one for weavers and the other for brass and copper workers in Tripoli.

As modern industry expands, a group of craftsmen is gradually developing to meet the demand for such servicing activities as the repair of bicycles, cars, radios and other electrical equipment. Their main problem is a lack of technical skill and of modern power-driven tools. Craftsmen of this kind can be expected to play an increasingly important role in the national economy, and they should be given every assistance in improving their efficiency. Such assistance might include special courses of instruction provided by the technical schools in Tripoli and Benghazi and hire-purchase facilities for obtaining modern equipment. We have included a sum of £L 30,000 for a hire-purchase scheme in our investment program, and we suggest that its implementation should be entrusted to the proposed Industrial Credit Department of the National Bank.

The promotion of handicrafts is particularly important for the Fezzan, where opportunities for establishing factory industries scarcely exist. We have devoted a special section in Annex XIV to a discussion of the problems involved in improving and expanding the existing Fezzanese handicrafts and in developing new ones.

FISHERIES

Fisheries is one of the least developed economic pursuits of the country, and its contribution to the national economy is negligible. Since no inland fishing is possible, all fishing is done at sea and takes one of three forms: inshore fishing operated by small boats; tunny fishing with traps; and sponge fishing by various methods such as diving and dredging. An appreciable number of foreign fishing boats of Italian, Maltese and Greek origin are exploiting the fishing grounds over the continental shelf off the Libyan coast; their catch, however, is not landed in Libyan ports but is sold in their respective home countries. Foreign companies, predominantly Greek, are licensed to fish sponges in Libyan territorial waters. The only contribution which these foreign enterprises make to the national economy is the payment of license fees to the government and the expenses incurred when their boats and crews use shore facilities in Libyan harbors, mainly Benghazi and Tripoli.

The total Libyan catch is estimated at 2,000-2,500 tons of fish a year, consisting half of sardinella and some quantities of high quality fish (e.g., red mullet and stone bass) and half of tunny. Approximately one-third of the catch is sold fresh, mainly in Tripoli, where the foreign community provides a good market for this product. The other two-thirds are processed in a number of small and primitively equipped plants located along the Tripolitanian coast, which produce salted and canned fish for domestic consumption and export. There are no fish processing plants in Cyrenaica. Only very limited quantities of sponges, varying between 10 tons and 20 tons a year, are landed in the country and processed for export abroad. The yearly value of the fish catch may be roughly estimated at £L 200,000-250,000 and of the sponge catch at £L 30,000 or about 0.5 percent of the present national product in total. The labor force engaged in the industry is currently estimated at around 1,000, but most of these are employed on a seasonal basis. This applies particularly to the tunny fish industry where some 500 workers find employment for two or three months of the year only. There are probably only about 200 fishermen who derive their main livelihood from fishing, the others being largely part-time workers. Since earnings are low (probably not more than 40 piasters per working day), there is a tendency for fishermen to seek other more remunerative and stable employment. A large proportion of the skilled workers in the industry, including the skippers of the boats, are foreign residents of Italian or Maltese origin.

The administration of fisheries is a responsibility of the provincial governments, whose main concerns are the collection of statistical material and the issuing of licenses for fishing boats. The only active step taken at present to help the industry is the distribution of salt at concessional rates to the fish processing industry in Tripolitania. The port manager in Tripoli, who has been made responsible for the fisheries administration in that province, is operating on the basis of fishery legislation dating from the Italian occupation, which was partly amended during the British military administration; no legislation has been enacted since Independence. These Italian regulations were revoked in Cyrenaica during the war and have not been replaced by more up-to-date legislation.

As early as 1952, the Libyan Government tried to find ways of exploiting the maritime resources of the Mediterranean, and with the assistance of the FAO two surveys have been made of the position of Libyan fisheries, their potential for development and the measures to be taken to promote their growth.[4] The government now has a project

[4] C. D. Serbetis, *The Fisheries of Libya*, FAO Report No. 18, Rome, 1952; Francois Bourgois, *The Present Situation of Libyan Fisheries*, FAO Report No. 817, Rome, 1958.

under consideration for developing trawler fishing on an enlarged scale.

Although the Mediterranean cannot be considered to be as rich in fish as the highly productive fishing grounds in the North Atlantic and the North Pacific, Libyan fisheries could certainly participate on a much larger scale than at present in operations on the continental shelf along the Libyan coast. In any case, this is a resource within reach of the Libyan economy that is not being fully utilized and that could, moreover, be used to improve the nutrition and health of the Libyan people, whose diet is currently unduly concentrated on a few items such as cereals, vegetables and a little meat. The mission therefore gives full support to the government's policy of developing the fishing industry. It must be recognized, however, that Libyans are not by inclination or tradition a seafaring nation, nor at present do they eat much fish. Unlike industry, where people can be trained in a comparatively short time into skilled operators, fishing is a way of life as well as an occupation, and its development will require considerable, concentrated and prolonged efforts on the part of the government. When embarking on a policy for fishery development, the government should be prepared to pursue a long-term promotional program in respect of training, the provision of fishery services, marketing and measures to popularize fish as a part of the Libyan diet. In the latter connection, it is most important that prices be reduced. The present price of fish, while somewhat lower than that of meat, is extremely high in relation to the earnings of the Libyan workers.[5]

As a preliminary to the institution of a program for the promotion of Libyan fisheries, the mission recommends the creation within the proposed Ministry of Agriculture and Natural Resources, of a Department of Fisheries, which would be responsible for formulating policies and projects. Since the success of a fisheries program will depend in large measure on the development of ancillary facilities to handle, process and market the catch (e.g., cold storage, fish canning and waste processing plants), the Fisheries Department will need to establish close liaison with the Ministry of Finance and Economics. For the same reason we recommend that responsibility for fisheries administration in the provinces should be transferred from the Nazirates of Communications to the Nazirates of Finance and Economics. In the administration of fisheries, the federal government should confine itself

[5] The average price of fish on the Tripoli market in 1958 was 20 piasters a kilogram against 34 piasters a kilogram for mutton and 32 piasters a kilogram for beef. Prices of both commodities are subject to wide seasonal variations.

strictly to the formulation of policies, including the drafting of special projects in cooperation with the provincial authorities, whereas the provincial governments should be made fully responsible for their execution.

A high-level fishery specialist should be appointed by the federal government for at least five years to take charge of the over-all development of fisheries in the country; he should maintain close contacts with the provincial authorities in the execution of any development program. Further, to create a cadre of qualified staff, four young Libyans should be sent abroad for two years' training in the administration of fishery development policies and programs. The total cost of this program is estimated at £L 40,000 for the period 1960/61 to 1964/65 inclusive.

Various suggestions for the regulation of sponge fishing and for assistance to the tunny fishing industry are made in Annex XV. So far as the development of surface fishing is concerned, this requires a thorough reorganization of the present primitive fishing methods. In particular, the use of dynamite for catching fish must be stopped since this is not only inefficient, but also destructive. The catch achieved by present methods is probably as low as 10 kilograms per man-fishing day, as compared with about 100 kilograms per man-fishing day in other Mediterranean countries where more modern techniques are employed. Only if productivity in the Libyan industry can be greatly increased will it be possible to boost sales by lowering prices and thereby make fishing a sufficiently attractive occupation for the workers.

As the mission sees it, the main objectives of a Libyan fisheries policy should be:

1. to teach the fisherman his trade, including navigation, the operation of motor trawlers, use of modern gear and methods of preserving the catch;
2. to provide the wherewithal for the establishment of small Libyan fishing enterprises, whether organized on an individual or a cooperative basis;
3. to build up a bigger market for fish in Libya both by ensuring larger, more regular and cheaper supplies and by stimulating demand through a sales promotion campaign; and
4. to encourage the participation of foreign firms in developing a Libyan trawler fishing industry.

The Libyan Government is considering a scheme for equipping and training a fisherman's cooperative in Benghazi, starting with the purchase of a motor trawler in 1960 and building up the venture step by step into a self-supporting enterprise. FAO is understood to be willing to provide technical assistance in establishing a vocational training center for Libyan fishermen, complete with demonstration equipment. The mission believes that it should not be difficult to reconcile these two approaches, and that an attempt should be made gradually to build up in each of the two coastal provinces a small fleet of Libyan trawlers under private or cooperative ownership, with the initial capital provided by government on a loan basis, with skilled instructors acting as skippers of the boats and with the crews consisting of young Libyans. Government should assist the operators to develop their own marketing organization or to make suitable arrangements with private traders for the sale of the catch.

The details of the scheme would have to be worked out between the government and FAO. Alternatively technical assistance might be obtained directly from one of the western countries with long experience of the fishing industry, possibly on the lines of the Norwegian fisheries training project in India. The scale of the project must depend essentially on the availability of technical assistance and on the response of Libyan fishermen. There is at present no body of skilled labor to draw on, and it may well be that better results will be obtained by the training of young men who have little previous experience of fishing than by the retraining of those already used to primitive methods of inshore fishing. The spread of education since Independence has resulted in much higher rates of literacy amongst the young than amongst those in the middle and older age groups, and this is a very important consideration when it comes to imparting skills in such fields as engineering and navigation.

While the mission does not underestimate the difficulties involved in introducing modern techniques of fishing in Libya, it sees no reason why the experiment should not be successful so long as fishing can be shown to pay. Close attention will therefore have to be given by government to improving the present arrangements for marketing, storage and processing of fish as well as to developing a taste for fish amongst the Libyan population.

One of the principal reasons for the high price of fish in Libya at present is that the market is controlled by a small number of merchants, who are able to keep the prices paid to the fisherman down and the prices paid by the consumer up. One or two foreign firms have tried to enter the market by developing their own trawler business in Libya, but their efforts have received no support from government, and they have been abandoned. The mission strongly recommends that the government should reconsider its policy in this matter. More competition in the supply of fish will help to bring prices down and encourage consumption of fish, thereby in the long run serving the interests of the Libyan fishermen as well as of the Libyan consumers. Moreover, foreign firms can provide employment for Libyans and help to train them in modern fishing techniques. As we see it, the best prospect for the development of a Libyan fishing industry lies in combining a government-sponsored training and production project with the maximum encouragement of private fishing enterprises.

The suggested fisheries project will have to be worked out in detail before its financial cost can be assessed. Tentatively the mission suggests that capital expenditures on the project over the next five years might amount to about £L 100,000, and that the net costs of operation, after taking into account proceeds from the sale of the catch, might average about £L 10,000 a year, excluding the cost of technical assistance, which we have assumed would be granted under one of the UN or other aid programs. The figure suggested for capital expenditures assumes the provision of four trawlers at a cost of £L 20,000 each, plus ancillary equipment and buildings costing another £L 20,000.

SUMMARY OF PROPOSED EXPENDITURES

The recommendations made in this chapter in respect of industry, handicrafts and fisheries would entail a total capital outlay in the public sector of about £L 800,000 over the five years 1960/61-1964/65. Further, *additional* recurrent expenditures would have to be carried on the budgets of the federal and provincial governments to the extent of another £L 71,000 a year, or a total of £L 355,000 over the five years. Details are as follows:

(£L '000)

	Five-Year Total	Annual Average
Capital expenditures		
Industry		
Industrial credit	500	100
Industrial estates	50	10
Pilot tanning plant	35	7
Handicrafts		
Tripoli and Benghazi emporia	35	7
Misurata training-cum-production center	50	10
Hire-purchase scheme for modern crafts	30	6
Fisheries		
Purchase of trawlers and other equipment	100	20
Total capital expenditure	800	160
Additional recurrent expenditures		
Industry		
Government administration[a]	75	15
Management training	15	3
Labor training	30	6
Curing and tanning	50	10
Printing	40	8
Contingent reserve for overseas training[b]	15	3
Handicrafts		
Government administration	25	5
Misurata center	15	3
Fisheries		
Government administration[c]	40	8
Operation of development project[d]	50	10
Total additional recurrent expenditures	355	71

[a] Includes £L 30,000 for the training of Libyan officials and the employment of an industrial adviser; also £L 45,000 for the consulting services to be provided by the Industrial Credit Department of the National Bank.

[b] Suggested as a reserve fund for training Libyans abroad in various industrial techniques according to need; should cover one-year training for 10 persons.

[c] Includes £L 15,000 for the employment of a trawler fishing expert to take charge of fisheries administration and £L 25,000 for the training of Libyans abroad.

[d] Allowance for initial losses that may be incurred during the five years in the operation of a trial fisheries project.

CHAPTER 10 *THE TOURIST TRADE*

Libya's Attractions for the Tourist

Libya has three different types of attraction for visitors from Europe and North America, who are the mainstay of the international tourist trade. First, nature has endowed it with a sunny climate, mild in winter and seldom excessively hot on the coast even in mid-summer; with a long Mediterranean coast line and numerous sandy beaches; and with a variety of landscapes, including desert, oases and mountains. Second, history has left behind a legacy of interesting monuments ranging from Greek and Roman antiquities through Islamic architecture to the battlefields of World War II. Third, Libya's life has a distinct mixture of African and oriental flavors which are reflected in the customs and dress of the people, in the town and village market places, in the mosques and in the Bedouin encampments in the desert.

The factors in Libya's favor as a tourist center are strengthened by the current trend for European tourists and Americans traveling in Europe to move south in search of the sun, a trend which has made the Mediterranean more and more the main center of international travel. Traditional holiday resorts in Italy, France, Spain, Yugoslavia, Greece and other Mediterranean countries are becoming increasingly overcrowded during the summer season and are generally too well known. Tourists are therefore looking for somewhere different to go, preferably "off the beaten track," and Libya could well satisfy this new pioneering spirit. Air transport, moreover, is bringing distant countries within easier reach than before of European and American tourists. The wide-spread use of charter flights, organized by travel agents or specialized companies, is making long-distance travel cheaper than it used to be and more accessible to middle-income groups. In 1958, for example, German air charter companies alone carried 58,000 tourists to the Mediterranean area.

Tourists from Germany, Scandinavia, Holland, Belgium, Switzerland, the United Kingdom, other countries in Northern Europe and Italy probably constitute the most promising tourist market for Libya to tap in the near future. The obvious line for the development of the tourist trade in Libya is to concentrate in the first place on attractive beach resorts equipped with modern hotels for visitors arriving by air or sea and to provide good facilities for local excursions to places of historical, scenic or cultural interest, especially the classical sites at Leptis Magna and Sabratha in Tripolitania, and at Cyrene, Apollonia and Tolmeta in Cyrenaica. Air trips to the Fezzan and other desert oases might be fitted gradually into this pattern.

At present few genuine tourists bring their cars to Libya, partly because vacations are seldom long enough for extended road travel, partly because of the high cost of transporting cars overseas and partly because of the political difficulties in the way of road travel along parts of the North African coast. Ultimately private motoring may become a more important element in Libya's tourist trade, but for the time being it is largely confined to foreigners who are residents in the country for fairly long periods.

Present Pattern of Libyan Tourism

Libya's actual tourist business is not very large. Statistics based on frontier checks indicate that about 38,000 nonresidents entered and left the country in 1958, and that a further 32,500 passed through in transit. About half the total traveled by air and most of the rest by sea. The great majority originated from countries in Europe and North America, but visitors from Tunisia and Egypt were also important.

Libya's figures are very slightly higher than those of neighboring Tunisia, but very small in comparison with the millions of tourists who visit countries on the European side of the Mediterranean every year. In fact, given the boom in Mediterranean tourism, neither Libya nor Tunisia has succeeded as yet in gaining more than a very small share of the trade.

Moreover, most of the nonresident visitors to Libya are not genuine tourists or holiday makers, but air crew, diplomats, businessmen, oil company staff, members of visiting missions, archaeologists, relatives of military personnel and so forth.[1] Indeed, on the basis of some

---

[1] In accordance with usual United Nations practice, the tourist is defined in this report as any person traveling for a period of twenty-four hours or more in a country other than that in which he usually resides (subject to the exception mentioned below). Persons who stay there for more than twelve months should be considered as immigrants and not as tourists. The same applies to members of the armed forces stationed in the country. However, visitors ashore from a sea cruise or a cruise by land are considered as tourists, even when they stay less than twenty-four hours.

statistics for 1955, it would appear that less than one-third of the non-resident visitors fall into the tourist category. This is not to say that the other categories of visitors are unimportant from the point of view of developing the tourist industry in Libya. On the contrary, they provide a continuous flow of visitors throughout the year, thereby reducing seasonal fluctuations and helping to support the hotel trade in the off-season. In addition, the large numbers of foreign troops, diplomatic personnel and oil company employees stationed in Libya for longer periods constitute a valuable basis on which to build up hotel and catering facilities and other amenities.

Objectives of Libyan Tourist Policy

The main purpose of developing tourism is to provide additional income and employment for the Libyan people. Tourism benefits not only the hotel, catering and transport trades, but also shopkeepers, wholesale merchants, local industries and handicrafts.

The tourist trade can also become an important source of foreign exchange earnings. No reliable statistics are available of either the gross or the net foreign exchange earnings of Libyan tourism in recent years, but there is no doubt that Libya has been spending more on foreign travel than it has been earning from it. If full advantages are taken of the opportunities for attracting more tourists to the country, the balance should be reversed.

There are too many uncertainties involved to attempt to forecast what contribution the tourist trade might make to Libya's economy in future years. The mission believes that the *potential* for the development of tourism in Libya is considerable. But many things have got to be done by government and private individuals if this potential is to be fully and rapidly exploited.

Difficulties to be Overcome

Present hotel accommodation in Libya is lacking both in quantity and quality. Few of the existing hotels are well maintained or have properly trained staff, and not a single hotel is located on a beach. Public transport facilities within the country are rather limited, and the absence of rest-houses and good eating places makes road transport over long distances uncomfortable.

Notwithstanding these deficiencies, prices for rooms and meals in the best Libyan hotels are generally well up to the levels of first-class hotels in European tourist resorts, and none but the best hotels in

Libya can offer the foreign tourist the comforts and conveniences he expects. Charges for car hire in Libya are likewise high. Libya is not therefore a cheap country for the foreign tourist, and he has no special incentive to go there on this account. This seems to be the main reason why cruise travel predominates. It is at present not a paying proposition for European travel agents and tour operators to convey regular groups of tourists to Libya by charter plane and keep them in the country for one or two weeks. Both Tunisia and Egypt offer cheaper rates and hence a more remunerative field for activity. One of the main things that Libya has to do to become competitive in the Mediterranean travel market is to grant substantial price reductions for the accommodation of parties.

Numerous and complicated entry and exit formalities are a serious handicap to the promotion of the tourist trade. Rapid progress has been made in Europe in recent years with the removal of restrictions on international travel, including the need for visas, and European tourists are frequently irked by the more exacting passports and customs formalities in Libya. Nor can they understand why it should be necessary to undergo passport and customs examination while traveling inside Libya from one province to another, as at present between Tripolitania and Cyrenaica.

Foreign travel agents also complain about the difficulties of organizing excursions to the main places of interest in Libya, especially to the Roman and Greek antiquities. In particular, they feel the need for more trained guides speaking several languages. Arrangements for welcoming foreign tourists in Libya therefore have to be improved. A proper organization should be built up to take charge of all activities connected with travel in Libya such as renting of cars, buses and planes, provision of meals, entertainments, guided tours and so forth. Existing travel agencies might be entrusted with this job, but it should be carried out under the supervision of the provincial tourist offices.

Finally, there is not as yet any real awareness in Libya of the value of tourism to the country, either among federal and provincial authorities or among the public at large, which is still far from being "tourist-minded." If Libya wants to develop tourism, it must spare no efforts to make the country as attractive as possible to foreign visitors. The truth must be faced that international tourism is a highly competitive business. The tourist normally has many countries to choose from, and he will only go to Libya if he finds what Libya has to offer more attractive in the circumstances than what is offered by other countries.

The mission believes that all the difficulties and shortcomings mentioned can in time be overcome by the joint efforts of the Libyan authorities and those engaged in the tourist trade. Some of the things which might be done in Libya to encourage tourism are indicated in the following paragraphs.

Expansion of Hotel Accommodation

Priority should be given to the expansion of hotel accommodation. At the time of the mission's visit there were only about 1,160 beds available in hotels suitable for foreign tourists, and many of these were more or less permanently reserved for the use of air crews, oil company employees and official visitors. Indeed, the mission itself was made very much aware of the shortage of hotel accommodation by the difficulty it had in obtaining rooms in Tripoli at short notice. It is true that accommodation in neighboring Tunisia is not very much greater, but three new hotels are already under construction, and plans are being carried out for adding 2,000 new beds to existing accommodation. Another North African country, Morocco, already offers between 7,000 and 8,000 beds in first-class and good second-class hotels. Accommodation in such countries as Italy and Spain is, of course, on a vastly larger scale.

A few new hotels, all rather small, have been completed in Tripoli and Benghazi since the mission's visit, but accommodation is still far from adequate to meet the demand in Tripoli. Discussions have now been going on for well over a year with various foreign hoteliers interested in building a modern hotel outside the city, and the idea is apparently supported in principle by both the federal and provincial governments. Yet all sorts of difficulties have been allowed to delay the successful conclusion of negotiations, and nothing had been decided when the mission was last informed of the position in February 1960. This is most discouraging, particularly as an International Fair is due to be held in Tripoli in 1962.

As the trend of Mediterranean tourism shows an increasing preference for group travel, new hotels must be built large enough to cater for parties. A capacity of at least 100 beds, and sometimes more, is indicated for the main tourist centers. Such hotels should be designed to meet all the requirements of the international traveler. There should normally be a sufficient number of rooms with bath, spacious public rooms, a restaurant and bar, heating in winter, air-conditioning in summer and a swimming pool. Well-trained staff speaking several languages is essential.

With the exception of some newly-built establishments, all the existing hotels in Libya are publicly owned—mostly by the municipalities, which put their hotels out to tender at regular intervals (usually every 10 years). This is a very unsatisfactory system. The highest bid tends to be accepted regardless of the professional qualifications of the bidder, while the experienced hoteliers at present running some of Libya's best hotels hesitate to invest more money without a guarantee of continuing the management after expiration of the limited lease. The mission therefore recommends the institution of new arrangements for tender under which offers should only be accepted when made by professionally trained hoteliers, and management should be unlimited in time so long as the hotel is operated successfully.

Every effort should be made to reduce the cost of hotel operation and to improve the quality of service offered. In this connection the mission strongly advises that the hotel trade should be exempted from the regulations of the labor law of 1957 relating to hours of work, under which the working day is limited to eight hours and overtime is payable for extra duty. As experience in a number of other countries has clearly shown, such restrictions on hours worked add greatly to the cost of running hotels and lower the quality of service (e.g., by limiting the hours at which visitors can get meals). Some tourist countries, including Switzerland, have special regulations for working hours in the hotel business.

Another matter requiring attention is the training of Libyans in catering schools and hotels abroad, for which use might be made of UN fellowships and bilateral aid from foreign governments. For a long time ahead, however, it will be necessary to employ foreigners in key posts in hotels, and the mission considers that it would be to Libya's advantage to adopt a more liberal policy in granting permits for the employment of foreign hotel staff.

If suitable encouragement is given by the government along the lines indicated above, the existing Libyan hotel interests should be ready and able to provide most of the capital needed for the modernization of the leading hotels in Tripoli and Benghazi. Additional capital might be provided by the government in appropriate cases through the proposed Industrial Credit Department of the National Bank (see Chapter 9). Some of the hotels need to be made more luxurious and brought up to Riviera standards with swimming pools and other amenities; standards of cooking could also be improved to great advantage in some cases.

For the construction of the new hotels required, every effort should be made to attract foreign investment. Foreign hotel and transportation interests would be particularly welcome as investors because they are well placed to secure part of their own clientele. To attract foreign investment the mission recommends that the Libyan Government should be ready to offer special tax concessions on the lines of those offered to industry under the law for the investment of foreign capital.

If difficulty is experienced in getting foreigners to invest capital in hotels in Libya, the government should try as an alternative to find qualified foreign hotel concerns which might be interested in operating hotels under a management contract on lines tried out successfully in some other Mediterranean countries. In such cases the capital has to be put up either by the government or by private local interests. We have made no specific provision for this in our program, but we have assumed that funds will be available to finance such investment if a suitable arrangement can be worked out. After detailed study of a proposition put forward to the Libyan Government recently by a group of foreign businessmen, the mission is satisfied that a well-run first-class beach hotel outside Tripoli, possibly costing somewhere in the region of £L 350,000, could be made into a paying proposition. Of course, this judgment holds good regardless of who puts up the capital, but experienced foreign *management* is necessary at this stage.

The most urgent need for new hotels is in Tripoli, and at least one beach hotel of the type mentioned above should be built close to the city, possibly with as many as 300-400 beds. Consideration might also be given to construction of a second beach hotel, which would be rather smaller and less expensive. Meanwhile, as a first step toward increasing hotel accommodation in the city, the mission suggests reconversion to its original use of the "Melograno," which was built in 1938 as an annex to the Grand Hotel and is used today as a residence for government officials and their families.

Benghazi is the only other center in Libya besides Tripoli where there is steady demand for hotel accommodation throughout the year from visiting officials, foreign missions, oil companies, air crews and so forth. The hotel situation there at the time of the mission's visit was far from satisfactory, but three new hotels were under construction as a result of private initiative, and these have since added, or will add shortly, between 250 and 300 new beds. Even so, there may still be room eventually for a beach hotel outside the town catering especially to holiday makers and to the employees of oil companies operating in Cyrenaica.

Opportunities for the profitable operation of hotels outside Tripoli and Benghazi are very much more limited in present conditions, and direct action by government will probably be necessary in the first instance to develop the facilities required to encourage tourism. A network of nine small hotels was established by the Italians in Tripolitania at Homs, Zliten, Misurata, Cussabat, Zuara, Garian, Jefren, Nalut and Gadames. The majority of these establishments have since been closed down, and the few still in operation are in poor condition. Only the hotels at Homs and Gadames would be suitable as holiday centers, and the mission suggests that the federal government should provide funds for these to be renovated and reopened. Management might be entrusted to existing hotel interest in Tripoli on a contract basis. The federal government might also provide capital for renovation of some of the other country hotels to serve as rest-houses for tourists traveling around Libya. Initially, most of these country hotels and rest-houses could be expected to operate at a loss, and this would have to be covered out of public funds.

The country hotels in Cyrenaica (at Cyrene, Apollonia, Derna, Tobruk and Beida) are in a rather less run-down condition than those in Tripolitania, but there is still need for better maintenance. Occupancy of existing hotels in Cyrene, Derna and Tobruk is very low, and efforts should be made to attract more patrons from amongst foreigners resident in Libya by improving the amenities. The mission has suggested elsewhere in this report (Chapter 12) that the deep-water anchorage at Ras el Hilal between Apollonia and Derna might be developed as a landing place for cruise ships. If this project turns out on closer examination to be feasible, the possibility of building a medium-sized beach hotel nearby would also be worth consideration. However, no immediate action is suggested since it will inevitably take several years to open up this area to the tourist trade, and existing hotel accommodation is more than adequate in quantity to meet present needs.

The desert oases of Libya, most of which lie in the Fezzan, offer a potential tourist attraction. Travel to the oases, especially to the more colorful ones like Gadames and Murzuk, would have a special fascination because so few countries in the world are able to offer similar attractions. If these can be coupled with rapid transport and reasonably good accommodation, they might become a useful addition to the other attractions that Libya has to offer. As for accommodation, the fortresses left behind in a number of these oases by the former Italian and French administrations might be converted into tolerably good rest-houses or hotels. Travel during the fall and the spring, and also perhaps during winter, could be organized on the basis of round-trip tours for groups and parties if the air companies will cooperate in such a venture. The government might be able to encourage this type of tourist trade by offering inducements in the form of low rentals on public buildings used as hotels, duty-free import for hotel supplies, special income tax concessions and improved maintenance of landing strips. The mission, however, would suggest implementation of this project at a somewhat later stage after facilities for the promotion of tourist traffic in the coastal areas are better established.

Transport Facilities

Improvements in facilities for getting to Libya and for traveling around inside the country will naturally be of assistance to tourism. Existing air services from Europe to Libya and within Libya between Tripoli and Benghazi appear to be adequate, and there is no reason to doubt that the airlines will be ready to provide additional services to meet any major increase in demand for travel over these routes. Private enterprise should also be given every encouragement to promote internal air travel. Special charter flights organized by one tourist agency at Easter 1959 to take parties from Tripoli to Gadames and back were apparently successful, and more desert trips of this kind can be visualized in future, especially if the hotel at Gadames is renovated and put back into use.

Cruise ships are another potentially important source of tourist traffic. In 1958 transit cruises brought approximately 4,000 tourists to Tripoli, and although the stay is generally limited to one day, appreciable sums of money are spent on handicrafts and souvenirs and on visits to Leptis Magna and Sabratha. Brief visits of this kind are of considerable value in making Libya better known to tourists, and contacts with the foreign companies running cruises should be actively promoted. One travel agency organized a series of cruises in 1959 which allowed passengers to stop over in Tripoli for one or two weeks, and arrangements of this kind might well be extended in future.

Tourist travel by road within Libya is essentially a matter for private enterprise. It is most important, however, that the authorities should allow tourists free choice in making use of the means of transport available, and that public interference should be limited to cases where action is needed to protect the tourist's interests (e.g., the regulation of taxi fares). An example of inappropriate government intervention was provided while the mission was in Tripoli in March 1959, when an edict was issued by the provincial government that buses would not in future be allowed to enter the port area to meet tourist ships. The idea behind this edict was understandable, namely to help the local taxi and horse-carriage drivers to secure more custom. But the right way to do this is to attract more tourists to the country and not to impose irksome restrictions which are liable to keep them away by causing inconveniences and adding unnecessarily to the costs of their visit.

Road traffic between Libya and Egypt and between Libya and Tunisia is very light. Few European tourists are likely to be interested at present in motoring from Libya to Egypt because of the distances involved, but something might be done to encourage motoring between Libya and Tunisia, which would be in the interests of the tourist industries in both countries. As one step in this direction, we suggest the construction of a small government rest-house with facilities for eating on the Libyan side of the Tunisian border. Use could also be found for a good rest-house at Marble Arch which lies on the coast road approximately midway between Tripoli and Benghazi. The capital cost of such rest-houses should not exceed £L 10,000 each.

Other Amenities

In addition to hotels, good restaurants or cafes serving Libyan as well as European food are required at all the principal places of tourist interest and at intervals on the main roads. A number of cafes have been established by the tourist authorities (e.g., between Barce and Derna in Cyrenaica), but they are poorly kept and have little but packaged and canned goods to sell. Tourists also want varied facilities for sports (swimming, sailing, fishing, tennis, golf, horse-riding, hunting and pigeon shooting) and amusements (cinemas, night-clubs, casinos, displays of Libyan music and dancing). Only Tripoli and Benghazi can hope to offer a comprehensive range of sporting activities and entertainments, but some variety is required in the smaller tourist centers such as Cyrene.

The two existing casinos in Tripoli and Benghazi attract a good deal of custom from foreign residents and visitors and provide a valuable source of income for the municipalities and the provincial departments of tourism. Provincial and municipal taxes on the gambling proceeds, at present 50 percent, might with advantage be raised to 60 percent, which would not be out of line with European practice and would yield additional revenues for the promotion of tourism.

Antiquities and museums are an essential feature of Libyan tourism, and by helping to maintain the classical sites and to continue excavations the federal and provincial governments are contributing to the promotion of tourism. Public expenditures on antiquities and museums have been running at the rate of around £L 45,000 a year. This amount might well be increased to enable more rapid progress to be made with the excavations at Leptis Magna, Sabratha, Cyrene, Apollonia, Tolmeta and other sites where considerable areas of great potential interest are still unexplored. The mission therefore recommends that an *additional* allocation of £L 15,000 a year be made for this purpose by the federal government. At the same time entrance fees to antiquities and museums (commonly only two or three piasters) should be considerably increased. This is a very small item in the budget of the foreign resident or tourist, and having come all the way to Libya he can easily pay at least 10 to 20 piasters for admission to such unique attractions as the ruins at Leptis Magna and Cyrene. (Concessionary rates could be charged for special groups, including Libyan students.) Additional revenues raised in this way should be reserved for the use of the provincial departments of antiquities.

Simplification of Formalities

Simplification of present immigration formalities is one of the most important steps that has to be taken to develop tourism. Following the example of Tunisia, the mission suggests that visa requirements should be abolished for tourists coming from Western Europe and North America, wherever possible on a reciprocal basis. Visas for other nationals should be granted without charge at the frontier or airports. At present the visitor has to make a written declaration for customs in respect of his personal effects, and the same procedure is required for import and export of currencies. We would suggest that in both cases examination be confined to personal questioning, with written declarations only asked for in special cases. It is a great advantage if customs officers, police officials and other staff at frontier posts can speak foreign languages, thus making visitors from abroad feel welcome, and language training for these officials could be arranged by the respective government departments.

Organization of Tourism

The promotion of tourism is at present mainly the responsibility of the provincial governments in Tripoli and Benghazi, while there is also a federal Director of Tourism and Fairs in the Ministry of National Economy. As in many other fields of government action, there is no clear division of function between the federal and provincial authorities and little coordination of their activities. None of the departments concerned appears to be equipped with adequately trained staff, and publicity is poorly handled. In the mission's view, a radical reorganization of the whole machinery is essential if real progress is to be made with promotion of the tourist trade. Both the federal and provincial governments might consider engaging advisers with expert knowledge of the travel business.

As the mission sees it, the federal government should concentrate on four main tasks:

1. Laying down general policies for tourist development in Libya covering such matters as entry and exit formalities, concessions to foreign investors and financial assistance to private hotel operators.
2. Providing capital assistance to the provinces for the construction or renovation of government hotels and rest-houses and for improving amenities (especially antiquities), such assistance carrying with it the responsibility for ensuring that the sums allocated to the provinces are spent in the ways intended.
3. Representing Libyan tourism abroad by giving information to potential visitors, and at a later stage by engaging agents to undertake publicity campaigns in selected countries.
4. Cooperation with other Mediterranean and Middle Eastern countries in reviewing common travel problems, eliminating frontier restrictions and organizing joint publicity campaigns.

The proposal to hold an International Fair in Tripoli in 1962 lends urgency to the tasks of improving the amenities for tourists in Libya and of overhauling the administration of tourism. Timely preparations have to be made for the reception and accommodation of visitors, careful thought must be given to the selection of exhibitors, much work has to be undertaken on the site and so forth. The success of the Fair could do much to enhance Libya's reputation as a tourist center; equally, any shortcomings in the organization of the Fair itself, or of the amenities provided for visitors, could have the opposite effect.

Summary of Proposed Expenditures

It is difficult to estimate with any precision the public expenditures that would be entailed in carrying out the recommendations in this chapter because much will depend on the type of arrangements made for financing construction of the new hotels proposed. The aim should be to induce private enterprise, Libyan and foreign, to put up as much as possible of the capital required for hotels, transport and other tourist facilities. On the assumption that the government will not have to finance the building of large new hotels, and that any public money required for improvement of existing hotels in Tripoli and Benghazi will be provided through the proposed Industrial Credit Department of the National Bank, we suggest the following program of government expenditures on tourism and antiquities for the five-year period 1960/61 to 1964/65:

(£L '000)

	Five-year total	Annual average
Capital expenditures		
Restoration of country hotels and rest-houses	130	26
Construction of new rest-houses on coast road	20	4
Additional recurrent expenditures		
Increased allocation for antiquities and museums	75	15
Initial losses on operating country hotels and rest-houses	50	10
Organization and publicity	125	25
Total Development Expenditures	400	80

First priority should be given to the expansion and improvement of hotel accommodation in Tripoli and Benghazi. The suggested program for the renovation and reopening of country hotels and rest-houses in Tripolitania and for improvements to existing publicly owned hotels in Cyrenaica should be carried out in stages over a period of five to ten years, priority being given to putting the hotels at Homs, Misurata, Jefren, Gadames, Cyrene and Derna into better shape. The allocation of £L 130,000 contained in the above capital budget should be sufficient for this purpose. At a later stage, work might be undertaken on renovation of other hotels in Tripolitania and possibly on the construction of desert rest-houses in the Fezzan.

We have suggested elsewhere in this report certain other expenditures which are primarily designed to encourage tourism. In particular, money has been included in the programs for roads and ports to finance a possible scheme for the development of Ras el Hilal as a calling place for tourist ships. This scheme, if it proves feasible, should make the main tourist attraction of Cyrenaica much more easily accessible to foreign visitors.

CHAPTER 11 *ELECTRIC POWER*

Organization of Power Supplies in Libya

The supply of electric power is the most important public utility in Libya. Gas is at present of minor importance; a private company provides a piped supply in Tripoli and also produces bottle gas for cooking and heating. Considerable sums have been involved in recent years in the expansion of electricity supplies (see Chapter 3), and details of the existing facilities are set out in Annex XVI.

Very little electric power is consumed in Libya in comparison with other Middle Eastern countries. There are no big industrial undertakings, and the total power sold by public utilities in 1958 amounted to less than 67 million KWH. The mission was not able to obtain a complete record of the output of existing private power plants, but has evidence that it amounts to less than a third of that of public utilities.

By far the largest public utility is that known locally as Tripoli Power, which sold 42 million KWH of electricity in 1958, or roughly two-thirds of the total for the whole of Libya. This undertaking was formerly owned by an Italian company, *Societa Electrica Commerciale Industriale* (SECI), but in 1956 the federal government purchased roughly 70 percent of the shares with funds provided as a grant by the LARC, SECI retaining the other 30 percent. The price paid was about £L 1,120,000 ($3.14 million). The LARC also lent about £L 300,000 ($928,000) to the undertaking for working capital, including the purchase of stocks of fuel and spare parts from SECI. The undertaking has two power stations in Tripoli, as well as small units at Homs and Misurata.

An independent public corporation has now been set up to run Tripoli Power. The chairman of the board is a senior official of the federal government, and there are six other members, two nominated by the federal government, two by the provincial government and two by SECI. The first meeting of the board was scheduled to take place early in 1960.

The other public power plants in Tripolitania are owned and operated by the municipalities (except that at Jefren, which is owned

222

and operated by the State Property Department), but they are maintained by the Nazirate of Public Works. Electricity supply undertakings in Cyrenaica and the Fezzan are owned and operated by the provincial Nazirates of Public Works. Except for Tripoli Power, which has been operating at a small profit, none of these undertakings keeps commercial accounts or is run on strict business lines. Electricity in Cyrenaica covers its operation costs, though not its capital charges. All the smaller plants in Tripolitania and the Fezzan are heavily subsidized.

Tripoli Power

Tripoli Power has two generating stations (one steam and one diesel) with a combined installed capacity of a little over 18,000 KW, but the "firm" capacity is at present somewhat less than 12,000 KW as some units are old and some of the boilers are being rehabilitated. Output and sales have both risen rapidly in recent years. From 1953 to 1958 the annual average rate of growth was over 10 percent, and the peak load in summer has reached nearly 9,500 KW.

About 44 percent of the power sold in 1958 was for lighting and domestic power, 39 percent for agricultural and other pumping and the rest for industrial purposes. Demand, however, greatly exceeds present capacity, and the undertaking has had to refuse connections and to resort to load-shedding. The tariff structure is complex, the charges for agricultural pumping being below the cost of supply, while those for industrial power are disproportionately high. This and the load-shedding explain why many factories, and even farms, have installed their own diesel plants.

Plans for the expansion of the undertaking were put forward five or six years ago, but the federal government had difficulty in securing a loan to finance the work. As an interim measure, the LPDSA placed orders in the United Kingdom for a 1,350 KW diesel generator and a 5,000 KW turbo-generator. The cost of these two units, including installation charges and consultants' fees, was about £L 200,000, and both are now in operation.

An offer by an American firm to supply two new 10,000 KW turbo-generators and miscellaneous ancillary electrical equipment was made to the Libyan Government in 1956, and early in 1957 the government signed a contract with this firm for $3.65 million on a deferred payment basis. No provision was made for the purchase of boilers to supply steam to the new generators. The U. S. Government subsequently agreed to finance the project, and early in 1958 the LARC engaged a firm of American consultants to design the plant, order much of the equipment and supervise construction and installation. Orders for boilers and certain other equipment were placed by these consultants in 1958 with American suppliers. At no stage does it appear that the Italian management responsible for operating the undertaking was fully consulted about the details of the expansion scheme.

The generators and some of the other equipment manufactured in the United States were ready for delivery in 1958, but at that time no decision had been made on the construction of a new power house. As a result, the equipment remained in the United States, where substantial expenses were incurred for storage and insurance. It was not until the summer of 1959 that agreement was reached between the Libyan Government and the U. S. Development Loan Fund on a further loan to finance the construction part of the project. The contract for the power house and installation of the plant was then let to another American firm, and the work is now proceeding. It is due to be completed some time in 1961.

In 1956 consultants to the firm supplying the generators estimated the total cost of the expansion scheme, including transmission and distribution facilities, at £L 3.7 million. More recently, early in 1959, the consulting engineers to the LARC re-examined the scheme and, allowing for the provision of much additional equipment and further consultants' fees, revised estimates of total costs upwards to £L 4.9 million or just under $14 million. Some of the work to which this latter figure relates has already been carried out by the management and financed out of the earnings of the undertaking, and it is impossible to say at this stage exactly what the final cost will be. It is clear, however, that costs have been greatly increased by the confusion and delays in planning and replanning of the project.

U. S. funds have so far been made available for the project as follows (amounts in U. S. dollars):

Private U.S. suppliers credit being repaid by LARC	3,648,550
Loans made in 1957 under U.S. Mutual Security Act	3,500,000
Loans made in 1959 by U.S. Development Loan Fund	5,000,000
Total	12,148,550

For the purpose of estimating investment in electric power facilities during the five years covered by its program, the mission has assumed that about £L 2.75 million (just under U. S. $8 million) of the expenditures on Tripoli Power will be incurred after March 1960.

In view of the fact that the costs of the expansion scheme have been so high (probably not much less than U. S. $700 per KW installed, transmitted and distributed), it seems unreasonable that the resulting capital charges should be passed on in full to the new corporation. The mission therefore recommends that part of the capital invested in the scheme should be written off by the government.

The expansion now in hand should, when completed, take care of the power needs of the area served by the undertaking until 1966 or later, though severe shortages may be experienced during the next two years pending installation of the new units. It is difficult to forecast the rate of growth of demand once supplies are fully available, as much will depend on the reliability of supplies and the schedule of charges. Agriculture is now making the greatest demand on power for electric pumping, but the cultivated area around Tripoli is being overexploited, and the water table is falling in places at an alarming rate (see Chapter 7). New areas in the vicinity are available for cultivation, and the demand for power will depend in part on how quickly these are developed. The demand for domestic lighting and power may slow down after a brief spurt to meet the recent pent-up demand, but if the foreign community in Tripoli should continue to grow as a result of oil operations or for other reasons, domestic and office consumption of electricity might well continue to rise quite fast with the extended use of air-conditioning and other electrical appliances. Once regular supplies are assured and the tariffs for industrial power adjusted, there is likely to be a big increase in the demand for industrial power as factories switch over from private plants to the public supply.

Costs of generating and distributing power in Tripoli (22 milliemes or 6.2 U. S. cents per unit sold in 1956-58) are very high in comparison with costs in other countries. This appears to be mainly due to the antiquated and ineffecient generation, transmission and distribution facilities, and a marked improvement should be looked for when the new plant comes into operation. Costs must certainly be reduced if Tripoli Power is to put its own finances on a sound footing and at the same time play its proper role in the development of the economy.

A great deal of essential work has already been done on the distribution system to reduce line and other losses and, in the power house, to reduce power consumption by the station auxiliaries, so that the total percentage loss was reduced from 24.75 percent in 1951 to 17.74 percent in 1958 and from 9.01 percent to 5.93 percent in these two sources respectively. Similarly the thermal efficiency at the Marconi steam station was improved from 10.75 percent in 1951 to 15.49 percent in 1958 and at Miani from 28.41 percent (for the diesel units) to 32.96 percent. Fuel costs for these stations fell in the same period from 9.373 milliemes per KWH generated to 5.206. All this reflects credit on the management.

The mission recommends that, as one of its first tasks, the new corporation should arrange for a full investigation to be made into the future financial position of the undertaking in the light of the most recent development, including the discovery of oil in Libya. This investigation should provide material for, and be followed by, a re-examination of existing tariffs with a view to devising a tariff structure that is adapted both to the development needs of the area and to the financial interests of the corporation. This re-examination should be undertaken in consultation with the federal and provincial governments and should have regard particularly to the urgent need to restrict the exploitation of groundwater in the Tripoli Quadrangle (see Chapter 7). If it is the government's policy to subsidize agriculturalists or any other class of users, the subsidy should be clearly identified, and government should reimburse the corporation to the same extent as it would reimburse a private company required to sell goods at subsidized prices.

The mission welcomes the decision to set up an independent corporation to administer the affairs of Tripoli Power. The responsibilities of the corporation should be confined for the time being to Tripoli Power, but the mission believes that it should in due course take over the management of all other public electricity undertakings in Tripolitania and, ultimately, in Cyrenaica and the Fezzan also. It is most important that appropriate arrangements should be made for the board to consult regularly with the main agricultural, industrial and other consumers.

Efficient operation requires that the undertaking should continue to be run on commercial lines and kept clear of political influences. Management and senior technical posts will have to remain in the hands of foreigners until Libyans are trained to replace them; the manager himself should be a qualified engineer. The corporation should regard the institution of a training scheme for Libyans as one of its most urgent tasks. Even so, it is likely to be at least 10 years before any Libyan can be expected to gain the necessary technical qualifications and practical experience to occupy any of the senior engineering posts.

Finally, the mission considers it to be of the utmost importance that the management of Tripoli Power—and of other public utility undertakings—should be given full responsibility for day-to-day operations and should be consulted on all proposals affecting future development of the undertaking. If consultants are employed to advise on particular problems, they should be employed by the corporation and not by any outside body or government department. Failure to observe these principles and the resulting confusion of responsibilities as between consultants and management have largely contributed to the delays and excessive costs of the present expansion scheme.

Other Power Stations

Benghazi is the most important center of power supply in Libya after Tripoli. Its power station was commissioned in 1952, replacing a station damaged in the last war, and it ran until 1955 in parallel with the existing plant left by the British administration. It has now an installed capacity of 6,150 KW, which is all diesel-driven and has all been financed by one of the foreign aid agencies. Output has increased from nearly 10 million KWH in 1953/54 to 16.84 million in 1957/58 or at the rate of more than 11 percent a year. The undertaking is managed by the Cyrenaican Nazirate of Public Works, as are also all the 14 other public power plants in the province. The revenue from all these undertakings has increased from £L 135,030 in 1953/54 to £L 337,710 in 1958, but working profits (excluding depreciation, for which no allowance is made) have decreased from £L 38,140 to £L 22,900 in the same period. There are various reasons for this decrease, including failure to adjust tariffs, short collection of revenue, redundant staff and other administrative deficiencies connected with noncommercial management.

The peak load of the Benghazi plant (4,020 KW in 1959) indicates the need for more installed capacity if growth in demand continues at anywhere near the present rate of 11 percent a year, and £L 180,000 has been provided for this in the mission's program of capital expenditure. The technical management is excellent, but too many staff are employed on maintenance and bill collection.

There are 18 small publicly owned power stations in Tripolitania, 14 in Cyrenaica and 3 in the Fezzan, but none of these is under commercial management. Most of the larger towns in Tripolitania are poorly served and improvements in policy direction are indicated almost everywhere. Where the utilities are both owned and operated by the Public Works Department, a reasonably high standard of technical efficiency appears to be maintained, but where there is a dual control, conditions are generally unsatisfactory.

As explained in Annex XVI, many of the installations in the existing power stations are old, the distribution systems are not always in good condition and hours of operation have not been fixed to meet the requirements of potential users. The mission has allowed in its program for the expenditures needed to put matters right, to replace obsolete plant and to provide for future expansion. Assuming replacement of 50 percent of the existing obsolescent plant and a growth of demand at the rate of 10 percent a year for half the installed capacity (other than Tripoli Power) and 5 percent a year for the rest, the capital investment required will be about £L 650,000 in the five-year period. This includes £L 180,000 for the Benghazi power station.

Summary of Proposed Expenditures

The recommendations which we have made in this chapter, together with projects already being undertaken, would entail a total capital outlay in the public sector of £L 3,400,000 over the five years 1960/61 to 1964/65. This total would be distributed as follows:

(£L '000)

Project	Five-year total	Annual average
Expansion of Tripoli power	2,750	550
Other power stations in Tripolitania	250	50
Benghazi electricity supply	180	36
Other power stations in Cyrenaica	220	44
Total	3,400	680

CHAPTER 12 *TRANSPORT AND COMMUNICATIONS*

Existing Transport Facilities

On the whole, the existing transport system serves the needs of the country adequately (see map facing next page). Internal transport is carried mainly by road, supplemented by air travel for passengers between the three provincial capitals. The railways play a very minor role and are run at a loss, while coastal shipping traffic is negligible. Privately owned motor vehicles are responsible for the bulk of the road traffic, but government also owns and operates large fleets of motor vehicles. Many of the main roads carry little traffic.

The bulk of Libya's foreign trade passes through the port of Tripoli, the only other harbor of significance being Benghazi which serves a much less densely populated hinterland and at present handles less than a fifth of the country's trade. There are a number of minor ports along the coast which were developed before the coming of road transport and were used in Italian times, especially for military purposes, but are now largely abandoned except by fishing vessels. The only natural harbor of any size in Libya is at Tobruk, but this is far from the main centers of population, industry and trade.

There are two main international airports, Idris airport near Tripoli and Benina airport near Benghazi. Both are served by a number of foreign airlines, with regular connections between the two on six days of the week. There is a landing strip at Sebha, which is connected with Tripoli by a weekly service. A number of other good landing strips exist in the desert at such places as Gadames, Hon, Brak and Ghat, and temporary strips have been laid out by the oil companies at many of the exploration sites. Important military airfields are located at Wheelus Base outside Tripoli (leased to the United States) and el Adem near Tobruk (leased to the United Kingdom).

THE RAILWAYS

Two small single-track narrow-gauge (95 centimeters) railways operate in Libya—the Tripolitanian railway (178 track kilometers

229

with 42 kilometers of sidings and branches) and the Cyrenaican railway (164 track kilometers with 20 kilometers of sidings and branches). Both railways operate at a considerable loss. The total loss in the six-year period 1952/53 to 1957/58 was £L 339,288, and revenue from goods transported in this period was only £L 60,908, or an average of £L 10,151 a year. Passenger revenue amounted to rather over two and a half times the goods revenue. The loss moreover has been increasing year by year, and in 1958/59 the deficit on the operations of the Tripolitanian railway alone amounted to over £L 50,000.

In an endeavor to attract traffic to the railways, passenger fares and goods tariffs have been kept very low (well below cost), but the railways have still been unable to compete effectively with road services, which in most countries have proved to be more economical for carrying traffic over short distances. The most modern rolling stock consists of one diesel car, dated 1939, in Tripolitania and a diesel locomotive and a diesel car, both dated 1952, in Cyrenaica. Most of the rest of the rolling stock is said to date from 1890 to 1929. In these circumstances it is creditable that the railway administrations have managed to keep the railways operating at all.

The mission has considered the possibility of rehabilitating and extending the railways, but this would cost a lot of money and in view of the very low volume of traffic offering, the limited area served by the railways (less than one-half percent of Libya or 10 percent of the settled area) and the deficit character of the railways operation, we have been forced to the conclusion that the railways, as such, should be closed down. The area served by the Libyan railways is for the most part served also by good roads, and as the roads will have to be maintained anyhow, there is no need to have the railways as well. Abandonment of the Tripolitanian railways would not increase the truck traffic on the parallel roads by more than a few percent. In Cyrenaica, once el Abiar is linked by road with Barce, as recommended elsewhere in this report, the roads should have no difficulty in carrying all the passenger and goods traffic that is likely to be offered in the area at present served by the railway.

The mission's detailed recommendations, and some of the facts on which they are based, are elaborated in Annex XVII. The existing sidings and branches in and around the port areas of Tripoli and Benghazi would be retained under our proposals, but they would be managed by the port authorities concerned. Valuable use can be made of railway lands in Tripoli, and to a lesser extent in Benghazi, if these are made parts of town improvement schemes.

The total staff employed by the railways at the time of the mission's visit numbered 265 in Tripolitania and 240 in Cyrenaica. Of these, 29 were salaried employees of government and could be transferred to other departments. There should be no great difficulty in finding alternative employment for the remaining skilled (197) and unskilled (279) labor as there is strong demand for both types of labor in Libya at the present time. No major problems have arisen in the past when the labor force on the railways has been curtailed. However, some employees may suffer hardship if their services are suddenly terminated, and we suggest that appropriate compensation should be made to all on the basis of so much for every year of service, special consideration being given to exceptionally hard cases.

ROADS AND ROAD TRANSPORT

The Road System

The most important road in Libya is the federal coast road, 1,822 kilometers in length, which runs the whole way from the Tunisian to the Egyptian border, passing through Tripoli, Benghazi and many of the smaller towns in Libya, including Zuara, Zawia, Tagiura, Homs, Zliten, Misurata, Sirte, Agedabia, Barce, Beida, Lamluda, Derna and Tobruk. It was constructed by the Italians between the wars and has a black-top surface throughout its length. There is a second link between Barce and Lamluda known as the "south road," which is 141 kilometers long. The other federal road, at present little more than a desert track in some places, runs from a point on the coastal road 120 kilometers south of Misurata through Sebha, the capital of the Fezzan, to Ghat near the Algerian border. The total length of this Fezzan road is about 1,250 kilometers, and there is a branch 260 kilometers long running from Uaddan to Sirte. The first section from the coast to Sebha (620 kilometers) is being improved and provided with a black-top surface, and the work is scheduled to be completed by the end of 1961.

In addition to the federal highways, Tripolitania has about 1,200 kilometers of black-top and macadamized roads and Cyrenaica about 500 kilometers (see map). The main groups of oases in the Fezzan are linked by rough roads and desert tracks. In fact, practically all the towns and villages of Libya, including the desert oases, are accessible by motor vehicle, but the going is sometimes extremely rough, and four-wheel drive is necessary in parts of the desert.

Road Maintenance

During the six years 1954/55 to 1958/59, about £L 4.3 million was spent on rehabilitating Libya's road system, which deteriorated badly during and after the war. Some of this work, especially in Cyrenaica, consisted in repairing war damage, but the bulk of it was for expensive reconstruction of long lengths of road where maintenance had been neglected for years. The majority of the black-top roads are now in fairly good condition, and it may be taken that practically all war damage has been fully restored except that a few large bridges on the coast road are still in the process of being rebuilt.

The mission urges that in future adequate budget provision be made for renewals of road surfaces, and that not less than 10 percent of the surfaces on all black-top roads in Libya be renewed every year for the next few years, the renewal of surfacing and upkeep of existing roads being given priority over new construction as a matter of government policy. Provision for road maintenance and renewals should be included in the ordinary budgets of the federal and provincial governments, and not in the capital budget, and all the money voted by Parliament under this head should be used strictly for the purpose indicated and not diverted to new construction, as has sometimes happened in the past. It should be the function of the Auditor General to draw the attention of Parliament to any cases in which this rule has been infringed. We would also suggest that, when Parliament is asked to approve expenditure on a new road, the consequent maintenance liability should be indicated for its information.

Annual requirements for expenditure on maintenance and renewals of surfacing during the next five years are estimated at about £L 900,000 divided as follows (amounts in £L):

Federal roads	484,500
Tripolitania	252,700
Cyrenaica	148,900
Fezzan	15,200
Total	901,300

The basis of this estimate is explained in Annex XVIII. It does not include any provision for maintenance and renewals to the new Fezzan road now under construction; this will fall due after 1965 and will add about £L 120,000 to the annual bill for maintenance and renewals.

New Construction and Improvements

At present there is very little traffic or potential traffic justification for new roads. Exceptions are a new road parallel to the railway from el Abiar to Barce (54 kilometers), some short lengths of new road near Tripoli (30 kilometers) and some local roads in Cyrenaica (40 kilometers). Short lengths of new agricultural feeder roads are also required in all provinces. The Tocra-Tolmeta road now under construction should be completed, but the mission sees no justification, economic or other, for the proposed extension of this road to el Hania and Susa, especially as this would involve very costly engineering in places where the escarpment comes down close to the sea.

As already noted, a decision has been taken by the Libyan Government to construct a new black-top road from the coast road south of Misurata through Hon to Sebha in the Fezzan. This decision cannot be justified on economic grounds, but the mission understands that important administrative and political considerations may be involved. A contract for the construction of this road has been let to a Libyan contractor, and work is already in hand. The value of the contract is understood to be £L 1.9 million, with a 10 percent allowance for escalation, although it is clear that the actual cost of completing the road to the agreed specifications would be well in excess of this figure. It was brought to the mission's attention that no instrument survey of the alignment was made before the contract was let, and for the reasons stated in Annex XVIII we feel that the procedures followed by the government in this matter are open to criticism.

Costly roads built to remote oases might facilitate administration, but would be of little benefit to the majority of the inhabitants. The mission considers that, when the main demand is for passenger movement between remote points, the need would best be met in these modern days by an air service (discussed below). Interest has been shown by the Fezzan Government in the construction of a new hard-top road linking Hon and Uaddan directly with the port of Sirte. It is just possible that this might have been a better route for the Fezzan road than the more westerly one actually chosen from Hon to Bugren on the coast road, but now that work on the latter has begun, there can be no economic justification at present for the construction of a second main road between Hon and the coast. If more traffic between the Fezzan and Cyrenaica should develop as a result of oil operations or for other reasons that cannot be foreseen, the question of improving the track linking Hon to Sirte might be reviewed later on.

The mission has suggested elsewhere in this report investigation of the possibility of developing Ras el Hilal in Cyrenaica as a calling point for tourist ships. If such a scheme were undertaken, the Cyrene-Susa-Derna road and the branch to Lamluda should be widened and improved, as also the approach road to the Ras el Hilal jetty. Similarly, widening and improvement of the roads Tripoli-Azizia and Suani ben Adem-Bivio Ghiran in Tripolitania and the approach road to Solluk in Cyrenaica should be undertaken if the railways are closed down as recommended. The only improvements needed to the federal roads are the straightening of some bad curves, reconstruction of bridges damaged during the war, and the upgrading and surfacing of short stretches in difficult country, and near oases beyond Sebha.

The cost of the new construction and improvements recommended above, including the road works connected with the Ras el Hilal scheme, is estimated at about £L 650,000 divided between the provinces as follows (amounts in £L):

Federal roads	200,000
Tripolitania	250,000
Cyrenaica	150,000
Fezzan	50,000
Total	650,000

We recommend that this program should be spread over the five years 1960/61 to 1964/65. Financial provision will also have to be made during this period for completion of the work on the Fezzan road as far as Sebha. The contract cost of the project was about £L 2 million, but the mission does not know how much of this will have been spent by March 1960, or what additional allocations will be needed over and above the sum contracted for. We have therefore made a notional allowance of £L 2 million for expenditures during the next five years. If this amount is added to the program recommended by the mission, the five-year total for new construction and improvements comes to £L 2,650,000.

Road Administration

The mission found some lack of coordination in the road programs of Libya. Each province seemed to be going its own way to satisfy local needs, while the federal government concentrated its attention on federal roads. No all-Libya policy direction exists on road widths, permissible vehicle weights and dimensions, road curves and gradients, traffic regulations or road maintenance standards. Nor are provincial and federal road projects always properly coordinated at the technical level (see Annex XVIII).

Much could be said in favor of appointing one administration to take responsibility for road policy and road upkeep in the whole country. By modern standards there is not enough road work at present, or in the foreseeable future, to employ fully four agencies with their technical staffs. In particular, there appears little justification for employing a federal agency to construct and maintain federal roads in the provinces. We recommend therefore that the Federal Roads Department should in future concern itself only with matters of policy, including the preparation of projects, and that federal road works should be handed over to the provincial Nazirates of Public Works for execution under federal direction, with the federal government retaining control over the use of funds.

Road Transport

Passenger and goods vehicles operated by private enterprise serve traffic needs at a not unreasonable cost. The number of civilian motor vehicles in the country increased by more than two-thirds between 1955 and 1959 and the consumption of motor fuel was more than doubled (see Annex XVIII). Traffic has expanded further during the past year with large fleets of trucks carrying supplies for the oil companies.

Licenses to run buses in Tripolitania are auctioned, and the fares are moderate. So are the charges for the carriage of goods, owing to keen competition among operators induced by the present surplus trucking capacity. The standards of vehicle maintenance are, however, generally low and suggest the need for a re-examination of the motor vehicles act and better enforcement of suitable regulations. Statistical information on motor vehicles is not readily available in convenient form, and there was no evidence that traffic counts with estimates of tonnages were being taken by the road authorities to determine road improvement needs.

An examination of road and rail traffic statistics showed that even an unsurfaced road running parallel with a section of the railway did compete successfully because of the limitations of the railway under "short haul" traffic conditions. Judging by past experience, when no difficulty was experienced in moving large quantities of imported food-grains in time of drought, and judging by the present keen competition in the trucking industry, the mission has no doubt that the existing trucking capacity in the country is ample, and that no difficulty will be experienced in transporting goods by road if the railways are abolished.

For both Tripoli town and Tripolitania, the rights to run buses are auctioned once every nine or ten years. The competition induced by such auctions is claimed to make for good service and low fares, but the argument cannot be accepted as valid in view of the long period between auctions. The mission recommends that auctions should be abolished, as they introduce an element of uncertainty which is detrimental to the growth of transport. Experience in the more developed countries indicates that bus and road haulage operations can best be controlled by rules and regulations issued under a comprehensive motor vehicles act. Under such an act, applications can be made to operate on specified routes at specified fares or rates, and licenses are granted in accordance with the needs of the route in question. Once an operator has been granted a license, his rights are safeguarded so long as he fulfills the conditions laid down. If a dispute arises over the granting of licenses, appeal can be made to an Appeal Tribunal. This system, if properly administered, allows scope for competition in the initial bidding for licenses, and also, where more than one carrier is licensed to operate over the same route, in the quality of service provided. On the other hand, it guards against the dangers of unregulated competition.

Government Transport

As a legacy from the times of the Italian occupation and the British army administration after World War II, the federal and provincial governments still own and operate fairly large fleets of private cars, landrovers and trucks. It was difficult to ascertain the total numbers of such vehicles as they are owned by many different departments and by the police, but the number owned and maintained by the Nazirates of Communications alone is over 770, and total expenditure by these departments on the purchase and operation of vehicles is more than £L 500,000 a year.

Operations are not conducted on commercial lines, and management is frequently subject to day-to-day political interference, particularly with regard to employment of staff. In Cyrenaica, for example, almost three workers are employed by the Transport Department of the Nazirate of Communications for every vehicle on the road. This is two and a half times as many as in Tripolitania. The proportions of new vehicles ordered each year and of vehicles scrapped are abnormally high, even allowing for the extremely adverse conditions under which many of them operate on desert tracks. In the Fezzan, for example, the life of a landrover is seldom more than a year and frequently very much less.

All in all, the present system appears to the mission to be very wasteful and inefficient, and we recommend that urgent attention be given to reorganizing the provision of government transport on a more economical basis. Where practicable, private enterprise might be invited to supply transport for the government on a contract basis. There appears to be ample capital available in the country for investment in the transport industry, as is evidenced by the surplus truck capacity on the roads. Insofar as operations remain in the hands of the government, workshops should be run on a strictly commercial basis, and sufficient foreign managers and technicians should be employed, as in the private bus undertakings, to ensure high standards of maintenance.

PORTS AND COASTAL SHIPPING

Tripoli

The port of Tripoli handles more than three-quarters of all the country's foreign trade and operates at a substantial profit. Its commercial cargo turnover has more than trebled since 1954, although there has been a decline in military cargoes. It is now handling over 400,000 tons of commercial dry cargo annually (see Table 6), and there is every indication that under present conditions its trade will continue to increase. About £L 500,000 has been spent on rehabilitation and improvements since 1952, and a further expenditure of about £L 325,000 is indicated on rehabilitation, deferred maintenance, buildings and equipment to bring the ports up to standard. The mission endorses the scheme to create a "free zone" in the port as an experiment since the initial cost (£L 65,000) will be relatively small and the prospects for increased trade appear favorable.

The port is run departmentally by the Nazirate of Communications. Its accounts are merged in the Tripolitanian budget and are not kept on a proper commercial basis; operating profits accrue to the provincial government and are not available for financing development of the port. The responsibilities carried by the manager and his assistant (both loaned from the Port of London Authority) are excessive, and there exists no proper machinery for consultation between the management and commercial interests. Efficiency is hampered by the inflexible procedures of governmental control and the difficulty in obtaining authority for expenditures. At the time of the mission's visit, for example, there was no port engineer because of the government's inability under its rules to offer the salary necessary to attract a competent man. With the growth of the port, the existing difficulties of handling cargoes (entailing much overtime employment) will be intensified, and labor problems will increase unless the present rigid rules restricting the freedom of management are relaxed.

The mission is satisfied that a strong case exists for the creation of an autonomous federal authority to run the port on a proper commercial basis with responsibility for financing its own expansion and with appropriate borrowing powers. The mission appreciates that there are constitutional difficulties in creating an autonomous port authority, but considers that, as in the case of the electricity authority, these difficulties can be overcome and suitable arrangements made to compensate the Tripolitanian Administration for its vested interest in the port. We also recommend a change in the present arrangements under which certain privileged users of the port, including the U. S. Government, receive specified facilities free of charge and in return render services to the port for which no charge is made. In order to facilitate good accounting, all services rendered to or by third parties should be charged for, if only by special vouchers which will show the details of the transactions for record purposes.

Benghazi Harbor

The port of Benghazi at present handles rather under one-fifth of Libya's foreign trade. It serves a hinterland with a population of about 300,000, and the amount of commercial cargo passing through the port in the years 1954-58 never exceeded 105,000 tons in any one year. In 1958 it was about 81,000 tons. About 30,000 tons of petroleum products are discharged annually by means of a special pipeline to storage tanks adjacent to the harbor, and varying quantities of military cargo enter and leave the port in accordance with the requirements of the British forces in Cyrenaica (see Table 6). Port revenues are about £L 50,000 a year.

Before the war the Italians developed Benghazi as a naval and military port, and a deepwater harbor was constructed for this purpose (the Outer Harbor on the plan facing page 242). As explained in more detail in Annex XIX, the Outer Mole has since been largely destroyed by the action of the sea and by naval and air action during the war, a process accelerated by defects in the original design, and only the Middle Harbor is now in use. This has two main drawbacks. It is sometimes inaccessible to shipping in stormy weather and it is limited at all times to vessels with a draft of 14½ feet or less, though many ships of much greater registered draft use the port when they are lightly laden.

TABLE 6   Statistics on Tripoli and Benghazi Ports, 1954–1958

(In Metric Tons and £L)

	Imports			Exports		Total Com-	£L	
Year	Com- mercial	Mili- tary	Pe- troleum	Com- mercial	Mili- tary	mercial Cargo	Reve- nue	Expendi- ture
Tripoli Port								
1954	158,801	52,484	154,603	75,286	16,897	234,087	212,599	108,406
1955	223,513	71,901	163,106	77,867	29,241	301,380	263,681	111,188
1956	253,342	47,239	165,227	74,898	18,051	328,240	344,233	145,733
1957	269,517	36,989	201,379	73,289	20,932	342,801	376,000	182,000
1958	308,591	28,488	173,656	95,823	18,373	404,414	392,184	190,000
Benghazi Port								
1954	48,517	46,639	19,907	20,578	27,359	69,095	27,310	40,860
1955	60,613	43,240	18,716	15,918	16,607	76,531	34,705	40,768
1956	87,343	37,606	18,062	16,287	20,808	103,630	40,527	38,751
1957	88,257	9,841	29,943	16,720	24,178	104,977	48,197	42,249
1958	71,447	3,133	28,430	9,244	17,176	80,691	61,770	49,550

To overcome these limitations, a number of schemes have been put forward in recent years for the reconstruction of a deepwater port at costs ranging from about £L 4.5 million to £L 7 million. The earlier postwar schemes envisaged abandonment of the Outer Mole and the Outer Harbor, but the Libyan Government specifically requested the restoration of the harbor to its prewar dimensions, and this is provided for in the latest specifications submitted by the consulting engineers. The rebuilding of the Outer Mole alone is estimated to cost over £L 4 million.

The mission has been aware of the keenness of the Cyrenaican Government to develop the facilities of the port and to render it accessible to large ships in all weather. The fact that Benghazi is one of the capitals of Libya, and also the capital of Cyrenaica, invests this project with a special importance: and there are other political and psychological considerations that were brought to the mission's attention in this connection. We have borne all this in mind in studying the project, and while our own examination has properly been confined to the economic, financial and technical aspects, we recognize that these are not the only criteria that have to be applied in a case of this kind.

Some action is needed immediately, in any case, to prevent further deterioration of the existing harbor installations, and any reconstruction or development of the harbor that is undertaken should have regard to the likely growth of trade in future as the Cyrenaican economy expands. The main issue for consideration, however, is whether there is justification, *in present circumstances,* for undertaking the large expense of rebuilding the Outer Mole and providing an all-weather harbor for ships drawing as much as 30 feet and more, or whether the funds likely to be used up by this large project, less whatever is needed to develop the existing Middle Harbor, could be better employed on more immediately productive investments. In examining this issue the mission's primary objective has been to decide whether the *economic* benefits to be derived from the construction of a deepwater harbor at present would be commensurate with the cost. It must be left to others to assess the noneconomic benefits.

In support of the case for a deepwater harbor, it is pointed out, first, that, because of the limitations of the existing harbor, certain cargoes destined for Benghazi have to be transshipped to smaller vessels at Tripoli, Malta or other ports, and that this adds to the cost of Cyrenaica's imports. Second, there is the danger of ships being unable to enter the port in bad weather, which gives Benghazi a bad name and tends to discourage even the smaller vessels from calling there. Third, most Mediterranean cruise ships are too big to enter the present harbor at all, and it is claimed that this deprives Cyrenaica of valuable tourist traffic. Fourth, since the discovery of oil in Cyrenaica, a port able to admit larger vessels might be useful for bringing in heavy equipment and other supplies for the oil companies.

There is an element of truth in all these points, but the following facts must also be considered. First, regular services to Benghazi in vessels up to 4,000 tons dead weight, some of them built specially for this trade, are at present provided by five shipping lines (two British, two Italian and one German) ensuring on the average seven or eight calls a month. In addition, there are many calls from small tramps or freighters belonging to Italian and Levantine countries. These ships now carry most of Benghazi's bulkier imports (cereals, sugar, cement, machinery, steel, transport equipment) direct from ports in Northern Europe, Italy and other Mediterranean countries. At least one of the lines concerned charges the same rates from the United Kingdom and Rotterdam to Benghazi as it does to Tripoli ($£L$ 6 per freight ton in each case in 1959), while for the other lines the differential ranges from $£$ 1 to $£$ 1.10.0d. per freight ton. These services appear to be adequate to handle the cargo at present offering; indeed, some of the ships visiting the port have difficulty in finding cargo, particularly in the outward direction. There is seldom any serious congestion in the port.

A few cargoes are still transshipped en route, but these are mainly goods coming from United States and Asia such as emergency supplies of grains, oil equipment and tea.[1] The most common place of transshipment is presumably Tripoli, and the total amount of cargo forwarded from Tripoli to Benghazi on transshipment bills of lading amounted to 4,437 tons in 1957 and 2,365 tons in 1958. Some foreign merchandise is no doubt unloaded at Tripoli and sent to Benghazi by road. No statistical data are available on this, but the quantity can hardly be large, as it would normally be much simpler and cheaper to use sea transport in such cases.

So far as cruise ships are concerned, plans to land tourists at Benghazi have had to be abandoned on several occasions in recent years because of rough seas. Difficulties have also been experienced in bad weather in embarking Libyan pilgrims on ships going to Arabia. But the additional income to be obtained from tourists passing through the port would cover only a tiny fraction of the costs of a development scheme. In any case, Benghazi lies over 150 kilometers from the main places of interest to foreign tourists in Cyrenaica, and it is for consideration whether, as suggested elsewhere in this report, it might not be better to develop an alternative calling place for cruise ships at Ras el Hilal, which is on the coast between Cyrene and Derna.

While Benghazi is hardly likely to be used as a port for the ship-

[1] Ships carrying tea from Asia normally off-load their cargoes by lighter outside Benghazi, but sometimes in bad weather they by-pass the port, and the cargoes have to be transshipped elsewhere. Even in such cases, however, the transshipment charges amount to less than one-half of one percent of the retail price of tea in Benghazi.

ment of oil produced in Libya, it is the nearest commercial port of any size to the recently discovered oilfields in the Sirte desert and could be useful for the movement of supplies for the oil companies. The companies will have the choice between bringing in their equipment and other supplies through the existing ports of Tripoli and Benghazi and building special facilities for this purpose in the Gulf of Sirte. In view of the fact that Tripoli and the Gulf of Sirte are both accessible to large ocean-going freighters, the lack of a deepwater harbor at Benghazi is unlikely to present major difficulties. On the other hand, if there were such a harbor, the companies would probably make some use of it.

In short, the mission can see no economic justification for the reconstruction of a deepwater harbor at Benghazi at present in view of the very heavy costs involved. Supposing that, in line with the consultants' latest estimates, the actual cost of such a scheme worked out at about £L 7 million, and that this money had to be borrowed at rates of interest in line with those now prevailing in most capital-exporting countries, with repayment spread over, say, 25 years, annual debt service payments alone would be equivalent to about ten times the present annual revenues of the port. Another way of looking at the problem is to consider what might be done with the £L 7 million if it was spent in other ways—say, on improving rural conditions in Cyrenaica, on building and equipping more schools or on providing better houses for the poorer people in the towns. While the scope for additional expenditures in these directions may be limited at the moment, the long-term need is great, and it will be evident from the other chapters in this report that much could eventually be done with a sum of this magnitude. It would suffice, for instance, to build houses for over one-quarter of the population of Cyrenaica.

The mission is satisfied nevertheless that some improvements to the existing harbor are needed both to prevent further deterioration of the structures and to provide for the expansion of trade which is to be expected as the economy develops. It is difficult to say how rapid this expansion will be. For one thing, if the measures suggested in this report for the development of agricultural production in Cyrenaica are successful, there might actually be some reduction in the imports of cereals, which in volume could more than outweigh any likely increase in exports of other agricultural and livestock products. The trend of other imports will depend in part on the general level of incomes and in part on the amount of construction work undertaken in Cyrenaica. All in all, and leaving aside the imports and exports of the oil companies and foreign military forces in Cyrenaica, it might be reasonable to expect Benghazi's commercial trade to grow at a rate of around 5-10 percent per annum. If anything, this estimate may be rather on the high side. It would be consistent with the trend over the past five years, but exceptional factors have operated during this period to raise the volume of imports (e.g., construction of the administrative center at Beida and the need for emergency imports of animal feed).

We accordingly recommend that consideration should be given to a modified scheme for the development of the Middle Harbor on the lines indicated in the plan facing page 242. Our proposal, which would require further technical examination to confirm its feasibility, is to limit the working area of the port to that portion only where the existing quays are situated. The extension of Rasif Libya No. 1 (item 5 in the plan) by 450 feet or so will permit three of the largest vessels now using the port to discharge their cargoes simultaneously. Other ships could use the existing quays or discharge by lighter. In this way, and because ships of 18 feet draft will be able to use the port under our scheme, we estimate its handling capacity will be increased to at least three times the present figure. Provision is also made (as shown in the plan) for constructing new quays on the northwest side of the harbor, but we do not anticipate that these will be required for many years. Wave action in the harbor should be reduced to reasonable limits by the extension of the Italian Mole and the construction of a new breakwater (items 3 and 4 in the plan).

Before the position of the breakwater is finally determined, the records of the hydraulic model tests carried out by the consulting engineers responsible for the original plans should be studied. The actual lengths of the mole extension and of the breakwater can only be decided after further detailed study of site conditions, but we do not anticipate that the final design will differ appreciably from that shown in our plan. The new breakwater, wherever sited, will have a section for most of its length very similar to that of the existing Cathedral Mole shown in the plan, as it will not traverse deep water except near its outer end. When the depths are greater than 10 feet or so, the breakwater and the Italian Mole extension will have sections similar to those proposed by the consulting engineers for similar work under their scheme.

We consider the work requiring most urgent attention is the rehabilitation of the Central Mole (item No. 1 in the plan) which is fast disintegrating. If this mole fails (as may happen at any time in the near future), there will be little shelter for vessels approaching the port itself. We recommend therefore that work on repairing the Central Mole be taken in hand at once pending consideration of our other proposals. We also suggest that the consulting engineers responsible for the previous plans should be asked to comment on our scheme. If they agree that it is technically sound, they should be asked to fill in details, draw up bills of quantities and prepare the project for world-wide tender. We tentatively estimate the cost of the scheme at around £L 1½ million, and we have made appropriate provision in our capital investment program.

Adoption of the scheme suggested here would not preclude consideration of the project for a deepwater harbor at a later stage. With the opening up of oilfields in Cyrenaica there are too many unpredictable factors in the situation for any final judgment to be passed now on the likely growth of trade in the area served by Benghazi, and as we have observed already, economic factors may not be the only ones that have to be considered by the Libyan Government in relation to this project.

The port of Benghazi and other ports in Cyrenaica are run by the Nazirate of Communications, and their accounts are merged in the provincial budget. While we do not consider that the operations of these ports are large enough to justify the appointment of an independent port authority, we would urge that their accounts be separated from those of general government and maintained on a commercial basis.

Minor Ports and Coastal Shipping

At present, some dozen minor ports exist along the coast of Libya (see Annex XX). Many of these were built by the ancient Greeks and Romans and were further developed by the Turkish and Italian rulers of the country before the advent of motor transport. The Italians used some of the larger ports for military purposes before the coastal road was built. Tobruk is the only port with a natural harbor. Derna and Zuara have artificial harbors, while most of the others have some protection afforded by natural reefs on which the remains of small ancient moles can generally be seen. Cargo handled by these ports is very small apart from military cargoes entering and leaving Tobruk.

With the exceptions of Derna and Tobruk, very little has been spent during the last five years on the upkeep of minor ports. Extensive repairs to the moles were carried out at Derna, and much dredging has been done, but the harbor silted up again within a year after dredging. It has been estimated that it would cost £L 125,000 to eradicate this trouble. Very large sums would also be required to restore the other ports. The mission does not recommend incurring any large expenditures during the next few years on these ports. The Zuara mole should, however, be repaired and the harbor dredged (estimated cost £L 20,000), and more attention should be paid to minimum essential maintenance of useful structures in the other ports against the possibility of a revival of the coastal shipping trade. For example, if the breach in the mole at Zuara had been attended to when the first signs of failure were noticed in 1950, the repair bill might have been a few hundred pounds instead of the £L 20,000 now required, and the harbor would not have silted up. The mission recommends that £L 12,000 be earmarked every year for essential maintenance of the minor ports, including dredging. As recommended in Chapter 10, Ras el Hilal might be developed as a calling place for tourist ships; the anchorage is sheltered by a headland, and deep water runs close into the shore. The cost of repairing the concrete jetty and making a turning place for buses is estimated at £L 30,000, and we have tentatively included financial provision for this in our program of capital expenditures.

The mission found it difficult to assess with any exactitude the comparative costs of coastal shipping and road transport. It noted that traders at present preferred to send their goods by road (even when the cost was slightly higher) because of the convenience of road transport (ensuring door-to-door delivery) and the inconvenience of coastal shipping, the liability to damage and breakage of goods, the delays and paperwork arising from customs proceedings and formalities, and the difficulty of finding shipping to take the small consignments usually offered. An attempt made recently to operate a coaster under the Libyan flag collapsed for lack of patronage. In fact, the main obstacle to the development of coastal shipping at present is the small amount of traffic offered. We would not rule out the possibility that coastal shipping might revive as the Libyan economy develops, but we see no immediate likelihood of this happening.

CIVIL AVIATION

Idris airport outside Tripoli is the largest civil airport in Libya. Traffic "movements" are fairly heavy (42,000 a year), but civil aircraft movements total only about 14,000 a year (5,948 in 1955), and many of these are accounted for by oil company planes. Passengers now number about 80,000 a year (23,000 in 1955). Benina handles much less traffic, the number of passengers in 1958/59 being about 10,300 (7,000 in 1955), and is losing its importance as a refueling station for transit aircraft with the introduction of the modern long-range jets.

Since Independence, about £L 800,000 has been spent on the development of Idris and Benina. The mission estimates that, if there is no abnormal growth of traffic at these airports, about £L 280,000 will be required for further development and equipment during the period 1960/61-1964/65 and roughly another £L 500,000 for resurfacing the runways when they begin to show signs of wear. Since much of the cost of traffic control at Idris arises from the large number of movements of foreign military aircraft in the vicinity, contributions toward the cost of this control should be sought under the existing foreign treaties. Sebha will require about £L 20,000 for fire fighting and other equipment. Very little need be spent on the other airports until the traffic begins to develop (see Annex XXI).

Idris and Benina airports are undoubtedly beneficial to the economy, especially as they benefit the tourist industry. They are at present operated (at a loss) directly under the provincial governments, as indeed are all the civil airports in Libya, with the help of foreign technical personnel. No change in the present organization appears necessary. Internal air services are operated at present by foreign airlines, which provide about nine services each way a week between Tripoli and Benghazi and one between Tripoli and Sebha. With the exception of the flight to Sebha these services require no subsidy from the government, and there does not appear for the moment to be any economic justification for creating a Libyan national airline. Such an airline could at present find traffic for only three or four services a week on the Tripoli-Benghazi route and for only occasional calls at other airports, and the mission recommends against the creation of a "prestige route network," which would have to be heavily subsidized. This question might be reconsidered later if air traffic grows rapidly.

On the other hand, the mission considers that light aircraft facilities should be provided for carrying passengers between Sebha and the desert oases in the Fezzan, with connections from Sebha to Tripoli and Benghazi. Outlying oases in Tripolitania and Cyrenaica (e.g., Gadames, Jalo and Kufra) could also be served in this way. The best method of supplying these facilities might be to employ a private company to organize and operate regular services between the more important centers, with provision for ambulance facilities as necessary.

Although these services will almost certainly be run at a loss in the beginning, the cost to the economy will probably be very much less than that of constructing new roads over long distances to remote oases, as is apparently at present contemplated. Moreover, if the inhabited areas of Libya are seen as a large number of islands in a vast sand sea, the passenger transport-communication problem must be solved, as the economy of the country develops, either by road or by air transport, and air transport will require much less capital investment and be more quickly established. Goods traffic could use the present desert tracks which serve the economy adequately at a not unreasonable cost. The mission believes that, as in other countries, the existence of air facilities will rapidly make people more air-minded, and the expansion of air travel seems to us in keeping with the more modern and progressive spirit that is developing in Libya. An allowance of £L 50,000 a year has been included in our program of current development expenditures for running the proposed services and maintaining the landing strips.

TELECOMMUNICATIONS AND BROADCASTING

Telecommunications and broadcasting services are now being developed on modern lines under schemes financed by the Government of the United States. The schemes have been radically modified on several occasions. Tripoli and Benghazi are now linked by radiotelephone. Telephone exchanges in both towns are being modernized, broadcasting services have been started, and two new studios are in the course of construction. The telecommunications project was designed to form part of a new international circuit linking Europe and the East by way of Italy, Tunisia, Libya and Egypt. As yet, however, neither the Tunisian nor the Egyptian links have been constructed, and the Libyan system will thus be left without connections at either end. This is a most unsatisfactory situation, and one that calls for urgent discussions between Libya and its two neighbors.

Approximately £L 2.35 million has been made available out of U. S. funds for the telecommunications project and £L 1 million for the broadcasting project. By the end of March 1960 all the money allocated for broadcasting will have been spent, and it is estimated that approximately £L 500,000 will remain to be spent on telecommunications. This sum has been included in our program of capital expenditures.

The telecommunications system is an expensive one to maintain since very highly qualified—and highly paid—foreign personnel have to be employed to operate it, and will have to be so employed for some time to come. Operating costs for personnel alone are currently in the region of £L 250,000 a year, and on top of this provision has to be made for spare parts and fuel, raising total operating costs to well above £L 300,000 a year. Costs of depreciation for the entire system have been estimated at about £L 160,000 annually on the basis of a twenty-year amortization schedule.

It is difficult to see how a system of this kind can be run at a profit without substantial international traffic, and there is little prospect of such traffic materializing within the next few years. The broadcasting services will also impose an increasing burden on the public exchequer. We have assumed that recurrent expenditures on telecommunications and broadcasting together during the next five years (net of additional revenues, but including depreciation) might average about £L 300,000 a year above the present level, and provision for this increase has been included in our program.

The contract for the telecommunications scheme provides for training of Libyans in telecommunications and broadcasting techniques and operation. The mission would urge that this training be put in hand as early as possible since effective training will take a long time. The UNESCO experts have already set up a school (with government funds) to train technicians for the broadcasting service, and this school is doing very good work.

Since the mission's visit the Libyan Government has submitted to the UN Special Fund a request for assistance in establishing a radio and telecommunications training school in Libya. This would cater for training in those telecommunications techniques which are not covered by "on-the-job" and other training provided in the contract; it could also train operators and mechanics in the police and army. It is suggested that the school should enroll 25-30 students a year in courses lasting from 12 months to 27 months. The cost of establishing the school and operating it for the first five years is estimated by the Libyan Government at just under £L 500,000. The mission has not had an opportunity to study the project and is therefore unable to express any judgment on it. However, we believe that some additional training facilities are urgently needed in this field.

The present intention is apparently that the new telecommunications service should take over responsibility, under the Post and Telecommunications Department, for all telephone and telegraph services in Libya. It is essential, in the mission's view, that all these services should be run on a commercial basis, with their accounts kept separate from those of general government. Management should be reasonably unfettered, and the existing civil service law should not apply to the staff. For the management of the broadcasting services, the mission suggests that advice be obtained from the UNESCO experts in Libya. This is a very specialized business, and it is inadvisable to try to organize it on hit-and-miss lines.

POSTAL SERVICES

When the new telecommunications service begins to operate, the Post, Telephone and Telegraph Department of the Ministry of Communications will be faced with many difficult problems. The mission advises that the opportunity should now be taken to reorganize the postal services, as there is considerable scope for improvement. Action is indicated on the general lines suggested in the "Report on Survey of Libyan Posts" by Dr. J. C. Russell and Mr. Sabri Husseni, especially in the matter of introducing reasonably unfettered management and a proper cost accounting system. A post office is essentially a business enterprise, and the rigid procedures and rules and regulations governing the running of an administrative government office, as set forth in the Civil Service Law of Libya, should not be applied without radical modifications.

TRANSPORT ADMINISTRATION

We have made a number of specific proposals earlier in this chapter for the organization and management of roads and road transport, ports, civil aviation, telecommunications and broadcasting. If these proposals are accepted, there should be no need for separate Nazirates of Public Works and Communications in the provinces, and we recommend that these two departments should in each case be amalgamated. At the federal level we recommend that the existing Ministry of Communications should be renamed the Ministry of Transport and Communications and made responsible for the formulation of national policies in this field. We further recommend that a standing ministerial committee on transport and communications should be established to secure better coordination between the activities of the federal and provincial governments and to ensure that the provinces are fully consulted at the policy-making stage. This committee would be presided over by the Minister and would include the three Nazirs of Public Works and Communications.

The ministerial committee would in its turn receive advice from a committee of technical officials which would include the Directors of the Nazirates of Public Works and Communications, the Directors of the federal Roads and Telecommunications Departments, the Director of Civil Aviation and such additional technical advisers as may be required. This committee, on which the Development Council should be represented, would deal with problems of transport and communications at the technical level. Room should be found in sub-committees or otherwise for representation at this level of the private transport and commercial interests concerned with road construction, road-making machinery, port construction plant, materials and other supplies.

SUMMARY OF PROPOSED EXPENDITURES

The recommendations which we have made in this chapter, together with projects already being undertaken, would entail a total capital outlay in the public sector of £L 5,805,000 over the five years 1960/61 to 1964/65. The breakdown of this total would be as follows:

(£L '000)

	Five-year total	Annual average
Fezzan road	2,000	400
Other road construction and improvements	650	130
Tripoli port[a]	300	60
Benghazi harbor	1,500	300
Ras el Hilal	30	6
Minor ports	25	5
Civil airports	800	160
Telecommunications	500	100
Total	5,805	1,161

[a] Includes £L 235,000 for capital works in the main port and £L 65,000 for the creation of a free trade zone. The remaining £L 90,000 required to bring the port up to standard (see page 237) has been treated as deferred maintenance chargeable to revenue.

So far as recurrent government expenditures are concerned, we envisage savings of about £L 75,000 a year from the closing down of the provincial railways and a substantial reduction in the costs of operating government road transport. On the other hand, the proposed desert air services might cost £L 50,000 a year, and we have recommended budgetary provision of £L 900,000 a year for road maintenance and renewals, which we estimate would represent an increase of £L 360,000 a year over actual expenditures in 1957/58 (the latest year for which we have a breakdown between capital and recurrent expenditures). Account has also to be taken of the heavy costs of operating the new telecommunications and broadcasting systems which might amount to as much as £L 300,000 a year (net of any increase in revenues likely to be achieved during the next five years). Allowing for all items, the combined budgets of the Ministry of Transport and Communications and the provincial Nazirates of Communications may show an increase of £L 600,000-700,000 a year. The port of Tripoli will be able to finance the suggested expenditures on deferred maintenance out of its own revenues.

CHAPTER 13 *EDUCATION*

The Priorities

Education is desired for its own sake, and not simply as an investment which will contribute toward raising the national output. Some types of education may not help to raise output at all, at any rate in the short run. On the other hand, a country's whole development effort may be held back by shortages of the more advanced skills, which can only be acquired through a long process of education and training. This is outstandingly true of Libya where the neglect of education prior to Independence has resulted in an acute lack of technicians, professional people and administrators in every field of economic activity. No matter how much money is available—be it foreign aid, oil revenues or domestic savings—development can usefully be pushed no faster than the supply of properly trained personnel to administer and execute it. That is why the mission places so much importance on the expansion of facilities for technical and vocational training and on programs of adult education.

In giving first priority to vocational training and adult education, we do not underestimate the value of general education or the desirability of achieving the objective of free compulsory primary education for all, which is laid down in the Libyan Constitution. At the time of Independence, when fewer than 10 percent of the adult population had ever been to school, it was entirely right to concentrate on laying down the foundations for a proper school system and opening the doors of education to a large number of children in the shortest possible time. The success of this effort is reflected in the rapid growth of school enrollment in the past six years. In 1952/53 there were 45,000 pupils in 234 schools, 42,000 of them in primary schools; by 1958/59 the number of pupils had been raised to 106,000 (of whom just under 100,000 were in primary schools) and the number of schools to 524. This is a very considerable achievement. So far as the mission can judge from the available statistics, between 60 percent and 70 percent of all Libyan children in the primary school age groups (6-12) are now in school, a proportion which stands up well to comparison with other underdeveloped countries.[1] In India, for example, the target for the end of the present Second Five-Year Plan in 1961 is 63 percent.

Now that a fairly broad base has been created, we believe that the emphasis in primary education should be shifted from the expansion of numbers to the improvement of the quality of the education offered. This is not to say that children seeking access to school should be denied admission, but that priority should now be given to measures to ease overcrowding, to provide better teaching equipment, to improve the curriculum, to secure better supervision of teaching and above all to increase the supply of trained Libyan teachers. Numbers in primary school will tend in any case to grow further, and we envisage that enrollment may rise to about 125,000 by 1964/65 (probably representing about 75 percent of all children of primary school age at that date). This would be a satisfactory advance. Further advances should be envisaged for succeeding years, and the ultimate goal of primary education for all might be realizable within 15 years from now. But the mission holds strongly to the view that during the next five years expansion of enrollment should be paced so that it does not run ahead of necessary improvements in standards of education.

Public school education in Libya is currently being reorganized on a twelve-year basis, in place of the eleven-year system followed hitherto. The primary school provides the first six years of instruction (nominally from the ages of 6 to 12), the preparatory school the next three (from 12 to 15) and the secondary school the last three (from 15 to 18). In 1958/59, as against 99,545 pupils in primary school, there were 4,368 in preparatory school (then a two-year course) and 2,165 in secondary school. In addition, about 1,000 children in the post-primary age groups were receiving vocational training at the two agricultural schools at el Aweila in Cyrenaica and Sidi Mesri in Tripolitania, at the Technical and Clerical Training Center and the School of Applied Engineering in Tripoli, at the Health Assistants and Sanitarians Institute in Benghazi and at various other institutions. A further 1,426 children were attending teachers' training schools.

The mission attaches high priority to strengthening and broadening the facilities for both general and technical education beyond the

---

[1] The percentage quoted is arrived at by comparing the numbers enrolled in primary school in 1958/59 with the total of all children of primary school age, which is estimated at around 160,000. However, this is not a true basis for comparison since some of the children in primary school are above the age of 12. On the other hand, it should be borne in mind that by no means all the children who enter primary school stay for the full six years.

primary stage. As a rough guide to the planning of post-primary education during the next 20 years, we suggest that about one child in every three or four entering primary school should go on to preparatory school or to a vocational school at the preparatory level, and that about half those who study at the preparatory level should continue with some sort of formal education at the post-preparatory stage, either at a general secondary school or at a technical or vocational training institution. On this basis, and allowing for the fact that the preparatory and secondary school course are only three years each as against six years for primary school, we estimate that enrollment in preparatory schools, together with vocational and technical training institutions at the preparatory level, should rise to about 15,000 by 1964/65 and enrollment in post-preparatory schools (general, technical and vocational) to about 7,500 by 1967/68 (i.e., to 15 percent and 7.5 percent of the present enrollment in primary schools). This expansion should proceed gradually, and special efforts must be made to ensure that the technical and vocational schools receive an appropriate share of the children leaving primary and preparatory schools, so as to combat the traditional bias in favor of a general education.

The supply of suitable teachers is likely to be the principal factor limiting the expansion of the school system at all levels, and while a large proportion of secondary school teachers must continue to be recruited abroad for the time being, the highest priority should be given to expanding the facilities for the training of Libyan teachers. The training of teachers for primary and preparatory schools will be mainly undertaken through teachers training colleges (pp. 258-259). The training of teachers for general secondary, technical and vocational schools will be one of the most important functions of the Libyan University, of the existing technical schools and ultimately of the proposed Higher Institute of Technology (pp. 264-266). Taking a long view, the mission urges that special efforts should be made to attract good people to the teaching profession and to raise the standards of teacher training. In so many countries the teacher is underpaid by comparison with other occupations and he does not enjoy the status that should properly be accorded to men and women who have such an important role to play in shaping a nation's destiny. When oil revenues materialize, the Libyan Government will have the money to ensure that its teachers are adequately equipped for their job and so rewarded for their service that it makes it attractive for men of ability to remain as teachers. We hope that it will do so.

Education of the child and adolescent is not enough. An attempt must be made to compensate for the lack of education amongst a large part of the adult population in whose hands the economic welfare of the country currently rests. Indeed, an effective adult education campaign, including agricultural extension, should yield quicker and surer economic benefits in terms of increased production than any program for the education of the young. The mission feels therefore that even greater stress should be placed on this aspect of education during the next five years.

Obviously no one branch of education can be given absolute priority over all the others; it is a question of striking the right balance between them. The recommendations put forward in this chapter are intended to help in achieving such a balance. It must, however, be remembered that the mission is looking at education in its relation to economic development rather than in the wider context of human and spiritual values. In other words, this is not a report on Libyan education, but a chapter on education in a report on Libya's economic development. From the point of view of such development we feel that the education authorities, while they have made remarkable progress in a short time, have tended to place too much emphasis on numbers in primary education rather than on quality, on general education at the post-primary levels rather than on technical and vocational trining, on the education of children rather than on the education of adults and on education for urban life rather than on rural needs. Our program accordingly strikes a somewhat different balance.

Long-Term Planning

In the field of education a five-year program should be regarded as only the first phase in a longer-term plan. Sound educational expansion requires a forward look of at least 20 or 30 years. For example, the quantity and quality of first-year primary education today will have an impact on the type and scope of specialized and higher education possible more than 15 years from now. The proper way to plan educational development is to establish ultimate objectives and then make sure that in the shorter term each phase contributes to attaining those objectives.

We have suggested above some very broad aims for educational development, but these need to be worked out in details, and the different parts of the program have to be carefully coordinated, so that expansion at all levels of the educational pyramid keeps in step. More primary schools, for example, mean that more primary school teachers must be trained at the preparatory and secondary levels. This in turn means that more teachers are needed for preparatory and secondary schools and teachers' training colleges which again means an increasing demand for university graduates. In Libya, where the numbers involved are comparatively small, it would be particularly valuable to have a comprehensive survey made of the likely demands over the next 20 to 30 years for the various types of professional skills—doctors, nurses, medical assistants, architects, surveyors, agronomists, veterinarians, foresters, engineers, scientists, school teachers and so forth— so that the educational system can be geared to supply them. This could be done by the Development Council, working in close consultation with the Ministry of Education and other departments concerned.

The mission recommends that the task of drawing up a long-range educational program should be entrusted to an experienced technical adviser, who should be recruited to work with the Ministry of Education. He should be assisted by the establishment of a Bureau of Research and Records. The first task of such an adviser should be to make a careful survey of educational facilities in relation to the distribution and growth of population and national needs, and to recommend long-term plans to take care of these needs.

The Primary School System

It will inevitably take time to reach the goal of universal primary education, particularly where social customs still tend to keep girls away from school. The expansion of primary schools has therefore to be undertaken gradually, and attention concentrated in the meantime on measures for improving the quality of the facilities provided. More emphasis must be given in the curriculum to practical training for everyday life. The number of adequately trained teachers must be increased. More and better school equipment, textbooks and teaching aids should be provided. There is undoubtedly need also in certain cases for better and more hygienic school buildings, but the mission regards this as a lower order of priority. Simple accommodation, provided it is clean, will often be adequate in rural areas, where there appears to be little justification for having school buildings which are much superior in standards of construction and cost to the ordinary dwellings.

The Curriculum. The program of primary studies is prescribed by the Ministry of Education, and every primary school in the land must adhere to it. This common program is looked upon as an effective means for welding the nation together through offering all children common knowledge and ideas. Government authorities believe that the great distances which separate the centers of population from one another and the short experience of the people with independence render such a uniform program essential. The mission noted, however, some dissatisfaction with the rigidity of the school program and its emphasis on words rather than understanding and experience. The mission also noted heavy migration from village to city among primary school graduates, an inclination to seek white-collar jobs and a disdain for manual work.

The mission's view is that the primary school should educate the whole child, helping to shape his physical, moral and intellectual character and emphasizing good habits of thought, work and conduct. The primary school, particularly in rural communities, should become a community center serving both children and adults. The principle of learning by doing should be practiced, with projects, field trips, manual work, plays and club activity supplementing learning from books. In such a school the teacher assumes a heavy responsibility. He is both an educator and community leader. Thus the primary school teacher should be carefully selected and well prepared for his work. Once he is well-trained, he should be given the opportunity of making some adjustment in his program in order to fit the needs of his pupils and the community which the school serves.

At present primary schools in rural areas follow exactly the same curriculum as schools in urban areas, and the teachers frequently have no background in rural matters. We would like to see this situation changed. The primary school can do much to stimulate an interest in agriculture and to encourage a proper appreciation of the advantages of rural life, and this is particularly important in Libya because of the absence of a tradition of settled agriculture and the consequent shortage of elementary skills which in other countries could be taken for granted. The program in rural schools should therefore be modified with this end in view. Wherever practicable, schools should have small gardens, and special arrangements should be made for the practical study of nature, animals and agriculture. At the same time a system of specialized training should be instituted for rural school teachers (see page 259).

Education of the Tribes. The education of the tribes presents a difficult problem, especially in Cyrenaica where a sizeable proportion of the population are nomads or semi-nomads. In attempting to solve this problem, the Nazirate of Education in Cyrenaica has opened boarding primary schools for the tribal children. It is estimated that the cost of maintaining a boarding student is approximately £L 100 per school year, while the cost of an outside or day pupil is approximately £L 10. Thus, because of the limited facilities for primary education and the great demand for it, the boarding of one child is basically at the expense of 10 day children.

The mission recommends that, wherever tribal groupings are large enough to provide sufficient pupils, the school be brought to the tribal children and not vice versa. The first four years of the primary schools should be taught in day schools attached to the tribes, and boarding facilities should be restricted to pupils of the fifth and sixth grades. Suitably qualified members of the various tribes should be attached to their respective tribes as teachers. Such tribal teachers should receive in-service training and careful supervision.

The migratory habits of the tribes in Cyrenaica and some other parts of Libya are such that we are convinced that the school-within-a-tribe concept can in part be adapted to the requirements of Libyan tribal living, as it has already been so adapted in Syria, Iraq and parts of Jordan. It may be added that schools traveling around with tribes have also worked successfully amongst the Touaregs in Libya. When tribal concentrations are small and scattered over large distances, the school-within-a-tribe concept may not be operative, but this should not discourage the attempt at such methods where relevant. As a long-range measure, we recommend the appointment in the Ministry of Education or in the Nazirate of Education in Cyrenaica of a special well-trained inspector who will concern himself solely with supervising and studying the problems of tribal education.

Capital Expenditures on Buildings and Equipment. Many of our recommendations with respect to the primary school system could be put into effect with little or no capital cost. Some of them indeed (e.g., the proposals for tribal education) should result in economies in capital expenditures. Nevertheless, increased enrollment will entail the building of some new schools and the enlargement or rehabilitation of existing ones. There will also be need for more furniture, equipment and teaching aids. Our estimate is that about 25,000 additional places will have to be made available in primary schools over the next five years, and that the average capital cost per place works out at just over £L 28 for buildings (assuming £L 1,000 per classroom holding 35 pupils) and about £L 2½ for furniture. We have therefore provided a total of £L 770,000 in our five-year investment program for the expansion of the primary school system.

Training of Primary School Teachers. Most of the primary school teachers are Libyans. They are trained in five training colleges, which they enter immediately after leaving primary school. Courses at these colleges, which normally last three or four years, are thus more or less on the same level as courses at the ordinary preparatory schools. Two of the colleges are in Tripoli, two in Benghazi and one, newly founded, in Sebha. Three branches of the Tripoli colleges have been established in Giado, Misurata and Zawia.

The number of teachers graduating from the existing colleges appears to be adequate to meet the needs of the primary schools, but standards of training leave much to be desired. Six years of primary school is clearly not an adequate preparation for admission to a teachers' training college, and however necessary it may have been initially to set the admission requirements so low, it is essential that they should be raised as rapidly as circumstances permit. Normally a prospective teacher should be expected to have had at least nine years in ordinary schooling before he enters a training college, and this should be the objective for the existing colleges in Libya, to be achieved in stages. Instruction at the colleges would then in effect be on the secondary rather than on the preparatory level. Such instruction must continue for the time being to be entrusted mainly to expatriates pending the graduation of more Libyans from the university.

Programs of rural teacher training should be separated from those of urban teachers and be transferred to the agricultural schools at el Aweila in Cyrenaica, at the Agricultural and Vocational Training Center at Sidi Mesri outside Tripoli, and at the projected agricultural college at Sebha. Admission requirements at these rural teacher training colleges should likewise rise gradually from six-year graduates to nine-year graduates, and candidates should be selected mainly from those who are themselves from rural areas. Although the course of study in rural teachers' training would follow the general three-year curriculum for other primary school teachers, special emphasis should be given to agricultural and other rural subjects. There should be a program of in-service training, augmented by special summer teachers' institutes at the agricultural schools, attendance at which would be rewarded by promotions and salary increases. Finally, in order to maintain standards of teaching, a selected number of rural school inspectors should be appointed and given one year of intensive training in an agricultural school.

After the Primary School

Under the twelve-year school system the six years at primary school, which are compulsory, are followed by an optional three years at preparatory school and another optional three years at secondary school. However, preparatory and secondary schools provide only a general education, and there are parallel institutions for technical and vocational training at both levels. Thus the Clerical and Technical Training Center in Tripoli offers three-year junior and senior courses for boys of 16 and upwards. Likewise the two agricultural schools recruit students both from those leaving primary school and those leaving preparatory school. The five training colleges for primary school teachers recruit students direct from primary schools and are thus broadly parallel with the preparatory schools.

As already noted, there were 4,368 pupils in preparatory schools and 2,165 in secondary schools in 1958/59. To arrive at the total number of children receiving formal education or training at the preparatory and secondary levels it is necessary to add in the 1,426 students at teachers' training colleges (mostly at the preparatory level) and the 1,000 or so students at other technical or vocational schools (most of them at the preparatory level, but some at the secondary level). On this basis it might be very roughly estimated that total enrollment at the preparatory level was about 6,500 and at the secondary level about 2,500. We have suggested that the numbers in the first group might be raised to 15,000 by 1964/65 and the numbers in the second group to 7,500 by 1967/68 (say, to 5,000 by 1964/65). These figures have been used for the purpose of estimating recurrent and capital expenditures on education over the next five years, but we have not attempted to specify exactly how the additional students should be split up as between the general preparatory and secondary schools on the one hand and schools with a technical or vocational bias on the other. It is, however, in the latter field that we see the most urgent need for expansion.

One of Libya's most pressing needs is for qualified artisans (mechanics, fitters, electricians, plumbers, carpenters, bricklayers, etc.), skilled agricultural workers and demonstrators and intermediate technicians (assistant engineers, surveyors, draftsmen, etc.). Such persons are of much greater value to the economy at the present time, and are required in larger numbers, than white-collar workers. They are wanted to staff the government's technical services, to participate in agricultural extension work and to take jobs on farms, in factories and workshops; and there will be a ready and continuing demand for them to work for the oil companies. Good wages and salaries await young people who are qualified in these fields, and there will be no lack of jobs for them. Such people should normally receive six to nine years of general education, followed by two to four years of specialized training, before they enter employment. Their training will then continue on the job, and outstanding workers can be given opportunities for more advanced study later on (e.g., for an engineering degree).

The mission considers that the present facilities for vocational training at the preparatory and secondary levels should be strengthened. There should not, of course, be too sharp a dichotomy between academic and vocational education: the curricula of the general preparatory and secondary schools should include some practical subjects (e.g., gardening, carpentry, bookkeeping) and the curricula of the vocational schools should develop knowledge in academic subjects. But we believe that the emphasis, particularly at the secondary level, should be increasingly placed on the technical and vocational aspects.

Agricultural Schools. A program of agricultural development such as we have proposed will call for a considerable number of trained staff to administer it and to operate the various government research and extension services. At present, there are two agricultural schools in Libya, one in temporary headquarters at Sidi Mesri outside Tripoli and the other at el Aweila in Cyrenaica. A third school is being established at Sebha. In principle, pupils at these schools have previously completed nine years of general education and have thus graduated from preparatory school; in practice, however, the educational background of some of the students is more limited. Twenty-two students graduated from Sidi Mesri in 1958/59 and nine from el Aweila. There is otherwise no source in Libya of persons trained in agricultural skills.

Current agricultural education thus fails to provide for training either above or below the intermediate level. While about 30 technicians a year might be sufficient to meet annual replacement requirements at the vocational agricultural school level, there is at present no prospect of obtaining replacements at the university level. Since the latter would be required at the rate of less than 10 a year, the mission feels that it would be unrealistic to establish an agricultural college at the University of Libya and recommends that suitable employees of the agricultural services should be sent abroad for agricultural training at the university level.

There also seems to be a need for a third group of agricultural technicians at a practical level, somewhat below that of the present vocational schools. A considerable number of practical demonstrators in agriculture, horticulture, animal husbandry and forestry will be required for the proposed extension services. This class of agricultural technician could well be trained in special centers of a temporary nature. The mission proposes that three such centers be established forthwith, each capable of accommodating 30 students a year for a two-year course. It is estimated that some 300 agricultural assistants will be required by the government services. Thus the temporary training centers will be able to produce the main corps of agricultural assistants in four or five years, after which the three centers could be consolidated into one continuing center which would thereafter be able to supply a sufficient number of annual replacements, and in addition begin to supply agricultural technicians of this level to the larger private farming enterprises. In our five-year program of capital expenditures we have allocated £L 30,000 for the establishment of such centers for agricultural assistants.

Agricultural schools, if they are to contribute effectively to the development of Libyan agriculture, must succeed in inculcating in their students a practical knowledge of farming and a readiness to apply this knowledge by working themselves in the fields. More emphasis should therefore be placed in the curriculum on field work and less on class work. We also suggest that the schools should aim to support themselves out of the proceeds from the sales of their own agricultural produce.

Other Technical and Vocational Training. As already noted, a number of institutions already provide facilities for technical and vocational training at the pre-university level. The Technical and Clerical Training Center in Tripoli has made a most effective contribution in this field, and the trainees have easily found jobs in government and private business. Eventually, there might be advantages in separating the clerical and technical sections into district centers serving the two coastal provinces. For the time being, however, we recommend that the present Center in Tripoli should be kept together as one unit and enlarged. Graduation from preparatory school should normally be regarded as a necessary entrance qualification.

The mission's second main recommendation relates to the School of Applied Engineering in Tripoli. This school was designed to train assistant engineers, but admission requirements are too low for this purpose, and the syllabus is inadequate. We suggest therefore that the school should be converted into a more widely based technical high school combining education in academic subjects with practical training in such fields as mechanics, carpentry, draftsmanship, surveying, building design and so forth. Courses would last three or four years, and students would have the option of specializing in a particular trade during their last year. We envisage that most of the graduates would take up jobs on leaving school, but a few might go on to the

Institute of Higher Technology (see page 264). The present school is housed in a large new building with some modern equipment, and this could be taken over and adapted to the needs of a technical high school.

Preparatory and Secondary Schools. Plans for general preparatory and secondary education have to take account of two considerations which point to the desirability of moderating the rate of expansion. The first is the shortage of teachers. At present over 90 percent of the preparatory and secondary school teachers are non-Libyans, mostly Egyptians, and it will be some years before the flow of Libyan graduates from the university will be large enough even to meet the demand for additional teachers, let alone replace expatriates. Second, while most young people in Libya exhibit a marked preference for white-collar jobs and tend to look down on manual labor, it is vital that this prejudice should be counteracted, and that a larger proportion of teenage children should be selected for technical and vocational training.

The primary, preparatory and secondary schools themselves can do much to disseminate vocational skills and create a public opinion more favorable to manual activities. We have already referred to the need for an agricultural bias in rural schools. Other schools should also include in their curriculum instruction in manual arts. This type of education requires well-trained teachers, and an in-service program for training teachers in practical handicrafts should be instituted immediately. In short, the mission urges that the values of practical training be emphasized throughout the general academic education system and not be left to the specialized schools alone.

Attention should be given to enriching the program of the preparatory and secondary schools. The present curriculum of both types of school is overcrowded. Thirteen subjects are taught during the first year of each school, thirteen in the succeeding years of the preparatory school and eleven in the last two years of the secondary school. As a measure for encouraging good habits of independent work, the number of subjects taught should be reduced and greater emphasis placed on thoroughness. Library work should be encouraged and library facilities improved. The secondary schools have to take care of the education of the intellectually more gifted children, who will eventually fill many of the higher administrative and professional posts in the government service, agriculture and industry, who will provide the teaching staff for the preparatory and secondary schools themselves and who will constitute most of the "leadership groups" in future Libyan society. There will naturally be a very strong demand for places in these schools. High standards should therefore be set for admission, and great care must be exercised in the selection of students so as to ensure the right type of student body.

Buildings and Equipment. Altogether we have envisaged the creation during the next five years of about 11,000 *additional* places in schools and training centers lying in the intermediate range between primary education at the bottom and university education at the top.[2] As a rough guide to the capital expenditures required to create these places, we have assumed that the average cost of buildings will be about £L 1,200 for a class of 25 students and the average cost of equipment about £L 4 per student. On this basis, and allowing a margin for contingencies, we arrive at a round figure of £L 600,000 for capital expenditure on buildings and equipment during the five-year period.

Supply of Teachers. The recruitment and training of teachers for preparatory and secondary schools and parallel technical and vocational schools is one of the most difficult problems Libya has to face. If an extra 11,000 pupils are to be enrolled over the next five years, at least another 400 teachers will be required, or an increase of 80 a year. This is more than the total numbers that will be graduating from the Libyan University during this period, and only a proportion of the university graduates will want to become teachers, though every encouragement should be given to them to do so. There is as yet no other institution in the country capable of turning out properly qualified teachers for schools at the preparatory and secondary levels, and though we envisage this as an important function of the proposed Higher Institute of Technology, the institute can hardly make any significant contribution during the next five years. Teachers must therefore continue to be recruited from abroad to fill the gap.

Institute of Higher Technology

Proposals for establishing an Institute of Higher Technology in Tripoli have been put forward by the Libyan Government, and the United Nations Special Fund has agreed to contribute £1 million (£L 357,000) to the project to provide equipment and to pay for the services of some of the foreign teaching staff, along with the grant of fellowships to train Libyan counterparts, who will eventually take

---

[2] Some of these additional places will already have been created in 1959/60, especially in view of the reorganization of the preparatory school system on a three-year instead of a two-year basis. The expenditure figures given here should therefore be regarded not as precise estimates, but as indications of the orders of magnitude involved.

over from the foreign teachers. The Libyan Government's contribution for the first five years of the institute's operations will be about $2 million, of which rather over half will consist of recurrent expenditures (including the provision of furniture) and rather under half of capital expenditure on land and buildings.

The project is to be executed by UNESCO, and the details have still to be worked out in consultation with the Libyan Government. The stated objective of the institute is to provide technical training at university level for students now graduating in mathematics and science from secondary schools (estimated at over 200 in 1960). It is intended that the institute should accept between 50 and 60 students a year, aiming at a total enrollment of 200 after four years. Four courses of up to five years each are proposed, one in civil engineering (to start in October 1962), one in electrical engineering (October 1963), one in mechanical engineering (October 1963) and one in food technology (October 1964). The Libyan Government will provide the site, buildings and furniture and will progressively take over financial responsibility for running the institute.

In principle, the mission strongly supports the idea of establishing an institute of technology. Its main functions, as we see them, should be to produce the many technicians required by government and private industry, particularly in the engineering and constructional fields, and at the same time to train Libyan teachers for technical and vocational schools. Technicians trained at the institute should be regarded as potential recruits to the ranks of senior technical administration. After several years in government service promising men should be sent abroad for advanced training in engineering and other applied sciences. The oil companies can also be expected to offer good opportunities for Libyans to acquire higher professional skills.

The mission's main doubt about the scheme concerns the level at which students are admitted to the institute and the length of the courses proposed. It might well have been better in our view to establish a polytechnic at the senior high school level, so that graduates could enter industry at an earlier age and develop their knowledge and skills on the job, where they could at the same time be making an effective contribution to the economy. As it is, we recommend that consideration be given to offering more shorter courses at the institute— that is, courses of two or three years duration rather than four or five.

Assuming that the institute is established at the university level, as now proposed, it should rank as equal in status to the University of Libya and be accorded the right to award diplomas or degrees comparable with those granted by the university. Otherwise it is likely to have difficulty in attracting a high caliber of students. Suitably qualified graduates of the institute should be guaranteed jobs in the government service unless they enter private employment. The mission has included a sum of £L 300,000 in its investment program for the purchase of land and construction of buildings to house the institute. The government's share of the costs of running the institute over the next five years should be covered by the general increase which we have allowed for in recurrent expenditures on education (see page 274).

University of Libya

The Libyan University was formally established in 1955 under the direct supervision of the Ministry of Education. The University opened in 1956. It is composed of three tuition-free colleges: College of Arts, Letters and Education (Benghazi); College of Science (Tripoli); College of Commerce and Economics (Benghazi). The numbers enrolled in the three colleges in 1958/59 were 151, 53 and 77 respectively, and there has been a big increase in enrollment in 1959/60. Four years of study are required for the B.A. or B.Sc. degree. A specialized B.A. degree may be attained by one additional year of study. Almost all teachers and professors of the university are non-Libyans.

In view of the decision to establish an Institute of Higher Technology the mission advises against adding other colleges and faculties to the university at this time. In too many fields the number of graduates required is too small for the establishment of a course of studies to be economical. The objective should be to make the University of Libya a medium-sized, well-organized, well-taught college of liberal arts and sciences, with particular attention given to strengthening the faculties of chemistry and geology in the College of Science at Tripoli now that oil apparently will play such an important role in the economy. Graduates should be qualified to enter classes in professional schools abroad, if they so desire, and reliance should be placed on overseas training to equip Libyans with the most advanced professional and technical skills.

Those who terminate their studies at the University of Libya should be equipped to enter the economic life of the country with a potential for leadership, both intellectual and material. Many graduates will enter the nontechnical ranks of the government's administration, while others will become teachers, particularly at the secondary schools. Since our economic development plans call for educated administrators in increasing numbers, and since our education proposals envisage an expansion, both proportionately and absolutely, of the latter years of the twelve-year school system, we recommend an eventual expansion in the university's enrollment to 700 or 800.

On the other hand, we strongly advise against too rapid an expansion in numbers. There appears to be a widespread belief in Libya that the majority of students attending secondary schools should go on to the university as a matter of course. This does not happen in other countries, and it would be a mistake to let it happen in Libya. The result, only too evident in some underdeveloped countries, is liable to be a surplus of arts graduates, who cannot find employment that measures up to their expectations, and a shortage of people with technical training capable of performing practical jobs in agriculture, industry and other sectors of the economy. Budgetary provision for the upkeep of the university has risen from £L 42,000 in 1956/57 to £L 176,000 in 1957/58 and £L 342,000 in 1958/59. Such a rate of growth in expenditures obviously cannot be maintained indefinitely, and a more selective approach to university education is needed.

The mission would further suggest that the Ministry of Education reconsider its present policy of granting free tuition, maintenance, books and special allowances to every university student. This is a wasteful use of public funds, and one that cannot be justified by considerations either of economy or of equity. In our judgment exemption from tuition fees should be the most that the university should offer all its students indiscriminately. A university scholarship board should be established to grant aid for maintenance to needy students on the basis of demonstrated special capacity and genuine need.

There should be greater emphasis on regular attendance and participation in the life of the university by its students. Of particular importance is the cultivation of habits of independent study and thinking through more emphasis on library work and on seminars where a stimulating exchange of views between teacher and students is carried on. The university is already moving in this direction and making efforts to achieve higher standards of intellectual attainment, but these still leave a good deal to be desired. While the university program and standards are being built up, it might be helpful if an examining commission of distinguished university professors from abroad were invited periodically to assist in the final examinations for degrees.

The university is in need of some new accommodation, particularly in Benghazi, and we suggest that £L 500,000 should be devoted to capital expenditure on buildings and equipment over the next five years. We have not made any specific recommendation with regard to recurrent expenditures on running the university. These would have to be accommodated within the increase of 10 percent a year for total budgetary expenditures on education suggested on page 275.

Adult and Fundamental Education

In Tripolitania a government program in adult education was started in 1957. Enrollment for 1958/59 was 11,000. Classes are held in 150 schools. This program is limited to evening classes which teach the curriculum of the first three years of the primary school. No adult vocational training has been undertaken so far. No women are enrolled. UNESCO has not undertaken any adult education program in this province.

In Cyrenaica the government program of adult education is less developed than in Tripolitania. It enrolls 5,000-6,000 adults. The program is mainly focused on combating illiteracy. There are evening vocational courses given to adults at the Trade School in Benghazi. There is also an adult program on the secondary level sponsored by a private benevolent organization. In 1958 UNESCO helped in starting a Fundamental Education Center near Benghazi. Twenty-one students are enrolled, all of whom are boarders. Candidates must have completed primary education. The center aims to assist in the preparation of rural teachers and village workers and to experiment with teaching materials appropriate for Libya. The program has four divisions: fundamental and adult education; women's education; rural education; and physical education and recreation.

There is no government-sponsored adult education program in the Fezzan, but the Fezzan Government operates a number of adult education and fundamental education centers with the help of UNESCO. The centers are located in some of the larger oases. The UNESCO team consists of three specialists with a mobile cinema unit. This is a small unit for the range of activities undertaken by it. Their program consists of teaching reading, hygiene and what might be called "social education." In 1958, 20 adult education centers were opened in the Fezzan. Enrollment in 1958/59 was 884 students. The Fezzan has an excellent program for women's fundamental education, in which UNESCO is collaborating. This project trains women community leaders, village workers and potential primary school teachers. For all this work, there is only one teacher at present, who is also expected to travel widely to enroll the pupils. The school offers day and evening classes. The program covers two years at present; it may be extended one more year shortly.

In spite of these inadequacies, the efforts in adult education have been highly productive. The mission feels, therefore, that even greater stress might be placed on this aspect of education in the next few years. Adult and fundamental education is essentially an attempt to bridge the gap between the past and the future: to ameliorate the lack of education among today's adults until the education of today's children can make itself felt in the future. Thus, adult education is an immediate priority since its need will eventually tend to disappear. As a matter of urgency, then, the mission recommends that the following steps be taken:

1. A special directorate for adult education should be created within the Federal Ministry of Education in order to study the problems of adult education in the country, advise the Nazirates on these problems and coordinate plans for the expansion of adult education in the country as a whole.
2. The Center for Fundamental Education near Benghazi should be strengthened. The staff, program, classrooms, equipment and boarding facilities of the center should be developed so as to render it a truly national center for the training of community leaders for the country as a whole. Both the women's and men's sections of this project should be developed, and it should be closely linked with the scheme for agricultural development in the Gebel Akhdar.
3. Short courses should be established for the teachers who are engaged in adult education.
4. The women's center for fundamental education in Sebha should be strengthened by the addition of at least two more staff members. The two aspects of its program should be developed: the women's fundamental education program and the women's teacher training program.
5. An adult education program should be established as an integral part of the programs of the various vocational training centers in Tripolitania and Cyrenaica.
6. A campaign against illiteracy should be conducted by establishing more adult education centers in preparatory and secondary schools, and by seeking the volunteer services of secondary school students and student teachers to join in the campaign.
7. Lecturers and students at the university should be encouraged

to participate in the adult education campaign by helping with night classes, extension lectures and summer courses.

8. Extensive use should be made of radio for adult education purposes. Special programs should be directed to urban and rural audiences and there should also be special programs for women.

Most of these measures can be undertaken with the use of existing buildings, but additional equipment will be required. In our five-year program we have suggested that £L 50,000 should be earmarked for this purpose.

In all fields of education, but particularly in adult education, there is considerable scope for coordination of effort between UNESCO and the other agencies concerned with such matters in Libya. At present such agencies appear to work without sufficient reference to the activities of others. The mission urges that attempts be made to improve methods of liaison and consultation with respect to educational programing.

Foreign Study

A number of Libyans will continue to go abroad for some phases of their education, both because of the limited requirements for certain types of professional men and other specialists and because of the lack of certain types of educational resources within Libya. In order to maximize the advantages accruing to Libya from such foreign study and in order to get the best possible value for the money so expended, there ought to be a considered policy on selection of scholarship recipients, their fields of specialization, numbers and conditions of appointment. The mission therefore welcomes the establishment of the Commission on Foreign Study.

During 1958/59 there were 255 students studying abroad on government or agency grants and about 50 studying at their own expense. In all over £L 300,000 had been allocated by the LARC for this purpose up to the end of March 1959, though less than £L 100,000 had actually been spent at that date. United Nations agencies have contributed extensively, and provision has also been made in the budgets of the Federal Ministry of Education (£L 77,500 in 1957/58 and £L 66,500 in 1958/59). Continuation of federal grants at around the current levels, together with the substantial carry-over of U.S. aid funds, should be adequate to meet requirements for overseas study during the next few years.

As the mission sees it, there are two types of suitable recipients of foreign study grants: the potential professional who has advanced as far up the Libyan education ladder as is possible, and the government administrator or technician who has advanced far enough in his practical functioning so as to warrant further training abroad. In both cases the requirements should be that the candidate be mature enough to be able to define the purposes of his course of foreign studies, that he has every intention of continuing to work in Libya and that his prior training and experience be such that the time spent abroad may be limited to obtaining instruction and orientation which could not have been obtained in Libya. The other important criterion for making a foreign study grant should be that the end-use of such study, namely the potential employment of the candidate, be assured. Students should thus be selected on the basis of posts to be occupied on return to Libya.

Administration

Central Ministry of Education. There are four educational authorities in Libya—the Central Ministry and the three Nazirates of Education in Tripolitania, Cyrenaica and Fezzan. The Ministry of Education is responsible for supervising the following aspects of education throughout Libya: formulation and modification of the programs of instruction; determining the duration of the academic year; examinations; standards and certificates; textbooks; qualifications of teachers; supervision of private schools and of the University of Libya. Other duties pertaining to education are in the hands of the provincial education authorities. Each Nazirate decides upon the number, location and kinds of schools which should be established in the province; the funds to be used and their allocation; salaries of teachers; regulations for the construction of school buildings and the provision of equipment. The pattern of organization of each Nazirate follows the central pattern rather closely.

The cost of the administrative organization is very high in relation to the number of people served. The total school population served does not justify the existence of four such elaborate administrative organizations, each with its complete cadre of personnel. Furthermore, the dual control of education by the federal ministry and provincial Nazirates of Education, without a clear-cut division of responsibility, tends to cause duplication of effort and to lower efficiency. Another weakness of the present system is that educational facilities are unevenly distributed. Some towns and cities are adequately supplied with schools—e.g., Benghazi, Derna, Tripoli—whereas large areas, especially rural areas, are without any schools at all. In a country where educational resources are limited and the need great, it is essential that schools be built where the need is greatest. There is no central bureau of records in the Ministry of Education which would make it possible to conduct continuing studies of the educational system on a national scale.

It was suggested earlier in this chapter that a high-level technical adviser should be appointed to the Ministry of Education, and that a Bureau of Research and Records should be established under his direction. In addition to the task of preparing a long-term program for education, this adviser should be asked to advise on the distribution of functions between the Ministry of Education and the Nazirates with a view to securing a rational division of responsibilities between the center and the provinces which would permit a streamlining of administration and substantial economies in headquarters staff. A possible solution might lie in the creation of interprovincial boards working alongside the Ministry of Education to administer the various branches of post-primary education—preparatory and secondary educations; technical and vocational training; and adult and fundamental education. There would then be no need to have separate staffs to deal with these subjects in each of the three provinces, and the three Nazirates of Education would be able to concentrate on looking after the primary schools, which is a big job in itself.

The review of functions should include an examination of the existing educational records with the object of determining what types of records should in future be kept centrally. The technical adviser and his staff might also be made responsible for publishing a regular bulletin dealing with educational problems, which could be distributed to all schools in the country.

Selected officials of the Ministry and Nazirates of Education should undergo a course of training designed to equip them for the work of carrying on the administration and implementing long-range development plans. The mission also recommends that the Higher Council on Education be strengthened through the addition of representatives from the Ministries of Finance and Agriculture. The main function of this enlarged advisory council would be to review policy changes suggested by the technical expert and make recommendations to the minister concerning their implementation.

Provincial Education Authorities. One of the most important administrative measures which could be adopted on the provincial level is the strengthening of the provincial Executive Education Committee by adding to its membership several leading educators in the province, such as representatives from the university and training colleges, and one or two of the more experienced inspectors and representatives from the Nazirates of Health and Agriculture. The major task of this committee is to see to it that education in the province really meets the needs of the province, and that high standards and quality of education are maintained. Some of the specific tasks which should be assigned to the Executive Education Committee are the following: coordination of health, agriculture and education in the school program; changes and modifications in the program that may be deemed necessary to meet special needs of different areas; and evaluating the significance of new educational experiments and policies.

In order to secure greater cooperation between home and school it is recommended that the government make every effort to establish local citizens' committees to work with local schools. Such matters as improving attendance, keeping the school buildings and equipment in a state of repair, securing the cooperation of parents in providing a more healthy life for the child—these are matters which even in the simplest of communities can be accomplished through such local school boards. If it is possible to secure the services of the more energetic citizens in the village for this purpose, the local committee could become an effective force for making the school a center for the social improvement of the community, and this would contribute to social development purposes even beyond immediate education objectives. The establishment of such local committees will, of course, require the leadership of capable teachers and inspectors to make them successful.

Inspection and Supervision. The inspector and school principal are in a particularly strategic position to help in the improvement of education in Libya. They are the link between the teachers and pupils, on the one hand, and the provincial and federal administration on the other. Traditionally the school principal and inspector have viewed their duties as those of an academic watch-dog, i.e., to see to it that the teacher attends his classes regularly, keeps records properly and teaches his classes in accordance with the dictates of the official syllabus. Modern education assigns a more positive role to the inspector and principal in the belief that the primary function of the inspector and principal is to help the teacher improve his methods and his knowledge. He is a teacher's guide. The mission is of the opinion that the number of supervisors should be increased, and that special in-service institutes concerned with modern methods of inspection and supervision should be organized.

Summary of Proposed Expenditures

The recommendations made in this chapter would entail a total capital outlay in the public sector of £L 2,250,000 over the five years 1960/61-1964/65. The total would be made up as follows:

(£L '000)

	Five-year total	Annual average
Primary schools	770	154
Preparatory and secondary schools[a]	600	120
Agricultural training centers	30	6
Higher Institute of Technology	300	60
University of Libya	500	100
Adult education	50	10
Total	2,250	450

[a] Including technical and vocational schools other than those specifically mentioned in this table.

The annual average level of capital expenditures proposed would be nearly double the estimated average for the three years 1955/56-1957/58 (see Statistical Appendix, Table S.8), but slightly below the level for 1957/58 alone and well below the level for 1958/59 when a large program of school building was financed by the LARC. It is not, however, in capital expenditures, but in recurrent expenditures that the main impact of the rapid expansion of educational facilities will be reflected.

The mission does not have complete figures of expenditures on education for any year later than 1957/58. This makes it extremely difficult to make even a rough forecast of the recurrent expenditures likely to be involved in implementing the program we have outlined. Total recurrent expenditures on education in 1957/58, excluding contributions from the United Nations, are estimated at about £L 2 million, and it would appear that they have since been increased to about £L 3 million a year.

During the next five years, we envisage a further 25 percent increase in enrollment in primary schools, as compared with 1958/59, while enrollment in schools at the preparatory and secondary levels will be more than doubled. Provision must also be made for the growth of the university, for increased expenditures on adult education and for improvements of standards in all branches of education and training. We feel that in these circumstances recurrent expenditures on education (mainly on teachers' salaries) must be expected to grow by at least 10 percent a year, or by about 60 percent over the five-year period as a whole. This would raise these expenditures from an estimated £L 3 million a year now to over £L 4.8 million in 1964/65 and would entail additional expenditures over the five-year period as a whole of about £L 5 million. Total public expenditures on education at the end of the period would then be equal to about 10 percent of the present gross domestic product. Even when due allowance is made for the possible growth of national income over the next five years, the percentage of total resources going into education would still be very high. There are few other countries in the world, developed or underdeveloped, in which the proportion exceeds 4 percent, and it appears to be more commonly in the region of 2-3 percent.

The mission has doubts about the advisability of attempting to raise numbers in school any faster than suggested in this chapter, even if the administrative problems attendant on the expansion of the educational system can be successfully handled. Nor do we favor overlavish expenditures on school buildings, particularly at a time when the resources of the local building industry are heavily engaged. On the other hand, a strong case can be made out for raising the salaries of Libyan teachers. The mission believes that measures to improve the teacher's lot and make the profession a more attractive one deserves a high place in any list of claims for additional funds, and we recommend that higher pay for teachers should be one of the items included in the Supplementary Program.

CHAPTER 14 *HEALTH AND COMMUNITY SERVICES*

PUBLIC HEALTH

Present Health Conditions

General health conditions in Libya have not given rise to any serious alarm during the last ten years. Although the rate of population growth is relatively low, this is apparently due more to the unusually high infant mortality rate than it is to any particularly heavy morbidity among the adult population. There have been no major epidemics, and the people have not seriously suffered from the endemic and debilitating diseases which cause so much illness in many countries of the Orient. No study has been made of the measurement of levels of health of the Libyan people, and in the absence of accurate health records in all areas, an assessment of the health of the people cannot be supported by statistics. However, general observation made it clear to us that relatively adequate curative services are available. Current sickness rates can therefore be primarily attributed to the lack of appropriate health education and insufficient stress on the other aspects of preventive medicine.

The three most important preventable diseases in Libya are infantile gastro-enteritis, eye infections—chiefly trachoma—and tuberculosis. The infant mortality rate in Libya, though it is showing some decline in recent years, is believed to be still three or four times the rate in neighboring countries. Something like one infant out of every two born alive in Libya dies during its first year. Gastro-enteritis and tetanus are by far the most important factors in producing this very high death rate among infants.

It is estimated that at least three-quarters of the population show signs of active or past inflammatory disease of the eyes. The complaint is particularly severe in lower age groups among school children. Trachoma causes serious late complications which often result in partial loss of sight and sometimes in total blindness. No survey of the total and partial blind in the country has been made, but most observers

276

consider that the number must be not less than one percent of the population.

From the observations of WHO and other experts who have visited the country since 1951 and from the yearly increase in the number of hospital admissions for pulmonary tuberculosis, it appears that the incidence of tuberculosis is increasing. Total admissions for pulmonary tuberculosis during 1958 in Cyrenaican hospitals numbered 1,194 (about 0.4 percent of the population). Poor nutrition, overcrowding and bad housing conditions—which exist all over the country, especially in the poor areas of Tripoli and Benghazi—are considered to be major factors in the spread of the disease. The incidence of pulmonary tuberculosis in the Fezzan is relatively low.

Hospital Services

The country is well covered by a network of dispensaries and hospitals. There are large central hospitals in Tripoli and Benghazi and one is being developed in Sebha. There has been an appreciable increase in the number of hospitals, beds and dispensaries during the last five years. Great stress has been placed on the construction of new hospitals and the expansion and improvement of existing ones, and a sizeable proportion of the foreign aid funds has gone toward this end. There is no doubt that this was necessary in the initial stages of development of Libya's health services, and some hospital units still need a good deal of rehabilitation and some expansion. The stage has now been reached, however, when there should be a shift of emphasis from new construction to the consolidation of existing services.

In Cyrenaica there are ten government hospitals in all—the central hospital in Benghazi, four large general hospitals at Barce, Messa, Derna and Tobruk, three smaller hospitals in Agedabia, el Abiar and Kufra, a tuberculosis hospital near Barce and a mental hospital also at Barce. There are no hospitals for infectious diseases or isolation hospitals, but all general hospitals have some isolation beds and the larger hospitals also have some beds for TB and psychiatric cases. Benghazi and Derna hospitals have large TB wings. We recommend a number of improvements in existing hospitals (see Annex XXII) and, in addition, suggest that a new isolation hospital be established in Benghazi. The estimated capital cost of this program over five years is £L 310,000.

A tuberculosis sanatorium of 120 beds has been built by the LPDSA near Cyrene (Shahat). The main building was completed two years ago, but work is still proceeding on construction of staff quarters. The estimate of total cost when completed and equipped is about £L 300,000. Although the project was undertaken on expert medical advice, the mission considers that the sanatorium's location is such that the cost of running and maintaining it is likely to be extremely high. The money could in our view have been better used for rehabilitation and expansion of the TB hospital at Barce and the TB wings of Derna and Benghazi hospitals. However, if the sanatorium is to be operated as the main center for the treatment of tuberculosis, economies should be effected in the facilities for treatment elsewhere.

In Tripolitania there is a great deal of centralization at Tripoli town. The Tripoli government hospital (1,267 beds) is really a hospital group in magnificent buildings, and the main blocks are well equipped with modern hospital apparatus and furniture. There are district hospitals at Misurata, Zawia and Jefran and a TB hospital at Busetta. Proposals for expanded facilities, costing an estimated £L 300,000, will be found in Annex XXII. A hospital building was started at Gadames by the LPDSA three years ago and has since been left unfinished. We recommend its completion forthwith. The present dispensary-hospital unit is quite inadequate in view of the size of the local population and the potential influx of tourists.

The mental hospital in the suburb of Feshlum is located in unsuitable old barrack buildings and is very overcrowded. A new site has been found for this hospital a few kilometers outside Tripoli in a group of old police buildings. Funds are required for modifications, alterations and additions to this building to make it a proper mental hospital of 450 beds. We also recommend that leprosy patients be removed to a leprosarium of 50 beds which should be constructed outside Tripoli with facilities for outdoor employment of the patients, e.g., gardening, basketmaking and so forth. This leprosarium should only be used for isolation of severe and complicated cases of leprosy. Non-infectious and uncomplicated cases of leprosy should be treated on an ambulatory basis.

In the Fezzan there is room for improvement in all four existing hospitals (see Annex XXII), while at Murzuk a new 20-bed hospital should be built and equipped with facilities for surgery. The capital outlay involved in these improvements is estimated at £L 90,000.

Ambulance Transport

Every hospital and many large dispensaries have at least one motor ambulance car attached for the transport of patients and medical staff. The larger institutions have two to four ambulance cars and some utility vehicles for stores and personnel. But all transport is under the control of the Communications Departments which also provide maintenance. This procedure of control by one department and usage by another sometimes creates operational difficulties and holdups. The mission recommends that the Health Department in each province should have full jurisdiction and control over its own ambulance service. There appears to be an over-all shortage of ambulance transport, especially in the Fezzan, and we have set aside £L 75,000 in our capital investment program for the purchase of vehicles. There is some justification for the Fezzan—where road transport is costly and unreliable—to maintain a light aircraft service for the transport of serious and emergency cases from distant areas like Ghat to the central hospital at Sebha (see Chapter 12). Provision is made for this in the suggested allocation of funds for transport.

Medical Supplies and Equipment

The three provinces maintain separate provincial medical stores, at Tripoli, Benghazi and Sebha. Methods of procurement differ in each case, and there is no uniformity in hospital pharmacopoeias. Tripoli obtains most of its drugs and medical supplies from Italy, Fezzan from Tunis or Algeria and Cyrenaica from England. There appears to be a strong predilection for proprietory drugs and expensive formulations under brand names.

The Federal Ministry, with the help of the three provincial Directors of Health, should make a standard list of drugs and medicines for use in hospitals throughout the country, basing this on the International Pharmacopoeia. A central medical stores depot in Tripoli should be organized under the federal government. Procurement should be on the basis of international tender and supplies should be obtained direct from the manufacturers or their representatives. The estimated cost of establishing a central store is £L 50,000. The provincial stores should receive their supplies by indenting on the central medical stores. This procedure could be expected to produce a very appreciable saving (10-15 percent) in the expenditure on drugs and medical stores, including all hospital equipment; this expenditure is currently believed to be in the region of £L 200,000 a year.

Port Health Control and Quarantine

The sanitation of seaports is fairly satisfactory, and there are dispensaries at Tripoli and Benghazi seaports for dock workers and passengers needing medical aid. There are no arrangements for isolation or quarantine at the ports or airports, and this has to be carried out, when necessary, on board or in hospital. With the development of the two major seaports and the two international airports, suitable quarantine arrangements must be provided for all, and the mission has suggested that £L 40,000 should be allowed for this in the five-year investment program.

Preventive Services

An appreciation of the importance of a preventive health service by the government and leaders of the country is the first prerequisite for the building up of that service. But even if the necessary institutions and the trained staff are available, nothing substantial can be achieved unless health education reaches every home in the country. Emphasis is now gradually shifting toward strengthening the preventive services and more attention is being paid to this need. There is a growing realization that better health conditions and economic development are interrelated. WHO, UNICEF and LAJS have done much toward development of community health programs in the country. WHO is currently helping in the development of health training institutions and maternal and child health development, while LAJS is providing the necessary funds for expanding activities in the field of basic public health and sanitation.

Ante-natal work is of special importance in a country where many women are anemic and undernourished and frequent pregnancies impose a period of severe strain during which extra nourishment and rest is needed. Special food supplements are being provided. The mission hopes this program will be continued.

Infant welfare needs special attention as most of the newborn are weak and underweight and require much care during the first year of life if they are to survive. To reduce the very high infant mortality rate, a concerted effort has to be made to improve and expand antenatal care, infant welfare and health education of the mother in infant feeding and general hygiene. The value of proper midwifery services in this connection cannot be overstressed. Care of children during the weaning period is equally important because of diarrhoeal diseases and other hazards.

LAJS has established four Maternity and Child Health Centers (MCH)—three in Tripolitania at Misurata, Garian and Zavia, and one in Cyrenaica at Barce. These are model institutions with respect

to buildings, equipment and staffing, but the scarcity of suitably qualified personnel is an ever-recurring problem. These centers provide
ante-natal and post-natal care, infant welfare, public health nursing
and public health education. WHO, with the help of UNICEF and in
cooperation with the Ministry of Health, has established two MCH
centers at Benghazi and Suk el Giuma near Tripoli, which, though
essentially training and demonstration projects, are assisting the existing public health services in this field. Tripoli has also one center in
the old town which is managed entirely by local staff and is doing
useful work. A center is being planned for Benghazi by the provincial
Health Department, with the help of UNICEF, and is expected to start
functioning in the near future. In the opening of new MCH and public
health centers and in the placement of trained MCH auxiliaries, better
coordination should be attained between the federal and provincial
governments and the various aid agencies. We recommend that these
MCH centers should be merged into an integrated system of general
health centers and sub-centers serving all towns and the larger villages
in the country (see page 287).

Children who survive the first five years of life are fairly healthy,
though rather undernourished and subject to skin diseases and, during
summer, inflammatory diseases of the eyes. A school health service as
an entity exists in Tripoli and Benghazi where school medical officers
have been appointed and regular medical examinations of school children are carried out and advice and treatment provided. In other
areas the local medical officers and, in some cases, the sanitary inspectors visit schools, though not regularly. The development of a good
school health service throughout the country should be an important
item in the long-term health program for Libya. This service should
be adapted to the conditions existing in Libya, and particular attention
should be given to school sanitation, to control of endemic diseases
such as communicable eye diseases and to the dissemination of simple
rules of personal hygiene. A school feeding program is essential, and
the mission recommends that the present program be continued for
at least the next five years, with as much use as possible being made of
locally grown foods like barley and dates.

Health education, though mainly the responsibility of the health
services, must also be carried out in the home, in schools and in public places not only by health educators, midwives, nurses and doctors,
but also by schoolteachers, employers and public men and women.
The international agencies have done a great deal of work in teacher
training in public health education, and simple hygiene is now taught

in most of the schools. Training courses have also been conducted for health educators and home visitors. All MCH centers are providing health education for mothers and children both at the centers and during home visits. LAJS includes health education activity in its health development program and provides in-service training courses in this field to overcome the restriction imposed by lack of adequately educated personnel for regular training. Health education activities should be continued and expanded, depending on the availability of trained staff, and health information dissemination among the general public should be intensified by audio-visual methods, films in the cinemas, broadcasting and holding of health weeks, baby shows and the like. Use should be made of the great stress laid in the Moslem scriptures and sayings of the Prophet on personal cleanliness and community hygiene.

Doctors

Out of a total of 152 doctors employed by the three provinces at the time of the mission's visit there were only five Libyans. There were five women doctors, all foreigners. Until full Libyanization can be effected, recruitment of foreign doctors should be the responsibility of the federal government operating on a nation-wide basis, and without undue consideration of any nationals in specific areas. The intake of specialists should be adjusted to the actual needs of the country for the different categories instead of being determined on a haphazard basis as at present. The mission found, for example, that although there was no specialist in medicine or general surgery in Tripolitania (apart from two in orthopedia), there were five specialists in V.D. and dermatology, four in tropical diseases, four in chest diseases and three in pediatrics.

All foreigners seeking employment should undertake to start learning colloquial Arabic early after arriving in the country, and extra emoluments should be allowed to those who reach a reasonable standard of proficiency. Pay scales should also be uniform throughout the country, and apart from consultants and specialists, doctors should be employed on a whole-time basis and should be debarred from private practice and given a suitable non-practicing allowance.

If this were done, the number of doctors in government service could be reduced, while maintaining efficiency and increasing scales of pay. At present there is a distinction in Tripolitania between locally recruited doctors and those recruited abroad, with the former receiving as little as £L 67 a month, while the latter receive a minimum of £L 100 a month, a minimum which is applicable to all government doctors in Cyrenaica and the Fezzan irrespective of where they are recruited. We suggest that the minimum of £L 100 be extended to all government doctors in Libya. The rise in the pay scale in Tripolitania could be effected without any increase in the total payroll, since the number of government doctors there would be reduced. Furthermore, we recommend that there should be some provision for periodic increments in pay in order to reward long service. In addition to basic pay, all government doctors should receive a flat non-practicing allowance of, say, £L 300 a year. Specialists should further receive an extra allowance, ranging perhaps from £L 300 to £L 500 a year, in accordance with seniority. We feel that doctors who have professional qualifications in public health should be regarded as specialists and remunerated accordingly.

At the time of the mission's visit there were 47 Libyans undergoing medical training abroad—31 in the three medical faculties of Egypt, 8 in the United Kingdom, 2 each in Turkey and Spain, 3 in Poland and 1 in Italy. Most of these were on fellowships or scholarships and all of them were in their first three years of training. As six years are required to graduate in medicine and at least another three to specialize, Libya will be dependent on foreign doctors for many years. It is recommended that in future Libyans should preferably be sent for medical training to those countries which have social conditions and environment similar to Libya. On graduation they should return to their country and spend at least two years in government service under qualified supervision before they proceed for specialization, which may be undertaken in advanced countries such as the United Kingdom and the United States.

In a country where the seclusion of women exists, it is essential to have a good proportion of women doctors, preferably from Arabic-speaking countries. As far as possible, the central hospitals at Benghazi and Tripoli should have at least two women doctors each, and all MCH centers should be staffed with woman doctors. These women doctors, apart from their professional value, would be an example to the Libyan women of the part women can and should play in the social services of the country.

As there will not be a large enough demand for doctors in the foreseeable future to justify the establishment of a medical school in Libya, we recommend that the scheme of medical training abroad of Libyan men and women should be a continuous one. With economic progress some young people may eventually be expected to be going abroad for medical training at their own initiative and expense.

Nurses, Midwives, Health Visitors

At present there are no female Libyan nurses, midwives or health visitors. The few qualified women working in hospitals and health centers or training institutions are all foreigners. Nursing in hospitals is mainly carried out by Italian nuns and Libyan male and female nursing attendants. Although there are three training institutions in the country for women, the response for enrollment has not been encouraging. This is due not only to the strict seclusion of women, but also to the traditional attitude of the middle class toward employment of females. This attitude may be modified with the passage of time and the spread of education, but in the meantime there will have to be continued reliance on non-Libyan nurses. While full use of the school of nursing should be made, we also recommend that four Libyan girls with secondary education—two each from Tripolitania and Cyrenaica—be sent abroad for a full diploma course in nursing and midwifery. Preference for overseas training would be a factor in attracting girls to undergo nursing training in the first instance. On their return, the pioneer trainees would be able to help in establishing training institutes in Libya, and in influencing others to enter the profession.

In the meantime, it is essential that there should be a balanced quota of foreign women to fill posts in the health services. The central hospitals in Benghazi and Tripoli should have at least a small proportion of qualified professional nurses—one matron and three ward sisters in Benghazi and one matron, one assistant matron and six ward sisters in Tripoli. This would form the nucleus of a good nursing service, with the help of Italian nuns and local available staff, and would also contribute to raising the standard of work of the semi-trained personnel. As trained Libyan girls become available from the school of nursing, they should be absorbed in the service.

We strongly recommend that, in addition to the Tripoli school for female nurses, a school for male nurses should be established at Benghazi, and WHO should again be requested for advice and help both in assessing the recruitment possibilities for such a school and in its establishment. Both schools should admit candidates from all three provinces and no provincial quotas should be prescribed. The need for properly qualified male nurses is obvious in Libya, and even when female nurses in sufficient numbers become available, male nurses will still have a place in the health services of the country. The school for male nurses should be of the graduate standard, and the in-take could be so phased as to keep pace with the expansion of secondary education.

Other Health Workers

There is a small number of Libyans who have been trained as pharmacists, radiographers and laboratory technicians, but there is need for many more. In-service training is the best means of filling present gaps, and suitable candidates should be sent abroad for advanced courses, preferably to other Middle Eastern countries. Qualified physiotherapists and dieticians are needed for the central hospitals in Tripoli and Benghazi. At the time of the mission's visit five Libyans were undergoing courses in pharmacy abroad—two in Egypt and three in the United Kingdom.

Cyrenaica has a Chief Sanitary Inspector who assists the Director in public health work. LAJS in its health and sanitation program had by the beginning of 1959 trained 32 Libyan health and sanitation personnel abroad, mostly at the American University of Beirut and some in the United States. This is a continuing program, and the only limiting factor is the availability of suitable candidates with basic education and knowledge of the English language. Short training courses have also been organized in Benghazi and Tripoli for Libyan sanitary inspectors.

A small corps of trained Libyan sanitarians now exists, distributed over the country. Twenty-two sanitarians, after completing one year's training at the Health Assistants and Sanitarians Institute in Benghazi, received their certificates in October 1958. Of these, nine each were from Cyrenaica and Tripolitania and four from Fezzan. A further 18 sanitarians graduated in 1959. The first class of health assistants will be graduating in 1960 and should constitute a valuable addition to the medical services, particularly in rural areas.

It is estimated that the requirements of the country for health assistants and sanitarians will be satisfied after three to four classes of each have passed out of the institute. It is suggested that the institute be used for training of other categories of medical auxiliaries, e.g., laboratory and x-ray technicians. This will require some additional equipment and staff and close cooperation with the Benghazi general hospital. The institute should arrange refresher courses for working personnel.

Registration and Licensing

There is no federal council of medical registration. Registration of doctors and dentists is carried out by the provincial Nazirates of Health who issue annual licenses for professional practice. An all-Libya Council of Medical Registration should be established, with the Director General of the Ministry of Health as chairman and with representatives of all three provinces as members. This council should be the registering authority for doctors, dentists, nurses, midwives, medical technicians, pharmacists and all qualified technical personnel connected with the medical profession.

Reorganization of Health Services

We feel that the medical administrative set-up could be made more effective by delegating responsibility for the routine day-to-day administration of the health services entirely to the medical administrators, with only questions of policy, finance and coordination to be dealt with at the ministerial (or Nazirate) level. To give due emphasis to preventive health measures, we recommend that the designation of "Director of Medical Services" be changed to "Director of Health Services." In the provinces of Tripolitania and Cyrenaica the director should have only one assistant director, who should be qualified in public health and who should be responsible for coordinating and supervising all community health work in the province. In the Fezzan the Medical Officer of Health at Sebha should act as assistant director of public health in addition to his other duties. It would be an advantage to have nonmedical Libyan administrative assistants for all nontechnical routine matters in the two major provinces, as is now the case in Tripoli town. The matrons of the general hospitals at Benghazi and Tripoli should also act as advisers to the directors in all matters connected with the nursing organization, pending the appointment of a well-qualified public health nurse administrator on a full-time basis with the central health administration.

Health services should be reorganized on the basis of integrated health centers in all sizeable urban communities, supported by district hospitals and the central hospital, and with integrated subcenters in rural areas. The health center should combine public health services with dispensary facilities and coordinate preventive and curative medicine in one organization. It should provide the following services: maternal and child health, hygiene and environmental sanitation, public health education and public health nursing, school health, immunization and BCG vaccination and a dispensary to provide routine out-patient treatment. It should be under the supervision of a medical officer of health who should also be responsible for all sub-centers, dispensaries and ambulatoria in the area. He should be assisted at the health center by a team of suitable medical and auxiliary personnel as they become available. The inclusion of a woman doctor would be ideal, but a beginning could be made by a team of at least one, and preferably two, nurse-midwives, a health assistant, a sanitarian and medical orderly or male nurse. The sub-centers should have a health assistant and a sanitarian and, if possible, an auxiliary nurse-midwife. Each health center should have an ambulance and a utility car attached to it, and sub-centers in sparsely populated desert areas should each be equipped with a sturdy cross-country vehicle. The locations of these sub-centers should be widely publicized amongst the nomads of the area.

The object of developing the health center system is to prevent disease, promote health and afford early treatment. It would reduce the necessity for people to be hospitalized and thus reduce the need for expanding hospital services. We thus recommend the conversion of existing MCH centers into integrated health centers. A beginning has been made at Suk el Giuma, and a center has also been built at Zawia which is expected to start functioning in the near future. In addition, there are plans for conversion of the MCH centers at Barce, Misurata, Tagiura and Garian into fully integrated health centers or sub-centers. We recommend the allocation of £L 200,000 for the further development of health centers in the next five years and of £L 90,000 to establish a network of rural dispensaries.

Nutrition

Little reliable information is available about food consumption and nutrition in Libya. In general, the typical Libyan diet is monotonous and is heavily concentrated on a few items of vegetable origin, particularly cereals, consumption of which in the coastal provinces is estimated at nearly 400 grams per head a day. Consumption of meat, eggs and fish is generally very low. Milk consumption is high among the pastoral tribes, but quite inadequate so far as the rest of the population is concerned. Sugar consumption is much higher than in most other countries with comparable income levels, being closely related to the consumption of tea. Fresh fruits are eaten only in small amounts, apart from dates, which are an important article of consumption in the areas where they are grown (but not elsewhere).

Clinical signs of malnutrition among adults appear to be rare except for some cases of calorie deficiency due to poor economic conditions. Among children, however, signs of malnutrition are found very frequently and are believed to be due to incorrect feeding and weaning practices. Young children usually look thin and underdeveloped, which suggests a low calorie intake and an inadequate supply of proteins.

In order to correct some of these deficiencies particular attention should be given to encouraging consumption of fish, milk and other foods rich in proteins. Education in nutrition can go a long way toward helping to solve the problems created by poor feeding and weaning habits, and the school feeding program is helping to make good some of the most serious deficiencies in the diet of children. From a nutritional point of view it is highly desirable that Libyans should spend a smaller proportion of their income on sugar and tea and a higher proportion on other foods, and this is a point that should be borne in mind in connection with taxation policy.

TOWN AND VILLAGE WATER SUPPLIES

In most towns water supplies are piped and are derived from bacteriologically protected wells and springs. The only treatment carried out in most towns, including Tripoli and Benghazi, is chlorination. Some of these chlorination plants were originally installed by the military authorities. The rural population obtain their water mainly from shallow wells which are subject to pollution. In some cases, especially in the Gebel and in the Fezzan, the source is artesian wells or springs, while in other areas the only source is rainwater collected from roof-tops and stored in cisterns. The town of Tobruk presents one of the more difficult water supply problems as the available supply is very saline and inadequate for its growing needs (see Annex XXIII).

Tripoli and Benghazi, together with about forty small towns and villages in Tripolitania, ten in Cyrenaica and three in the Fezzan, have piped water supplies. The pumping capacity of the municipal waterworks in Tripoli is about 36,000 cubic meters in 24 hours. A shortage of water is known to exist in certain parts of the city, and several big industries were found to have bored wells and pumped their own water. Most of the other drinking water utilities in Tripolitania are owned and operated by municipalities, but maintained by the Nazirate of Public Works. In Cyrenaica and the Fezzan all utilities are owned and operated by the corresponding Nazirates. The reservoir capacity in no town seen was found to be adequate. None of the utilities keeps commercial accounts, and except for Tripoli, where revenue is only a little less than operating costs, all are heavily subsidized by government because water rates are everywhere very low.

The government has spent over £L 1 million since Independence in developing town water supplies in Libya and a great deal more on hydrological surveys and investigations. There are no perennial rivers in the country, and few places where shallow wells can be dug to supply villages with drinking water. Reliance has therefore to be placed on supplies from occasional springs and rain water collected in cisterns fed from roofs of houses and from paved areas in the towns. These sources of supply are unsatisfactory, and considerable efforts have been made in recent years to tap deep underground water.

For capital development in the period 1960-65, the mission recommends that £L 700,000 should be set aside to augment existing installations and provide new ones. Of this £L 300,000 would be for Tripolitania, £L 350,000 for Cyrenaica and £L 50,000 for the Fezzan. We attach particularly high priority to the scheme for boring three new wells to supply water to Tripoli, as the present source of Tripoli's water shows signs of overexploitation, and there has been a marked rise in its salt content in recent years (see Annex XXIII). The Nazirate of Public Works and the Municipality of Tripoli should work in close association in this matter with the proposed Geological and Hydrological Department recommended in Chapter 7 of this report. In Cyrenaica the mission attaches particular importance to the schemes for increasing the reservoir's capacity at Benghazi at an estimated cost of £L 80,000, for providing better water supplies at Barce, Cyrene and Derna (£L 100,000) and for drilling wells in villages (£L 80,000).

The mission suggests that the present arrangement in Tripolitania, whereby one authority is responsible for the operation and another for the maintenance of waterworks, is unsatisfactory and recommends that all town waterworks (except at Tripoli, where the municipality employs its own maintenance staff) should in future be vested in the provincial Nazirates of Public Works, which should also collect the revenue as in Cyrenaica and the Fezzan. Any subsidy that is necessary would then appear in the accounts of the Nazirates. The existing rates charged for water piped to private premises appear too low. The use of piped water for gardens should be forbidden where supplies are short, and charged for at commercial rates where permitted. The revenue losses (at present more than £L 100,000 a year) should be kept constantly under review and an endeavor made to reduce them by raising rates in appropriate cases, by imposing charges where no charge is at present levied and above all by better collection of monies due.

We do not, however, suggest imposing any charge for water obtained from public fountains and standpipes, which for some rural communities is the principal source of supply.

The mission considers that there is a good case on welfare grounds for including the supply of water to towns and villages amongst the projects for which additional provision should be made in the Supplementary Program. Great hardship is often experienced, particularly during hot weather, by people living in places where drinking water is scarce. It was noticed, for example, that in Zliten drinking water brought into the town on donkeys sold at about 1 millieme a liter; and at Hon even the hospital had to be supplied with drinking water by animal transport. A Supplementary Program should not, however, be considered until steps have been taken to establish a better organization for the construction and operation of waterworks in line with the recommendations outlined above.

For the Supplementary Program we suggest that capital expenditures on the provision of piped water supplies might be increased by anything up to £L 250,000 over the five years. This additional expenditure should be distributed over all three provinces, with an allocation of not less than £L 50,000 to the Fezzan.

We do not envisage the need to make additional financial provision in our program for losses incurred in the operation of water undertakings in Libya. As already noted, these losses are currently in excess of £L 100,000 a year. The federal government should as a matter of policy require the provincial governments to raise charges to the public at least to the extent necessary to cover any increase in operating costs resulting from further expansion of facilities.

SANITATION

The general standard of cleanliness in towns and even in villages, both large and small, is good. Abundance of sunshine and the dryness of the environment are important factors in the maintenance of such cleanliness and the prevention of water-borne disease. Flies, however, constitute a serious hazard to health during the summer months.

Sewerage

Tripoli and Benghazi have water-carriage sewerage systems, both discharging into the sea without treatment of any kind. Substantial improvements were carried out in the Benghazi sewerage system after a UN expert in 1952 reported it to be inadequate and in poor condition. The most urgent need now is to construct treatment plants at both capital cities, and we suggest that consulting engineers should be engaged to carry out surveys to determine the most economical methods of handling the problem. Sludge from the plants should be sold as manure, possibly composted with refuse, and it may be practicable to use the effluent for irrigation. As a tentative estimate of costs, we suggest that a total sum of £L 800,000 should be included in the capital investment program for this purpose, of which £L 450,000 would be for Tripoli and £L 350,000 for Benghazi.

In the majority of towns and larger villages, where water supplies permit, a limited water-carriage system exists with cesspits for each building or group of buildings. These cesspits are emptied periodically by municipalities, and this method appears to work fairly satisfactorily. However, further studies are needed to ensure disposal of sewage in a way that would avoid the contamination of ground or surface water, as well as the contamination of the ground surface. If these handicaps can be overcome, the present system might be extended to other localities. Its advantages are that the water consumption is low, the pits can be constructed by semi-skilled labor, little or no imported material is required and generally plenty of space is available for new pits when necessary.

The problem of latrines remains an urgent one. Priority should be given to the construction of individual family latrines. This would need governmental aid, and we recommend a self-help program be instituted, supported by the provision of construction equipment and of superstructures at low cost, for which £L 25,000 has been included in our five-year investment program.

Refuse Collection

Garbage and trash collection is carried out by the municipalities in the towns, either by their own staff or on contract, and disposal is by means of dumping outside the inhabited area or by the controlled-tipping method, as in the case of Benghazi. The cost of refuse collection results in substantial deficits as the charges levied by the municipalities, even if fully collected, do not cover the costs. As part of its sanitation project, LAJS has recently provided refuse receptacles and subsidized the purchase of refuse carts in some municipalities. We recommend the continuation of this program, but we see no reason why the municipalities themselves should not bear a larger share of the cost. We have not therefore made any specific financial provision for this item in our program.

Control of Pests

Rodent infestation is not a serious health hazard, though the economic loss due to infestation of granaries, flour mills, bakeries and food markets must be considerable. This can be kept down by periodic poisoning campaigns, construction of rat-proof storage godowns and general clean-up measures. The only insect of special importance to health authorities all over the country is the housefly. Flies breed abundantly during the summer months, almost disappearing during the winter. It is probable that flies play some role in the transmission of all the three most prevalent diseases in Libya. Primative latrines and aggregations of large numbers of animals in towns and villages are responsible for most of the breeding. Fly control measures and clean-up campaigns are necessary and should be scientifically organized and continuous to be effective. An example of accomplishment in this respect is provided by the LAJS fly control campaign conducted in the Suk el Giuma area for three successive summers in support of the Wheelus Base sanitation, resulting in a drop of 75 percent in the dysentery admission rate in the Base hospital. There was also a considerable reduction in the incidence of gastro-intestinal disease treated at the Suk el Giuma government dispensary, although accurate records are not available. We strongly urge that such fly control campaigns be extended to other parts of the country.

Food Hygiene

In all towns food vendors are registered and fairly regular sanitary inspection by inspectors and overseers is carried out, though it is not always effective. Fresh milk is not very popular with the town dwellers, but a good deal of butter-milk (laban) is consumed and a certain amount of homemade cheese. There is sanitary supervision of milk vendors in towns, but there is no control of milk producers and there is no bottling or pasteurization either in Tripoli or Benghazi. Boiling of all milk is necessary. There are municipal slaughterhouses in all large towns and slaughtering is usually carried out under some sort of veterinary and medical supervision. In towns meat is taken to retailers in closed vans. LAJS has recently taken up the project of slaughterhouse rehabilitation in the larger towns as part of its community health activities, and a chilling plant is currently under construction at the municipal abattoir in Benghazi. Standards of markets for fresh food range from the open village market with vendors squatting on the ground among their produce to the central market in Tripoli where the level of hygiene is very satisfactory. Market places are usually cleaned up after the day's business and are generally fairly well maintained, but much improvement could be effected by the provision of an ample supply of water where possible and the construction of public latrines. More generally, there is plenty of room for improvement in enforcing proper standards of food hygiene.

Industrial Hygiene

There are no factory laws in operation, possibly because until now there have been few large industrial plants in the country. Standards of hygiene in food-processing establishments are not high, and there is considerable room for all-round improvement to bring these up to the level of modern requirements. Any outlay for this purpose would be economically productive, since foods processed under acceptable hygienic standards would find bigger markets in Libya and possibly abroad. Working conditions in most of the smaller industries are often unsatisfactory, and the provision of wash places and latrines for workers is often inadequate. We recommend that consideration be given to the enactment of appropriate legislation, and that provision be made for its subsequent enforcement.

HOUSING

A feature of the recent history of Libya is the considerable movement of landless labor toward the towns, and this trend may well continue for some years to come. Large "shanty towns" can be seen on the outskirts of Tripoli and Benghazi where people live under depressing slum conditions. Similar conditions were observed in and near several other towns. A few years ago the problem created by migration into the city of Tripoli got out of hand, and large numbers of migrants had to be forcibly returned to their places of origin.

A slum clearance scheme was initiated by government in 1954, and a shanty-town settlement to the west of Tripoli was rehoused on a more suitable site (Porta Azizia) and the shanties dismantled. However, the layout of the settlement (in the form of a grid) and the design of the 464 housing units (each consisting of two rooms and a courtyard built up in blocks of four units) leaves something to be desired. No trees were planted, and the only redeeming feature in the layout is a small mosque which makes an attractive central focus point. Later, 262 similar housing units were built in five towns in Cyrenaica (in this case there were eight units in a series of open-ended blocks) and 120 in Wadi Caam. In Tripoli the average cost per unit, including outside water standards and latrines, roads and other ancillary services, was £L 130; in Cyrenaica, where the units had interior sanitation and septic tanks, average cost per unit was £L 343; and in the Wadi Caam the cost was £L 333.

The traditional Italian colonial methods of buildings were adopted in all these settlements, the walls being made of local stone blocks plastered over with cement and the roofs of cement concrete or pre-cast beams with hollow clay tiles. All the units were of the same size, with no provision being made for large families, windows were placed in the outside walls (now often seen blocked up by the inhabitants), and the layouts made no attempt to provide privacy or to conform to the social habits of the people. In several of these settlements the inhabitants have been "improving" them by adding palm-leaf and clay lean-tos and enclosures. Nevertheless, these houses are very popular and are occupied immediately they are completed, so great is the demand for housing among people in the low-income groups. The scheme is now known as the "Popular Housing Scheme," and in most cases the occupants are not people from the shanty towns but those much higher up in the social scale. A nominal rent is charged, but the mission understands that it is not always enforced. In the Tripoli settlement a "Sheikh" has been appointed as community leader, and his discipline has been well accepted and the settlement is clean and tidy.

The 1954 census shows that 3,591 families were homeless in Tripoli city alone (the number is probably much greater today), and one of the five-year plans of Cyrenaica provided for 5,000 housing units as a first requirement. However, the attention so far given to popular housing by the provincial authorities falls far short of the need. It is sometimes argued that the provision of better houses in the towns will merely encourage people to move there from rural areas and thus aggravate the problems of urban concentration. We do not consider this a convincing argument against popular housing schemes, though it reinforces the case for financial assistance to be given by the federal government to the local housing authorities. A properly balanced housing program should anyhow include provision for new units in rural as well as urban areas.

The mission places the construction of low-cost housing very high on its list of priorities, and it suggests that the following principles should be observed in planning and executing a public housing program for Libya as a whole:

1. Before construction is started careful plans should be drawn up for community settlements that accord with the social customs of the people, including a community center, a mosque, shops, roads and trees.
2. Maximum use of local materials should be encouraged, and in rural areas construction should be organized wherever possible on a self-help basis.
3. Rent rules should be drawn up and strictly enforced. Rents should be fixed at levels which will enable capital costs, including interest, to be recovered over a reasonable period—say twenty years—with provision for special remissions to meet cases of hardship. Rents should never exceed a maximum of, say, one-tenth of a family's income.

The subject has been studied by UN experts under the technical assistance program, and they have drawn up schemes which provide for the greater use of local materials, including gypsum, of which there are large deposits in Tripolitania. They hope to be able to house people at from £L 33.5 to £L 55 per person in dwelling units without septic tanks. It is claimed that gypsum concrete walls are about 45 percent cheaper than walls made of local stone, and that methods of gypsum construction tried out with success in other countries could be adapted for use in Libya, where the dry climate is a favorable factor.

The mission recommends that a few experimental houses should be built of gypsum without any further delay with a view to determining whether the suggested methods of construction would be economic and practical. If the results are encouraging, the government should invite tenders from private firms for the supply of quantities of gypsum required for a housing program and should be ready, if necessary, to provide financial assistance for setting up the necessary plant.

Whatever methods of construction are employed, we recommend that the federal government should prepare plans in consultation with the provincial and local authorities for the housing of 2,000 families in Tripolitania and 1,000 families in Cyrenaica over the next five years.

The preparation of plans should be supervised by the technical adviser to the Development Council, and an experienced housing development officer should be appointed to assist him. The execution of the program should be entrusted to the provincial governments and the municipalities, but the federal government should retain strict control over the use of the funds allotted. In view of the interest currently displayed by foreign building contractors in taking on work in Libya, these contractors might be invited to tender for the construction of some of the larger urban housing settlements. Competition would be an important factor in keeping costs down.

The mission suggests that a sum of £L 1 million should initially be earmarked for the housing program suggested above, and we have included this in our list of proposed capital expenditures. We attach the greatest importance to low-cost housing projects as a means of promoting community welfare and ensuring that all sections of the population benefit from the increased income accruing from foreign aid and oil revenues. If the program already outlined is carried out successfully and further funds become available, the mission would be in favor of additional allocations for housing under the Supplementary Program.

There is little hope that private enterprise will be able to provide enough houses for the middle and lower income groups so long as the building boom, at present in evidence in all the large towns, continues. This boom is due to the rapid growth in trade and the large influx of foreigners into the country, including employees of the oil companies. Also many Libyans employed by foreign companies are now much better off than before and are demanding better houses. In addition, many public buildings have been erected, and the building industry is fully occupied and making such large profits that no attempt is being made to develop new and more economic designs or to make better use of local materials. If the government pioneers with a low-cost housing scheme, as here proposed, there is every prospect of private enterprise coming in to help at a later date when the present building boom subsides.

Low-cost public housing can only be provided for a small section of the population. Most of the better-paid artisans, clerks, government officials and other town-dwellers will continue to live in private houses or apartments. To assist such people to raise the money to buy their own houses, the mission suggests that consideration might be given to the institution of a government housing fund or mortgage bank. Finance for such an institution could be raised by local borrowing (see Chapter 15), and we have made no specific provision for it in our program of public expenditure.

COMMUNITY DEVELOPMENT

The concept of communal effort directed toward the achievement of communal objectives is one that fits in well with the traditional pattern of tribal society in Libya, but it is only recently that an organized community development program has been introduced as a feature of the current drive for economic development. Such a program was inaugurated in Cyrenaica in February 1958 with the help of USOM, and in the first two years of its existence it has achieved encouraging results. Not far short of a hundred small projects have been initiated, ranging from the building and repair of schools and mosques to the digging of wells and the construction of irrigation channels. Much of the work has been contributed voluntarily by local farmers and villagers.

The mission believes that there is considerable scope for wider use of this approach to the improvement of social and economic conditions in rural areas. The success of a community development program depends essentially on the quality of local leadership and on the ability of local authorities to organize practical schemes and arouse enthusiasm for them. Wherever the right spirit can be created, community development projects can make a valuable contribution in a variety of fields, including the improvement of village amenities, improvement and construction of rural roads, building of schools, health education and the expansion of agricultural production. Substantial investment can often be achieved from the expenditure of comparatively small sums of money. We recommend therefore that the federal and provincial governments should give full support to the existing program in Cyrenaica, and that the introduction of similar programs in the other provinces should be considered.

SUMMARY OF PROPOSED EXPENDITURES

The proposals made in this chapter in respect of public health, town and village water supplies, sanitation and housing would call for an estimated capital expenditure of £L 3,700,000 over the five years 1960/61-1964/65. The total would be divided as follows:

(£L '000)

	Five-year total	Annual average
Public Health		
Hospital buildings and equipment	700	140
School of nursing (male), Benghazi	20	4
Central medical store, Tripoli	50	10
Health centers and rural dispensaries	290	58
Ambulances	75	15
Port and airport quarantine stations	40	8
Total public health	1,175	235
Town and Village Water Supplies		
Cyrenaica	350	70
Tripolitania	300	60
Fezzan	50	10
Total water supplies	700	140
Sanitation		
Tripoli sewerage scheme	450	90
Benghazi sewerage scheme	350	70
Rural sanitation	25	5
Total sanitation	825	165
Housing		
Low-cost housing construction	1,000	200
Total housing	1,000	200
Grand Total	3,700	740

A number of the mission's recommendations, if adopted, will involve an increase in the present running costs of the health services. We have proposed, for example, that all doctors should be employed and paid on a whole-time basis, instead of on a part-time basis as many are at present (particularly in Tripoli), and that they should receive additional allowances in certain cases. The programs for new hospital construction and the establishment of a system of health centers and sub-centers throughout the country will involve a steady increase in expenditures on staffing and on the maintenance of the new buildings. Provision has also to be made for the administration of port health control and quarantine facilities (page 279), for the recruitment of more foreign women doctors and nurses (pages 283 and 284), and possibly for some initial increase in expenditures on medical training abroad (page 283). On the other hand, centralized purchase of medical stores might result in a saving of £L 20,000-30,000 a year (page 279).

The mission was unable to obtain sufficiently detailed information about the present costs of the health services to make any reliable estimates of the additional recurrent expenditures involved in carrying out each of these recommendations, but on the assumption that the health services are at present costing approximately £L 1½ million a year to run (Statistical Appendix, Table S.9), we consider it would be reasonable to allow for these to rise in total over the next five years at the rate of 5 percent a year. This would raise recurrent expenditures to around £L 1,900,000 by 1964/65 and would entail additional expenditures of about £L 1,200,000 over the five-year period as a whole. The level of recurrent expenditures on health envisaged for 1964/65, combined with the investment expenditures proposed by the mission, would account for 7 or 8 percent of all the public expenditures envisaged for that year and possibly for about 2 or 3 percent of the total real resources available for use in Libya. This latter percentage would be rather higher than in most other underdeveloped countries, where it appears that expenditures on health seldom exceed 1 percent of gross national product.

The mission has recommended that, as a matter of government policy, the losses incurred by public authorities in the supply of water to towns and villages should not be allowed to increase beyond their present level. No provision is therefore made in our program for additional recurrent expenditures under this head. The additional running costs of sanitation and other municipal services should likewise be met out of local rates and taxes.

Additional provision for investment in town and village water supplies and low-cost housing is recommended as part of the Supplementary Program.

CHAPTER 15 *GENERAL FINANCIAL AND ECONOMIC POLICIES*

The financing of the program of public expenditures recommended in this report has been discussed in Chapter 5. With foreign aid running at about £L 12 million a year, with the possibility of oil revenues materializing within the next few years and with the cash reserves held by the federal and provincial governments, we have assumed that no major difficulties will be encountered in raising enough money to cover total public expenditures ranging from £L 22 million to £L 27 million a year over the next five years, which is the level implied by the mission's programs of capital expenditures and additional current expenditures related to development.

It has been argued earlier in the report that, in the mission's view, the limits to the pace of economic development are more likely to be set by shortages of trained personnel and by organizational and administrative problems than by lack of money as such. However, to the extent that these limitations can be successfully overcome by the energy and ingenuity of government and private enterprise, the mission has suggested that there may be room for supplementary expenditures in such sectors as the development of water resources, afforestation, education and training, popular housing and agricultural credit. This makes it all the more important for the government to concentrate its efforts on raising the efficiency of public administration and eliminating wasteful expenditures and superfluous controls which impede economic development. At the same time, in anticipation of the day when the country's capacity to execute useful economic projects is greater than at present, attention should be given to possible ways of mobilizing additional internal resources for development through taxation and voluntary savings. Quite apart from these considerations, changes in the present tax system are needed to ensure that increases in income are more equitably distributed among the different sections of the population.

It is now widely recognized that the government of a country has a responsibility for trying to ensure not only that the national income grows, but that the strains and stresses of growth are kept to a minimum, and that employment is provided for all who are able and willing to work. The Libyan Government has many dangers to contend with in the new era which has been opened up since Independence, first, by large-scale foreign aid and military expenditures and, more recently, by the discovery of oil. There is the danger that a few people will become very rich while the mass of the population remain very poor. There is the danger that prices will go on rising in an inflationary spiral, causing hardship and discontent among such classes as government officials and small farmers who constitute the most stable elements in society. There is the danger that the gulf between town and country will be widened, with the main benefits from the increase in external income accruing to trade and industry and passing by most of the rural population. There is the danger of a steady drift of population from the rural areas to the major cities in search of jobs, resulting in the creation of a depressed and uprooted urban proletariat, which could become a source of social and political instability.

The government can do much to guard against these dangers by pursuing wise financial and economic policies. This is not simply a matter of how the resources available for development are distributed between the different sectors of the economy, which has been the main theme of the preceding chapters of this report. It is also a matter of budgetary management in the widest sense, covering all aspects of public revenue and expenditure; a matter of social policies in such fields as minimum wage provisions and social security legislation; a matter of monetary policy involving control over the currency in circulation and the credit created by the banking system; and a matter of import and export policy, customs administration, exchange control and trade and financial relations with other countries. Each of these areas of policy is briefly reviewed in this chapter.

THE PROBLEM OF INFLATION

The present economic situation in Libya is characterized by widespread shortages and rising prices resulting from the sudden increase in demand for goods and services required in connection with oil operations. Where additional supplies can be freely imported, or where local production can be readily increased to meet the demand, the situation should be largely self-correcting, especially as there is a fair amount of competition in the wholesale and retail business. Nevertheless, traders take time to adjust themselves to the increased tempo of activity and to get used to handling a larger volume of business, and they have a strong incentive in the meantime to charge what the traffic will bear. This time-lag probably helps to explain why prices even of many imported goods have risen sharply during the past 12 months; if so, some of the price increases that have occurred may prove to be only temporary.

However, there are some shortages which cannot be easily overcome by increasing imports or local production. For example, the demand in Tripoli for offices, houses and apartments has been sharply increased not only by the oil boom, but also by the return of the federal government from Benghazi. New building is proceeding apace, but it may be quite a long time before supply catches up with demand. A similar situation has arisen in the case of hotel accommodation and many types of personal services. The resulting price increases mainly affect the foreign community and the upper Libyan income groups, but the rest of the Libyan population must also be feeling the effects in certain directions, and there is evidence that the general cost of living in Tripoli rose appreciably during 1959 (see Chapter 2).

The interaction of "demand inflation" and "cost inflation" is seen in the strong upward pressure exerted on wages and salaries by the oil boom. This pressure and the inflation of profit margins have raised costs of production and prices in the manufacturing, building and service trades. No reliable information is available about movements in wages and salaries, and the experiences of different groups must have varied greatly. But outside the civil service and agriculture there has clearly been a considerable rise in average wage and salary rates during the past two years.

There are limits to what the government can do to control an inflationary process of this kind in which the initiating factor has been increased expenditures by foreign governments and oil companies. This is no argument, however, for standing aside and doing nothing. The first essential is a liberal import policy, and we recommend later in this chapter that most of the remaining restrictions on imports should be removed. With substantial foreign exchange reserves and every prospect of a sharp increase in foreign exchange income in a few years' time, Libya can well afford to allow both consumer goods and capital goods to enter the country freely. Elsewhere in the report we have recommended various limited measures of tariff protection to assist the development of agriculture and local industries, but with the exception of wheat and flour (and possibly gold) we can see no good economic reason for retaining quantitative restrictions on imports.

Following the example of other oil-producing countries which have been faced with a similar situation in the past, the Libyan Government should encourage the immigration of skilled workers from abroad to fill jobs for which there is a shortage of qualified Libyans. Many people left Libya during the Italian occupation to live in Tunisia, Egypt, the southern Sahara and other neighboring countries, and it is understood that some of these would now like to return to Libya. We believe it to be in Libya's interests that they should be given every facility to do so, particularly if they have special skills to contribute to the development of the economy.

For broadly similar reasons we recommend that Libya should encourage foreign building contractors to establish branches and bid for contracts in the country. If a major program of public investment is to be carried out simultaneously with oil exploration and development, it is essential that the limited resources of the Libyan building industry should be supplemented by the import of organization and technical skills from abroad. As much competition as possible is desirable in this field to keep building costs down and expedite work. Cheaper and quicker private building will do more than anything else to bring down the present extortionate rents in Tripoli and Benghazi and to alleviate the shortage of housing accommodation for Libyans living in these towns.

The gap between earnings in the oil industry and earnings in other industries is already large enough to be a matter of serious concern, especially to the government, which is under increasing pressure to raise the pay of its own employees. In these circumstances the government should refrain from lending its support to claims for an all-round increase in the minimum wage in the oil industry. Such an increase, if granted, would ultimately be at the expense of the rest of the community, both because it would reduce the profits accruing to the government from oil production and because it would give an added stimulus to cost inflation in other sectors of the economy.

One of the government's principal aims in dealing with inflation should be to restrain excessive demands for private consumption by channeling a substantial proportion of the increased incomes generated by the oil boom into the public exchequer and by taking steps to encourage private saving. The government should also exercise restraint over its own expenditures to avoid adding fuel to the flames and accentuating existing shortages. These aspects of fiscal policy are discussed in more detail in the following section.

General monetary and credit restrictions are unlikely to be of much avail in dealing with the present situation. The expansion of money supply in Libya is in any case more an effect than a cause of the boom in oil activity. It may be appropriate for the National Bank to urge the commercial banks to exercise restraint in extending credit for certain purposes such as hire purchase. However, a more effective way of controlling hire purchase is for the government to impose restrictions on the terms of hire purchase agreements, and we recommend that consideration be given to the introduction of suitable legislation for this purpose.

Direct controls over prices and distributive margins may be necessary in some cases to check profiteering and to protect the poorer sections of the community against increases in the cost of basic commodities such as foodgrains and clothing. In fact, prices of some commodities such as bread and pharmaceuticals are already subject to control. It must be recognized, however, that direct controls of this kind, and especially controls over rents, are notoriously difficult to enforce on any wide scale, and they should only be employed in exceptional cases. Particular care is necessary to ensure that prices are not fixed too low or too rigidly to discourage domestic production. Experience in other countries has shown this to be a very real danger.

Inflationary pressures are likely to continue in Libya for some time, and it would be unrealistic to imagine that they can be eliminated altogether when activity is expanding so rapidly. It should be the special responsibility of the National Bank to keep a watch on developments and to advise the government on appropriate action. The compilation of reliable and up-to-date indices of the cost of living in the main towns should be regarded as an essential guide to the formulation of policy.

FISCAL POLICY

Broad Objectives

Sound management of public finances is essential to the success of any well-directed economic development program. The main objectives of fiscal policy should be to raise the funds needed to finance projects in the public sector, to eliminate wasteful expenditures which impede development, to preserve a reasonable measure of internal financial stability and to ensure that all classes of the people have opportunities to share in the additional income generated in the process of economic growth. In a private enterprise economy these objectives have to be pursued in such a way that the best use is made of private capital, initiative and skills in promoting the expansion of the country's production and wealth. Particularly taxation policies may have an important bearing on the results achieved, and when tax changes are contemplated, account has to be taken of their likely economic impact as well as of their effects on government revenues. In Libya this is particularly necessary in the case of customs duties which constitute the principal source of domestic revenues.

Public Expenditures

The mission was disturbed by the apparent lack of appreciation in Libya of the importance of economizing in government expenditures. This can no doubt be explained in part by the fact that a large part of these expenditures has hitherto been financed out of foreign grants and loans, and a greater sense of financial responsibility is to be looked for in future as Libya becomes increasingly self-dependent. Certainly, an entirely different approach to public spending will be required if a program of the dimensions indicated in this report is to be carried out successfully during the next five years when oil revenues will probably not be very large.

As can be seen from Table S.3 of the Statistical Appendix, the rate of growth of government expenditures in recent years has been phenomenal. Thus between 1954/55 and 1958/59 public expenditures on defense and education were roughly trebled and expenditures on health, transport and communications and public buildings were more than doubled, while expenditures on law and order rose by about 80 percent.

In some cases the growth of expenditure has slowed down in the last two or three years, but in others it has continued at a rate that obviously cannot be sustained, even on the most optimistic assumptions about oil revenues. For example, in one year alone (1957/58 to 1958/59) expenditures on law and order rose by about 25 percent and expenditures on education by over 30 percent. We have pointed out in Chapter 5 that recurrent expenditures in some fields must be expected to go on rising, but limits have to be set to the rate of growth. In education, for example, we have suggested a growth rate of 10 percent a year over the next five years and in health of 5 percent a year. The Ministry of Finance should be very reluctant to allow these limits to be exceeded unless and until really large oil revenues are assured—a contingency which has been provided for in our Supplementary Program.

The Budgetary System

Details of public expenditures in recent years, insofar as the mission was able to ascertain them, are set out in the Statistical Appendix, and the salient features have been described in Chapter 2. The need to strengthen the machinery for controlling expenditures at all levels has been stressed in Chapter 6. Attention was also drawn in Chapter 6 to the lack of reliable information about the financial operations of government and the failure to make a proper distinction in the government accounts between current and capital items. Secrecy in public finance is wrong in principle, and both Parliament and public should be kept informed of what is going on.

The mission strongly recommends that in future all transactions of the federal government, including the agencies or agency responsible for development, should be brought together into a single comprehensive budget. Expenditures should be grouped into three main categories: (a) current expenditure, including grants-in-aid to the provinces and to nongovernment bodies (e.g., the Libyan University) and subsidies to revenue-earning government enterprises; (b) capital expenditures for economic development and other purposes, including grants to the provinces for investment projects approved by the Development Council; and (c) loans and capital subscriptions (e.g., to the Agricultural and Industrial Credit Departments of the National Bank of Libya).

We envisage that, with some exceptions, the items under (b) and (c) will comprise the capital budget, which should correspond broadly in coverage with the five-year program of capital expenditures recommended in this report, and the money for which should be provided by the Ministry of Finance in accordance with the recommendations of the new Development Council as approved by ministers. Some of the investment projects in this capital budget will be for execution by the federal government, some by the provincial governments and some by autonomous public bodies such as the Tripoli Electricity Authority. The federal projects will be shown in detail in the federal budget. In the case of projects to be carried out by the provinces, which we assume will normally be financed out of special federal grants, the federal budgets should show the allocations of funds by the Ministry of Finance to each of the provinces under broad headings (e.g., roads, electric power, health, education, etc.), and only the larger projects need be itemized (say, those costing £L 100,000 or more). It would then be for the provincial Nazirates of Finance to show in detail in their budgets how they were proposing to spend the money allocated to them for investment in education, health and so forth. Loans made to independent public authorities and special agencies under item (c) above should be separately listed in the federal budget. The capital budget will not, of course, include recurrent expenditures related to development (e.g., routine road maintenance or the pay of school teachers), which should be carried on the revenue budgets of the federal and provincial governments.

Ideally, expenditures should be classified in two ways in the budgets of the federal and provincial governments, in addition to the usual classification under the heads of the different spending departments. First, there is the functional classification under which expenditures are grouped in accordance with the different functions of government such as defense, foreign affairs, police, agriculture, education and health. This is the classification we have followed in the tables of the Statistical Appendix. Second, there is the economic classification which distinguishes between the various categories of current expenditure on goods and services, transfer payments and capital expenditures.[1] With the present acute shortage of trained accountants and economists it would be premature at this stage for the Libyan authorities to go into all the refinements of an economic classification, but the attempt should eventually be made as experience in budgetary analysis is developed.

On the revenue side the general budget of the federal government should embrace three main groups of transactions: (a) current revenues, including foreign grants, oil revenues and the profits of government enterprises; (b) proceeds from the sale of state property; and (c) receipts from long-term borrowing by the government, including foreign loans, and from the repayment of loans to the government. It is not, of course, suggested that capital expenditures should be financed solely through borrowing. On the contrary, it is to be anticipated that there will normally be a substantial surplus of current revenues over current expenditures available for financing investment. All oil revenues accruing to the federal government, including those reserved under existing legislation for projects approved by the Development Council, should be included in the general budget under item (a). The arrangement under which 70 percent of oil revenues are earmarked for allocation by the Development Council appears sensible.

The accounts of the posts and telecommunications services and of the Libyan broadcasting system should be set out under separate heads, which enable them to be distinguished from the general transactions

---

[1] For a full treatment of this subject reference should be made to *A Manual for Economic and Functional Classification of Government Transactions*, UN Department of Economic and Social Affairs, New York, 1958.

of the federal government. The same procedure should be followed in the provinces for revenue-earning undertakings such as civil airports, ports, urban water supplies and government newspapers, which are run directly by departments of government. Where the undertakings are run at a loss, the extent of the loss should be clearly indicated in annual financial statements to Parliament and provision made in the budgets for the necessary subsidies. All these undertakings, together with autonomous authorities such as the Tripoli Electricity Authority and the suggested Tripoli Port Trust, should submit to the federal government annual statements of capital expenditures proposed for the coming year, indicating how far these can be financed out of their own funds. This information is needed to enable the Development Council to prepare a comprehensive program of capital expenditures and to advise ministers on the allocation of funds set aside in the budget for development.

Taxation

Over 70 percent of the domestic revenues of the federal and provincial governments in 1958/59 were derived from indirect taxes, including customs duties, the profits of the tobacco and salt monopolies and government trading in sugar. Direct taxes, mainly provincial income taxes, contributed about 15 percent, and rather over 10 percent was made up of motor vehicle taxation, miscellaneous fees and dues and the surpluses of revenue-earning public enterprises, notably Tripoli port and the government press in Tripoli (see Statistical Appendix, Table S.2). Domestic tax and non-tax revenues, including the profits of the monopolies and state trading in sugar, are now probably equal to over 20 percent of the gross domestic product, which is a high figure for a country at Libya's stage of economic development. A significant proportion of these revenues, however, is paid by the resident foreign community and foreign companies.

Heavy reliance on indirect taxes, and especially customs duties, is a normal feature of the revenue systems of underdeveloped countries. This is primarily because indirect taxes are generally simpler to collect and administer than income tax. Indirect taxes have the disadvantage that they tend to be "regressive" in their impact—that is to say, they absorb a larger proportion of the incomes of the poor than of the rich. This is probably less true in Libya, however, than in some other countries. Import duties are much the most important form of indirect taxation in Libya, and comparatively few imports apart from wheat and flour, tea and sugar enter largely into the consumption of the rural population. The imports which make the largest contributions to customs revenues, between them accounting for well over half the total yield from this source, are petroleum, sugar, textiles and clothing, tea, motor cars, flour, electrical equipment, iron and steel manufactures and alcoholic beverages. By and large, with the exceptions of sugar, tea and flour, these commodities are consumed mainly by the foreign community and by comparatively well-to-do Libyans in the towns. The same applies with even greater force to luxury items such as cameras, films, watches and cosmetics which collectively account for a significant proportion of customs revenues. The duties on certain of these items (e.g., cosmetics, wines and spirits) were sharply increased in the summer of 1959, and this has further reduced the regressive bias of the tax system.

In general, and apart from a few items mentioned elsewhere in this report, the mission feels that the structure of the tariff is well adapted to Libya's needs. A notable deficiency at the time of the mission's visit was the absence of any duty on gold, which was being imported in substantial amounts (over £L 500,000 in 1958) partly for use in handicrafts, but mainly for other reasons, including re-export to neighboring countries. A duty of 15 percent has since been imposed, and import controls have been tightened up. As a result, gold imports have declined. The mission considers, however, that a considerably higher duty would be justified (say, 50 percent at least).

The mission has suggested in Chapter 4 that the import duty on kerosene should be reduced to encourage the use of kerosene as a fuel in place of firewood and charcoal. When oil is produced and refined in Libya, the wider use of kerosene could be a significant factor in checking despoliation of the country's limited forest resources.

The revenue from import duties has risen rapidly in recent years along with the growth of imports, which has been made possible by the increase in income from foreign aid, foreign military expenditures and oil exploration. Details are as follows:

(£L '000)

	1954/55	1955/56	1956/57	1957/58	1958/59
Imports, c.i.f.[a]	11,333	14,338	16,601	23,069	24,422
Receipts from customs duties[b]	2,455	3,381	3,873	4,899	6,400

[a] Figures refer to calendar years and exclude equipment and supplies imported directly by oil companies, some of which are liable to duty.

[b] Including minor receipts from export duties (about £L 50,000 a year).

Some further increase in imports may be expected as the local expenditures of the oil companies reach a peak,[2] and government receipts from customs duties should average at least £L 6-7 million a year during the period covered by our program and quite possibly more. Excise duties as such are of minor importance at present, but if oil is produced and refined in Libya, the existing customs duties on petroleum products will have to be converted into excise duties. With this prospect in view the mission considers it to be of the utmost importance that excise duties should be made a federal subject. The present position under which customs duties are a matter for the federal government and excise duties a matter for the provinces is in any case anomalous and out of line with the usual practice in other countries.

The operations of the tobacco and salt monopolies have been reviewed in Annex XIII. Demand for cigarettes can be expected to grow with the continued rise in incomes, and if the mission's recommendations for the better management of the monopolies are accepted, revenues obtained by the provincial governments from these two sources (over £L 1 million in 1958/59) should be appreciably increased. Under the present system of government trading in sugar, the price charged to the consumer (11 piasters per kilogram in Tripoli) is nearly three times the landed import price, and after deducting distribution costs the government derives a revenue equivalent to nearly 6 piasters per kilogram, of which rather under half accrues to the federal government in the form of customs duty and rather over half to the provincial governments as a trading profit. The revenue obtained by the provincial governments from sugar amounted in 1958/59 to about £L 500,000, and this figure can be expected to rise in line with the general growth of personal incomes since the income elasticity of demand for sugar appears to be fairly high.

Recommendations for the reform of the existing systems of income tax and agricultural taxes were put forward in the report of a UN adviser in 1954.[3] At present each of the coastal provinces has its own income tax law, although a draft federal law has been under consideration by the government for a number of years. As mentioned in Chapter 6, the mission strongly recommends that income tax should

---

[2] Machinery and equipment imported directly by the companies for use in oil exploration and development are exempt from customs duties. On the other hand, other supplies obtained from abroad, whether directly or through local contractors, are normally liable to duty.

[3] *Problems and Recommendations on Taxation in Libya*, S. H. Ahmed, United Nations, New York, 1957.

be made a federal subject. As a first step, immediate action should be taken to implement the present draft law, which lays down a sound basis for a uniform system of income tax throughout Libya. The second step would be to make the federal government responsible for the collection and distribution of income tax and the tax on businesses. Use should be made of the existing machinery for tax administration in the provinces, and the revenue obtained should be allocated between the center and the provinces in accordance with the recommendations of a Finance Commission. The standard rates of tax should be higher than the present 10 percent for companies and 8 percent for individuals (4 percent for those earning less than £L 15 a month), but we suggest that the exemption limits should be raised to exclude from the scope of the tax all persons earning less than, say, £L 180 a year (instead of £L 80 a year as at present). Tax moreover should be applicable only to that part of the income which exceeds the exemption limit and not to the whole income as at present. This recommendation would be in line with that made in the 1954 UN report.

Ultimately the objective should be to introduce a progressive scale under which liability to income tax would be related to ability to pay. A graduated income tax is, however, more difficult to administer than a flat rate, and it will be better to concentrate first on improving the machinery for collecting taxes and on extending the scope of income tax. At present the provincial income taxes apply to registered companies and traders, professional people and employed persons. In practice, it would appear that incorporated enterprises and employed persons bear the brunt of the tax, while many unincorporated traders and merchants manage to avoid it altogether. Vigorous efforts should therefore be made to tighten up the administration and to extend the list of registered taxpayers.

Greater use should be made in Libya of property taxes, particularly on houses and other forms of real estate. There is a house tax in Tripolitania and a miscellany of taxes on property in the principal Tripolitanian and Cyrenaican municipalities, but their yield is extremely small. Property taxes are comparatively easy to assess and collect, and we suggest that, as a first step, they should be more widely adopted in urban areas for the purpose of raising municipal revenues.

Agricultural taxes in Libya are levied by the provincial governments on cereals, animals, trees and irrigated land. These taxes were conceived as tithes on production. Their total yield is very small, generally averaging between £L 100,000 and £L 300,000 a year according to variations in rainfall, and it is clear that there is widespread evasion.

Exemptions are frequently granted; as an extreme example, the Cyrenaican Administration has remitted all taxation of agriculturists throughout the entire province for the past two years.

The present system of agricultural taxation in Libya is both complex and inefficient, and a strong case can be made out in principle for replacing the existing taxes in each province by some simpler form of land tax. The mission does not favor increased taxation of the small farmers or pastoralists who are eking out a meager subsistence on marginal land. On the other hand, the larger and more prosperous farmers and landowners in the more fertile districts can well afford to pay higher taxes than at present and should be required to do so. The main problem, and it is certainly not an easy one, is to find some way of assessing capacity to pay.[4] An agricultural income tax would probably be too difficult to administer in Libya under existing conditions. But it should be possible to make a rough and ready distinction between fertile and nonfertile land and to levy a tax on the former, either at a uniform rate per hectare throughout the country or at rates varying from one district to another according to the average productivity of the land in the district concerned. A further distinction could be made, within the category of fertile land, between irrigated and nonirrigated land. Selective remission might be allowed in case of drought, flood or other special circumstances.

If a solution is sought along these lines, the existing agricultural taxes might be retained for the time being, but the aim should be eventually to get rid of them altogether. The experience of other countries has shown that the absence of a complete cadastral survey is no insuperable bar to the introduction of land tax, nor would it be necessary to wait for the enactment of a land law, since individual rights to the more productive land which would be initially subject to tax are in most areas already quite well known. Indeed, it could be laid down that failure to register land for taxation would jeopardize subsequent claims to ownership at the time when a cadastral survey is undertaken.

Revenue is collected by the federal and provincial governments from a variety of minor taxes and fees, including stamp duties, motor vehicle licenses, court fees and so forth. In addition, the municipalities in Tripolitania and Cyrenaica raise revenues from taxes on industry and commerce and from numerous miscellaneous levies—and in the case of Tripoli and Benghazi from the proceeds of the municipal

---

[4] For a useful discussion of this problem see Haskell P. Wald, *Taxation of Agricultural Land in Underdeveloped Economies*, Harvard University Press, 1959.

casinos. The mission has not examined these taxes in detail and has no special comments to offer. By and large, they appear reasonable. As a matter of general financial policy, however, the municipalities should be discouraged from relying too heavily on subventions from the provincial governments, and where improvements are made in municipal services, the costs should generally be met by the municipalities themselves. We have made no special provision for municipal services other than electricity and water in this report on the principle that the additional expenditures required (e.g., on refuse collection, street lighting, public playgrounds) should be financed through increases in local taxes, for which we believe that there is ample scope.

Charges for Public Services

There appears to be little recognition in Libya of the principle that revenue-earning public enterprises, like private firms, should generally aim at least to cover their own costs, including capital charges and depreciation, and further that, wherever possible, they should earn a profit which can either be reinvested in the enterprise itself or used to finance other forms of public investment. The mission, in its travels around the country, found a widespread expectation amongst members of the public that economic services should normally be provided by government without charge or at any rate at well below cost, and it encountered many instances where, for instance, piped water or water for irrigation newly made available as a result of a development project was being supplied free to householders or farmers. Indeed, the levying of a charge for services of this kind appeared to be the exception rather than the rule. Even with long-established public enterprises such as railways and municipal power stations it is accepted as quite natural that they should be run at a loss, and in fact, with the notable exception of Tripoli port, the great majority are.

Such attitudes are easily understandable in view of Libya's history. The Italian settlements in Libya were supported by large subsidies from Italy before the war, and the economy has depended heavily on foreign assistance since. Nevertheless, losses incurred by public enterprises are in the last resort a charge on the purse not of the foreigner, but of the Libyan taxpayer, and it is in the public interest to eliminate such losses except where there are special reasons for subsidizing a particular group at the expense of the rest of the community. The mission believes that subsidies may occasionally be justified—for example, for the supply of drinking water to outlying towns and villages, where living conditions are austere. These cases, however, should be the exceptions and not the rule. As normal practice, economic services provided at the public expense such as water piped to houses, water for irrigation, electricity, transport and communications should be charged at commercial rates, and the costs of development projects should be recovered over a period of time from the beneficiaries. Indeed, it will often be advisable for a public utility enterprise to go further than this and charge rates designed to realize a profit or surplus which can be used for reinvestment.

More specifically, the mission urges the federal and provincial governments and the Tripoli Electricity Authority to re-examine the charges made for water and electricity, posts and telecommunications with these considerations in mind. We have also suggested at various places in the report that subsidies to the provincial railways should be discontinued and the railways closed down, that stricter measures should be taken to enforce payments of rent by tenants of houses built at public expense, and that entrance fees to museums and antiquities should be increased. All these proposals, if adopted, will have the effect of mobilizing more capital for development or alternatively of making possible a reduction in indirect taxes for the benefit of the lower income groups and thereby distributing the costs of development more fairly.

Government Borrowing

The mobilization of voluntary savings can be viewed in one sense as an alternative to taxation as a means of raising money to finance public development projects. The savings habit is in any case one that may well be considered worth encouraging for its own sake. In Libya, as in other Moslem countries, religious attitudes toward usury have tended to discourage the formation of an organized savings movement. The mission nevertheless gained the impression from talks with leaders of opinion in the country that these attitudes are becoming more flexible, and that there would be no strong opposition to the introduction of a small savings scheme. The National Bank of Libya recently put forward proposals for a scheme to be operated through the post office, and we understand that this is at present under consideration by the government. While we are not familiar with the details of the proposals, we consider that the idea is worth pursuing in principle, and we commend it to the government's attention. Care must be taken, before a savings scheme is introduced, to ensure that adequate machinery exists for its administration, and that it can be operated efficiently without making excessive demands on already overburdened public servants.

The absence of an organized capital market in Libya, lack of experience in public finance and the relatively comfortable financial position of the government have hitherto discouraged the issue of government securities. As a result, Libya at present has no internal public debt.

The mission has carefully considered the pros and cons of trying to institute in Libya a scheme for the sale of government securities to financial institutions and members of the public. On the one hand, borrowing from the banking system could in certain circumstances encourage extravagant expenditures and add to the inflationary pressures in the economy. On the other hand, there is the point that, although the government does not really need to borrow from the public at present, it may do so in future when the present technical and administrative limitations on the preparation and execution of development programs have been overcome. It takes time to create the necessary institutional framework for mobilizing private savings. Procedures will have to be tried out, advance publicity may be required, and confidence will have to be built up gradually. It may be desirable therefore that the ground should be prepared now.

On balance, the mission inclines to the view that a strictly limited measure of public borrowing would be justified over the next five years, particularly to the extent that this takes the place of further borrowing abroad and is linked with provision of finance for specific purposes. As a general principle, there appears to be little justification for Libya to borrow abroad to meet local currency expenditures (e.g., for agricultural credit) if the money can be raised at home. Local borrowing by the government would help to encourage voluntary savings, and it would also provide the commercial banks and insurance companies with a local outlet for surplus funds. From its talks with commercial banks the mission gained the impression that the banks would welcome the opportunity of investing part of their funds in sound interest-bearing federal issues instead of keeping substantial sums lying idle as they sometimes do at present. This would not in itself, of course, justify the issue of government securities, but it is an indication that, if such securities are issued, a market could be found for them. Initially the banks might hesitate to commit large sums for any long periods, and for this reason the government would be well advised to concentrate first on the issue of comparatively small amounts of short-term and medium-term certificates, interest on which should be free of tax.

The mission accordingly recommends that the National Bank of Libya and the Ministry of Finance should work out detailed proposals for the issue of certificates of this kind. Consideration might be given to the possibility of linking government borrowing with the institution of a government housing fund which would make loans to private individuals for building or purchasing houses (see Chapter 14). No building society or mortgage institution exists in Libya at the present time, and although some of the commercial banks do finance private building for selected customers, it is often difficult for prospective house-owners to borrow money privately except at exorbitant rates of interest. The creation of a public institution to fill this gap would, in the mission's view, meet a real need. Such an institution would need a small staff to administer the funds, scrutinize applications for loans and give advice to borrowers.

SOCIAL SECURITY LEGISLATION

Statutory Minimum Wages

A statutory minimum wage of 25 piasters a day is laid down for employees of government and industry under the Labor Law, which also provides for one day's paid holiday a week and two weeks' paid holiday a year. Workers in the oil industry are guaranteed a minimum of 35 piasters a day under a separate agreement between the government and the companies. There is no statutory minimum wage for agricultural workers.

The mission fully sympathizes with the desire of the government to protect workers against possible exploitation by employers, and the absence of a well-organized trade union movement admittedly adds to the risk of such exploitation. Even so, we are doubtful that a statutory minimum wage is appropriate in Libyan conditions, especially if applied to industry and not to agriculture. Care must be taken to guard against the danger of inflating industrial costs to the point where Libyan industries are unable to compete with imports, and even less able to compete in export markets. At the same time, by increasing the attraction of employment in government service and industry relative to agriculture, the minimum wage regulation is liable to hamper agricultural development and to encourage the drift of labor from the rural areas to the towns.

We do not suggest that the existing legislation should be changed, but we strongly recommend that there should be no increase in the minimum wage for the time being. There is keen competition for labor in Libya, especially for skilled and semi-skilled workers, and most of those employed in industry are already earning more than the statutory minimum. In these circumstances there is no pressing need for wage regulations, least of all for any upward revision of the minimum in the oil industry (see page 303).

Social Insurance

A Social Insurance Act, drafted with the assistance of an ILO expert, was introduced in 1957 and was brought into force in Tripoli toward the end of 1958. It is to be extended later to other parts of Libya. All persons gainfully employed under a written or oral contract of employment are to be compulsorily insured in accordance with the provisions of the act. The object of the act is "to establish a National Social Insurance scheme for the purpose of protecting employed persons in the event of sickness, employment injury, maternity, death, invalidity, old age and unemployment." The scheme is to be financed out of weekly contributions from the insured person and his employer, generally in the ratio of two to three; the employer is responsible for deducting the employee's contribution from his wages. Benefits include medical care in case of sickness or industrial injury, funeral expenses, unemployment pay and retirement pensions.

The mission has no comments to offer on the individual provisions of the act, which have been adapted from pre-war Italian legislation and follow the pattern of similar legislation in other countries. The scheme is understood to have been well received by the workers so far eligible. It is an essential principle of the scheme that the benefits received by the insured person are directly related to the contribution he makes, and the principle should be firmly adhered to.

MONEY AND BANKING

The functions and present position of the National Bank of Libya are described in Annex II. The bank was established in 1956 with an authorized capital of £L 1 million in order to "regulate the issue of bank notes and coins, to keep reserves with a view to maintaining monetary stability in Libya and the external value of the Libyan pound, to influence the credit situation to the Kingdom's advantage and to act as banker to the Government, and to the Provincial Administrations" (Article 6 of the National Bank Law). The National Bank now has three branches, and in addition to acting as a central bank, it has established a commercial department, which represents the first Libyan venture in this field, since all the private commercial banks in the country are under foreign ownership and control. The Governor of the Bank is a Libyan, while the Deputy Governor and many of the senior officials are expatriates with experience of banking in other countries.

Of the authorized capital of £L 1 million, only £L 700,000 has so far been subscribed. The mission recommends that the remaining £L 300,000 should be subscribed by the federal government in order to strengthen the basis of the National Bank's operations, and we have included provision for this in our program of capital expenditures.

The National Bank's ability to regulate the issue of bank notes and coins in Libya has been governed by a provision in the National Bank Act requiring that the currency should be backed up to 100 percent by foreign exchange. In actual practice, therefore, the expansion or contraction of currency becomes self-regulatory, in accordance with variations in the balance of payments, and the question of independent action by the National Bank to regulate the flow of currency does not arise. Such a system can be disadvantageous if the country wishes to pursue an independent monetary policy and regulate changes in the supply of currency to suit the requirements of domestic economic activity.

While this argument has force in it and would suggest the need for a revision of the Act, it does not appear to the mission that in the particular context of Libya's economic circumstances the matter is of great urgency. The levels of activity and incomes in Libya at present are largely dependent on foreign aid, foreign military expenditures and the expenditures of the oil companies. At the same time any increase in internal demand is liable to have a direct and immediate impact on imports because the import content of most investment and consumption expenditures is high. There is in these circumstances little scope for the pursuit of independent monetary or credit policies designed to insulate the domestic economy from movements in the external balance of payments. The government can do something to restrict the inflationary pressures resulting from a large inflow of income from abroad. But in the event of a sharp and prolonged decline in external income the scope for the exercise of independent regulatory powers would be extremely limited, since measures for maintaining demand and employment at home would tend to put added pressure on the balance of payments and increase the loss of foreign exchange reserves. Fortunately, the latter situation is hardly likely to arise in the foreseeable future, as there is every prospect of a steadily rising income from oil. Furthermore, Libya's official holdings of foreign exchange (over £L 25 million at the end of January 1960) are well in excess of the amount required as currency cover (£L 9.8 million at the same date). The 100 percent currency provision does not therefore impose any effective restriction at present on the expansion of the money supply.

While, therefore, the argument that 100 percent currency backing prevents the National Bank from playing an active role in monetary management is theoretically sound, it is rather academic in present circumstances. On the other hand, there is nothing sacrosanct in a 100 percent reserve system, and the Libyan authorities should certainly be free to substitute an alternative arrangement in future if the circumstances warrant it. However, Article 4 of the 1953 Financial Agreement with the United Kingdom requires in effect that any change in the existing Libyan currency arrangements shall be subject to the agreement of both governments. We suggest, therefore, that the Libyan Government discuss this matter with the Government of the United Kingdom.

Every country needs to maintain external reserves in the form of gold or foreign exchange, but there is no simple formula for determining how large these reserves should be in any particular case. It will depend among other things on the magnitude of the country's imports and on the extent to which its external receipts are liable to fluctuate with changes in world trading conditions. Libya's imports are high in relation to its national income, and this is an argument in favor of holding relatively large reserves. On the other hand, once oil revenues are assured, Libya should be less exposed than most countries to the vicissitudes of international trade.

If it should be felt desirable at a later date to change the present reserve arrangements, there are various alternatives that might be considered. The minimum reserve could be set either at a certain fraction (say, 50 percent or 75 percent) of the currency in circulation or at an absolute figure. Some countries have no fixed foreign exchange reserve requirement at all, but the mission would strongly advise Libya to adhere to the principle of a statutory minimum, which is often an important factor in maintaining confidence in the currency.

As to the composition of official foreign exchange holdings, the National Bank Act requires that 75 percent of the foreign exchange holdings of the Issue Department should be invested in sterling assets.

It was suggested to the mission that this imposed undue restriction on the Bank's freedom of action in investing its reserves in the most advantageous way. Against this, it must be borne in mind that the bulk of Libya's trade is conducted in sterling, and that this makes it in certain respects advantageous for a high proportion of reserves to be held in sterling rather than in other currencies. The whole question is closely tied up with Libya's membership of the sterling area and, as such, is essentially a subject for discussion between Libya and the United Kingdom. We suggest therefore that it might be examined by the two governments in the context of the discussions on Article 4 of the 1953 Financial Agreement mentioned above.

The Banking Law of 1958 raises issues of a different kind relating to the control of commercial banking. Under this law the Minister of Finance is given the power to prescribe minimum cash reserves to be held by commercial banks (over and above the statutory liquid reserves amounting to 20 percent of their deposit liabilities), and he is also responsible for considering applications for examination of bank affairs and various other functions. The exercise of these functions calls for considerable technical knowledge and experience, and in many other countries they are entrusted to the central bank as the agency primarily responsible for the regulation of currency and banking. We recommend that the same practice should be adopted in Libya.

At present the commercial banks, which are all branches of foreign banks, are under no obligation to hold any of their capital in Libya, and only three of them in fact do. The Banking Law of 1958 states that no bank with a head office abroad shall be granted a license to operate in Libya unless the issued and paid-up capital is at least the equivalent of £L 500,000, but this does not require any of the capital to be assigned specifically to the Libyan branch. Moreover, most of the commercial banks hold the greater part of their liquid assets outside Libya for lack of local investment opportunities. In time, if a market for Libyan government securities is developed, the attractions of holding funds in Libya should be increased. Meanwhile we suggest that, in line with the arrangements in most other underdeveloped countries, 20 percent of the liquid reserves which the commercial banks have to maintain under the present banking legislation should be kept within the country, in the form either of currency or of deposits with the National Bank of Libya.[5] The mission considers such action as a first step in the

[5] This would be equivalent to 4 percent of the total time and sight liabilities of the commercial banks, since the present liquidity reserve requirement is set at 20 percent of these liabilities.

direction of a system under which all, or at least the bulk, of the statutory liquid reserves should be maintained with the National Bank. In order to prevent the National Bank from using funds so deposited as a basis for additional commercial business, we suggest that the compulsory deposits made by commercial banks should be kept in a special account entirely separate from the general banking division of the National Bank.

The National Bank is empowered under existing legislation to extend credit to the federal government by means of temporary advances and the purchase of government securities, but limits are imposed on the amount of credit that may be granted.[6] In the mission's view it is desirable that the National Bank should be protected in this way against excessive demands for lending directly to government, and we do not in any case consider that substantial lending of this kind would be justified at the moment. More generally, the mission urges that the greatest caution should be observed with respect to government borrowing from the banking system.

The mission considers it highly desirable that the National Bank of Libya should in time play a more active role in the management of the economy, with particular reference to the maintenance of the stability of the currency. Experience in other countries underlines the value of having an independent central bank, which is free to offer advice and criticism to the government and which can also help to foster better public understanding of economic, fiscal and monetary problems. To do this effectively the National Bank of Libya needs a reliable statistical and research department. It has already made a beginning in this direction by establishing a small research department staffed with young Libyan graduates and supervised by an expatriate economic adviser. As recommended in Chapter 6, this work should be developed with particular attention to monetary and banking matters, the balance of payments, industrial finance and agricultural credit. Economic studies and forecasts should be prepared for the information and guidance of the board in determining the bank's policy, and the research staff should be granted access by government departments to all records and data required to carry out this function. Prompt and regular publication of results of research should be provided through the issue of a monthly or quarterly statistical bulletin.

6 For example, temporary advances may not exceed 10 percent of the total revenue approved by Parliament in the budget law of the year. If any such advance remains unpaid after the end of the financial year in which it is made, the bank cannot make any further advances until the amounts due have been repaid.

FOREIGN TRADE AND PAYMENTS

Import and Export Policies

Libya's merchandise exports at present earn less than one-quarter of the foreign exchange needed to pay for its imports. The rest is obtained from receipts of foreign aid and from payments made by foreign governments for goods and services procured in Libya. In some ways the picture presented by the figures is rather deceptive. A sizeable but indeterminate proportion of Libya's imports is consumed by the "foreign sector," i.e., by foreign governments and oil companies and their non-Libyan employees.[7] It can thus be said that these governments and companies have helped to create the "gap" in the balance of payments as well as to fill it. Even so, the present situation is a rather precarious one, and the Libyans would naturally like to see their economy become self-supporting as soon as possible. Until recently the possibility of any such development appeared remote, but the discovery of oil has entirely changed the picture, and there is a good chance that within five to ten years oil revenues will provide a basis for viability.

If this happens, the arguments in favor of special policies to promote exports and save imports will carry less weight in the determination of national economic policy than would otherwise have been necessary. The mission believes nevertheless that export promotion should continue to receive close attention from the government, and it also advocates a determined effort to develop certain types of domestic agricultural and industrial production to replace goods at present imported. The growth of production in agriculture and industry is needed to provide local employment and to secure better utilization of existing capacity, and this growth can in some cases only be achieved at the expense of imports.

We have indicated in earlier chapters a number of fields in which we consider that producers will require protection against imports, at any rate in the initial stages of development. Except for one or two special cases such as imported wheat and flour, quantitative restric-

---

[7] Supplies imported into Libya directly by the United States and United Kingdom forces, together with machinery and equipment for oil operations, are exempt from customs duties and do not appear in the import figures quoted in this report. On the other hand, substantial quantities of imported goods are bought by foreign governments and oil companies through local contractors and merchants, and these are included in the returns of commercial imports.

. . . nor should tariffs be raised to pro-tion provides a valuable stimulus to costs, and the interests of the consumer well as those of the producer. It is ulti- to pay the price for tariff protection, and esent circumstances that protection will be istries which are being promoted by influ-n there may be no sound economic justifica-

trend toward greater liberalization of imports is to u. A big step forward was taken early in 1959, when a wide ported commodities was placed on open general license. subject to control include cereals, sugar, alcoholic drinks, uit and vegetables, tobacco, petroleum, hides and skins, private cars, boots and shoes, fresh fish, meat, carpets and rugs, radio sets, refrigerators and cameras. Most of these restrictions could prob-ably now be safely dispensed with. We recommend therefore that a study be undertaken by the Ministry of Finance, in consultation with the Customs Department and the provincial Nazirates of Finance and Trade, with a view to further narrowing down the list of items under control. This study should include a detailed examination of the pos-sibilities of substituting increased tariffs for quantitative restrictions as a means of protecting domestic producers.

Exports from Libya are at present subject to license, and although licenses are seldom refused, the filing and approval of applications takes up the time of businessmen and officials. An export license is even required for the dispatch by sea freight or mail of goods bought in Libya by tourists and visiting businessmen, and this can be a real deterrent to making such purchases. Export controls were defended to the mission in Tripolitania on the grounds that they were necessary, first, to ensure the maintenance of adequate standards, particularly in respect of the grading of agricultural products, and second, to prevent under-invoicing of exports, which is sometimes resorted to as a means of evading exchange controls. Political and strategic arguments are also sometimes advanced in this context. The mission was not con-vinced that there is any good economic or commercial reason for re-taining export controls, and it strongly recommends that they should be abolished, subject possibly to one or two exceptions justified on noneconomic grounds. This is not to say that the efforts being made in Tripolitania to enforce proper quality standards should be abandoned, but the necessary inspection can be carried out without the elaborate paperwork involved in the present system of export licensing. The regular export documents provide all the information needed to keep a watch on under-invoicing.

Foreign trade policies in Libya, as in other federal states, should be laid down at the national and not at the provincial level. The present arrangements under which each of the coastal provinces has its own system of import licensing are anomalous and have the undesirable result that restrictions are imposed on trade between the two provinces. This is a case where policy finds expression not in the law, but in the regulations issued under the law. We strongly recommend therefore that in future all regulations relating to the control of imports and exports should be issued by the federal government, after consultation with the provinces. This will help to promote trade between Tripolitania and Cyrenaica, which is desirable in the long-term interests of integrating the economies of the two provinces and achieving a more unified national economy.

As Libya moves into the new phase of economic expansion heralded by the discovery of oil, an increasing number of foreign businessmen and tourists will be visiting the country and an increasing number of Libyans will be traveling abroad. At the same time more goods will be moving in and out of the country, including supplies required for oil development. It is in Libya's economic interest that everything possible should be done to facilitate these movements of trade and people. All restrictions and controls that are not absolutely necessary should be removed, customs procedures should be speeded up and made more flexible, and visas for foreign visitors should either be abolished or else made very much easier to get. These arguments apply with even greater force to traffic within Libya between one province and another. Present controls on the movement of goods and passengers between Tripoli and Cyrenaica, while the reasons for their introduction are understandable, are entirely out of place in a modern and growing economy and are a source of amazement and sometimes of frustration to foreigners who are traveling or doing business in Libya. Their removal is particularly desirable from the point of view of encouraging the tourist trade.

Exchange Control

Libya has a system of exchange control modeled on the usual sterling area pattern, with, however, no significant discrimination between one foreign currency and another. Since the beginning of 1958 the regulations have been administered by the National Bank. This is a considerable improvement over the previous arrangements under which each coastal province had its own system of exchange control, and the mission gained the impression that the present administration is reasonably efficient, though inevitably subjected to political pressures, which it may find it difficult to resist. Restrictions on the use of foreign exchange have been considerably relaxed in recent years in line with similar trends in the rest of the sterling area, and the main purpose of the controls now is to keep some check on the export of private capital.

Even in countries with long experience of administering exchange controls, it has proved very difficult to exercise efficient control over capital movements. In Libya, too, it is the mission's impression that substantial amounts of private capital are evading the control and finding their way abroad. When large oil revenues materialize, which we do not expect to happen for some years, the remaining arguments in favor of exchange control in Libya may lose a good deal of their force, and consideration might then be given to abolishing the controls altogether. We recommend, however, that the present system be kept in operation for the time being, and that efforts of the National Bank to prevent the illicit export of capital should be fully supported by the federal and provincial authorities.

International Trade Relations

Libya's foreign trade is mainly oriented toward European markets, with Italy and the United Kingdom between them supplying over 50 percent of Libya's civil imports (excluding oil equipment) and taking over 50 percent of its exports. Italy is much the largest single market for Libyan exports and has traditionally granted special duty-free quotas for selected Libyan produce, including olive oil, dates, oilseeds, fresh and canned fish. This arrangement has necessitated a waiver under the rules of the General Agreement on Tariffs and Trade. During the annual meeting of GATT in 1959 the waiver was extended until December 31, 1961.

The tariff concessions granted by Italy are of considerable value to Libya, and it is important to Libya that they should not be affected by the establishment of the European Common Market. The Libyan Government is understandably concerned about this point, and we would hope that suitable arrangements can be negotiated between Italy and other Common Market countries to safeguard Libya's interests.

Libya has close trading and financial relations with the United

Arab Republic, but its trade with the rest of the Arab world is comparatively small, and it is Europe rather than the Middle East which offers the most promising markets for its exports. There may nevertheless be some opportunities for increasing exports to the United Arab Republic and to Lebanon (e.g., in meat), and these should be energetically explored. There are also certain spheres of economic activity such as tourism in which Libya stands to benefit from closer cooperation on a multilateral basis with other Mediterranean and Middle East countries.

Italy and the United Arab Republic are the only two countries with which Libya has special bilateral trading arrangements. Libya has accumulated a large credit balance under its payments agreement with the United Arab Republic, and difficulties are apparently being experienced in liquidating this credit. The mission can see little scope for the conclusion of further bilateral trade and payments agreements, and in general it believes that Libya's economic interests are best served by conducting its external transactions on a multilateral basis without discrimination between one country and another. Maximum diversification of export markets is desirable so as to avoid undue dependence on any one country.

PROSPECTS FOR THE LIBYAN ECONOMY

The program set out in this report is intended to serve as a guide to the planning of economic development activities during the next five years. We see this period essentially as one of training and preparation for the time after 1965 when large oil revenues may permit a marked acceleration in the process of economic development. The most urgent task is to build up the administrative machinery and to train the people that will be needed to execute a much larger program of capital formation than any that should be contemplated at the present time.

Investment in people through better education, medical services, nutrition and housing will at this stage often be more rewarding, though also more difficult, than investment in construction of such things as public buildings and transport facilities. The rate at which the economy grows will be powerfully influenced by the supply of skilled professional and technical personnel. The investment program should be tailored to the talent available. Here the Libyan people have a choice in deciding how many foreign technicians and administrators they wish to employ. The mission is fully conscious that there are disadvantages to Libya in having to depend heavily on outsiders. On the other hand, if a faster rate of progress is desired in the short run, extensive use will have to be made of the services of foreigners in the preparation and execution of programs.

The matters discussed earlier in this chapter illustrate the important, often indeed the decisive, role which government action can play in stimulating economic growth. Perhaps the most important task of government is to foster the kind of economic and social climate in which private enterprise can function most effectively in the national interest. No hard and fast rules can be laid down with regard to the division of functions between public and private enterprise. The relative inexperience of the Libyan Government in the administration of economic affairs provides a strong argument for leaving as much as possible to private enterprise, with government stepping in only where private enterprise is unable or unwilling to act. The mission was impressed by the apparent determination of the Libyan authorities to rely mainly on private capital and private initiative for the promotion of activity in industry, trade and agriculture, and it believes that this approach is sound. However, as indicated elsewhere in this report, we believe that government should play a more active role in the development of certain branches of economic activity which have tended to be neglected by private enterprise, notably agriculture, fisheries and tourism. We have also recommended that, where private enterprise is given a job to do, it should not be hampered by unnecessary regulations and controls.

The process of economic development in Libya can best be assisted through continuous cooperation and consultation between government and the private sector and by measures to encourage the participation of foreign capital and technical assistance on mutually advantageous terms. Government can give a lead to public opinion in setting out clearly the objectives of economic planning and explaining the means by which these objectives are to be attained. The mission attaches considerable importance in this context to the dissemination of economic information through the radio, newspapers and other channels. At the same time wise leadership will oppose strong resistance to pressures from sectional interests, who seek special privileges at the expense of the wider interests of the nation as a whole. Several instances of such pressures have been mentioned in this report.

One of the most difficult problems facing any country in an early stage of economic development is to strike the right balance between

considerations of equity on the one hand and the need to provide incentives for increased output on the other. In Libya at the moment the
main danger appears to be that increases in the national income will
be too unevenly distributed, and that savings will be concentrated in
the hands of those who do not wish to use them for purposes of productive investment. For this reason special emphasis in our report has
been placed on the need for a more equitable distribution of income
and for government assistance to small producers in agriculture and
industry who lack capital for development.

Economic development will in time bring great changes in Libya.
We have not attempted in this report to assess in any detail the impact
which the program we have recommended might have on foreign
trade, national income, employment and prices because there are so
many unknowns in the equation, and the discovery of oil has introduced a new dynamic and unpredictable element into the situation.
Oil production and exploration will almost certainly be much the
biggest single factor contributing to the rise in national income over
the next five or ten years, and the possibilities range within very wide
limits. We do not, however, foresee long-term employment in the oil
industry absorbing more than about 5 percent of the present labor
force (say, 15,000-20,000 people), and the proportion might well be
significantly smaller. Moreover, it should not be overlooked that much
of this employment has already been created by the initial work of
exploration. A peak may be reached during the next five years when
exploration and development activities are proceeding simultaneously,
and there is always the risk of some decline in employment thereafter
as the construction of major pipelines and terminal facilities is completed.

Production and employment in manufacturing, distribution and
other service trades should be stimulated by the expansion of incomes
associated with oil development. These sectors would also be affected
by any change in either direction in the level of foreign military expenditures in Libya. On balance, the rise in output is likely to be
greater than the rise in employment, especially as a number of industries and trades are at present working at well below their full
capacity (e.g., flour-milling and road goods transport). Demand for
building is certain to remain high, and the amount of work done will
depend on how fast the capacity of the building and civil engineering
industries can be expanded by the import of organizational talent and
skilled manpower from abroad.

One of the main conclusions of this report is that there will not be enough jobs available in the towns (or in the oil industry) to provide employment for more than a small fraction of the 200,000 people at present engaged in agriculture and animal husbandry. This will not prevent workers from continuing to leave the rural areas in search of better opportunities elsewhere, nor will it prevent wages in non-agricultural occupations from rising. But it is liable to result in the growth of unemployment and underemployment in and around the towns and in the fostering of social discontent and unrest.

That is one reason why so much emphasis has been placed in the mission's program on measures to improve the lot of the small farmer and pastoralist. This will be a slow process, and any increase in output in this sector may initially be dwarfed by more striking developments in oil production and trading activities. But progress in agriculture will not be the less important because it is unspectacular, and though it may take a long time to achieve major results, the mission is convinced that agriculture, forestry and water resources must be accorded high priority in planning for the longer-term development of the Libyan economy. This conviction is reinforced by the consideration that, although the present rate of growth of the Libyan population appears to be comparatively small, it could easily be doubled by improvements in education and health leading to a sharp decline in infant mortality.

A growth rate of between 2 percent and 3 percent a year, which would not be out of line with trends in other North African and Middle Eastern countries, would result in a doubling of the existing population in 25-35 years. The present territory of Libya almost certainly supported a population of at least 2½ million in Roman times, and there is no reason why it should not do so again.

The most important of the Mission's recommendations are listed together in this appendix for convenience of reference. They are grouped under subjects corresponding broadly to Chapters 6-15 of the main report, where the details of the recommendations and the reasons for them are elaborated. The list does not include recommendations for possible increases in expenditure under the Supplementary Program.

GOVERNMENT ORGANIZATION

1. Strengthening of the federal government through the creation of a federal Ministry of Agriculture and Natural Resources in place of the existing Ministry of National Economy, reorganization of the Ministry of Finance as a Ministry of Finance and Economics with a much stronger staff, and the enactment of a law to govern the allocation of federal grants-in-aid to the provinces, with a Finance Commission to review the principles on which such allocations should be made.

2. Transfer of responsibility for income tax and excise duties from the provincial administrations to the federal government.

3. Gradual unification of the federal and provincial civil services and establishment of a single system of civil service recruitment for Libya as a whole, together with regular interchange of officials between the center and the provinces.

4. Arrangements for closer day-to-day consultation between the federal and provincial governments and for more regular consultation between government and private interests.

5. Streamlining of the organization of the provincial governments and a reduction in the numbers of their departments and staffs.

6. Creation of an independent authority to administer the affairs of Tripoli port.

7. Reorganization of the Development Council along the lines at present proposed, with a technical wing and a strong permanent staff of administrators and economists to take charge of the planning and coordination of economic development programs in place of the foreign aid agencies.

8. Measures to strengthen the government statistical and economic services and to improve existing knowledge of the economy, including the unification of statistical services on an all-Libya basis, recruitment of more trained statisticians, transfer of the Central Statistics Office to the Prime Minister's Office and enlargement of the statistical and research staff of the National Bank of Libya.

9. Stricter control over public expenditures at all levels, involving the strengthening of the staff of the Ministry of Finance and improvements in the arrangements for auditing government accounts.

10. Measures to improve the efficiency of the civil service, including an immediate review of pay scales, adoption of a 40-hour work week, rearrangement of working hours and the institution of special schemes for the training of Libyan officials.

11. Continued reliance on technical assistance from the United Nations and foreign countries, and on the recruitment of expatriate officials, where necessary to ensure the effective administration of economic development programs.

12. Observance of standard rules and procedures in the award of government contracts.

13. Strengthening of the staff of the Petroleum Commission and recruitment on a part-time basis of a high-level petroleum consultant to advise the government on future dealings with the oil companies.

GEOLOGY AND WATER RESOURCES

14. Establishment within the Ministry of Agricultural and Natural Resources of a federal Department of Geology and Hydrology to study and extend knowledge of the geological, mineral and ground water resources of Libya.

15. Enactment of a federal law, supported by provincial regulations, for the proper control of water resources.

16. Establishment of Water Resources Branches in the provinces to take over from the foreign aid agencies the execution of water development projects and to control the use of water in areas where there is danger of overexploitation.

17. Urgent measures to restrict the use of ground water for agricultural purposes in the "Tripoli Quadrangle," coupled with investigations into the possibilities of opening up new areas for farming in the Bir Ghnem area southwest of Tripoli.

18. Establishment of sentinel wells along the coast of Tripolitania

to guard against salt water intrusion and enforcement of rigid restrictions on pumping in areas where signs of such intrusion are discovered.

19. A five-year program in Cyrenaica for the construction of wells, renovation of cisterns, terracing and diking and provision of irrigation facilities at an estimated cost of £L 1,780,000, including recurrent expenditures.

20. A similar program in Tripolitania estimated to cost £L 1,190,000.

21. A special five-year program for the provision of wells and irrigation facilities to serve the needs of small farmers in the Fezzan at an estimated cost of £L 570,000.

22. Execution of a new project for the control of floods and soil erosion in the Wadi Megenin in Tripolitania involving soil and water conservancy works, flood protection works, afforestation of part of the catchment area and the removal and resettlement by stages of the present inhabitants in this area. (The cost of the first stage of this project is estimated at £L 500,000, including £L 100,000 for afforestation).

23. Preliminary investigations into the possibilities of developing water resources for irrigation at Ain Mara and Ain Zeiana in Cyrenaica and at Taorga and the Wadi Tareglat in Tripolitania.

24. Research into the water requirements of different crops and into more efficient methods of irrigation and drainage in the coastal areas and the desert oases, coupled with education of farmers in the economical use of water.

AGRICULTURE, LIVESTOCK AND FORESTRY

Agriculture

25. Appointment by royal decree of a Commission on Land Rights to formulate a land policy promoting the permanent settlement of the tribal population and to prepare a draft land law for the government's consideration.

26. Creation of a federal Land Survey Department to undertake a cadastral survey of all agricultural land in Libya.

27. Establishment of an Agricultural Credit Department within the National Bank of Libya to take over the work of the National Agricultural Bank, with an immediate enlargement of the funds available from £L 1 million to £L 2 million and a further increase to £L 3 million in the course of the next five years; the additional funds for agricultural credit to be provided by the Libyan Government.

28. Measures to foster the development of credit and marketing cooperatives of small farmers.

29. Creation of an Agricultural Marketing Department as part of the proposed Ministry of Agriculture to assist in the marketing of agricultural produce at home and abroad, including sales to the oil companies and foreign government establishments in Libya.

30. Improved facilities for agricultural training and greater emphasis on the development of agricultural extension services.

31. A project for the development of the former Italian farms in Cyrenaica at a total estimated capital cost of around £L 1,100,000 (including credit), the project to be undertaken in stages by a specially appointed Gebel Akhdar Development Board and to be spread over five years starting in 1962.

32. An intensive campaign to raise wheat yields, combined with measures to encourage the cultivation of wheat in the Barce Plain and other suitable areas, including the introduction of a price support scheme, continued regulation of wheat imports, restriction of flour imports and maintenance of controls over bread prices.

33. More extensive use of barley as a feed for livestock coupled with measures to increase production of high quality barley for export to Europe.

34. Integration of cereal cultivation, wherever possible, with the growing of pastures and fodder crops to meet the feed requirements of livestock.

35. Continued purchase of dates for the school-feeding program; investigation of the possibilities of making greater use of dates as a concentrated feed for livestock and building up reserve stocks for use in times of drought; concentration of date research on developing by-products such as syrup, paste and alcohol; study of the Italian market for packaged dates.

36. Programs for the planting of 30,000 new olive trees a year in Tripolitania and 10,000 trees a year in Cyrenaica; abandonment of the scheme for rehabilitation of wild olives in Cyrenaica.

37. Changes in the arrangements for growing tobacco in Tripolitania, including progressive reduction of subsidies and termination (after two or three years) of the present licensing system.

38. Deferment of the proposals for growing sugar beet in Tripolitania pending more careful study of the technical and economic factors involved.

39. Abandonment of the scheme for large-scale cultivation of cotton in the Fezzan.

40. Efforts to stimulate output of cereals, fodder and livestock products in desert oases for local consumption; more attention to cultivation of early vegetables and oilseeds for local consumption and export.

41. A survey of agricultural experimental stations and farms in Libya with a view to securing better coordination of research work and a reduction in the number of research centers; wider and more prompt distribution of the results of research; collection of the results of previous research work in a central reference library, including translations of pre-war Italian studies; more emphasis in future research work on practical investigations bearing on actual farming conditions in Libya, with particular reference to the problems of the small farmer.

42. Systematic classification of agricultural land in Libya, followed by a general soil survey to be carried out on a contract basis by a commercial firm under the supervision of the Ministry of Agriculture.

43. Measures to combat soil erosion by encouraging the use of better tillage methods, contouring and the planting of windbreaks, especially on Italian farms in Tripolitania.

44. Measures to promote the further mechanization of agriculture.

45. Research and extension activities directed toward the control of plant diseases and insect pests, with particular attention to the olive fly and the Mediterranean fruit fly; stricter enforcement of control measures.

Livestock

46. Concentration on raising the quality of livestock through the closer association of livestock farming with settled agriculture; ecological studies to provide basic information required for a long-term pasture improvement program.

47. Government action to build up emergency reserves of feeding-stuffs and to establish fodder stations on the Libyan side of the Egyptian border.

48. Enactment of a veterinary law and related measures of livestock improvement, which are necessary preconditions to the development of an export trade in meat.

49. Encouragement of poultry farming with a view particularly to increasing sales of eggs and poultry to the foreign community in Libya.

50. Continuation of the pilot dairy project in Benghazi with a view to determining the feasibility of producing economically for the local market.

Forestry

51. Creation of a federal Department of Forestry as part of the Ministry of Agriculture and Natural Resources; enactment of a federal forest law; allocation of an additional £L 30,000 a year for strengthening the staffs of the provincial forestry services; establishment of an all-Libya forestry experimental station.

52. A five-year program for Tripolitania covering the afforestation of an additional 16,000 hectares for soil and water conservation and the production of fuels and timber, the fixation of 9,000 hectares of sand dunes and the supply of 6 million seedlings at an estimated capital cost of £L 1,090,000 (including £L 100,000 for afforestation in the Wadi Megenin catchment area).

53. Allocation of £L 400,000 for a five-year program of forestry improvement in Cyrenaica, with a further £L 70,000 to cover roadside planting and the planting of windbreaks.

INDUSTRY, HANDICRAFTS AND FISHERIES

Industry

54. Measures for strengthening the administration of industrial policy at both the federal and provincial levels, including the recruitment of a foreign industrial adviser and the training of Libyan university graduates abroad.

55. Reconsideration of the draft law for the registration and protection of industries; introduction of a simple system of industrial registration; extension of the Law for the Development of National Industries to include associations of very small enterprises which do not at present qualify for government assistance.

56. Creation of an Industrial Credit Department in the National Bank of Libya with an initial capital of £L 500,000 to make loans to private industries and assume responsibility for technical assistance to industry; allocation of £L 45,000 out of public funds to cover the cost of consulting services provided by the department.

57. Various other steps to promote industrial development, including (a) the establishment of an industrial estate in Tripoli at an estimated cost of £L 50,000, (b) training schemes for industrial managers, workers and trade union leaders and (c) special assistance to the leather and printing industries through the establishment of a pilot tannery

training and demonstration center and the institution of an apprentice training program for the Government Printing Press in Tripoli.

58. Careful investigation of the economic and technical problems involved in manufacturing cement in Libya before government support is given to private projects for establishing cement factories.

59. Further study, as a matter of urgency, of the organizational and supply problems involved in running the proposed cold storage plant in Benghazi and of the possibilities of finding overseas markets for Libyan meat, particularly in the Mediterranean area.

60. Examination of the scope for further developments in fruit and vegetable canning, the manufacture of date syrup and the establishment of a tomato paste factory in Cyrenaica.

61. Improved arrangements for running the tobacco factory in Tripoli directed primarily toward the earning of additional revenue for government; reorganization of the salt monopoly on commercial lines.

Handicrafts

62. A five-year program costing about £L 150,000 for the development of Libyan handicraft industries, including the establishment of a training-cum-production center at Misurata, the opening of government emporia in Tripoli and Benghazi and the provision of technical advice and financial assistance to small operators in modern crafts such as bicycles and radio repairing.

63. Continued support of the small-scale industries center in the Fezzan.

Fisheries

64. Creation of a federal Department of Fisheries in the Ministry of Agriculture and Natural Resources, with a trawler fishing expert to take charge of fisheries administration and a program for training a cadre of qualified Libyan staff.

65. An experimental project for the development of trawler fishing to be undertaken with foreign technical assistance at an estimated cost of £L 150,000 over the five-year period, coupled with measures to expand the market for fish in Libya.

THE TOURIST TRADE

66. First priority to be given to the expansion and improvement of hotel accommodation in Tripoli and Benghazi, active efforts being made to interest foreign hotel operators in building and running modern hotels (with or without capital assistance from the government) and better arrangements being devised for the management of existing hotels.

67. Application to the hotel trade of all concessions offered under the existing Law for the Investment of Foreign Capital, including appropriate tax remissions; exemption of the hotel trade from the provisions of the Labor Law regulating hours of work in industry and the adoption of more liberal policies in granting visas for the employment of foreign hotel staff.

68. A five-year program for the renovation, and where necessary, reopening of existing country hotels and construction of two new government rest-houses on the coast road at a total estimated cost of £L 180,000.

69. Measures to encourage tourist air travel to the desert oases, possibly coupled with the conversion into rest-houses of some of the old military forts.

70. Investigations with the help of competent consultants into the possibilities of constructing a deep-water jetty for tourist ships at Ras el Hilal in Cyrenaica, coupled possibly with the erection of a modern hotel nearby.

71. Additional federal allocations of £L 15,000 a year to the antiquities departments of the provincial governments to enable more rapid progress to be made with excavations at the principal classical sites; raising of admission charges to antiquities and museums.

72. Simplification of present immigration formalities for tourists, including the abolition of the visa requirement for tourists from Western Europe and North America, easier customs clearance and removal of all formalities in the case of movement within Libya from one province to another.

73. Reorganization of government tourist administration at both federal and provincial levels.

ELECTRIC POWER

74. Full responsibility for the management of Tripoli Power to be undertaken immediately by the new electricity authority, and eventual extension of the responsibilities of the authority to cover all public power undertakings in Libya.

75. An investigation into the future financial position of Tripoli Power in the light of the latest developments, including the discovery of oil, to be followed by a review of existing electricity tariffs and other steps to ensure that the expanded power facilities are used to the best advantage for the development of industrial and agricultural production in the area (subject, however, to the overriding need to restrict water pumping in the immediate vicinity of Tripoli).

76. A five-year program for the development of electricity supply in other parts of Libya at an estimated capital cost of £L 650,000, including £L 180,000 for extensions to the Benghazi power station.

TRANSPORT AND COMMUNICATIONS

Railways

77. Closing down of the two provincial railways, both of which are running at a substantial loss, and transfer of rail traffic to the roads; suitable compensation to be provided for railway employees, although no difficulty is envisaged in finding alternative employment for them; railway properties in Tripoli and Benghazi to be adapted for use in connection with town improvement schemes.

Roads and Road Transport

78. Closer attention to highway maintenance and the allocation of larger sums for the upkeep of existing roads, which in general should be given priority over new construction. (Annual requirements for maintenance and renewal of surfacing during the next five years are estimated at about £L 900,000.)

79. A five-year program costing £L 650,000 for minor new construction and improvement of roads in all three provinces, including a new road from el Abiar to Barce in Cyrenaica to replace the railway, the widening of the coast road from Cyrene to Derna and improvements to

roads in the immediate vicinity of the more important oases in the Fezzan.

80. Uniform policies to be laid down at the federal level in respect of road standards and traffic regulations; transfer of executive responsibility for federal road works from the Ministry of Communications to the provincial Nazirates of Public Works.

81. Measures to improve efficiency and reduce costs in the management of government road transport.

Ports

82. Creation of an autonomous federal authority to run the port of Tripoli on a proper commercial basis with responsibility for financing its own development and with appropriate borrowing powers, the Tripolitanian Administration being compensated for its vested interest in the port.

83. Further expenditure over the next five years of about £L 325,000 on the rehabilitation and improvement of Tripoli port and of £L 65,000 on the creation of a "free zone" in the port.

84. A scheme for the rehabilitation and development of Benghazi harbor involving deepening of the Middle Harbor, repair of the Central Mole and provision of additional quays and other facilities at an estimated cost of £L 1½ million.

85. Improvements to the port of Zuara and minimum essential maintenance of other minor ports at an estimated cost over the five years of £L 85,000, including dredging.

86. Subject to preliminary studies of the engineering and tourist aspects, adoption of a project for the development of Ras el Hilal as a calling place for tourist ships involving estimated expenditure of £L 30,000 on repairing the jetty and providing a turning place for buses.

Civil Aviation

87. A five-year program for the further development and equipment of the civil airports at Idris and Benina and for the resurfacing of runways at these airports, together with the provision of fire-fighting and other equipment for Sebha, at a total estimated cost of £L 800,000.

88. Postponement for the time being of the proposal to establish a Libyan national airline; development of light air services for the Fezzan and other outlying oases on a charter basis with financial assistance from the federal government at an estimated cost of £L 50,000 a year.

Communications

89. Expansion of the programs for training Libyans in telecommunications and broadcasting techniques; measures to ensure better management of postal services and introduction in the post office of a proper cost accounting system.

Transport Administration

90. Amalgamation in each province of the Nazirates of Public Works and the Nazirates of Communications; conversion of the existing Ministry of Communications into a Ministry of Transport and Communications responsible for formulation of national policies in this field; establishment of ministerial and technical committees on transport and communications to coordinate the activities of the federal and provincial governments.

EDUCATION

91. Concentration on improving the quality of primary school education, with particular attention to the supply of teachers, the provision of more and better equipment, textbooks and teaching aids and reorientation of the curriculum to give greater emphasis to practical training in everyday life.

92. A program costing £L 770,000 for the provision of primary school buildings and equipment needed to raise standards and to accommodate an additional 25,000 pupils over the next five years.

93. A five-year program costing £L 630,000 to expand facilities for education at the preparatory and secondary school levels, with special emphasis on vocational training, including the establishment of three new centers for training agricultural technicians and the conversion of the School of Applied Engineering in Tripoli into a comprehensive technical high school.

94. Endorsement of the proposal to establish an Institute of Higher Technology in Tripoli with assistance from the United Nations Special Fund, this institute to be accorded equal status with the University of Libya.

95. Gradual development of the University of Libya into a medium-sized college of liberal arts and sciences, construction of new buildings to house the University and measures to raise academic standards, including the appointment of an examining commission of university professors from abroad to assist in the final examinations for degrees.

96. Greater emphasis on adult and fundamental education; strengthening and extension of the present adult education program which is being carried out with the help of UNESCO; creation of a special directorate for adult education in the Ministry of Education.

97. Continuation of existing programs for foreign study with special care being given to the selection of students for scholarships.

98. Appointment of a high-level technical adviser to the Minister of Education to prepare a long-term program of educational development, to review the distribution of functions between the ministry and the Nazirates and to establish a proper system of educational records (with the help of a Bureau of Records and Research).

99. Recruitment of additional school inspectors; broadening the membership of the provincial executive education committees; encouragement of local citizens' committees to assist in raising standards in primary schools.

HEALTH AND COMMUNITY SERVICES

Public Health

100. Shift of emphasis in public health policy from the curative services to preventive medicine, with special reference to maternity and child health.

101. A five-year program for improvements to existing hospitals, establishment of a new isolation hospital in Benghazi and the building of one or two new district hospitals (e.g., at Murzuk in the Fezzan) at an estimated cost of £L 700,000, of which £L 310,000 would be for Cyrenaica, £L 300,000 for Tripolitania and £L 90,000 for the Fezzan; purchase of additional ambulances for the three provinces at an estimated cost of £L 75,000.

102. Merging of the existing Maternity and Child Health Centers into an integrated system of health centers and sub-centers serving all towns and the larger villages in Libya at an estimated capital cost of £L 290,000 over five years (including £L 90,000 to establish a network of rural dispensaries).

103. Centralization of arrangements for procurement of drugs and medicines, establishment of a central medical store and preparation of a standardized list of drugs and medicines for use in hospitals throughout Libya.

104. Establishment of suitable quarantine arrangements at the major ports and civil airports at an estimated capital cost of £L 40,000.

105. Revision of existing scales of pay and allowances for doctors on a uniform all-Libya basis, with larger allowances for specialists; recruitment of additional women doctors for the main hospitals and health centers; continuation of medical training for Libyans abroad.

106. Measures to strengthen the nursing services and to encourage more Libyan girls to take up nursing and midwifery; establishment of a school for male nurses in Benghazi.

107. Various changes in the organization of the health services coupled with the establishment of an all-Libya Council of Medical Registration.

Town and Village Water Supplies

108. A five-year program of further improvements and additions to town and village water supplies costing £L 700,000, of which £L 350,000 would be for Cyrenaica, £L 300,000 for Tripolitania and £L 50,000 for the Fezzan; high priority to be given within this program to boring new wells for Tripoli and increasing reservoir capacity at Benghazi.

109. Re-examination of water rates and better collection of charges with a view to reducing the losses incurred by the water supply undertakings (currently in excess of £L 100,000 a year).

110. Municipal waterworks in Tripolitania, except in Tripoli itself, to be taken over by the Nazirates of Public Works, which is at present responsible for maintenance but not for operations.

Sanitation

111. Allocation of £L 450,000 for the construction of a sewage treatment plant at Tripoli and £L 350,000 for a similar plant at Benghazi; government-aided program for construction of family latrines.

112. Measures to raise standards of environmental sanitation, including anti-fly campaigns, stricter food inspection and the insistence on higher standards of hygiene in food processing establishments.

Housing

113. Organization of a low-cost housing scheme, a sum of £L 1 million being provided initially to cover the housing of some 2,000 families in Tripolitania and 1,000 families in Cyrenaica in properly planned communities; housing in rural areas to be carried out whenever possible on a self-help basis; use of gypsum for construction.

114. Investigation of the possibilities of establishing a government-housing fund or mortgage bank, financed out of local borrowings, to provide financial assistance for private house purchase.

Community Development

115. Support for the community development program in Cyrenaica and the introduction of similar programs in the other provinces.

GENERAL FINANCIAL AND ECONOMIC POLICIES

Public Finance

116. Strenuous efforts to achieve economies in public expenditures, particularly in the staffing of government departments; limits to be set to the growth of recurrent expenditures in education and other fields.

117. Maintenance of existing capital assets generally to be accorded priority over new construction in the allocation of funds; continuing costs of projects to be carefully assessed before additional investments are undertaken.

118. Better methods of budgetary accounting, distinguishing between current and capital expenditures and separating the accounts of revenue-earning public undertakings from those of general government.

119. Implementation of the draft income tax law; higher standard rates of income tax and business profits tax; vigorous efforts to tighten up income tax administration and to extend the list of registered taxpayers.

120. Greater use of property taxes, particularly for the purpose of raising additional revenues for municipalities to cover the extra cost of local services.

121. Replacement of existing agricultural taxes by a land tax applicable to cultivable land in the more fertile districts.

122. Special tax remission for kerosene used for heating and cooking, coupled with action to ensure an adequate supply of cheap kerosene stoves (with the object of reducing demand for fuel wood and thereby helping to preserve the country's forest resources).

123. A review of charges made for public utilities, irrigation and other economic services provided at the public expense with a view to mobilizing additional revenues for financing economic development.

124. Measures to mobilize voluntary savings through the institution of a post office savings scheme; consideration to be given to a

limited issue of short-term and medium-term Libyan Government securities, coupled possibly with the establishment of a government housing fund or mortgage bank.

Banking

125. Transfer of certain powers relating to the control of commercial banking from the Minister of Finance to the National Bank of Libya, the exercise of such powers remaining subject to the Minister's approval; measures to ensure that at least 20 percent of the liquid reserves maintained by the commercial banks under present banking legislation are kept within Libya in the form either of currency or of deposits with the National Bank.

126. The capital of the National Bank of Libya to be raised by government subscription to £L 1 million; measures to enable the National Bank to play a more active role in the management of the economy, with particular reference to the maintenance of currency stability, such measures to include the strengthening of the Bank's statistical and research department.

Economic Policy

127. A liberal import policy and removal of most remaining restrictions on imports to help counter inflationary pressures; abolition of export controls; assumption by the federal government of sole responsibility for issuing regulations for the control of imports and exports; removal of all restrictions on interprovincial trade.

128. General reliance on tariffs rather than quantitative restrictions on imports to protect local producers, subject, however, to certain exceptions in the case of agriculture; specific changes in tariffs on selected items to assist local industry (e.g., vegetable oils, caustic soda and household utensils); a further increase in the tariff on imports of gold.

129. Encouragement of private foreign investment in Libya and liberal application of the provisions of the existing Law for the Investment of Foreign Capital.

130. Measures to stimulate competition in the building and civil engineering industry in order to keep construction costs down and expedite work.

131. Encouragement of immigration of skilled workers from abroad, particularly Libyans who left the country during the Italian occupation.

STATISTICAL APPENDIX

TABLE S.1   Public Revenues and Expenditures in Libya

(£L '000: fiscal years beginning April)

	1954/55	1955/56	1956/57	1957/58	1958/59[a]
Domestic Revenues					
Federal Government	2,561	3,565	4,100	5,090	6,532
Tripolitania	1,784	2,243	2,605	2,986	3,709
Cyrenaica	726	774	932	943	1,189
Fezzan	40	51	64	94	119
Municipalities[b]	438	428	446	482	500
Total domestic	5,549	7,061	8,147	9,595	12,049
External Assistance					
Grants from United Kingdom	3,750	3,750	4,000	4,250	3,250
Grants from United States[c]	1,786	2,500	3,214	6,099	6,785
Loans from United States	—	—	—	1,250	—
Other[d]	105	20	20	470	1,010
Total external	5,641	6,270	7,234	12,069	11,045
TOTAL REVENUES	11,190	13,331	15,381	21,664	23,094
Expenditures					
Federal Government[e]	1,501	2,120	2,719	3,589	4,948
Tripolitania	3,652	3,805	3,992	4,614	5,008
Cyrenaica	2,062	2,340	2,646	2,751	3,178
Fezzan	398	404	504	635	892
Municipalities[b]	431	408	452	464	500
LARC	—	2,485	4,038	3,851	3,938
LPDSA	753	1,416	1,082	1,127	715
TOTAL EXPENDITURES	8,797	12,978	15,433	17,031	19,179
Surplus or deficit of revenues over expenditures	+2,393	+353	−52	+4,633	+3,915

[a] Many of the figures for 1958/59 are budget estimates and as such are not comparable with the figures for earlier years.

[b] Includes all municipalities of Tripolitania and Cyrenaica, except Derna.

[c] Technical cooperation grants and gift wheat and other commodities supplied under PL 480 are excluded.

[d] Grants from France, Italy, Egypt, Pakistan and Turkey, the figures showing actual receipts (as distinct from the allocations shown in Table 1 of Chapter 3). UN technical assistance and U. S. technical cooperation assistance are excluded from both the revenue and expenditure sides of the account.

[e] Including expenditures under the "Exceptional Budget."

TABLE S.2   Analysis of Domestic Revenues

(£L '000: fiscal years beginning April)

	1954/55	1955/56	1956/57	1957/58	1958/59[a]
Federal					
Customs (gross)	2,455	3,381	3,873	4,899	6,400
Post and telecommunications (net)	40	50	82	54	—
Miscellaneous	66	134	145	137	132
Total	2,561	3,565	4,100	5,090	6,532
Tripolitania					
Income tax	512	638	680	862	1,118
Other direct taxes	133	156	231	276	350
Indirect taxes	209	270	302	362	406
Tobacco and salt monopolies	315	443	576	584	714
Sugar trading	211	190	241	193	350
Miscellaneous	404	546	575	709	771
Total	1,784	2,243	2,605	2,986	3,709
Cyrenaica					
Income and property tax[b]	150	175	218	279	419
Indirect taxes	86	102	127	152	169
Tobacco monopoly	195	194	233	277	285
Sugar trading	218	212	235	118	192
Miscellaneous	77	91	119	117	124
Total	726	774	932	943	1,189
Fezzan					
Direct taxes	8	16	22	28	37
Indirect taxes	22	15	28	39	52
Public services	10	20	14	27	30
Total	40	51	64	94	119[b]
Municipalities					
Tripolitania	246	274	291	301	n.a.
Cyrenaica	192	154	155	181	n.a.
Total	438	428	446	482	500[b]
TOTAL DOMESTIC REVENUES	5,549	7,061	8,147	9,595	12,049[b]

[a] Property tax varies around £L 15,000 a year.
[b] Estimates, not actuals.

TABLE S.3   Public Expenditures by Main Categories

(£L '000: fiscal years beginning April)

	1954/55	1955/56	1956/57	1957/58	1958/59
General administration and defense					
Law and order	1,517	1,676	2,022	2,179	2,745
Tax collection	173	169	172	192	314
Development administration	40	70	106	271	303
Other civil administration	1,362	1,840	2,011	2,006	2,060
Public buildings	555	533	739	1,314	1,576
Defense	313	352	464	629	1,033
Sub-total	3,960	4,640	5,514	6,591	8,031
Social services					
Health	630	968	1,508	1,392	1,480
Education	1,177	1,342	1,741	2,499	3,322
Popular housing and other relief expenditures	421	208	259	402	236
Municipal services	386	368	405	406	433
Sub-total	2,614	2,886	3,913	4,699	5,471
Economic services					
Agriculture and irrigation	608	1,944	2,165	1,796	1,371
Industries and minerals	20	120	70	58	72
Tourism and antiquities	50	56	90	49	77
Transport and communications	1,407	1,669	2,269	2,873	3,306
Electric power and water supply	138	963	1,412	965	851
Capitalization of National Bank of Libya	—	700	—	—	—
Sub-total	2,223	5,452	6,006	5,741	5,677
GRAND TOTAL	8,797	12,978	15,433	17,031	19,179

TABLE S.4   Public Expenditures on Agriculture, Water Resources and Forestry

(£L '000: fiscal years beginning April)

	1954/55	1955/56	1956/57	1957/58	1958/59
Federal Government[a]	5	234	267	204	182
Tripolitania	255	348	218	341	378
Cyrenaica	107	123	149	156	189
Fezzan	24	26	23	27	28
LARC[b]	—	822	1,238	871	510
LPDSA	217	391	270	197	84
Total	608	1,944	2,165	1,796	1,371
Of which:					
General Administration	96	122	151	148	161
Soil and water conservation	83	366	454	377	146
Irrigation and wells	93	116	236	230	82
Water investigations	6	15	42	68	42
Forestry and dune fixation	90	119	176	228	196
Land settlement	32	49	48	61	92
Horticulture	5	40	91	40	64
Animal husbandry	66	191	201	129	130
Agricultural tools and machinery	—	23	26	22	156
Agricultural credit	—	500	500	—	—
Assistance to cooperatives	7	45	6	15	18
Grain storage	—	—	12	28	48
Training and research	80	86	155	267	165
Extension services	5	14	19	41	25
Miscellaneous[e]	45	258	48	142	46
Total	608	1,944	2,165	1,796	1,371
Of which:					
Recurrent expenditure[d]	342	803	697	932	900
Capital expenditure[d]	266	1,141	1,468	864	471
Total	608	1,944	2,165	1,796	1,371

[a] Includes expenditures out of the Exceptional Budget. The figures for 1955/56 and 1957/58 contain £L 211,000 and £L 89,000, respectively, for expenditures on locust campaigns.

[b] Includes £L 500,000 in each of the years 1955/56 and 1956/57 for capitalization of the National Agricultural Bank.

[e] The figures for 1955/56 and 1957/58 contain £L 211,000 and £L 89,000, respectively, for expenditures on locust campaigns.

[d] The distinction between recurrent and capital expenditures, being largely based on the mission's own estimates, is subject to a considerable margin of error.

TABLE S.5 Public Expenditures on Industries, Fisheries and Minerals

(£L '000: fiscal years beginning April)

	1954/55	1955/56	1956/57	1957/58	1958/59
LARC	—	64	47	53	70
LPDSA	20	56	23	5	2
Total	20	120	70	58	72
Of which:					
Vehicle workshops and equipment	—	40	31	38	15
Agricultural processing	20	69	28	5	52
Fisheries	—	—	1	—	—
Minerals investigation	—	11	10	15	5
Total	20	120	70	58	72
Of which:					
Recurrent expenditures[a]	—	7	—	—	—
Capital expenditures[a]	20	113	70	58	72

[a] The distinction between recurrent and capital expenditures, being largely based on the mission's own estimates, is subject to a considerable margin of error.

TABLE S.6 Public Expenditures on Electric Power and Water Supplies

(£L '000: fiscal years beginning April)

	1954/55	1955/56	1956/57	1957/58	1958/59
LARC	—	715	1,180	646	637
LPDSA	90	205	182	252	137
Municipalities	45	40	47	58	67
Fezzan	3	3	3	9	10
Total	138	963	1,412	965	851
Of which:					
Purchase of Tripoli power	—	700	423	—	—
Tripoli power expansion	—	—	541	574	523
Other power stations	35	86	91	48	191
Water supplies and miscellaneous	103	177	357	343	137
Total	138	963	1,412	965	851
Of which:					
Recurrent expenditures[a] [b]	n.a.	52	54	70	90
Capital expenditures[b]	n.a.	911	1,358	895	761

[a] The only recurrent expenditures shown in this table are the government subventions required to support municipal power and water undertakings in Tripolitania and public utilities in the Fezzan.

[b] The distinction between recurrent and capital expenditures, being largely based on the mission's own estimates, is subject to a considerable margin of error.

TABLE S.7   Public Expenditures on Transport and Communications

(£L '000: fiscal years beginning April)

	1954/55	1955/56	1956/57	1957/58	1958/59
Federal Government	301	392	272	259	479
Tripolitania	530	470	427	510	548
Cyrenaica	330	305	312	328	381
Fezzan	50	60	65	48	66
LARC	—	100	972	1,439	1,476
LPDSA	196	342	221	289	356
Total	1,407	1,669	2,269	2,873	3,306
Of which:					
General administration	105	84	95	110	153
Roads	487	615	1,227	1,161	810
Railways[a]	56	57	54	75	79
Ports and lights[b]	94	140	130	161	174
Civil aviation[c]	202	202	126	151	256
Telecommunications[d]	—	18	60	336	724
Meteorological Department	38	43	41	47	102
Broadcasting	—	—	64	373	409
Road transport	378	378	427	451	557
Posts	47	132	45	8	42
Total	1,407	1,669	2,269	2,873	3,306
Of which:					
Recurrent expenditures[e]	1,054	1,035	923	1,105	1,225
Capital expenditures[e]	353	634	1,346	1,768	2,081

[a] Figures represent subsidies paid to railways by provincial governments to cover their operating losses and capital expenditures.

[b] Capital expenditures only, financed by LARC and LPDSA.

[c] Figures include operating losses covered by government subventions, plus capital expenditures which have been mainly financed by LARC and LPDSA.

[d] Expenditures by LARC on the telecommunications project plus capital expenditures financed through the ordinary budget of the Ministry of Communications.

[e] The distinction between recurrent and capital expenditures, being largely based on the mission's own estimates, is subject to a considerable margin of error.

TABLE S.8   Public Expenditures on Education

(£L '000: fiscal years beginning April)

	1954/55	1955/56	1956/57	1957/58	1958/59
Federal Government	49	68	224	376	549
Tripolitania	630	691	824	1,116	1,136
Cyrenaica	397	420	491	549	676
Fezzan	32	42	58	101	143
LARC	—	18	97	331	790
LPDSA	69	103	47	26	28
Total	1,177	1,342	1,741	2,499	3,322
Of which:					
General administration	87	109	129	160	195
Teacher's salaries	620	755	900	1,034	1,353
Schools	385	362	375	699	890
Teacher and vocational training	42	59	95	142	213
Libyan University	—	5	42	176	342
Higher Institute of Mahomed el-Senussi	—	—	110	130	160
Scholarships abroad	42	52	59	94	98
Adult education and miscellaneous	1	—	31	64	71
Total	1,177	1,342	1,741	2,499	3,322
Of which:					
Recurrent expenditures[a]	1,070	1,216	1,637	2,034	2,779
Capital expenditures[a]	107	126	104	465	543

[a] The distinction between recurrent and capital expenditures, being largely based on the mission's own estimates, is subject to a considerable margin of error.

TABLE S.9   Public Expenditures on Health

(£L '000: fiscal years beginning April)

	1954/55	1955/56	1956/57	1957/58	1958/59
Federal Government	9	14	58	60	114
Tripolitania	329	415	568	635	596
Cyrenaica	242	287	300	349	394
Fezzan	29	41	47	76	101
LARC	—	40	399	214	224
LPDSA	21	171	136	58	51
Total	630	968	1,508	1,392	1,480
Of which:					
Recurrent expenditures[a]	609	781	1,120	1,276	1,328
Capital expenditures[a]	21	187	388	116	152

[a] The distinction between recurrent and capital expenditures, being largely based on the mission's own estimates, is subject to a considerable margin of error.

TABLE S.10   Analysis of Expenditures by Agencies

(£L '000: fiscal years beginning April)

	1954/55	1955/56	1956/57	1957/58	1958/59
Federal government[a]					
General administration and defense	1,128	1,388	1,761	1,992	2,525
Development administration	9	18	19	23	36
Agriculture, water resources and forestry	5	234	267	204	182
Education	49	68	224	376	549
Health	9	14	58	60	114
New Capital at Beida	—	—	96	630	1,008
Transport and communications	301	392	272	259	479
Tourism	—	6	22	1	—
Social welfare	—	—	—	44	55
Total	1,501	2,120	2,719	3,589	4,948
Tripolitania					
Civil administration	1,572	1,769	1,825	1,908	2,133
Agriculture, water resources and forestry	255	348	218	341	378
Education	630	691	824	1,116	1,136
Health	329	415	568	635	596
Transport and communications	530	470	427	510	548
Relief and welfare	305	82	103	75	169
Tourism	31	30	27	29	48
Total	3,652	3,805	3,992	4,614	5,008
Cyrenaica					
Civil administration	960	1,181	1,366	1,344	1,509
Agriculture, water resources and forestry	107	123	149	156	189
Education	397	420	491	549	676
Health	242	287	300	349	394
Transport and communications	330	305	312	328	381
Relief and welfare	7	7	8	8	8
Tourism and antiquities	19	17	20	17	21
Total	2,062	2,340	2,646	2,751	3,178
Fezzan					
Civil administration	260	232	308	374	544
Agriculture	24	26	23	27	28
Education	32	42	58	101	143
Health	29	41	47	76	101
Transport and communications	50	60	65	48	66
Electric power	3	3	3	9	10
Total	398	404	504	635	892

[a] Including expenditures from Exceptional Budget.

TABLE S.10 Continued

(£L '000: fiscal years beginning April)

	1954/55	1955/56	1956/57	1957/58	1958/59
Municipalities					
I. Tripoli	180	160	170	190	n.a.
Other Tripolitania	100	95	93	95	n.a.
Total	280	255	263	285	300
II. Benghazi	126	125	153	139	n.a.
Other Cyrenaica[b]	25	28	36	40	n.a.
Total	151	153	189	179	200
GRAND TOTAL	431	408	452	464	500[c]
LARC					
Administration	—	21	50	200	226
Agriculture, water resources and forestry	—	822	1,238	871	510
Education	—	18	97	331	790
Health	—	40	399	214	224
Transport and communications	—	100	972	1,439	1,476
Public buildings	—	—	38	37	3
Capitalization of National Bank of Libya	—	700	—	—	—
Electric power and water supplies	—	715	1,180	646	637
Tourism	—	—	17	—	—
Popular housing	—	5	—	60	2
Industries and minerals	—	64	47	53	70
Total	—	2,485	4,038	3,851	3,938
LPDSA					
Administration	31	31	37	48	47
Agriculture water resources and forestry	217	391	270	197	84
Education	69	103	47	26	28
Health	21	171	136	58	51
Transport and communications	196	342	221	289	356
Electric power and water supplies	90	205	182	252	137
Tourism and antiquities	—	3	4	2	8
Relief and welfare	109	114	148	215	2
Public buildings	—	—	14	35	—
Industries and minerals	20	56	23	5	2
Total	753	1,416	1,082	1,127	715

[b] Excluding Derna.
[c] Estimates, not actuals.

FOREIGN TRADE AND PAYMENTS

TABLE S.11   Libya's Balance of Payments

(£L million)

	1954	1955	1956	1957	1958
Current Account					
Exports and re-exports, f.o.b.	3.5[a]	4.3	4.0	5.2	4.8
Imports, c.i.f.	11.3	14.3	16.5	22.8	23.9
Trade balance	−7.8	−10.0	−12.5	−17.6	−19.1
Imports of non-monetary gold	n.a.	n.a.	n.a.	−0.5	−0.7
Foreign military expenditures	+5.6	+6.2	+10.8	+9.8	+6.9
Other services (net)[b]	−2.1	−1.3	−4.6	+4.4	+9.7
Balance of goods and services	−4.3	−5.1	−6.3	−3.9	−3.2
Private donations and transfers (net)[c]	−0.5	−0.6	−0.6	−0.8	−1.2
Official donations[d]	+5.1	+8.4	+10.1	+7.5	+9.4
Current account balance	+0.3	+2.7	+3.2	+2.8	+5.0
Capital Account					
Private capital receipts (net)	+1.2	+0.6	+1.3	+1.0	+0.3
Change in net foreign assets of official and banking institutions (increase −)	−2.6	−3.9	−4.5	−4.6	−5.1
Capital account balance (improvement −)	−1.4	−3.3	−3.2	−3.6	−4.8
Errors and Omissions	1.1	0.6	—	0.8	0.2

[a] Excludes net value of raw sponges.

[b] Including oil company expenditures in Libya, which explain the marked improvement in this item in 1957 and 1958.

[c] Mainly outward remittances by Italians resident in Libya.

[d] These figures differ from those given in Table 1 of Chapter 3 on account of two main factors: (i) they relate to calendar years, not fiscal years, and to receipts, not allocations; and (ii) they exclude surplus commodities supplied by the U. S. under PL 480. The first of these two factors largely explains the difference between this table and Table S.1.

SOURCE: Government of Libya, Central Statistics Office.

TABLE S.12   Foreign Exchange Holdings of the National Bank

(£L '000, end of March)

	1957	1958	1959	1960[b]
Issue Department				
Foreign government securities	4,622	5,687	7,497	7,848
Deposits with foreign banks	1,495	1,500	545	1,944
Total (equivalent to currency in circulation)	6,117	7,187	8,042	9,792
Banking Department				
Foreign currency notes	3	14	9	19
Balances with overseas banks[a]	724	2,176	5,223	8,165
Foreign government and other securities	4,614	7,947	6,400	7,393
Total	5,341	10,137	11,632	15,577
Total holdings of National Bank	11,458	17,324	19,674	25,369

[a] Including net claims on National Bank of Egypt under the bilateral trade and payments agreement—£ 756,887 at the end of March 1959 and £ 2,117,395 at the end of January 1960.

[b] End of January 1960.

SOURCE: National Bank of Libya.

TABLE S.13 Composition of Exports

Commodity	Value in £L '000 f.o.b.					Percentage of domestic exports				
	1954	1955	1956	1957	1958	1954	1955	1956	1957	1958
Groundnuts	583	633	818	848	1,020	16	15	21	18	24
Live animals	567	749	744	500	838	15	17	19	11	19
Scrap metal	225	410	479	439	155	6	10	13	9	4
Esparto	610	532	403	348	272	17	12	11	7	6
Olive oil	261	513	61	1,171	447	7	12	2	25	10
Wool and animal hair	302	320	241	218	113	8	8	6	5	3
Hides and skins	223	237	225	222	219	6	5	6	5	5
Sponges	373	252	188	131	134	10	6	5	2	3
Others	524	637	646	876	1,115	15	15	17	18	26
Total domestic exports	3,668	4,283	3,805	4,753	4,313	100	100	100	100	100

SOURCE: Government of Libya, Central Statistics Office.

TABLE S.14 Destination of Exports

Country	Value in £L '000 f.o.b.					Percentage of domestic exports				
	1954	1955	1956	1957	1958	1954	1955	1956	1957	1958
Italy	1,093	1,683	1,452	2,772	1,596	30	39	38	58	37
United Kingdom	1,129	886	801	810	654	31	21	21	17	15
Egypt	197	466	515	438	722	5	11	14	9	17
Malta	251	267	291	173	240	7	6	8	4	6
Germany	138	368	283	168	327	4	9	7	4	8
Greece	636	333	155	93	157	17	8	4	2	3
Others	224	280	308	299	617	6	6	8	6	14
Total domestic exports	3,668	4,283	3,805	4,753	4,313	100	100	100	100	100

SOURCE: Government of Libya, Central Statistics Office.

TABLE S.15 Composition of Civil Imports[a]

Commodity	Value in £L '000 c.i.f.					Percentage of total civil imports				
	1954	1955	1956	1957	1958	1954	1955	1956	1957	1958
Cereals	1,465	1,495	1,877	1,775	1,420	13	10	11	8	6
Tea	1,048	1,248	865	1,317	1,001	9	9	5	6	4
Fruit and vegetables	671	430	615	680	730	6	3	4	3	3
Sugar and sweets	381	656	638	1,240	994	3	5	4	5	4
Dairy products	215	208	235	303	339	2	1	1	2	1
Wines, spirits, soft drinks	108	81	112	185	230	1	1	1	1	1
Other food and drink	189	224	309	156	620	2	2	2	1	3
Total food and drink	4,077	4,342	4,651	5,656	5,334	36	31	28	26	22
Tobacco and cigarettes	102	151	85	211	138	1	1	1	1	1
Vegetable oils	92	241	453	257	138	1	2	3	1	1
Perfumes and soap	130	141	168	206	300	1	1	1	1	1
Pharmaceuticals	202	230	259	358	484	2	2	2	2	2
Textile yarns and fabrics	995	1,408	1,496	1,682	2,432	9	10	9	7	10
Clothing	580	710	761	954	1,237	5	5	4	4	5
Footwear	179	202	213	329	323	2	1	1	1	1
Total food, clothing etc., as above[b]	6,357	7,425	8,086	9,653	10,386	57	53	49	43	43

[a] Figures for 1957 and 1958 exclude goods directly imported by petroleum companies.
[b] Sub-total broadly represents value of imports of food and finished consumer goods, excluding durables.

TABLE S.15 Continued

Commodity	Value in £L '000 c.i.f.					Percentage of total civil imports				
	1954	1955	1956	1957	1958	1954	1955	1956	1957	1958
Coal and coke	180	725	321	301	253	2	5	2	2	1
Petroleum	596	710	757	1,463	1,403	5	5	4	6	6
Machinery[e]	946	1,123	1,690	2,408	2,873	8	8	10	10	12
Transport equipment	832	1,027	1,265	2,883	3,426	7	7	8	12	14
Base metals and mfrs.	549	861	1,101	1,491	1,592	5	5	7	6	6
Building materials[d]	259	606	844	880	723	2	4	5	4	3
Fertilizers	136	134	228	234	258	1	1	1	1	1
Other chemicals	189	203	280	647	680	2	1	2	3	3
Rubber tires	114	142	156	259	299	1	1	1	1	1
Other materials and mfrs.	1,175	1,382	1,873	2,847	2,529	10	10	11	12	10
Total imports	11,333	14,338	16,601	23,066	24,422	100	100	100	100	100

[e] Including radio sets and household electrical appliances.
[d] Cement, bricks and tiles, timber, stone, natural asphalt, etc.

SOURCE: Government of Libya, Central Statistics Office.

TABLE S.16   Source of Civil Imports[a]

Country	Value in £L '000 c.i.f.					Percentage of total civil imports				
	1954	1955	1956	1957	1958	1954	1955	1956	1957	1958
Italy	3,730	3,833	4,968	7,391	7,299	33	26	30	32	30
United Kingdom	2,478	3,594	3,662	5,177	6,130	22	25	22	22	25
Germany	579	1,462	1,732	2,039	2,326	5	10	10	9	10
France	305	801	996	1,154	1,467	3	6	6	5	6
Egypt	468	845	986	927	697	4	6	6	4	3
Holland	621	695	823	929	1,113	5	5	5	4	5
Ceylon	736	766	663	954	823	7	5	4	4	3
United States	256	244	599	1,335	1,281	2	2	4	6	5
Others	2,160	2,098	2,172	3,160	3,286	19	15	13	14	13
Total	11,333	14,338	16,601	23,066	24,422	100	100	100	100	100

[a] Figures for 1957 and 1958 exclude goods directly imported by petroleum companies.

TABLE S.17   Quantities of Selected Imports[a]

(metric tons)

	1954	1955	1956	1957	1958
Foodstuffs					
Wheat meal and flour	17,770	35,242	46,003	n.a.	41,518
Rice	3,418	4,658	6,042	n.a.	4,681
Barley	3,050	3,210	3,397	n.a.	—
Wheat and other cereals[b]	18,151	1,545	1,279	n.a.	—
Total cereals	42,389	44,655	56,721	n.a.	46,199
Tomatoes (preserved)	n.a.	930	2,125	n.a.	1,608
Apples	n.a.	1,086	1,012	n.a.	1,045
Potatoes	3,957	4,579	5,057	n.a.	7,375
Sugar	7,058	14,176	13,676	n.a.	17,884
Tea	2,137	2,491	2,062	n.a.	2,770
Vegetable oils	483	2,024	3,171	n.a.	1,247
Building materials					
Tar and asphalt	n.a.	4,206	5,649	n.a.	3,118
Stone	n.a.	2,129	2,286	n.a.	2,835
Cement	n.a.	n.a.	51,170	n.a.	71,771
Bricks, tiles, pipes, etc.	5,057	n.a.	18,174	n.a.	n.a.
Other materials and fuel					
Coal and Coke	26,116	75,371	33,672	n.a.	36,242
Iron and steel	2,267	n.a.	7,527	n.a.	8,753
Fertilizers (manufactured)	6,965	7,474	9,232	n.a.	11,531
Vehicles (numbers)					
Railway locomotives, wagons, etc.	n.a.	n.a.	10	n.a.	—
Passenger cars	960	986	981	n.a.	2,417
Motor cycles	n.a.	761	616	n.a.	879
Buses, trucks, lorries, etc.	191	371	398	n.a.	1,114
Bicycles	n.a.	6,245	7,271	n.a.	6,294

[a] Figures for 1958 exclude goods directly imported by petroleum companies.
[b] Excluding gift wheat and other cereals provided by the U. S. under PL 480.

CURRENCY AND BANKING

TABLE S.18 Money Supply

(£L '000, end of December)

	1956	1957	1958	1959
Total currency issued	5,927	7,182	7,842	9,552
Currency holdings of National Bank and commercial banks	927	959	652	596
Currency outside banks	5,000	6,223	7,190	8,956
Sight deposits (including government deposits with National Bank)	10,742	11,996	14,604	19,533
Money supply	15,742	18,219	21,794	28,489
Government deposits with National Bank	1,907	4,430	6,550	9,013
Total money supply, excluding government deposits	13,835	13,789	15,244	19,476
Percentage increase over previous year	—	−0.3%	+10.6%	+27.8%

TABLE S.19   Consolidated Statements of National Bank

(£L '000)

	1957 March 31	1958 March 31	1959 March 31	1959 December 31
ISSUE DEPARTMENT				
Assets				
Foreign government and other securities	4,622	5,687	7,497	6,856
Deposits with foreign banks	1,495	1,500	545	2,696
Total	6,117	7,187	8,042	9,552
Liabilities				
Notes issued	6,117	7,187	8,042	9,552
Total	6,117	7,187	8,042	9,552
BANKING DEPARTMENT				
Assets				
Cash	71	109	157	97
Bank balances	724	2,176	5,223	7,830
Foreign government and other securities	4,614	7,947	6,400	7,245
Advances and discounts	47	350	359	419
Other assets	894	264	285	287
Total	6,350	10,846	12,424	15,878
Liabilities				
Capital and reserves	700	1,194	1,366	1,356
Federal and provincial balances	1,123	4,840	6,334	9,013
Other customers balances	3,154	4,179	4,029	4,383
Other liabilities	1,373	633	695	1,126
Total	6,350	10,846	12,424	15,878

SOURCE: National Bank of Libya.

TABLE S.20 Combined Balance Sheet of Private Commercial Banks

(£L '000: end of month)

	December 1958		December 1959	
Assets				
Cash on hand or in transit	507		517	
Balances with National Bank	741		1,942	
Foreign currency on hand and balances due from banks abroad	1,879		2,522	
Total liquid assets		3,127		4,981
Total credit extension (advances, over-drafts, bills discounted and other loans)		8,374		10,766
Fixed and other assets		7,258		9,913
Total assets		18,759		25,660
Liabilities				
Capital and reserves		1,042		1,031
Demand deposits	6,080		8,510	
Time and savings deposits	4,163		5,358	
Total deposits		10,243		13,868
Borrowing from banks abroad		326		710
Other liabilities		7,148		10,051
Total liabilities		18,759		25,660

Note: Comparable statistics for earlier periods are not available.

SOURCE: National Bank of Libya.

ANNEXES

ANNEX I *NATIONAL INCOME AND EXPENDITURE*

Gross Domestic Product

The Libyan Central Statistics Office in June 1959 published a preliminary estimate of the national income of Libya in 1958, following broadly the definitions recommended by the Statistical Office of the United Nations in its publications on "A System of National Accounts" and "Classification of Government Transactions." The gross domestic product at factor cost was estimated at £L 52.2 million, made up as in Table A.1.

TABLE A.1 Industrial Origin of Gross Domestic Product at Factor Cost in 1958

Economic activity	£L millions	Percent
1. Agriculture, forestry and fishing	13.6	26.1
2. Petroleum prospecting and quarrying	3.6	6.9
3. Manufacturing and repairing	6.0	11.5
4. Construction	1.8	3.4
5. Electricity and gas	0.8	1.5
6. Transportation, storage and communication	2.9	5.6
7. Wholesale and retail trade	7.3	14.0
8. Banking, insurance, ownership of dwellings, other services	9.5	18.2
9. Public administration and defense	6.7	12.8
Gross domestic product at factor cost	52.2	100.0

The main sources used in compiling this estimate were as follows:

Agriculture and forestry—Very rough estimates of production by quantity and value made by the provincial Nazirates of Agriculture and FAO statisticians.

Fishing—Numbers employed obtained from 1954 population census.

Manufacturing, repairing, construction, electricity and gas, transport and communications, wholesale and retail trade, banking and insurance and miscellaneous services—Census of Employment and Production taken by the C.S.O. in Tripoli, Benghazi and certain other urban areas in January-May 1959, except for domestic service, which was estimated on the basis of 1954 population census.

Public administration and defense—Analysis of government accounts made by IBRD Survey Mission; relates to financial year 1957/58.

For the purpose of these estimates of domestic product the boundary of the Libyan economy was drawn so as to include all Libyan nationals, the resident Italian community and foreigners more or less permanently resident in the country such as expatriate officials of the Libyan Government, expatriate teaching and medical staff and the foreign business and banking communities. On the other hand, it excludes U.S. and British forces stationed in Libya, together with UN and USOM personnel, other employees of foreign governments and non-Libyans employed by the oil companies. Expenditures of foreign governments and oil companies in Libya are treated as "invisible exports"; these expenditures, however, exclude goods directly imported into Libya for their own use by foreign governments and oil companies.

The mission believes, on the basis of some rough calculations of its own, that the official estimates represent a fair approximation to the size of the domestic product as a whole. On the individual components, however, we incline to the view that the official figures rather overestimate the contributions of manufacturing industry and petroleum prospecting and underestimate those of wholesale and retail trade and construction.

Some rough estimates of national expenditures were made by the mission while in Libya. These relate, for the most part, to the calendar year 1957 and the fiscal year 1957/58 and are set out in Table A.2. The estimates do not include any allowance for changes in inventories on which the mission was unable to obtain any information.

TABLE A.2 Expenditures on Gross Domestic Product and Imports, 1957/58

(£L millions)

1. Private consumption expenditure (1957)	28.3
2. Government consumption expenditure (1957/58)	12.0
3. Fixed capital formation in public sector (1957/58)	5.0
4. Private fixed capital formation (1958)	3.5
5. Exports and re-exports of goods (1957)	5.2
6. Exports of services (1957):	
(a) foreign government expenditure in Libya	10.7
(b) oil company expenditure in Libya	4.1
(c) other	1.7
7. Total expenditure on gross domestic product and imports	70.5
8. *Less* imports of goods and services (1957)	25.5
9. Gross domestic product at factor cost	45.0

Notes to Table A.2

Item 1. Based on estimates of food production at market prices plus imports, less exports, less consumption of food by foreign governments, oil companies and the Libyan army and police forces. Other consumption has been arbitrarily assumed to be 50 percent of food consumption in line with the ratio commonly prevailing in other countries with a low per capita income.

Items 2-3. Estimates derived from analysis of accounts of federal and provincial governments, foreign aid and municipalities.

Item 4. Largely guesswork. The gross value of private building in Tripoli alone is officially estimated at about £L 1½ million in 1958. In addition, allowance has to be made for private residential and industrial building in Benghazi and other towns and for private investment in agriculture (especially on the larger foreign-run farms in Tripolitania). Exploration investment by the oil companies is excluded, being treated as an invisible export to the extent that it involves expenditures on goods and services bought in Libya.

Items 5-6 and 8. Based on the official balance of payments estimates.

No attempt is made here to reconcile the two sets of estimates, which in any case relate to different years. The mission considers, however, that it would be reasonable to conclude from the limited data available that the value of the domestic product in 1958 was in the region of £L 50 million. It will certainly have risen further in 1959.

Agricultural and Livestock Production

Agriculture and animal husbandry are two of the sectors of the Libyan economy where statistical information is particularly unreliable. The mission made the following very tentative estimates of output in these two sectors in the agricultural year 1957/58:

TABLE A.3 Agricultural Output in Libya

(£L millions)

Tripolitania	
Cereals (excluding fodder crops)	1.2
Olives (mainly used for oil)	2.3
Fruit and nuts	2.1
Vegetables	1.2
Other agricultural production	0.8
Animal products	2.7
Total (excluding fodder)	10.3
Cyrenaica	
Cereals (excluding fodder crops)	0.9
Olives, fruit and nuts	0.4
Other agricultural production	0.4
Animal products	1.2
Exports of live animals	0.8
Total (excluding fodder)	3.7
Fezzan	
Agricultural and livestock production	0.5
All Libya	
Gross value of agricultural output	14.5
Less input of fertilizers, machinery, seed, etc., say	2.0
Net value of agricultural output, say	12.5

The breakdown of the estimate shows the large elements of guesswork entering into the calculations. Estimation of livestock production in Libya is wildly hazardous, since there is huge uncertainty about the numbers of animals in existence at any given time. A rough check of numbers made by the agricultural departments in May each year has produced the following figures:

TABLE A.4   Livestock Numbers

(In '000; May each year)

	1955	1956	1957	1958
Tripolitania				
Sheep	429	503	574	631
Goats	436	469	573	631
Cattle	49	45	47	52
Camels	70	74	81	89
Cyrenaica				
Sheep	1,032	815	545	785
Goats	691	586	524	661
Cattle	86	60	33	59
Camels	76	76	76	83

These figures look high when compared with estimates for previous periods made by the Italian authorities before the war and by a Four-Power Commission after the war. The U.S. Embassy in Libya has compiled estimates of maximum and minimum numbers of livestock in Libya as a whole during the period 1950-56, and these are as follows:

	Minimum Numbers	*Maximum Numbers*
Sheep	300,000	1,236,000
Goats	667,000	1,232,000
Cattle	50,000	96,000
Camels	93,500	197,000
Horses, mules and asses	59,500	95,000
Pigs	2,000	3,000

The area of uncertainty covers not only the numbers of animals, but also the production derived from any given number. Widely differing conversion factors have been used at various times in calculating the amounts of meat and milk consumed in Libya per head of livestock. The estimates used by the mission give a per capita consumption of 7-8 kilograms of meat a year in Cyrenaica and 8-9 kilograms a year in Tripolitania. For milk and milk products the corresponding figures are 70 kilograms a year in Cyrenaica and 50 kilograms a year in Tripolitania.

The other main livestock products in Libya are hides and skins, wool and hair, poultry, eggs and honey. A considerable proportion of these products is consumed by the producer, particularly in the case of the nomadic and semi-nomadic population. A large element of guess-work therefore inevitably enters into the calculations, since no detailed survey has been made of consumption patterns.

Changes in stocks (inventories) of animals must be an important element in the Libyan national income. In drought years the number of animals brought to market may actually increase, and output estimates may be seriously misleading unless they take account of slaughterings and losses due to natural causes. This is not so important when it is simply a question of calculating output in a single year, as has been done here. But it makes a lot of difference in measuring changes from one year to another, and serious study should be given to the problem as national income statistics in Libya are developed.

Industrial Output

The official estimates of value added in Libyan industry (see Table A.1) were based on the urban census of production. A breakdown is given in Table A.5.

TABLE A.5   Value Added in Manufacturing and Repairing, 1958

Industry	£L '000	Percent
Food	1,584	26
Beverages	459	8
Tobacco	889[a]	15
Textiles	214	4
Footwear and clothing	440	7
Wood products, furniture and fixtures	283	5
Printing, publishing and paper	232	4
Nonmetallic minerals (excluding petroleum)	174	3
Metal manufacture, machinery and appliances	229	4
Transport equipment (mostly repair)[b]	921	15
Miscellaneous	563	9
Total	5,988	100

[a] Includes the monopoly profit accruing to government. If this is excluded, value added in tobacco manufacture is only about £L 200,000.

[b] Includes repair workshops operated by British and American forces in Libya.

THE NATIONAL BANK

Background

Prior to Independence, a Preparatory Currency Committee dealt with monetary matters. This committee, composed of representatives from Libya, France, Italy and the United Kingdom, signed a financial agreement in 1951, whereby the British Government undertook to provide 100 percent sterling backing for the initial issue of Libyan currency. Subsequently, the Libyan Currency Commission was established and started in March 1952, to issue Libyan pounds in place of Egyptian pounds in Cyrenaica, British Military Authority lire in Tripolitania and Algerian francs in the Fezzan. The Libyan pound is now legal tender in all these provinces. It is officially at par with sterling, and there is a fixed exchange rate with the Egyptian pound of 97½ Egyptian piasters to the Libyan pound for settlements under a bilateral payments agreement. Exchange rates for other currencies are based on London quotations or are negotiated.

In April 1955 a law was passed setting up the National Bank of Libya, and the Bank opened its doors in Tripoli in April 1956. Subsequently, two more offices were opened, one in Sebha (April 1957) and the other in Benghazi (August 1957).

Organization and Objectives

The National Bank is organized along the lines of the Bank of England with an Issue Department and a Banking Department. It also conducts commercial banking business on a small scale. The authorized capital is £L 1 million, of which £L 700,000 has been subscribed and paid in by the Libyan Government. All or part of the remaining £L 300,000 may be offered for public subscription if the Board of the Bank and the federal government deem it appropriate.

Although the Bank maintains only three offices altogether, both the Tripoli and the Benghazi branches are designated as "joint chief

377

offices." The Bank's objectives are "to regulate the issue of bank notes and coins, to keep reserves with a view to maintaining monetary stability in Libya and the external value of the Libyan pound, to influence the credit situation to the Kingdom's advantage and to act as banker to the Government and to the Provincial Administrations" (Article 6 of the National Bank Law). To achieve these aims, the Bank is in theory armed with the following powers: (a) manipulation of the discount rate; (b) open-market operations; and (c) prescription of compulsory deposits for commercial banks.

In practice the National Bank has not been able to exert any appreciable influence on the monetary situation by any of these means. The discount rate, initially 4 percent, was raised to 5 percent in October 1957, when inflationary pressures began to threaten monetary stability. Because of the excess liquidity of the commercial banks, however, they generally had no need to discount paper with the National Bank, and this instrument was thus rendered ineffective. The raising of the interest rate in these circumstances was merely a "signal" to the banking system that inflation actually had become a problem. In fact, only two private banks have had recourse, on a limited scale, to National Bank credit as a source of funds. Effective open-market operations are also out of the question as there are no Libyan government securities. Even if the government decided to issue securities, the National Bank appears to be restricted by law to operating only in bills that have already been sold by the government to the market.[1]

The power of prescribing cash reserves to be held by the commercial banks over and above the 20 percent liquid reserve required by the Banking Law of 1958 is potentially a more effective method of restricting private bank lending to the public. However, according to the present law, the executive power in regard to this provision is conferred on the Minister of Finance. The Minister also has the authority to grant bank licenses and to consider applications from shareholders and/or depositors for examination of bank affairs, together with a number of other executive functions (Articles 4-7, 9, 10, 11 and 17 of the Banking Law). In all these matters he is required to consult the National Bank before taking action.

A more fundamental reason why the National Bank is not in a position under the present circumstances to regulate the money supply independently lies in the existing currency reserve system. Following the provisions of the former Currency Commission Law, the National

[1] The relevant article of the National Bank Law (Article 24 (viii)) is vague on this point, and the above interpretation is open to question.

Bank Law stipulates a cent-per-cent foreign reserve for the Libyan currency. These foreign assets may consist of (a) sterling balances, (b) sterling Treasury Bills of the British Government, (c) sterling securities of, or guaranteed by, the British Government, (d) securities issued or guaranteed by other governments and (e) foreign exchange balances other than pounds sterling. However, non-sterling assets (items (d) and (e)) may not exceed 25 percent of the assets of the Issue Department of the National Bank. This system is in effect an automatic sterling exchange standard. Consequently, the volume of Libyan currency cannot be determined at the discretion of the National Bank at all, as the law suggests, but is instead automatically regulated by the public's preference for and its capacity to tender or hold approved foreign assets or Libyan pounds. The foreign exchange holdings of the National Bank of Libya are given in Table S.12 of the Statistical Appendix to the main report.

THE COMMERCIAL BANKS

Origin and Location

All private commercial banks operating in Libya are branches of foreign banking institutions. Three of the head offices are in Italy, two in Great Britain, one in Egypt, one in Jordan and one in France. All these banks operate in Tripoli, and five have also opened offices in Benghazi; one British bank maintains offices in a number of towns along the coast. None of the private banks is represented in the Fezzan. However, the National Bank provides commercial banking facilities in Sebha.

Financial Characteristics

A comprehensive balance sheet for all private banks in Libya is reproduced in Table S.20 of the Statistical Appendix and shows the positions at the end of 1958 and 1959. Comparable returns for earlier periods are not available because it was only toward the end of 1958 that the National Bank began to collect systematic and detailed information on the financial operations of the commercial banks.

The balance sheet figures immediately point to one basic characteristic of Libyan banking, namely the caution private banks observe in their operations. Total liquid assets at the end of 1958 aggregated

£L 3.1 million, of which 60 percent consisted of foreign currency reserves mostly in the form of balances with head offices abroad. Only three banks have their own capital and reserves in Libya, amounting to slightly over £L 1 million.

A second characteristic of private banking practice in Libya is a high degree of liquidity compared to deposits, pointing to a lack of suitable investment opportunities as well as to the cautious attitudes

TABLE A.6   Analysis of Customers' Liabilities to Private Banks

	1958		1959	
	Credits outstanding at year end (£L '000)	Percentage distribution	Credits outstanding at year end (£L '000)	Percentage distribution
Agriculture				
Livestock and agricultural bodies	1,015	12.1	1,047	9.7
Industries				
Food, drink, tobacco	313	3.7	489	4.5
Textiles and clothing	130	1.6	186	1.7
Soap and oils	135	1.5	116	1.1
Metal products and machinery	100	1.2	181	1.7
Stone, cement, bricks	72	0.9	87	0.8
Other	199	2.4	294	2.7
Construction	400	4.8	347	3.2
Wholesale Merchants	3,527	42.1	4,512	41.9
Retail Merchants	863	10.3	805	7.5
Motor Vehicles and Transport Services	785	9.4	1,481	13.8
Professional and Private Individuals	117	1.4	201	1.9
Mortgages	194	2.3	167	1.6
Miscellaneous[a]	524	6.3	853	7.9
Total	8,374	100.0	10,766	100.0

[a] This item includes small loans extended to municipalities, public utilities, wood and paper firms, chemical firms, hotels and restaurants, insurance companies and credit cooperative societies.

SOURCE: National Bank of Libya.

of the managements. According to the Banking Law (Article 9 (i)), "every bank shall maintain at all times a reserve of cash or money on short call not exceeding ten days equal to not less than 20 percent of the deposit liabilities of the bank in Libya." The actual cash/deposit ratio in December 1958, however, stood at 30.5 percent and in December 1959 at 35.9 percent. This seems to be an unusually high liquidity ratio. On the one hand, the banks find it difficult to extend more loans and advances to the public on account of the risks involved; on the other, there are no local government securities to provide an outlet for excess funds.

The excess liquidity of the commercial banks and the lack of investment opportunities also explain the absence of any efforts on the part of the banks to recruit additional local savings. Out of the £L 13.9 million of deposit liabilities of the banking system at the end of 1959, only about 14 percent represent balances on savings accounts. Small-scale bank saving is restricted to a few areas predominantly populated by foreigners. The bulk of the banks' deposits are temporary surplus funds, primarily accumulated by trading firms.

Commercial Bank Credit

Commercial banking in Libya is characterized by the predominance of short-term advances, usually for periods of 3-12 months. Renewal of credits, however, is possible, and it appears that the commercial banks are compelled to adopt this procedure quite frequently. In general, advances are given without any tangible security, a natural response to local conditions and in particular to the shortage of suitable assets to serve as collateral for bank credits. As a result of these factors, banks tend to confine their lending operations to relatively few sectors, represented by a small number of customers who are well-known to the management.

Table A.6 shows that the bulk of the loans are extended to the tertiary sectors of the economy (distributive activities and service industries). The largest single item, credits to wholesale merchants, accounted for over 40 percent of total credit extension both in 1958 and 1959; practically all of these funds were used to finance imports and exports. Another sizeable amount was granted for the purchase of motor vehicles and other transport equipment (13.8 percent at the end of 1959), some of which went to private individuals. Nevertheless, directly productive loans in the strict sense of the word were not negligible. The agricultural sector's share at the end of 1959 was about 10 percent, construction accounted for 3.2 percent, and all industrial firms together received another 12½ percent. Thus directly productive sectors probably took a share of close to one-quarter of all credits granted. The extent to which commercial banks have financed the purchase of durable consumers' goods is not known, but there are indications that this field of activity is becoming increasingly important, at least to some banks. For the time being, installment buying is restricted to Tripoli and Benghazi.

Interest Rates

The information available on interest charges is necessarily restricted to bank loans. The rates charged by the noninstitutional money lenders are not known, but they are presumably well above the rates charged by the banks.

On the liabilities side of the balance sheet, current accounts are by and large noninterest-bearing deposits. Some banks, however, do allow interest on a limited number of accounts held by favored customers, presumably to prevent them from dealing with other banks. Rates on savings accounts vary from 1 percent to 4½ percent, with 2½ percent to 3½ percent being the usual range. Whether a particular bank pays a rate nearer the minimum or the maximum again appears to depend on the customer and the amount deposited. The rates offered by the National Bank vary according to the category of deposit: 2½ percent for 7 days, 3 percent for 30 days and 3½ percent for 90 days and longer.

Rates charged for secured loans generally extend from 6 percent to 9 percent, with 6½ percent to 7½ percent being the usual range. For unsecured advances, which represent the bulk of the credits, the rates appear to be only slightly higher (7 percent to 10 percent, but mostly around 7 percent). The narrow spread between secured and unsecured loans is surprising. But some banks seem to charge additional commission fees on unsecured advances. The practice of charging special commission fees varies from bank to bank, and within one bank from customer to customer. Nevertheless, to the extent that extra fees are charged, they represent a higher effective interest rate.

No rediscount rates are quoted by the commercial banks as the majority of bills are being held to maturity. The National Bank, on the other hand, charges a minimum rate of 5 percent, though this has never really been effective for the reasons mentioned above.

MONEY SUPPLY

Table S.18 in the Statistical Appendix contains the detailed components of the money supply over the period 1956-58. The amount of sight deposits, as compared to currency outside banks, is unusually large. At the end of 1959, for instance, notes and coins held by the public aggregated almost £L 9 million, while sight deposits totaled more than twice that amount. It is, of course, true that the federal and provincial governments held balances with the National Bank of £L 9 million (which are included under the item "sight deposits"). But even if these holdings are deduced the volume of sight deposits exceeded that of currency in each of the past four years.

In 1957 and 1958 the money supply (currency outside banks plus total sight deposits) increased by £L 2.5 million and £L 3.6 million respectively. The increase in 1957 was entirely due to a sharp expansion of government deposits, and there was a slight reduction in the volume of private money. In 1958, government deposits and private sight deposits both increased considerably. A large increase in money supply took place in 1959, reflecting the general rise in public expenditures and the increased activity of the oil companies. Total money supply, excluding government deposits, rose during the year by £L 4.2 million (28 percent).

ANNEX III *PROPOSAL FOR A FINANCE COMMISSION*

The mission has recommended that a statutory finance commission be set up by the Government of Libya for the purpose of making recommendations on the allocation of finance between the federal government and the provinces. It is proposed to outline here briefly some tentative suggestions on the composition of such a commission, its procedures and methods of work. These suggestions might serve as general guidelines. The detailed functioning of a finance commission would have to be adapted to the circumstances and needs in Libya as deemed appropriate by the government.

The allocation of resources between the federation and the provinces is a challenging problem. Both the federation and the provinces have responsibilities for administration and development and both of them derive their revenues from the same public; however, the provinces are rarely alike in population, revenue, resources and needs. In such a situation differences arise as to who should bear how much of the burden and how much should be retained or received by each unit for the needs of its own administration and development in the area of its own responsibility. An effective way of resolving such differences is by the establishment of grants commissions or finance commissions, as has been done in Australia and India, for example. Such commissions are composed of representatives of the federal and provincial governments, together with economic and other experts, and recommend to the federal government the size of the various allocations of available revenues. They determine the specific principles on which allocations should be made and base such principles on criteria justifiable on grounds of economy and equity. We suggest, therefore, that a similar effort should be made in Libya, and that such a commission should be set up as soon as possible. It should be reconvened at least every five years.

The commission should be established on the initiative of the federal government and should consist of a chairman and four members, of whom at least one should be conversant with the problems of finances in the provinces, one with knowledge and training in the field of economics and one with the rank and experience of a judge in the Supreme Court. It would also be desirable to have a representative of the Development Council—possibly its senior economist—as an ex-officio member. The chairman should be selected from among persons who have had wide experience in public affairs and command a wide measure of approval as between the federal and provincial governments. As the work of the commission concerns relations between the central government and provincial governments, it is essential that the federal government as well as the provinces should have confidence in the personnel of the commission. To this end, prior consultations between the governments concerned as to the acceptability of the members of the commission is desirable.

The commission should be charged with the responsibility of making suggestions for grants-in-aid to provinces out of funds derived from (a) customs and excise duties, (b) income tax revenues (which we have recommended in future be raised by the federal government) and (c) the funds derived from financial agreements with the United Kingdom, the United States and other countries, insofar as these are not earmarked for financing specific development projects.

Once appointed, the commission should generally determine its own procedures of work, but in the discharge of its functions it should have the powers of a civil court so that it can summon and enforce attendance of witnesses and require the production of any documents relevant to its work. The commission should hold both public and private sessions, and summary records should be kept of all of its discussions.

The federal and provincial governments should furnish the finance commission with detailed information regarding the financial situation, with a forecast of revenues and expenditures for a period of years and with a statement justifying those expenditures. At an early stage, the commission should issue a notification to the press inviting suggestions from interested members of the public, experts and organized bodies such as Chambers of Commerce, labor unions, banking or other organized bodies which have an interest in the commission's work, and asking for their views and suggestions on the problems with which the commission is charged. This will enable the commission to collate and sift public opinion as widely as possible. The finance commission should visit the three provinces as well as the federal capital to have discussions with ministers and officials of the respective governments. Discussions should also be carried on with other interested persons such as the commissioners of income tax, the Auditor General and the Development Council staff.

The finance commission should proceed on the assumption that, although the federal and provincial governments prepare their budgets on an annual cash basis, planned programs extending over a period of years require some degree of continuity in budget expenditures. The commission would be primarily concerned with advising on the allocation of funds for financing current expenditures, but in doing this it would need to take into account the distribution of capital expenditures. It should normally be sufficient to appoint a finance commission once every five years, although in special circumstances the interval might be reduced—for example, if a sudden increase in oil revenues should take place. The records of each commission's work should be preserved, since they will provide a useful basis for the work of the succeeding commissions. The commission would have to be assisted by an appropriate staff of experts and administrative personnel and, at least in the first instance, it would be advisable to try to obtain from abroad for this purpose people who have had experience of similar work elsewhere. The commission should normally deliver its report to the government as early as possible, but never later than a year after its appointment.

A finance commission of this kind is designed to serve as an instrument for a thorough discussion of federal and provincial financial relations on a systematic and expert basis, with a view to working out compromises on important points of difference. The commission, in other words, should be useful in establishing principles that embody the largest measure of agreement and harmonize principles of finance with public attitudes and political considerations. For this reason, the commission should endeavor to produce a unanimous report incorporating all necessary compromises on important issues under its purview and not leave a host of divergent views for the government to settle afterwards. So long as the commission undertakes its task with this objective in mind, the federal and provincial governments should accept such recommendations with as little change as possible.

In making allocations of funds as between the various units of government, the finance commission will have to bear in mind the needs of the federal government for defense and national development and the need to raise the less developed provinces to a level approaching the more developed ones by planning for a more rapid growth of their resources. In such a process, it is natural that the economically advanced provinces will feel that they are not getting their fair share of the resources subject to allocation. It is precisely for this reason that finance commissions are set up, so that their recommendations may be framed with a view to fulfilling *national* requirements and serving the collective good of the country as a whole. A disposition on the part of all concerned to accept such a judicial and expert adjudication is essential to a successful management of a federal union.

ANNEX IV *MINERAL RESOURCES*

Except for remote occurrences of the oldest Archaen formations, which might be prolific in mineral deposits of the heavy and more valuable minerals, such as gold, silver, copper and uranium, the geological constitution of Libya is not favorable for the occurrence of minerals of great economic importance. It appears that promise of the development of mineral resources in the near future may be more or less confined to industries which are related to nonmetallic minerals, such as gypsum, potash, phosphate and natron, which are associated with sedimentary formations.

The desert conditions and difficulties of transportation militate against detailed exploration and successful exploitation of mineral deposits which may be beyond easy access to the coast. Such obstacles, however, do not apply to the petroleum companies, whose large financial reserves enable them to take risks commensurate with the promise of greater returns. Exploration—in addition to the search for oil—will also provide much valuable information regarding the general geology of Libya. Emphasis should thus be placed on the necessity for close liaison with the petroleum companies, and immediate and continuous recording and correlation of such data at a central point.

We feel that it should not be a function of a government service to undertake detailed investigations of mineral deposits, such as the "proving" of reserves and their value. It is important, however, that preliminary work should be done, as in the case of the Fezzan iron deposits and the gypsum deposits near Jefren. Prospecting programs on such a scale are justified by the information which is thus to be gained regarding the structure of the deposits and the nature of their mineralization. At present, the following mineral resources are known to exist.

Iron Deposits

Hematitic iron deposits occur in the neighborhood of Brak in the Fezzan. The region is, however, devoid of facilities for modern mining exploration, including transportation and power. The iron deposits

387

occur in the Tournasian series of carboniferous age, composed of lenticular shallow-water deposits of light-red and brown sandstone, greenish-grey and brown strata and clay stone. Most prominent in the series are the massive hematitic structures which lie near the base. No igneous rocks occur in the neighborhood, but not far north of Brak there are elevated outcrops of a black basic rock, which may be related to the volcanic rocks of Gebel Soda, south of Hon. The basal beds of the series contain small amounts of petroliferous or asphaltic materials. The general dip of the formation is about one to two degrees south. The ore is oolitic, composed of minute oolites of chamoisite and hematite, and contaminated with sand in varying amounts. In places it resembles a highly ferruginous sandstone. Unoxidized portions contain abundant finely-disseminated pyrite. It is believed that considerable petrographic research on thin and polished sections of the ore is required to determine definitely the composition of the ore for the purpose of understanding the metallurgical treatment which will be required. However, it is definitely a high-silica ore, which is costly to treat on account of the abnormal consumption of coke and flux in the blast furnaces. Other factors, which tend to lower the value of the ore, are the increased cost of freight due to impurities, and the large amount of slag to be removed, which greatly reduces the output of the furnaces. The phosphorous content of the ore, although higher than other African ores, is considered to be reasonable.

Exploratory drilling operations were completed in 1957, and information gained from 42 holes, for a total length of 950 meters, and over a distance of 82 kilometers. The drill holes have been carefully logged, and more than 400 samples were analyzed in the LAJS chemical laboratory. However, it is still not possible to estimate the ore reserves. The appropriate investigations required to prove reserves as a prelude to mining development would require drilling on a regular pattern as well as detailed topographic mapping, and this should only be done if an industrial corporation can be found which would be interested in exploiting the deposits. The iron deposits are not comparable in grade and extent with those of North and South America or Sweden, nor with other deposits in North Africa, as in Algeria, Morocco and Tunisia, where ores contain more than 50 percent iron. It is apparent that they are comparable in grade with similar deposits in Western Europe. The latter, however, are usually situated in centers of large population, where such facilities as abundant labor, power and easy transportation are available. Circumstances for exploitation in the Fezzan are much less favorable.

The value of iron may range from 5-10 U.S. cents per unit of iron (22.4 lbs.) for low-grade ores to 20-30 U.S. cents for high-grade ores or concentrates. Libyan ore, if its grade could be enhanced by benefication from 45 percent to 60 percent ferrous content, might be able to fetch from $6.75 to $9.35 per ton at the port of shipment. However, even if a black-top road is constructed to link the deposits with the coast, the cost of road transport from Brak to Tripoli alone would probably work out at around $20 per ton, and this would rule out any possibility of the ore finding a market abroad.

In countries where there is the desire for a local iron and steel industry, but which lack a supply of coking coal, there is an increasing interest in "direct reduction" processes, using natural gas as fuel for the treatment of low-grade ores containing 25 percent to 45 percent iron. However, this is a process requiring much larger initial capital investment than could possibly be justified in Libya at the present time. For example, the capital cost of a plant to reduce 2,200 tons of ore per day is estimated at $23 million.

Gypsum

Deposits of gypsum occur in many parts of Tripolitania, and those which appear to be of greatest importance occur near Bir Ghnem on the Jefren road, 95 kilometers from Tripoli. The deposits are intercalated with shale and limestone strata of Jurassic age and, of the 100 meters of gypsiferous formation measured, 5 meters to 10 meters of massive gypsum occur near the base. Many outcrops of gypsum occur in the wadis in the area and in deep cuts at the foot of the Gebel, indicating the extensive and impressive nature of the deposits. A program of exploration by core drilling is being carried out under the auspices of LARC. Analyses show that the deposits would yield gypsum of high quality. Beds of gypsum ($CaSO_4.2H_2O$) occur in the same geological formation with beds of anhydrate ($CaSO_4$). The latter usually occur below the gypsum and constitute the original rock formation. Near the surface, through contact with atmospheric influences, water has combined with the anhydrate to form gypsum.

The principal use of gypsum is in the building trades. By calcining at a temperature of 700°F., plaster of paris is produced, which is employed in the manufacture of wallboard, lathes and molding. Care must be taken in heat control in the calcining (dehydration) of gypsum in order to obtain an evenly calcined product. Gypsum (uncalcined) is also used as a retarder for portland cement. High-grade natural gypsum may be mixed with anhydrate in the proportion of 75:25. It is employed in the manufacture of ammonium sulfate, which is a valuable fertilizer, and for making sulfuric acid, which gives sulfur as a by-product.

It is recommended that publicity be given to the existence of these important deposits, in order to attract either foreign or local capital. We have suggested elsewhere in this report investigating the use of gypsum for construction of low-cost housing, and if this proves feasible, an assured market might be provided for about 1,000 tons of gypsum a year. This would provide a stimulus to the exploitation of gypsum deposits by private enterprise and capital assistance could be extended by the government under the industrial credit scheme recommended in Chapter 10.

Potash (Carnallite)

Potash deposits at Marada consist of carnallite, which is a hydrous combination of potassium chloride (KCl) and magnesium chloride ($MgCl_2$) contaminated by admixture of ordinary salt (sodium chloride) in varying amounts. The Marada area lies in a topographic depression, of which the northern part is a desolate salt marsh. The oasis itself is occupied by some 1,000 inhabitants, and contains many fresh-water springs; potable water may also be obtained by drilling wells at the southern edge of the salt marsh. The geological formations of the region are of Lower Miocene and Oligocene ages, and the potash deposits are believed to derive from saline residues presumably left by a receding Miocene sea.

An attempt was made by the Italians to estimate the reserves of potassium salts, and preliminary results of drilling indicate the existence of a stratum below the marsh bed, eight meters thick, containing chlorides and sulfates of potash and magnesium. On this basis, inconclusive estimates were made pointing to the existence of 1,600,000 tons of potassium salts containing 40 percent to 42 percent K_2O, together with 7,500,000 tons of magnesium chloride.

During the investigations by the Italians it was found that, over an area of some 15 square kilometers, a relatively high concentration of potassium salts exists; and a system of exploitation was established, comprising 20,000 pits, two meters square and 10 centimeters deep, into which the brine seeped from the sandy soil. Within a week, under normal summer conditions, the pits would contain about 80 kilograms of a mixture of salts consisting of magnesium sulfate, magnesium chloride, sodium chloride and potassium chloride. Labor was abundant and cheap. Of the 700 laborers who were employed 500 were Libyan prisoners. A refining process of resolution and fractional crystallization produced a potash salt containing 40 percent to 50 percent K_2O.

During 1939, when operations by the Italians were begun, 21,000 tons, containing 40-42 percent K_2O were produced and said to have been exported to Italy. Operations were terminated by the war, and insignificant amounts of potash were subsequently sent to Italy. Communications had been established by road from Marada to el Ageila, 125 kilometers over desert and thence by coastal highway to a small harbor 43 kilometers west of el Ageila. The shipping facilities there were destroyed during the war, and little remains of the road across the desert, which is exceptionally rough and partially covered with dune sand.

The cost of transport of refined KCl from Marada to the coast is estimated to be £L 3.75 per ton ($10.50), and from there to Tripoli (by road) £L 3.5 ($9.80). Total transport cost would be $20.30 per ton. However, this cost might be appreciably reduced if improved road communications are developed to the oilfield south of Marada.

The cost of potash is relatively small in proportion to the total cost of a mixed fertilizer. The grade or purity of potash as fertilizer is not vitally important because of its admixture with nitrates and phosphates and other plant foods. However, pure potash has the advantage of the saving on freight charges.

Potash is used principally as a component of a mixed fertilizer, and in the United States 90 percent of the production is thus employed. In Tripolitania it is used for such crops as potatoes, tomatoes, groundnuts, vegetables and tobacco. Experiments by the FAO in Libya, on both dry land and irrigated farms of wheat and barley, suggest that little, if any, benefit results from such use. It is estimated that about 2,000 tons of potash might be consumed annually as fertilizer in Libya. A small amount of potash is used in the glass and chemical industries— also in the manufacture of liquid and soft soaps, dyes, disinfectants and matches.

In 1938, a concession was granted to the Societa Anonima Industrial Libica, for 50 years, covering 700 hectares. No work has been done since 1941, nor has any application been made for the restoration of the concession. We consider the data which has already been obtained is sufficient, by way of basic information, to permit foreign interests to determine whether or not the deposits may have importance to the industry. Publicity in trade journals would direct attention to the existence of the potash deposits, the future of which depends on exports rather than production for domestic consumption. Some publicity has been given in trade journals to the existence of the potash deposits, but only marginal interest has been evoked.

It is possible, nevertheless, that the proximity of the recent petroleum discoveries might stimulate renewed interest. A nearby potential source of natural gas enhances the prospects for the Marada deposits. Concentration of the salts through solar energy could now be supplemented by a process of evaporation by fuel, and could be continuous throughout the year. It appears doubtful if such operations could be performed at the coast because of the problems connected with the pumping of solutions through pipelines, the interiors of which would soon become caked with salt liberated from solution. Any plan of operations would thus have to envisage the bulk transportation of the potash products to the coast from the Marada deposits.

The salt flats (*sebchas*) of Posida, on the coast 145 kilometers west of Tripoli near the harbor of Zuara, are a possible source of potash. Deposits consist of a thin layer of evaporites 10 centimeters to 20 centimeters thick, which has been tested in 19 holes. The analysis showed that the potassium chloride (KCl) content was between 5-10 percent. Samples of the brine gave 0.5 percent KCl, 8-9 percent M_gCl, and a maximum of 35 percent NaCl. The cool and humid climate along the coast is not conducive to excessive evaporation and concentration of the saline content of percolating marine waters, which may explain the low concentration of potash and other valuable salts in the *sebchas*. However, there are indications of the presence of an appreciable amount of potassium and magnesium in the soil underlying the deposits. The value of these deposits as a source of potash is currently being determined by a USOM investigation. If potash in sufficient amounts to satisfy domestic demands can be produced economically, it would appear that the Pisida deposits would have an advantage over the Marada deposits as a source of supply.

The Idris deposits consist of sporadic *sebchas* scattered over an area of approximately 20 square kilometers, about 150 kilometers west of Brak in the Fezzan. The area is devoid of transportation facilities, which would confine distribution of the potash to local centers. Rainwater flowing over the Devonian rocks has dissolved their saline constituents, which have been concentrated in the lower parts of the closed depression. The crusts, resulting from evaporation, are relatively rich in potassium. Investigation, by means of 14 pits excavated below the water table into which the brine was allowed to seep and evaporate, has revealed that the saline crusts contain about 3.1 percent potassium, which is equivalent to about 6 percent potassium chloride (KCl). Experiments at Sidi Mesri laboratory indicate that fractional distillation will yield a high-potassium product. The desert climate is favorable for concentration of the salts.

Alum

Small alum (aluminum sulfate) deposits occur in the Fezzan near Serdeles in small evaporite basins. The salt is derived from the neighboring Devonian sandstones and forms a crust on the *sebchas* after evaporation of the saline waters. Production is in small quantities and is shipped to Sebha and Tripoli where it is used in the tanning industry.

Natron

In the Fezzan, east of Ubari, there are several small saline lakes from which natron crystals are harvested during the hot season, when the degree of evaporation is highest. The best quality comes from Mantan (Trona), and other localities are Fredga and Nashnush. The chemical composition of the salt is Na_2CO_3; $10H_2O$, or sodium carbonate plus 10 water-of-crystallization. It is exported to Sebha by camel under the supervision of the provincial government. Production is about 200 tons per year. In 1957, 66 tons were sold for £L 12,234. It is used for making snuff, cosmetics and in the glass industry.

Celestite (Strontium Sulfate)

In the southwestern corner of Concession 59 of the Oasis Oil Company in the el Haderiat area, celestite occurs at the surface. It occurs in a bright yellow marly limestone bed of Eocene (Tertiary) age as crystal masses or clusters of crystals in geodes, irregularly distributed throughout the parent rock. It has a bluish or smoky tinge and is transparent. It is believed to be associated with igneous basalt flows and "plugs" which lie to the west and south west of Concession 59. The area, over which crystals of celestite are abundant, is about three kilometers long and 500 meters wide. Celestite is employed in the manufacture of strontium nitrate for pyrotechnics, particularly for fireworks and tracer bullets. Strontium salts are also used in the recovery of sugar in beet-sugar refining and in medical preparations. Because of its high specific gravity (3.89) it may possibly have a local use in oil-drilling operations, instead of barite, in the preparation of "heavy mud." Strontium minerals are, however, numerous and widespread throughout the world, and little or no export trade could be expected.

Cement

The principal raw materials used in the manufacture of portland cement are limestone and clay or shale, the latter to supply alumina and silica. The ideal material is an argillaceous (clayey) limestone (cement rock) which combines the essential ingredients, and may be obtained in a single mining operation. The limestone must be relatively pure, containing not more than five percent of magnesia. Gypsum is added, in the proportion of 9 to 12 pounds per barrel, as a retarder to control the setting of the cement.

In Libya, where limestone formations are abundant, it is likely that good limestone will be readily available in many localities. The occurrence of clay or argillaceous shale, however, is believed to be rare, and has been reported in few instances. One such occurrence of what is believed to be a good combination of clay and limestone is in Tripolitania, about four kilometers west of Homs, north of the coastal highway in the hills called Ras el Mergeb and Ras el Marhunia. Another occurrence of material suitable for cement is in Cyrenaica on the coast south of Barce, and occurrences have also been reported near Benghazi. The position with regard to the investigation of these various deposits is discussed in Chapter 9.

Building Stone

Limestone and marl beds have wide distribution in Libya and constitute convenient local sources of supply of building material in most parts of the northern regions. Where limestone is absent, substitution may usually be made with sandstone. In Tripolitania the Muschelkalk limestone at Azizia has been used extensively as road metal and for other purposes. Softer, less compact limestone (marl), which is easily quarried and shaped, is extensively used in many localities. In Cyrenaica, the middle Eocene formation contains fine limestone beds which provided material for ancient monuments at Cyrene.

Other Minerals

Other minerals also occur in various parts of Libya, but in negligible quantities without economic significance. *Manganese*, for example, is to be found in small quantities at Ulad Mahmud, near Nalut, in the Wadi Ubari and in the Shatti Valley. *Phosphate* is also found, but insignificantly concentrated, in the Wadi Sofeggin, east of Beni Ulid. Small amounts of *sulfur* are to be found in the Sirte desert. Low-grade *lignite* is found in scattered locations—in the regions of Giosh-Sheksut and Chicla at the foot of the Gebel, in the Cussabat region and near Ubari, in the Wadi Ajal and near Ghat in the Fezzan—but the amounts are considered negligible.

The general geography, topography and geological structures of Libya suggest the possibility that bauxite, platinum, diamonds and uranium might also be found in the country, although no such deposits have been discovered to date. Once the federal Department of Geology and Hydrology has been established and further information on the geology of the country has been obtained, an investigatory search for these minerals could be considered.

ANNEX V *GEOLOGY AND HYDROLOGY*

Described briefly, the geological formation of Libya is sedimentary. The only exceptions are the large eruptive mountain mass of Gebel Soda, situated in the desert about half-way between the sea and Sebha in the Fezzan, and a few scattered eruptive dikes.

Cyrenaica is largely composed of fractured and fissured calcarious rock systems of the Tertiary Period, and the most pronounced geological features there are the two great escarpments of the Gebel Akhdar which run from south-west to north-east. These escarpments divide most of the central part of Cyrenaica into four zones parallel with the coast: the coastal plain below the first escarpment, the plateau between the first and second escarpments (250 to 550 meters above sea level), the plateau above the second escarpment (400 to 600 meters above sea level), and the southern desert slopes of the Gebel. To the west of the Gebel toward Sirte and to the east toward the Egyptian border, desert and semi-desert conditions obtain, but on the coastal zone and plateaus on the top of the two escarpments preponderately heavy clay soils (*terra rossa*) are prevalent.

Although the whole of the Gebel may be classed as fissured and porous limestones, there exist some impervious marly beds giving rise to springs which issue at various levels along the escarpments, and give progressively higher yields from west to east.[1]

Hydrologically, the central or Gebel part of Cyrenaica is remarkably complex, and although extensive exploratory work has been done in the past, much still remains to be done before its potential water resources are fully known.

With the relatively high rainfall of the Gebel country and the porous nature of the limestone rock, the infiltration to ground water storage should be high, but so far it has been comparatively little used for agriculture. This is chiefly because the planes of water movement are irregular and difficult to define and are usually inaccessibly located.

On the southern slopes of the Gebel and in the desert to the east, south and west, the water-bearing strata are seldom accessible, while

[1] *The Hydrology of Cyrenaica*, Dr. Marco Marchetti, Italian Colonial Agricultural Institute, Florence, 1938.

the wells are often of poor yielding capacity and the water from them
is often highly saline. These conditions, combined with low rainfall,
make settled agriculture impossible except in the wadi bottoms and in
oases.

In Tripolitania, the Gebel Nefusa and the formations to the south
are sedimentary types of the Secondary Period. The Gebel escarpment
is denuded and exposed to severe erosion. The few springs there and
on the southern slopes are small and the wells yield meager supplies.

The western coastal plain between the Gebel and the sea consists
of water-saturated, consolidated and unconsolidated sedimentary formations, dipping gently seawards. The phreatic water table is relatively
near the surface along the sea coast, but it may be 60 meters below the
surface at the foot of the Gebel. Below this are artesian aquifers, the
piezometric height of which is generally below ground level on the
Gefara, but near the coast, where the land is lowest, the piezometric
surface is above land surface and the wells will flow.

The Fezzan occupies a large erosional basin which is underlain by
a great thickness of sedimentary rocks, ranging in age from Cambrian
to Quaternary, and which lie on gneisses and crystalline schists of the
pre-Cambrian age. These sedimentary rocks make a large, nearly
circular, basin forming a great artesian reservoir, the center of which
may lie to the south of Murzuk. Recharge into the aquifers is from
rare precipitation falling on the upturned edges of the strata which
form the higher elevations of the region and generally make the
perimeter of the basin. The areas of recharge are extensive and a large
proportion of the rainfall is absorbed and moves downward into the
underlying sandstone. The only dependable source of water in the
Fezzan is the underground supplies in the unconsolidated alluvial deposits and the artesian water in the deeper lying consolidated aquifers.[2]

[2] *A Reconnaissance Report on the Geology and Hydrology of the Western Part
of the Province of Fezzan*, H. A. Whitcomb, U. S. Department of the Interior, Geological Survey, Washington, 1957.

ANNEX **VI** *PROPOSALS FOR A WATER LAW*

After a study of various Moslem law codes and the Italian water law for Libya[1] and after discussion with officials concerned with the use of water in Libya, the mission concludes that none of the previous laws will operate satisfactorily under the conditions now pertaining in those parts of the country where fixed agriculture has been or is likely to be developed. The mission therefore recommends that the government should take the actions outlined below in order to control and develop the use of water.

An Interim Law

Until a Libyan federal water law be drafted and passed, an interim law, based on the Italian water law for Libya of 1913 and the subsequent supplementary edicts, should be enacted by the federal government as the present water law of the country. This interim law should then be operated on a provincial level to control the use of water in certain specified areas where overuse, wrongful use and wasteful use is occurring. The two basic principles of the Italian law are that all water in the ground or flowing from springs or in streams is the property of Libya and that the use of this water must be sanctioned by the government.

The mission advises that the interim water law should contain the following clauses:

1. *Reasons and Objects.* The water resources of Libya are limited and their full exploitation, but without overexploitation, is necessary for the prosperity of the State. The object of the law is to ensure that the use of water drawn from underground sources, springs, streams, wells and reservoirs is controlled in specified zones by the provincial governments acting through

---

[1] *Water Laws in Moslem Countries*, FAO Paper No. 43, Rome, 1954. *Water Control and Legislation in Ethiopia*, FAO, Report No. 550, Rome, 1956. *Emergency Water Law in Libya*, J. L. M. Solignac, FAO, /57/7/5911, Rome, 1957. Italian Royal Decrees: No. 87 of February 6, 1913; No. 2433 of July 29, 1928; No. 374 of March 13, 1930; No. 1755 of April 3, 1937.

398

provincial water control boards so as to ensure full and equitable use of the resources available in these zones.

2. *Definitions.* These will include federal government, provincial government, provincial water control board, licensing authorities, authorized officers, water resources, water (underground water, springs, streams, well water), well and spring fittings (water pumps, pump motors, windmills), access to water, specified zones, registers, licenses.

3. *Ownership of Water.* All underground water, all water derived from springs, streams, reservoirs and wells shall belong to the State.

4. *Enabling Clauses.* (a) The enforcement of the law will rest with the provincial governments acting through their agents, the provincial water control boards and the authorized officers of the boards.

(b) The provincial water control boards shall be legally constituted boards having powers to authorize and refuse to authorize the uses of water. These powers shall be valid only within the specified zones.

5. *Rules and Regulations.* The provincial governments shall submit to the federal government for approval, drafts of such rules and regulations as are necessary to enforce the law. If the federal government approves these rules and. regulations, they shall be enforced by the boards with the full authority of the law. These rules and regulations shall authorize license fees, lay down procedures for prosecuting offenders against the law in the provincial law courts, fines, penalties, etc. They shall lay down the procedures for the appointment of members of the board and the appointment of chairman and secretary, board meeting procedure, quorum, keeping of registers, issue of licenses, court procedure, financial procedure, etc.

6. *Specified Zones.* The federal government shall approve from time to time an application submitted through the provincial governments for the establishment of specified zones and the law shall be operative only within these zones. The federal government shall take cognizance of the objections of interested parties when considering these provincial applications, and the applications will be given due publicity in the press and elsewhere for a certified period before being approved or otherwise. The boundaries of the proposed specified zones will be clearly defined in the applications.

7. *Use of Water.* (a) No water may be drawn from underground sources, springs, streams, wells or reservoirs within the specified zones without the consent of the board.

(b) All present users of water in the specified zones must register a claim with the board to continue to enjoy this use. The board shall confirm this use in full or in part or may refuse to confirm it. There shall be a right of appeal against any decision of the board in respect of confirmation of claims to enjoyment of existing water rights.

(c) All claims confirmed in full and in part shall be registered and licensed. The registers and licenses will state the ownership of the claim, the quantity of water which may be used, the method and place of extraction of the water.

(d) All further use of water must be authorized by the board to whom an application for a license to use water must be submitted. This shall apply to existing licensed users of water wishing to increase the quantity of water beyond the amount stated in their license. The applications for license to use water shall state the quantity required, the place and method of extraction and all other information required by the board. The board may approve any application in full or in part or may refuse it. There shall be a right of appeal to all decisions of the board in respect of applications to use water.

8. *Inspection.* The board's authorized officers shall have powers of inspection of wells and springs, well and spring fittings on privately and publicly owned land in the specified zones. The inspections may be made without notice by authorized officers producing a written authority from the board to do so.

A New Federal Law

The proposed new Libyan federal water law, while retaining the two basic principles of the Italian water law described above, should be an enabling law, and the application of the law should be entrusted to provincial water control boards, set up by the provincial governments, with powers of enforcement under rules and regulations drafted by the provincial governments but approved by the federal government. There should be a right of appeal to the law courts against any decision of the provincial control boards under the water law.

An ad hoc committee should be appointed by the federal government to draft the new federal water law; the committee chairman should be a law officer of the Ministry of Justice and the members of the committee should be agricultural and engineering representatives of the provincial governments, the UN agencies, the USOM and the federal Ministry of Agriculture. A senior technical officer of the Department of Geology and Hydrology should be secretary to the committee.

A standing provincial committee should also be established in each of the provinces to operate the interim water law and to prepare drafts of the rules and regulations for subsequent operation of the new federal water law. The standing provincial committees should be under the chairmanship of the Director of Public Works and have official and unofficial members representing agricultural and forestry interests; an officer from the Water Resources Branch should be secretary. The mission envisages that the standing provincial committees will be the forerunners of the provincial water control boards to be established when the federal water law is promulgated.

Administration of the Law

The mission recommends that *inter alia* the provincial control boards be assigned the duties enumerated below and that they be required to execute these duties through the provincial Water Resources Branches:

1. The control boards, being established by law, should have powers to authorize or refuse to authorize the use of water. They should also have powers to make inspections and to promulgate prosecutions in court for infringements of the water law.
2. They should have powers to ensure, where necessary, the full utilization of all water resources, irrespective of ownership or usage claims. This should include control of the distribution of water and the siting of canals and drains.
3. They should have powers to specify zones where further exploitation of water resources will be prohibited and to demand the registry of all existing claims within these zones.
4. They should have powers to regulate the siting of wells, and the water quantities drawn from wells, within specified areas.
5. They should have licensing authority and should charge fees for licensing and inspecting within the specified zones.
6. They should keep minutes of their board meetings and submit

copies to the Minister of Agriculture, keep records of their inspections and prosecutions under the water law, and keep licensing registers.

The Italian law permitted the licensing of applications for the use of water, but doubt has been expressed on whether it gave power to control the quantity of water taken by existing users. The proposed interim law and new federal law should be drafted to ensure that the power to control water quantities is given to the provincial water control boards, but subject to the right to appeal from their decisions.

ANNEX VII *ADMINISTRATION AND COSTS OF WATER RESOURCES DEVELOPMENT*

THE FEDERAL DEPARTMENT OF GEOLOGY AND HYDROLOGY

The federal department would be organized as an investigational research and advisory unit. Its basic duties would be to carry on the geological and hydrological studies now being made by the agencies, to obtain the detailed information required for application of the proposed water law and to advise the provincial governments on the location and dimensions of the ground water resources. Much of the time of the technical staff would have to be spent in the field. Adequate provision should therefore be allowed in the estimate for transport, equipment and field allowances.

The library and the laboratory are integral parts of the department. In the library would be filed the records, reports and books concerning the work done previously in this field; where necessary, these would be translated. Records of all current field work would be sent to the library for study and filing. Text books and current literature on geology and hydrology should be available in the library. The laboratory is required for the analysis of mineral samples, including water. Provision has been made in the estimates below for staffing, equipping and maintaining the department's office, library and laboratory, but no provision has been made for a building to house them. It has been assumed that suitable accommodation will be available in either Tripoli or Benghazi for the department and that the building maintenance will be done by the P.W.D.

The exploratory drilling which the department would require would be carried out by the provincial Water Resources Branches and provision has been made to reimburse the provincial governments for expenses incurred on this work.

Summary Budget (1960/61 to 1964/65)	(£L)
Staff (at £L 20,000 annually)	100,000
Recurrent charges (at £L 54,000 annually)	270,000
Plant and equipment (nonrecurrent)	15,000
Federal total	385,000

PROVINCIAL WATER RESOURCES BRANCHES

Cyrenaica

The Cyrenaican estimates give details for staffing and financing adequate to undertake annually the construction and rehabilitation of 16 wells, 5 irrigation systems, 200 cisterns, 20 kilometers of terracing and an unspecified number of dikes across wadis.

The well estimate is based on wells being provided with an average depth of 100 meters and 8 inches average casing diameter. It is assumed that the P.W.D. or Nazirate of Agriculture in Benghazi will provide office and store accommodation and workshop facilities.

These estimates are based on a larger program of routine work being undertaken there than in Tripolitania where the water resources are much better developed than in Cyrenaica. A sum of £L 5,000 has been included to finance expert hydraulic study and planning required to assist the preparation of specific schemes for such unused resources as Ain Mara and the Ain Zeiana—el Coefia springs complex.

Summary Budget (1960/61 to 1964/65)	(£L)
Staff:	
Headquarters (at £L 8,000 annually)	40,000
Drilling staff (at £L 10,000 annually)	50,000
Water resources development staff (at £L 7,000 annually)	35,000
	125,000
Recurrent charges (at £L 45,000 annually)	225,000
Plant and equipment (nonrecurrent)	100,000
Capital works (at £L 266,000 annually)	1,330,000
Cyrenaica Branch Total	1,780,000

Tripolitania

The Tripolitanian estimates are based on the staff and finance necessary to expand the existing well boring and irrigation branches of the Nazirate of Agriculture into a Water Resources Branch capable of undertaking the continuation of the program of work now undertaken by the Nazirate of Agriculture and by the aid agencies. The program envisaged includes funds for cistern repairs, terracing and diking on a self-help basis, for the exploitation of the unused water resources of the province, such as the unused artesian wells at Crispi near Misurata, and for the Wadi Megenin flood mitigation scheme. The first stage of the Wadi Megenin scheme, costing £L 300,000, appears as a separate financial item and is discussed separately. A sum of £L 10,000 has been included to finance studies of utilization of flows from the wadis between Tripoli and Homs. Staff for control of water use in coastal areas and the Tripoli Quadrangle has been provided. It is assumed that office, store and workshop facilities will be provided and maintained by the Nazirate of Agriculture, and that the Nazirate will take over the technicians and drilling equipment at present employed by the aid agencies.

Summary Budget (1960/61 to 1964/65)	(£L)
Staff:	
Headquarters (at £L 8,000 annually)	40,000
Drilling staff (at £L 10,000 annually)	50,000
Water resources development staff (at £L 7,000 annually)	35,000
	125,000
Recurrent charges (at £L 35,000 annually)	175,000
Plant and equipment (nonrecurrent)	60,000
Capital works (at £L 166,000 annually)	830,000
Tripolitania Branch Total	1,190,000

The Fezzan

The Fezzan estimates are based on the staff and finance necessary to conserve, control and develop artesian water resources, to finance a self-help program of repairs and improvement of wells and to implement the mission's general agricultural recommendations for the Fezzan. It is presumed that office, store and workshop facilities will be provided by the P.W.D. or Nazirate of Agriculture, and that the drilling rigs and equipment of the agencies will be handed over in due course to the Water Resources Branch. The Libyan technicians trained by the agencies in ground water exploration and development should be taken over as required by the branch. Staff for enforcing rules and regulations under the water law has been provided for.

Summary Budget (1960/61 to 1964/65)	(£L)
Staff:	
Headquarters (at £L 3,500 annually)	17,500
Drilling staff (at £L 5,000 annually)	25,000
Water resources development staff (at £L 2,500 annually)	12,500
	55,000
Recurrent charges (at £L 20,000 annually)	100,000
Plant and equipment (nonrecurrent)	5,000
Capital works (at £L 82,000 annually)	410,000
Fezzan Branch Total	570,000

WADI MEGENIN FLOOD MITIGATION PROJECT—FIRST STAGE

Capital Works	(£L)
Movement of 200 families from Wadi Huelfa Catchment to irrigated resettlement area below Ras M'daur Dam with provision of irrigation works and low-cost housing accommodation.	
(i) Movement and resettlement, including housing, school, wells and access roads	150,000
(ii) Irrigation works for 200 families on 2,000 hectares of land.	25,000
Execution of soil and water conservancy works, terracing, contour ditching, retaining walls, check dams, dikes, etc.	60,000
Road improvement works in the vicinity of Tripoli to prevent flood damage and interruption of traffic	25,000
Improvement to the flood channel of Wadi Megenin in the neighborhood of Tripoli to ensure uninterrupted flow to the sea of flood water reaching the city.	25,000
Contingencies (5 percent)	15,000
Total for five years	300,000
Annually Recurrent Maintenance Charges	
Maintenance of Wadi Huelfa Forest Reserve	2,000
Maintenance of flood channel around Tripoli	2,500
Maintenance of flood water diversion schemes	15,000
Contingencies	500
Annual total	20,000
Total for five years	100,000
Project total	400,000[a]

[a] Provision of an additional £L 100,000 for establishing the Wadi Huelfa Forest Reserve is made under the heading of the forestry program for Tripolitania, as set out in Chapter 8.

ANNEX VIII WATER RESOURCES PROJECTS REQUIRING FURTHER INVESTIGATION

CYRENAICA

Ain Mara Springs

There are four abundant springs at Ain Mara rising close together at levels between 420 and 450 meters above sea level and about 100 meters below the level of the Gebel plateau. The total flow of the springs fluctuates and no reliable maximum and minimum flow figures are obtainable, but at one time the Italian Government considered a scheme for using the combined springs flow to irrigate 100 hectares of adjacent flat land, and this would presuppose a minimum flow of 100 cubic meters per hour. The mission recommends that a development survey be carried out by the Water Resources Branch to prepare a plan for making full use of the Ain Mara springs; the plan would provide for construction of spring copings and aprons, canals, controls and terraces. A layout for a village should also be prepared and a cropping pattern, tied to marketing potentials, should be worked out. Assuming a minimum irrigable area of 100 hectares, the mission estimates that, on a cropping pattern suitable to semi-irrigated farming, the annual value of the crops produced would at current prices be £L 5,000 and that capital works up to the value of £L 30,000 would be justified. But the mission stresses that these works should be started only after careful study of soil and water availability and preparation of the fully detailed plans and estimates mentioned above. The question of the ownership of the water rights and the land tenure system required for settled agriculture, which at the present moment are not clear, must be resolved before development work is started.

Ain Zeiana and el Coefia Springs

In the neighborhood of Ain Zeiana and el Coefia (14 kilometers north-east of Benghazi), there is a complex underground water system leading several springs to the surface near the edge of the sea. The largest of these springs is Ain Zeiana, which discharges into a salt-water lagoon. The combined flow of the springs has been estimated at 1,500 cubic meters per hour and the water is highly saline in quality. The Italian Government carried out extensive surveys and experiments to determine a suitable method of utilizing the spring water, but no successful project was conceived, chiefly because the spring water is accessible only in such close proximity to the sea that continuous pumping has resulted in marked increase of the salinity of the water, making its use for agriculture impossible. The mission recommends that an intensive geological and hydrological survey be carried out on the coastal plain to the south of the springs, between the sea and the first Gebel escarpment, with the object of confirming that the springs are fed by underground channels, and, further, that these channels are accessible for exploitation of the water available, without salt water infiltration. Some geodetic investigation may be necessary to complete the survey and the Department of Geology and Hydrology should call in expert assistance for this. The mission considers that departmental and specialist expenditure on this survey up to £L 10,000 is justified.

TRIPOLITANIA

The Bir Ghnem Area

There is a zone of moderate ground water supply situated to the west and south of the settlements of Bianchi and Micca, between Zawia and Bir Ghnem. The land and water conditions there are similar to those prevailing in the adjacent Italian settlements, but rainfall is lighter. This zone is favorably situated within a distance of 50 kilometers of Tripoli and could be developed for semi-irrigated farming, using electric power from the Tripoli Electricity Authority for pumping, which might be supplied at a low unit rate during off-peak hours.

A previous study of this development proposal[1] indicates that, assuming an average water lift of 25 meters (the ground water table ranges from 10 to 30 meters below the surface of the ground in the area), some 50,000 hectares of land could be given a pumped water supply if a total power load of 24 million KWH were available over a period of some 4,000 to 5,000 working hours annually, the range being dependent on rainfall, which in the area under discussion averages

---

[1] The Role of Electric Power in Libya, Dr. Abdul Azez Ahmad, UN Technical Assistance to Libya, 1952.

over 200 mm. annually. The semi-irrigated farming suitable for the soil conditions in the area includes olive trees planted at 10 meters spacing with crops of vegetables, cereals, alfalfa and herbaceous plants interspersed. Farms of 10 hectares extent are a suitable size for Libyans engaged at present in this type of farming, but larger farms should be available to those wanting them. The normal annual requirements of pumped water would be 40,000 cubic meters per farm of 10 hectares. The capital cost of installing irrigation facilities for semi-irrigation is estimated at £L 750 for a 10-hectare farm. The costs of the administrative centers, access roads and farm buildings are not included in the estimates.

The area is at present partly sand dune land and partly used for grazing and shifting cultivation. It is, however, similar in condition to that of the adjacent Italian farms before they were taken over for settled agriculture. The mission recommends that a development plan should be prepared for this area by the provincial Nazirate of Agriculture in conjunction with the Nazirate of Public Works and the Tripoli Electricity Authority and that the plan should set out the lines for development of land settlement, utilities, roads, windbreaks, well spacing and administrative centers. This development plan could be put into operation in stages to keep pace with the demand for land for farming in the area. While the mission has some doubts as to the existing demand for land there by smallholders, it suggests that there may now be some demand for land for larger scale farming and recommends that, if so, this be met. The mission stresses, however, that there should be no expenditure of capital by government or provision of utilities in the area ahead of the demand for land and urges caution in this respect. The development of utilities should go hand in hand with agricultural development, it should be extended from the Italian settlements southwards, and it should not be piecemeal.

The mission also suggests that small farming should be developed there initially as part of the second stage of the Wadi Megenin Flood Mitigation Scheme. The 200 families from the proposed Wadi Hamman forest reserve, who have to be moved by government when the Wadi Hamman is closed to farming, could be settled on 10-hectare farms in the Bir Ghnem area. This resettlement would probably cost £L 300 per family for house and land, or a total of £L 60,000. The provision of the irrigation system at £L 750 per 10-hectare farm might be financed as long-term loans. We do not, however, envisage that the second stage of the Wadi Megenin project will be carried out before 1965, and we have not therefore made any specific provision in our program for the resettlement of families in the Bir Ghnem area.

While the primary purpose of this development is to meet the needs of the Libyan population for land on which settled agriculture is possible, it will also have several other advantages. It will allow for agricultural expansion without further demands on the already overtaxed groundwater resources of the Tripoli Quadrangle; it will use the underexploited water resources elsewhere; it will provide an off-peak load for Tripoli Power, when the new generators are installed; and, finally, it will develop the full agricultural potential of little used land within 50 kilometers of Tripoli and so within reasonable distance of the principal market of the country.

The ownership of the land in question is uncertain, but there undoubtedly exist squatters rights over most of it, and it would be the responsibility of those who wished to develop semi-irrigated farming there to make private arrangements for meeting the claims arising from these rights. Government at this stage would confine its responsibility to the following:

1. making a soil and water resources survey of the area;
2. preparing a well-location and well-capacity plan based on the water resources available;
3. preparing crop pattern plans for various sizes of holdings and suited to soil types and water resources;
4. preparing a projection of crop marketing and costing potentialities for holdings of various sizes;
5. preparing development plans showing the layout of holdings, access roads, electricity power lines and substations and administrative centers;
6. guaranteeing construction of roads and an electric power supply, in stages, as the area is developed;
7. providing long-term agricultural loans to suitable intending settlers for the cost of wells and irrigation systems; and
8. providing agricultural extension services to the settlers.

Taorga Spring

The Taorga oasis is situated amidst an extensive *sebcha* plain about 40 kilometers south of Misurata. Rainfall is meager in this region and is usually less than 150 mm. annually, but the oasis was developed in ancient times around a large spring, which has a variable flow of water, estimated at between 12,000 and 18,000 cubic meters per hour, so that it is possibly the largest spring in Libya. The water is saline and its irrigation uses would probably be severely limited. An analysis at one particular time showed the nature of the water to be:

Fixed Residue at 110°	3.19 percent
Chlorine	.85 "
Sulfate	.84 "
Calcium	.30 "
Magnesium	.11 "
Potassium	—
Sodium	—

The oasis has the remains of canals built by the Phoenicians, the Romans and the Arabs, and there was a time when the spring waters, carefully distributed, made date palm growing possible on 5,000 hectares of land around the oasis, but this land is now mostly *sebcha,* with sterile alkaline soil. At another time, a wide canal led the waters of the spring for 10 kilometers across the *sebcha* land, in a northwesterly direction, to good fertile land in the neighborhood of Gioda, where the remains of the feeder branches, which irrigated the crops, can still be traced.

Only a small amount of the water available is currently used at the oasis, and much of it flows to waste, through salt marshes, to the sea. The Agricultural Department now operates a small irrigation and drainage scheme for growing barley on about 25 hectares of land adjacent to the spring, where water, pumped from the spring, is led to the fields in a raised canal, and where drains have been dug to keep the water table low. In addition, some of the spring water is used by the inhabitants of the oasis to irrigate date palms. At one time the Italian Government had prepared plans to pump the water to fertile land on the west side of the road from Misurata to Sirte, but the war intervened and the scheme, though started, was never completed. About the same time the discovery and the exploitation of the artesian acquifer at Crispi and Gioda lessened the value of Taorga spring in Italian eyes.

The source of the waters of the spring has not yet been established by geologists, but the opinion most usually accepted is that the waters rise from the same acquifer that feeds the artesian wells at Crispi, and a comparison of the water analysis data gives support to this opinion. However, the source may be the underground water which has traveled underneath the bed of the Wadi Soffegin and other smaller wadis which debouch onto the coastal plain about 10 kilometers to the south-west of the oasis. Whatever the source of the water, it is likely to be more economic to develop it at places away from the *sebcha* land, and this could be done either by locating and exploiting the artesian acquifer to the west of the road, or by the interception of accessible ground water supplies there and planning for irrigating by pumping. A detailed geologic, hydrologic and soils survey of the area extending 20 kilometers to the west of the Taorga oasis is required, and this survey should be given a place on the programs of the Nazirate of Agriculture and the federal Department of Geology and Hydrology.

Meantime, in case these investigations prove that the spring water cannot be intercepted under good land situated to the west of the oasis where more valuable crops can be grown, the possibility of irrigating land around the oasis, as was done in ancient times, should also be investigated. If gravity irrigation from the springs is possible, this, combined with proper drainage, might make barley growing there an economic crop, and this possibility also should be investigated by the departments concerned. The mission recommends that these investigations be given a high priority as the utilization of the large volume of water available at Taorga spring will greatly enhance the agricultural potential of the area. Should an economic development scheme fructify from these investigations, we recommend that funds should be made available for the necessary irrigation works as part of the Supplementary Program. We attach considerable importance to diversifying the very limited range of occupations at present open to the 11,000 inhabitants of the Taorga oasis and providing these people with a better standard of life.

Wadi Tareglat

The Wadi Tareglat is one of the large wadis draining the southern slopes of the Gebel, and a special study of the whole of its catchment should be carried out to discover its hydrological and agricultural potential. The catchment of Wadi Tareglat is about 2,000 square kilometers in extent and the mean annual rainfall there varies, being 300 mm. at Cussabat, 250 at Tarhuna, 200 where it enters the sea between Homs and Zliten (where it is known as Wadi Caam) and between 200 and 100 in the southern part. The wadi discharges flood water into the sea four or five times each year. Near the sea, there are springs issuing from the bed of the wadi, which yield good quality spring water and have a total estimated flow of about 360 cubic meters per hour; half of the springs' flow is now used for irrigating crops at the Wadi Caam project, the rest being lost to the sea. The spring water is thought to originate from ground water traveling underneath the bed of the wadi.

During the Roman era the land in the wadi catchment was extensively cultivated, and the remains of Roman conservancy works and buildings are still everywhere evident. Before World War II the Italians started an investigation to discover the possibility of storing water behind a high dam, sited about 30 kilometers inland from the sea, and after the war the LPDSA employed a French firm of consulting engineers to complete this investigation. This was very thoroughly done and showed that storage potential was unexpectedly low, that the proposed reservoir site provided extensive shallow storage with probable seepage losses, and that expensive underground works would be necessary at the dam site. The consultants therefore reported adversely on the scheme.

Recently LAJS developed, in conjunction with the Nazirate of Agriculture, a scheme to irrigate 240 hectares of land near the bank of the Wadi Caam on the coastal plain. The capital cost of the irrigation works, land preparation, roads, houses and overheads was £L 256,000, or over £L 1,000 per hectare, and only half the flow of the springs was utilized. The mission is of the opinion that the scheme was overcapitalized, and that the size of the land holdings developed, which allows only 2 hectares for each farmer, is below the optimum size.

Meanwhile, on the fertile middle reaches of the wadi, about 60 kilometers southeast of Tarhuna, over 20 rock-fill dikes have been recently constructed by LAJS across the wadi which here forms a broad, flat valley, without any well-defined channel, over which the flood water spreads. Most of the dikes have been constructed on the upper flats, where the soil is sandy, and some have already been breached by the floods. Lower down the valley, where there is a clay soil, earth dikes were built with rock spillways on each side of the valley and these have been successful. There are no wells in this area, therefore no permanent houses or gardens, so that when water in the cisterns is exhausted, usually in July, the farmers leave the wadi. The mission recommends that a hydrological survey be carried out to locate possible sites for wells, and if this survey proves that wells can be drilled to provide water for domestic and stock requirements, a program can be prepared for the agricultural development of about 1,500 hectares of flat land in the middle reaches of the wadi. This program would involve making four wells with windmills and storage tanks, improving the road from Tarhuna (say 80 kilometers), building a school and providing agricultural extension services to get fruit trees and windbreaks planted. The mission estimates that the development required might cost £L 60,000 or £L 40 per hectare developed, providing a greatly improved living for about 150 families. We recommend this scheme for possible inclusion in the Supplementary Program, should the survey prove that a ground water supply is available in sufficient quantity at an accessible depth and in suitable localities.

ANNEX IX *REVIEW OF SELECTED CROPS*

Cereals

Barley is the principal cereal crop in Libya, normally accounting for between two-thirds and three-quarters of all cereals grown. Wheat accounts for most of the remainder. Small quantities of millets are also grown. Some statistics of production and imports are set out in Table A.7 on the following page; they are probably subject to considerable margins of error.

Cereals are grown mainly on dry land (except in the Fezzan), and production fluctuates widely with variations in rainfall. Because of its earlier maturity, barley is less liable to be affected by drought than wheat; it is also more tolerant to soil alkalinity. The area seeded annually to cereals varies directly with rainfall and ranges between about 200,000 hectares and 400,000 hectares.

Small fields of barley and wheat are grown in Tripolitania in the coastal area; barley is the principal crop in the Gebel, particularly in the wadis where some run-off water is held in the soil. In Cyrenaica, wheat is widely grown on the red clay soils of the northern Gebel, while barley is more important as a crop in the southern pre-desert area where shifting cultivation is practiced. These grain crops are planted after the rains come, usually in November and December. Even in years of good rainfall, yields are generally low because of broadcast seeding, planting seed mixtures and inefficient threshing methods.

Most of the grain produced in Libya is stored in bags on the farm in houses, caves or in small earthen pits. Damage due to diseases, weevils and rodents probably varies between 15 percent and 20 percent. Communal storage by the nomadic tribes is practiced in many areas. There is also considerable storage capacity owned by the Libyan Government. The purpose of these government storage facilities is to store local wheat, imported wheat, or any gift wheat or barley that may arrive. Five relatively modern grain storage silos are located over the country near population areas with a total bulk-storage capacity of 15,000 tons and 4,800 tons of temporary sack storage. There are also ten other buildings remodeled for grain storage which have a capacity of 5,750 tons. The total modern storage capacity is now 25,500 tons, which is adequate for the present needs of Libya.

415

TABLE A.7 Libya's Production and Imports of Cereals, 1943–58

(In metric tons)

	Average 1943–47	Average 1948–52	1953	1954	1955	1956	1957	1958
Production								
Wheat								
Tripolitania	5,600	6,000	3,400	5,400	2,700	4,500	23,000	12,400
Cyrenaica	4,700	4,000ᵃ	n.a.	9,000	11,000	8,400	21,300	13,600
Libya, exc. Fezzan	10,300	10,000	n.a.	14,400	13,700	12,900	44,300	26,000
Barley								
Tripolitania	50,000	55,000	15,000	37,500	30,000	30,000	84,000	37,000
Cyrenaica	13,000	n.a.	n.a.	n.a.	n.a.	18,000	25,000	23,000
Libya, exc. Fezzan	63,000	n.a.	n.a.	n.a.	n.a.	48,000	109,000	60,000
Wheat and Barley								
Tripolitania	55,600	61,000	18,400	42,900	32,700	34,500	107,000	49,000
Cyrenaica	17,700	n.a.	n.a.	n.a.	n.a.	26,400	46,300	36,600
Libya, exc. Fezzan	73,300	n.a.	n.a.	n.a.	n.a.	60,900	153,300	85,600
Net Imports (all Libya)								
Wheat and flourᵇ	n.a.	14,900	32,300	49,800	42,400	62,500	63,000	51,620ᶜ
Gift wheat	—	—	—	2,235	33,756	25,707	14,642	3,000
Barley	n.a.	−11,700ᵈ	4,000	3,000	3,200	3,400	neg.	−3,200ᵉ
Wheat and barley	n.a.	3,200	36,300	55,035	79,356	91,607	77,642	51,420

ᵃ Estimate for three years only (not stated which years).   ᵇ In terms of wheat equivalent, excluding gift wheat.

ᶜ Commercial imports in 1958 consisted entirely of flour, but 3,700 tons of wheat were exported (valued at £L 93,000), mainly to Lebanon.

ᵈ During the years 1948–50 exports of barley averaged 22,000 tons a year.

ᵉ No barley was imported in 1958, but 3,200 tons were exported (valued at £L 63,000), mainly to Lebanon and Saudi Arabia.

SOURCES: 1943–47, estimates made by Four Power Commission; 1948–52, FAO Yearbook of Food and Agricultural Statistics; subsequent

Consumption of cereals in Libya appears to have risen considerably in the past 10 years. Immediately before World War II total cereal consumption was probably in the region of 110,000 tons a year or 110 kilograms per head; much of this was no doubt accounted for by the Italian population. More than half the requirements at that time were supplied by imports. During the British military administration immediately after the war, when imports were hard to get, Libya seems to have reverted to a position of near self-sufficiency in food-grains (as in Turkish times) at a level of consumption that may have been in the region of 80,000 tons a year—say, 80 kilograms per head. Since Independence, however, imports have risen rapidly, and this has made possible a big increase in consumption, which is now officially estimated at around 128 kilograms per head (just over 350 grams a day)— the equivalent of 160,000 tons a year.[1] At present, in an average year, about three-quarters of domestic consumption of wheat and flour appears to be supplied out of imports. Libyan production of barley, on the other hand, is normally sufficient to meet the demand for human consumption, with a surplus available for livestock feed.

The mission was unable to obtain reliable data on cereal yields in Libya. Under the methods of shifting cultivation commonly practiced in Cyrenaica and the Tripolitanian Gebel the cultivator broadcasts the seed over a wide area and is more concerned with the multiplication of the seed than with yields per unit of land. Where wheat has been grown by modern methods, as it was in the Barce Plain under the British military administration, yields have not compared very favorably with other countries in North Africa and the Middle East. According to FAO figures, average wheat yields in these areas in 1948-52 ranged from 5 quintals per hectare in Iraq and Tunisia to 7 quintals per hectare in Jordan, Lebanon and Northern Morocco and 18 quintals per hectare in Egypt (where wheat is grown under irrigation). Yields obtained in Cyrenaica under the British wheat scheme over the five years 1944/45-1948/49 averaged just under 5 quintals per hectare.[2] In Tripolitania yields of 18 quintals per hectare have been achieved under irrigation, but the average for settled farming on dry land in the province is believed to be only about 4 quintals or 5 quintals.

Considerable scope appears to exist for raising cereal yields in Libya

[1] *Report to the Government of Libya on Nutrition,* FAO Report No. 920, Rome, 1958. See also *Food Balance Sheet for Cyrenaica,* 1957, Nazirate of Agriculture, Cyrenaica, 1959.

[2] See *Agricultural Development in Cyrenaica, Present Position and Future Needs,* Sir Herbert Stewart, C.I.E., March 1950.

by planting improved varieties of seeds, by drill seeding in rows instead of broadcast seeding, by the application of commercial fertilizers to wheat grown in rotation on irrigated and semi-irrigated land and by improved methods of threshing. Losses in storage and handling could also be reduced by better arrangements for marketing and education of the farmer.

Dates

No one really knows either how many date palms there are in Libya or what quantities of dates are produced. The number of date palms in the Fezzan alone has been estimated at between 10 million and 12 million, but many of these are stunted and unproductive trees. Tax records for Tripolitania and Cyrenaica in 1957/58 put the number of palms in these two provinces at 1,678,000 and 600,000 respectively. The FAO Yearbook gives a figure of 30,000 tons for annual average production of dates in Libya during the years 1948-55, and according to some estimates this is still the approximate scale of production today. On the other hand, estimates made by the provincial governments suggest that over the three years 1955/56-1957/58 production in Tripolitania alone averaged 28,000 tons a year and in Cyrenaica 8,000 tons, with perhaps a further 6,000 tons in the Fezzan—making a total of 42,000 tons for Libya as a whole. Yet other estimates put the total as high as 70,000 tons.

The *khadrai* variety, the best grown in Libya, is found in the Uaddan oasis near Hon; other good dates grown in the Fezzan are the *adhwi* and *sililu* varieties which are found in the Shatti Valley. Some good dates are also grown around Zliten in Tripolitania and in the Kufra oasis in Cyrenaica. However, few date gardens are well tended, and poor methods of harvesting frequently make the dates unpalatable.

Practically all the dates produced in Libya are consumed at home, mostly in the areas where they are grown. Baskets of pressed dates are a common sight in village markets in the coastal areas of Tripolitania. The highest per capita consumption of dates is in the Fezzan. Both in the Fezzan and in Tripolitania dates are fed to livestock. Small quantities are bought by the two date packing plants in Tripoli and Kufra for distribution under the school-feeding program; these plants have a combined output of 1,000 tons a year and are working at well below capacity (see Annex XIII). Another 500 tons of dates a year are used by distilleries in Tripoli for making alcohol, and an experimental plant has recently been constructed for the manufacture of syrup. Some of the better quality dates produced in the Fezzan are sold in Tripoli. Dates, in fact, constitute the principal agricultural export of the Fezzan.

Before the war Libya exported about 2,500 tons of dates a year, mainly to Italy. Since the war exports have been negligible. Only 286 tons (valued at £L 6,188) were exported in 1958, mainly to Italy, Germany and Malta. Hopes have recently been expressed in Tripolitania that a larger market might be developed in Germany.

Groundnuts

Groundnuts are grown under irrigation as a summer crop in Tripolitania, where production has increased from 200 tons in 1943 to about 1,900 tons in 1950 and an average of over 10,000 tons a year from 1955/56 to 1957/58. The area planted has expanded from 1,250 hectares in 1952 to 4,500 hectares in 1958. Groundnuts have become increasingly popular in Libya, where they are often eaten with tea. The bulk of the crop, however, is exported, and the value of exports has risen from £L 583,000 (5,150 tons) in 1954 to £L 1,020,000 (10,539 tons) in 1958. The principal export markets in 1958 were Italy (3,706 tons), Germany (2,344 tons), the United Kingdom (1,802 tons) and Holland (1,539 tons). The Libyan product is mainly eaten as nuts or used in the manufacture of cakes and confectionery. No facilities exist in Libya for processing the nuts into oil. Proper grading of nuts for export is essential, and a system of quality control has been established by the Tripolitanian Government. Root rot and fungus diseases have been causing increasing damage to the crop, and research is at present being undertaken to discover disease-resistant varieties.

Castor Seed

Castor seed is well adapted to climatic conditions in Libya and is cultivated mainly in small patches in Tripolitania, covering an area of 2,200 hectares in 1958. The plant is valuable for windbreaks on sandy soils in low rainfall areas. Practically the whole of the crop, estimated at rather over 5,000 tons in 1958, is exported, mostly to Italy, which took 4,281 tons in 1958. Libyan castor seed is admitted to the Italian market free of duty. Small quantities of castor oil are also exported (42 tons in 1958, mainly to Egypt).

Esparto Grass

For many years one of Libya's principal exports, esparto grass, has recently been declining in importance. The grass grows wild over parts of the Tripolitanian Gebel (mainly between Tarhuna and Garian). It is collected by hand by local tribesmen and is delivered for baling to collection points, where agents of the government-controlled Esparto Grass Corporation take it over and transport it (mainly by truck) to Tripoli.

On the production side careless and uncontrolled methods of harvesting have resulted in a progressive diminution of esparto grass reserves and have thereby helped to aggravate the problem of soil erosion. Under the Italian administration a law was enacted in 1914 to regulate the harvesting of the grass, but this is no longer enforced. The grass is generally pulled up by the roots in clusters with the aid of a stick, and this does not give it a chance to renew itself.

On the demand side, esparto grass, which is mainly used for the manufacture of bank notes and high-quality paper, has to face growing competition from wood-pulp and other paper-making materials. This competition has forced down prices from about £L 40 per ton f.o.b. in 1952 to about £L 13 per ton in 1958, affecting not only Libya, but also Tunisia, which is a much larger exporter. Lower prices have reduced the incentive to collect esparto grass in Libya, and this has been a major factor contributing to the decline in production. Libya's exports go almost entirely to the United Kingdom. The trend is shown in the following table.

TABLE A.8   Exports of Esparto Grass

	Quantity in Tons	Value in £L '000
1954	49,519	610
1955	35,549	532
1956	27,248	403
1957	n.a.	348
1958	20,458	272

Prospects of reviving the trade in esparto grass appear rather remote. Theoretically, better arrangements for harvesting and collecting the grass should be able to check the progressive despoliation of esparto grass reserves and at the same time ensure a better return to the pickers. Efforts should certainly be made in these directions. But even allowing for the development of possible new uses (e.g., in the manufacture of sacking, mats and ropes) the mission is doubtful whether production can be expanded on an economic basis in present conditions in Libya.

Sugar Beets

Sugar beets have never been grown as a commercial crop in Libya, but for several years they have been grown experimentally under irrigation in the coastal belt of Tripolitania. Seeding takes place in the autumn, and the beets are usually harvested in the latter part of April when the weather starts to become warm. Once harvested, the roots are liable to rot very quickly in hot weather—a factor which would make prompt transport to the processing plant essential if commercial production were to be attempted.

Data collected by the Nazirate of Agriculture in the 1957/58 season indicated a high variability in root yields per hectare as well as in sugar percentage, regardless of variety. The plot yields were generally low, though some were very good. Observations made by mission members in 1959 on variety tests at Sidi Mesri, Misurata and Crispi indicated that few or none of the varieties would yield more than 25 tons per hectare. Sugar beets are poorly adapted to sandy soils, such as those that occur widely in the coastal belt of Tripolitania. The best yields are generally obtained when the crop is grown in silty or clayey soils, such as some found in the vicinity of Misurata and Crispi. The red clay soils in the Barce Plain of Cyrenaica appear suitable for sugar beets, but irrigation water is not available there for the crop. The crop requires large amounts of good-quality irrigation water. Sugar beet production in Tripolitania would also be handicapped by the presence of nematodes, for which a four-year crop rotation is generally considered the minimum for adequate control. The crop demands precise cultivation techniques for high yields.

Almonds

Almonds appear to grow well in Libya. The crop is adapted to climatic conditions in the Gefara and around Misurata where there is an annual average rainfall of 170 mms. or more. Almonds can also be grown around Benghazi and on the Barce Plain. Irrigation is not required, even during the hot summer months. The danger from frost is limited to the Gebel area. Almond plantations can be established and maintained at less cost than for other crops. The number of trees per hectare varies with rainfall conditions with about 44 trees per hectare on the sandy soils of Tripolitania to 100 in the higher rainfall belt. The tree begins to bear fruit after 3 to 4 years of planting and attains full production in 10 to 12 years. Thievery is said to be a common problem on almond plantations, but a plantation would have to be at least 10 hectares in size in order for it to be economic to employ a guard. The practice of interplanting almonds and olive trees has adversely affected almond production, especially on the Italian farms, because of competition for soil moisture. When almond trees are planted alone, the crop is much more successful. The almond harvesting season comes in July and August when labor is plentiful; storage offers few problems. A mature almond plantation is said to yield some 7 kilograms of nuts per tree, which at the rather low price of 7 piasters per kilogram yields something like £L 34 per hectare.

Official estimates for 1958 put production at just under 4,000 tons in Tripolitania and about 700 tons in Cyrenaica, though these figures should be treated with considerable reserve. Exports from Libya in 1958 (including small quantities of other nuts) amounted to 671 tons valued at just over £L 200,000. The United Kingdom (390 tons) and Germany (183 tons) were much the largest markets. Libya has only a very small share of the European markets for almonds, and the mission feels that this crop has considerable promise for further development.

Citrus Fruits

Citrus fruits are well adapted to the coastal area of Tripolitania on deep fertile soils where non-saline irrigation water is available. Oranges, tangerines, lemons and grapefruit were grown on about 1,260 hectares in the province in 1957/58. There were 606,800 citrus trees with a total estimated production of 8,000 tons. Oranges account for about 75 percent of the total, but lemons and grapefruit appear to offer better prospects for expanded cultivation, since they are more dependable crops than oranges and both have produced excellent yields in Libya.

Tripolitania grows sufficient citrus fruits for local needs, with a small amount available for export. Owing to lack of water for irrigation, production in Cyrenaica is very small (only a few hundred tons in 1957/58). Details of exports in recent years are set out in Table 9.

TABLE A.9   Exports of Citrus Fruit

	Quantity in Tons	Value in £L '000
1955	3,864	112
1956	3,165	100
1957	n.a.	60
1958	3,279	84

Libya's exports of citrus fruit receive a substantial subsidy from the Tripolitanian Government. Most of them go to Malta; sales in other European markets are very small. If Libya is to compete effectively with other Mediterranean growers, great improvements will be needed in standards of production and marketing, and costs will have to be reduced. The number of varieties grown should be reduced, grading should be improved and more energetic action is required to control pests, particularly the Mediterranean fruit-fly. Spraying of the trees should be made compulsory.

If these difficulties can be overcome, Libya may be able to develop a larger market for citrus fruit in Europe; it should in any case be possible to expand sales to the oil companies and foreign military bases in Libya. There may be opportunities to develop the canning of citrus fruit and fruit juices if the quality and grading of the locally grown fruit can be improved, and there should also be scope for making greater use of citrus fruit in the manufacture of soft drinks for local consumption (see Annex XIII).

Grapes

The cultivation of vines was introduced under the Italian administration, mainly to produce wine for local consumption. Grapes grow well both in Tripolitania and Cyrenaica and require little or no irrigation. Present production, including table grapes, is estimated to be in the region of 3,000-5,000 tons a year in Tripolitania and 1,500-2,000 tons a year in Cyrenaica. With the contraction of domestic demand for wine since the war many of the vineyards have been abandoned, but good prices are still paid by the local winery for the grapes that are produced, and vines appear to yield a better return to the grower in the Gebel Akhdar than most other crops cultivated in Cyrenaica. Quite a palatable red wine is produced, and number of enquiries have been made in Libya about the possibilities of producing for export (e.g., to Germany). The mission believes that the possibilities of developing an export market for Libyan wine are worth exploring further. Meanwhile, the activities of the oil companies should present opportunities for expanding consumption by the foreign community in Libya.

Other Fruits

Other fruits in Tripolitania are grown principally for home consumption. The present area is estimated at 1,200 hectares planted to apples, pears, apricots, peaches, plums, figs, pomegranates and loquats. Apples, pears, apricots, peaches, plums and figs are grown in Cyrenaica, mostly in small units in the Gebel area. Many young trees have not begun to bear fruit. Fruits like apples, pears, apricots and peaches are adapted to the Gebel area in Tripolitania on deep soils where the average annual rainfall is 250 mm. to 350 mm. The coastal plain is suitable for apricots, plums and loquats under irrigation. Figs are adapted to both areas. Early varieties are damaged less by the Mediterranean fruit-fly than are late ones. In Cyrenaica, apples, pears and peaches are adapted to the Gebel area where the annual rainfall averages from 450 mm. to 600 mm., provided the soil is one meter or more in depth. Apricots are grown in the coastal area under irrigation. Figs grow in all areas without irrigation. They have been introduced as an experimental crop in the Fezzan, but have proved very susceptible to damage from *ghiblis.*

There is little encouragement for farmers to grow deciduous fruits in Tripolitania because of the Mediterranean fruit-fly, transport difficulties and the uncertainties of local markets. Sometimes the fruits remain unpicked on the trees because of low prices. In Cyrenaica, local markets are good for all deciduous fruits, but high prices charged by merchants tend to reduce the demand.

The mission feels that market conditions, as well as fruit quality, must be improved before there will be sufficient incentive for farmers to expand the production of deciduous fruits in Libya. Cold storage facilities are also desirable in order to spread market supplies of fruits beyond the harvest season. Control of the Mediterranean fruit-fly, as well as other insect pests, is essential for the production of high quality fruits. With these conditions corrected, it would be feasible to expand production, particularly in Cyrenaica, for local consumption.[3] There

[3] About 1,000 tons of apples and over 200 tons of other fresh fruits were imported into Libya in 1958.

may also be long-range possibilities for the development of an export market to Egypt for apples.

Vegetables

A variety of vegetables are grown in all three provinces of Libya for local consumption. These include potatoes, onions, tomatoes, peppers, broad beans, chickpeas, melons, lettuce, carrots, pumpkins, cabbages, cauliflowers and garden peas. The total annual value of the vegetables grown, at producer prices, may be around £L 1 million in Tripolitania and about one-third of this amount in Cyrenaica. The only fresh vegetables exported in any quantity are potatoes (1,143 tons valued at about £L 32,000 in 1958) and tomatoes (184 tons valued at just under £L 9,000 in 1958). The potatoes go mainly to the United Kingdom, with small quantities sold also in Malta, Germany, Italy and Holland; most of the tomatoes go to Malta. Imports of vegetables, mainly for the Italians and the foreign community, are considerable, as shown in Table A.10.

TABLE A.10   Imports of Vegetables in 1958

	Quantity in Tons	Value in £L '000 c.i.f.
Potatoes	3,418	64
Seed potatoes	1,034	29
Crude vegetable products	1,358	49
Onions	1,798	44
Other fresh vegetables	163	10
Dehydrated vegetables	345	20
Preserved tomatoes, tomato sauces	1,608	209
Other preserved vegetables	281	44
Total fresh and processed	10,005	469

Tomatoes are grown mainly in the coastal plain of Tripolitania, a substantial part of the crop being sold to the tomato paste factories in Tripoli. In Cyrenaica local market needs from December to March are supplied almost entirely from the Jalo oasis where early production is stimulated by ample irrigation water, a sandy soil and warm climate. Many tomatoes are shipped from Jalo every year during this period.

For the remainder of the season, local needs in Cyrenaica are supplied from the coastal area. In flood years—three years out of ten—tomatoes are grown on the Barce Plain as the flood waters recede. The retail price then drops to one piaster or less per kilo, as against the usual price of 3 piasters or 4 piasters. The mission believes that there is room for a tomato paste factory in Cyrenaica and recommends that the economics of such a factory should be investigated, along with the possibilities of establishing a larger and more stable production of tomatoes in the Jalo oasis and elsewhere.

Potatoes are widely grown under irrigation on sandy soils in Tripolitania, production in 1957/58 being estimated at around 12,000 tons. Exports to European markets consist mainly of early potatoes grown on a large mechanized farm near Tripoli, which has been developed by a British firm. Physical conditions in parts of the coastal plain in Tripolitania appear to be well suited to the cultivation of new potatoes and other *primeur* crops such as asparagus, carrots, green peas and cauliflowers for the European market, and every effort should be made to attract the skills needed for the organization of this trade and to ensure more regular shipping arrangements.

Onions are grown widely in Tripolitania in the irrigated gardens of the coastal area; they are also grown in the Gebel without irrigation. Onion production in Cyrenaica is largely confined to the coastal area where they can be irrigated from springs or wells. Good crops are sometimes obtained in the Gebel Akhdar when early rains permit November plantings. The crop also does well in the Fezzan as a winter crop. In view of the substantial imports of onions, the mission considers that the expansion of local production would be worth pursuing in conjunction with the development of better storage facilities.

More generally, there appears to be considerable scope for increasing production of vegetables in Libya to meet local demands, including the demands of the oil companies, foreign military bases and the resident foreign community. It is essential, however, that the quality of vegetables should be improved, that more effective action should be taken to control diseases and pests, and that marketing facilities should be improved, including facilities for transport, warehousing and cold storage. Efforts to develop exports should be directed particularly to vegetables that can be placed on the European market during the winter and spring and to the production of vegetable seeds, for which there is a good demand in Northern Europe. Grading, packaging and rapid transport all require the closest attention if Libya is to compete successfully in this trade.

ANNEX X *THE FORMER ITALIAN FARM SETTLEMENTS*

Pre-War Colonization

The first attempts to settle Italian farmers in Libya were made in 1914. The effort had to be abandoned during World War I, but was renewed in the 1920's. During the first phase of colonization, up to 1928, the administration granted private concessions in land to Italian settlers and businessmen, without, however, extending any special assistance for development. From 1928 to 1933 settlement continued on a private basis, but with direct financial help from the government. From 1933 onwards, under legislation passed in 1928, colonization was mainly carried out directly by the State, and few private concessions were granted.

Over 500 Italian farms were established in Tripolitania by the end of 1933, and about 1,500 Italian families were settled on them. The total area privately owned by Italians or let out in concessions was about 110,000 hectares, of which one-half was actually under cultivation. Rather over two-fifths of the farms were 25 hectares or less in extent and nearly another one-quarter had an area of between 25 hectares and 75 hectares. The remaining farms ranged upwards in size to 1,000 hectares and more. Settlement in Cyrenaica was much less advanced, with only about 90 Italian families established in agriculture by 1933.

State colonization was started in Cyrenaica in 1932 when the *Ente per la Colonizzazione della Cirenaica* was founded as a combined administrative, technical, economic and financial agency. This agency was converted in 1935 into the *Ente per la Colonizzazione della Libia* to extend its activities into Tripolitania. Colonization in Tripolitania was also undertaken by the *Instituto Nazionale per la Previdenza Sociale* which started operations in 1936. Yet a third government organization, the *Azienda Tabacchi Italiani,* settled a few Italian farmers on a small area around Garian in Tripolitania to cultivate tobacco for the monopoly. In Cyrenaica colonization was also undertaken on a small scale by the *Instituto di Credito per il Lavoro all'Estero.*

The activities of these agencies were directed towards the establishment in Libya of family farming units, the so-called "demographic farms." Altogether by 1940 more than 2,000 such farms had been established in Tripolitania at various points near to the coast and in the Gebel around Tarhuna and another 1,800 in the Cyrenaican Gebel between Barce and Derna.[1] Particulars of the total areas developed to settled farming by Italians in Libya in 1940 are as follows:

	Area in Hectares
In Tripolitania	
"Demographic farms"	65,479
Italian Tobacco Co.	2,300
Private concessionaires	80,366
In Cyrenaica	
"Demographic farms" ⎱	79,832
Private concessionaires ⎰	
	227,977

SOURCE: Italian Government Statistics.

The settlement of Italian peasant families in Libya took place on contract.[2] The contracts varied in accordance with local circumstances, but all contained regulations regarding the financial aid to be given by the Italian Government, the conditions under which the settlers would eventually receive titles to their farms and the steps required for proper land development and utilization. Each family received a plot of land which was regarded as sufficient to support him at a reasonable standard of living on the basis of planned cropping patterns. With the land he received a ready-built house, equipped with furniture, household utensils, a cistern and accommodation for livestock. Livestock, trees, seeds and other requisites were also supplied on credit.

Two different types of contract were in use in Cyrenaica. The one normally applied to holdings in the Barce Plain stipulated that the farmer should start to develop an area of about 50 hectares and that after ten years this should be split into two farms of 25 hectares each, one of which would become his property, while the other would be given to a new colonist. The tentative cropping pattern for each 25

[1] For details see two publications of the Instituto Agricolo Coloniale, Florence: *La Colonizzazione Agricola della Tripolitania*, and *La Colonizzazione della Cirenaica*, Rome, 1947.

[2] Marassi, A.: *I Contratti Agrari nella Colonizzazione Demografica della Libia*, L'Agricoltura Coloniale, XXXIII, No. 9, pp. 536-547, Florence, 1939.

hectares included 10.75 hectares of annual field crops and 14.25 hectares of olives, almonds, vines and other fruit trees. In Cyrenaica most contracts were for farms of around 30 hectares each, of which 19.5 hectares were to be planted to field crops and the remainder to fruits and nuts.

Libyan-Italian Agreement of 1956

World War II put an end to further Italian colonization in Libya. The whole Italian population was withdrawn from Cyrenaica in 1942. Many of the Italian farmers in Tripolitania also left the country during and after the war, but the majority have remained.

The future status of the Italian demographic farms in Tripolitania is governed by an agreement concluded between Libya and Italy in October 1956. Under this agreement all the former Ente farms in Cyrenaica were formally returned to the Libyan Government, along with a number of farms abandoned by the Italians in Tripolitania. The demographic farms still occupied by the Italian farmers in Tripolitania are to remain Italian property, and the Italian Government has undertaken to provide the financial assistance required to complete their development up to 1960. Thereafter the present occupants will obtain rights of ownership to their farms, and the farms will remain free of taxation by the Libyan Government for a period of 25 years from the date at which they were first established. The Italian farmers concerned are entitled to obtain machinery and materials required for developing their farms free of import duties until 1960. The duty-free concessions granted by the Italian Government on imports of olive oil (up to specified limits) are also designed to benefit the Italian farmers in Tripolitania.

Ente Farms in Cyrenaica

Details of the former Ente farms in Cyrenaica are set out in Table A.11, which is based on information supplied to the mission by the Cyrenaican Government.

TABLE A.11   Ente Farms in Cyrenaica, 1958

			Area in hectares		
			Arable land		
		Number of Ente farms	Total	Average per farm	Total in wheat and barley
Mutasarifa	Mudiria				
Barce	Barce	624	10,433	16.7	9,625
	Tolmeta	387	5,534	14.3	4,969
	Bayada	76	1,439	18.9	979
	Tecnis	10	300	30.0	160
	Total	1,097	17,706	16.1	15,733
Beida	Messa	112	2,128	19.0	1,721
	Beida	161	3,519	21.9	2,807
	Cyrene	32	704	22.0	427
	Fedia	132	2,121	16.1	1,622
	Omar el Mukhtar	70	1,266	18.1	848
	Total	507	9,738	19.2	7,425
Derna	Labrag	92	470	5.1	460
	Gubba	44	418	9.5	362
	Ras el Hilal	32	117	3.7	107
	Total	168	1,005	6.0	929
	GRAND TOTAL	1,772	28,449	16.1[a]	24,087

[a]Average per farm in wheat and barley is 13.5 hectares.

Ente Farms in Tripolitania

The two former Italian colonization agencies, the *Ente per la colonizzazione della Libia* and *Instituto nazionale per la previdenza sociale,* have combined forces to supervise the remaining development of the Ente farms in Tripolitania. They supplied the mission with the details which are set out in the following table:

	Number of Farms				Area in hectares		
						Approx. average per farm	
Locality	Originally established	Returned to Libya	Retained by Italians	Since abandoned	Approx. total still Italian	Total	Of which irrigated
Azzahra (Bianchi)	170	2	168	15	4,550	27	27
Annasira (Giordani)	194	15	179	17	4,850	27	27
Al Amiria (Micca)	148	9	139	19	3,750	27	27
Giud Daiem (Oliveti)	124	—	124	—	2,100	17	—[a]
Hascian	19	—	19	—	350	18	18
Funduk Al Togar	27	—	27	—	710	26	—[b]
Azzazia	31	9	22	—	900	41	—[c]
Garabulli (Cast. Verde)	58	56	2	—	140	70	nil
Ghanima (Coradini)	64	12	52	2	2,200	40 to 50	nil
Tarhuna-Sidi Essed (Tazzoli)	179	160	19	—	1,200	63	nil
Al Khadra (Breveglieri)	168	—	168	3	8,140	20 to 48	nil
El Gusea (Marconi)	131	130	1	—	70	70	nil
Dafnia (Garibaldi)	318	105	213	12	6,500	31	—[d]
Tummina (Crispi)	370	126	244	6	3,500	14	10
Kararim (Gioda)	101	78	23	—[e]	350	15	15
Total	2,102	702	1,400	74[f]	39,310	—	—

[a] 74 farms fully irrigated, 50 farms 3 to 6 hectares each.
[b] With 1 to 5 hectares irrigated each.
[c] With 2 to 5 hectares irrigated each.
[d] 20 percent of farms nonirrigated; 20 percent with 1 to 2 hectares, 50 percent with 2 to 3 hectares, and 10 percent with 3 to 8 hectares irrigated each.
[e] With the exception of a few, most are abandoned.
[f] Excluding the unknown number of abandoned farms of Kararim (Gioda).

ANNEX XI *THE GEBEL AKHDAR DEVELOPMENT PROJECT*

Proposals for a Development Board

An Agricultural Development Board would be established as an autonomous public body, charged with the responsibility of instituting and conducting an intensive campaign to promote agricultural production in the Barce-Beida area of Cyrenaica. Its principal objective would be to achieve a fuller utilization of the ex-Italian demographic farms in the area, on which considerable investments have already been made. Suggestions with regard to the composition of the board are set out in Chapter 8. An annual budget of £L 35,000 has been allowed to provide for staffing and operational expenses on the assumption that the board would have attached to it advisers from the UN and U.S. technical assistance missions, whose salaries would not be a charge on the board's funds. The board would need to have its own administrative, technical and financial staff, including a heavy machinery section. The work of restoring farm buildings would be contracted out to private enterprise. Credit operations would be conducted by the Agricultural Credit Department of the National Bank, working closely with the Development Board. While one of the main functions of the board would be to build up extension services in the area, it is assumed that the extension workers would be employees of the Nazirate of Agriculture rather than of the board itself.

Development of Ex-Italian Farms

The work of developing the demographic farms in Cyrenaica should be spread over five development years following a period of about two years required to organize the board and to prepare the initial plans for operation. It is suggested that in each development year a certain number of farms should be selected, increasing through the years on some rough pattern as indicated in Table A.13, so as not to concentrate all the development in one district of the area.

Some of these farms are as large as 50 hectares to 60 hectares, and the board might consider limiting the size of an average farm to about

432

25 hectares to 30 hectares or select for development, by arrangement with each farmer, only 25 hectares to 30 hectares of each farm in the first instance. Such a size would appear to be a reasonable economic unit for a family, but more research is required to establish the optimum size of a family farm in present Libyan conditions.

TABLE A.13 Numbers of Ex-Italian Farms in Cyrenaica to be Developed in a Five-Year Period

| | Location in Mudiria and Mutasarifa | | | | | |
	1st Year	2nd Year	3rd Year	4th Year	5th Year	Total
Barce	125	125	125	125	125	625
Tolmeta	50	50	75	100	112	387
Bayada	—	—	—	—	76	76
Tecnis	—	—	—	—	10	10
Mut. Barce	175	175	200	225	323	1,098
Messa	—	25	25	25	37	112
Beida	25	25	25	50	36	161
Cyrene	—	—	—	32	—	32
Fedia	—	25	50	57	—	132
Omar el Mukhtar	—	25	25	20	—	70
Mut. Beida	25	100	125	184	73	507
Labrag	25	25	25	17	—	92
Gubba	—	—	—	—	44	44
Ras el Hilal	—	—	—	—	32	32
Mut. Derna	25	25	25	17	76	168
Mut. Beida and Derna	50	125	150	201	149	675
Whole Cyrenaica	225	300	350	426	472	1,773

The board would bear the initial capital cost of renovating farm buildings, and farmers would be required to pay back the cost over a period of years. The selected farms should be provided with tilling facilities with the help of the board's heavy machinery section. Credits would be provided through the proposed Agricultural Credit Department of the National Bank for a number of purposes. In the first place, loans should be provided for the purchase of livestock, tools, seeds and tree saplings. Initially, the farmer might also need to borrow to meet minimum family consumption needs during the period before these special measures yielded a return. The collective cost of all these credits would be a liability which the farmer would be required eventually to repay: long-term loans in 20 years to 25 years and seasonal credits within a year. Long-term loans would be regarded as the farmer's liability only after he is finally granted the rights of ownership in land.

Heavy Machinery

The heavy machinery section should be staffed by a mechanical engineer and a deputy, and operating personnel appropriate to the number of machine units obtained. The heavy machinery should be set up in practical units, and each unit might consist of five 50-h.p. tractors, together with an adequate complement of disc harrows, stump-jump cultivators, seed drills, harvesters and threshers. Assuming each unit to be able to work at the rate of about 8 hectares per working day, and depending on the number of hectares selected each year for servicing, the units of machinery required will go up from two in the first year to about seven to eight for the Barce area, and from one in the first year to about five in the Beida-Derna area, giving a total of about twelve units in all. This calculation is based on the assumption of a 20 percent reserve capacity. The board should take over and expand the existing farm machinery unit at Barce, and a small mobile workshop should be established to service the equipment. Hire of the units should be on a fee-paying basis, although in the initial years it may be necessary to contemplate some deficit on operational costs.

Financial Arrangements

The financial section should be broadly in charge of the funds and the accounting of the board's operations. The board's capital requirements, which the mission has estimated at £L 500,000 for the first five years, should be covered by a grant from the federal government. Credit would be handled separately by the proposed Agricultural Credit Department of the National Bank of Libya. The administrative expenses of the board should be regarded as a charge on the current revenues of the government, and provision should be made for them in the annual budget of the Nazirate of Agriculture.

Credit Requirements

An effort should be made to work out an estimated necessary development credit pattern per farm somewhat on the lines of the following model:

Estimated Necessary Development Credits Per Farm in £L

	Short Term	Medium Term	Long Term Barce	Long Term Beida-Derna
Repair costs on buildings	—	—	300	300
Tractor tilling	15	50	—	—
Purchase of fruit tree saplings	—	—	57	140
Purchase cost 2/3 of seeds	31	—	—	—
Purchase cost 2/3 of livestock	—	59	—	—
Purchase cost 2/3 of equipment, etc.	—	40	—	—
Windbreak material	—	—	10	10
Chemicals and drugs for plant-animal protection	10	—	—	—
Fodder (first six months)	20	—	—	—
Total cost per farm:	76	149	367	450

For the whole project, which includes 657 farms in the Barce area and 740 farms in the Beida-Derna area, these credits will amount to:

in short-term credits	£L	134,672
in medium-term credits		264,028
in long-term credits		706,349
	£L	1,105,049

Linking these requirements with the number of farms selected for development during each of the years, the mission has worked out a tentative and very rough cost estimation as follows:

Necessary Credits per Development Year in £L

Year	Barce Area	Beida-Derna Area	Total
1st (1962/63)	103,600	33,750	137,350
2nd (1963/64)	103,600	84,375	187,975
3rd (1964/65)	118,400	101,250	219,650
4th (1965/66)	133,200	135,675	268,875
5th (1966/67)	190,624	100,575	291,199
Total	649,424	455,625	1,105,049

As indicated in Chapter 8, credit requirements for the first three years of the scheme, including the cost of repairing farm buildings, would amount on the above estimates to approximately £L 550,000. These figures would have to be adapted, brought up to date and rendered more precise by the board, taking into account the prices prevailing as of the date of operation.

Farm Output Projections

Estimates should be prepared of possible returns from farm units of average size for various cropping patterns. Values should be imputed for the output that may be expected from these farms, and assuming either the present or some other reasonable price for the output, rough estimates should be made of income patterns under different combinations of crops. Although only very approximate, such calculations would give some preliminary guidance as to the appropriate cropping patterns. The mission has assumed that wheat, barley and fodder would be the principal annual crops in the Barce Plain and that these would be supplemented by olives, almonds, fruit trees and vegetables, including tomatoes. In the Beida-Derna area only about 10 percent of the land on average would be suitable for cereals, and the main emphasis would be placed on olives, vines, pears, apples and other fruit trees, together with pasture. The farmers might also be encouraged to rear poultry and small numbers of other livestock. Further study, however, is required of the economics of different farming patterns, and we have suggested that this should be undertaken as part of the program of agricultural research and experimentation (see Chapter 9).

ANNEX XII APPRAISAL OF INDUSTRIAL CONDITIONS

Location

Apart from typical rural industries such as olive oil pressing, the curing of hides and skins, flour milling and fish canning, nearly all industrial establishments are concentrated in Tripoli and Benghazi.[1] According to the 1956 Census of Employment and Production, more than half are located in Tripoli. Both capital cities together account for 77 percent of the total number of industrial units and for 90 percent of the industrial labor force. Sebha, as the third provincial capital, lags far behind with only a few industrial enterprises.

TABLE A.14 Location of Industry, 1956

	Number	Percentage
Tripoli		
Establishments	1,773	57
Employment	11,493	79
Benghazi		
Establishments	628	20
Employment	1,631	11
Other Urban Areas		
Establishments	720	23
Employment	1,380	10
Libya		
Establishments	3,121	100
Employment	14,504	100

This marked preference for industrial location in Tripoli is understandable. The city of Tripoli, together with its adjoining semi-urban

[1] Industrial establishments refer to manufacturing, processing and servicing activities, irrespective of the number of workers per establishment.

437

settlements, has an aggregate population of 250,000 and provides the largest single market in the country. A sizeable foreign community and the proximity of the U.S. Air Force base at Wheelus add to the demand for manufactured goods. Purchasing power in Tripoli may well account for nearly half of total expendable income in the country, and it would appear that the bulk of the goods manufactured there are consumed within the city and its immediate environs. Only a very limited range of its manufactures find their way to rural Tripolitania, to the Fezzan or to Cyrenaica; these consist largely of processed food products (canned fish, pasta and tomato paste), olive oil, salt, textiles and tobacco.

Other factors adding to the attraction of Tripoli and Benghazi as industrial centers include ready access to imported materials, the availability of public utility services, a relatively high concentration of skilled labor (particularly in Tripoli) and a variety of supporting services made available through the concentration of trade, commerce and public administration in the two cities.

This is not to say that in every case the establishment of industries in the two capital cities is justified from a strictly economic point of view. The two tomato paste factories in Tripoli could have found a better location in the center of the tomato-growing areas; the same applies to stone and marble cutting and date processing. But, by and large, the present distribution of industry in the country is well justified by the pattern of available resources and markets.

The concentration of industry in the two big cities has nonetheless distinct disadvantages from a social point of view. It contributes to the drift of rural workers to the towns at the expense of agricultural development; it makes it more difficult for the farmers to secure a fair share in the material, social and cultural progress of the country; and it tends to aggravate the problem of seasonal unemployment, which is a serious one in Libya. Industrial agglomeration has the unfortunate tendency to perpetuate itself, particularly in countries in an early stage of economic development, and it is likely that the trend towards concentration in Tripoli and Benghazi will continue unless special steps are taken to counteract it.

The mission suggests that, in the interests of more balanced economic growth, the government should encourage decentralization wherever practicable through measures to improve the relative cost advantages of production in rural areas. We do not suggest that legislation should be enacted to regulate the location of industry, but would rather see incentives given for the establishment of new industries in rural areas. These could include special preferences accorded under the law for the promotion of national industries and liberal financial and technical assistance. Industries which, prima facie, are suitable for location in rural areas include leather tanning, agricultural and fish processing, quarry products, and repair and servicing undertakings for agricultural tools and machinery.

Raw Materials

Domestic raw materials for industry are confined to a few commodities of agricultural, mineral and maritime origin. Agricultural produce which is currently being processed by industry includes, in order of importance, olives, barley and wheat, grapes, tobacco, dates and tomatoes. Wool is the main fiber available and is largely used in the home textile crafts; the industrial use of hides and skins is mainly confined to curing, since negligible quantities are being processed into leather.

One of the major problems confronting agricultural processing is the considerable fluctuation in supplies from year to year. For example, during the three years 1955/56 to 1957/58, olive crops are estimated to have varied between 15,000 tons and 85,000 tons a year, barley and wheat between 61,000 tons and 153,000 tons and grapes between 5,000 tons and 7,000 tons, thereby causing appreciable differences in processing costs. An additional difficulty arises from the large number of varieties, particularly of olives and grapes. The quality of the processed product is likewise variable and, in the case of the wine, it is inferior to what could be produced if the supply of grapes was homogeneous.

Minerals used in sizeable quantities by industry include sandstone and low quality marble. Scattered clay deposits provide the basis for the manufacture of bricks and tiles and simple household pottery; the use of gypsum in the housing industry is negligible. Limestone and clay deposits could probably be used for cement manufacture. Silica sand is reported to be available in the Tripolitanian Gebel, but has so far not been sufficiently investigated as to quality and quantity. As far as maritime products are concerned, salt is manufactured on a substantial scale. On the other hand, only a small part of the yearly catch of fish is processed by industry. Since industry is largely confined to the manufacture of final consumer goods, interchange between industrial trades of domestically manufactured materials is comparatively unimportant; examples are wrapping paper, and ice, salt and olive oil for the fish canning and curing industries.

A substantial part of industrial output is based on imported commodities such as cotton and other yarns, leather, paper, metals and a great variety of miscellaneous materials required in light manufacturing industries. Transport costs for imported materials are generally low, but this advantage is to some extent offset by the relatively high prices that have to be paid for small consignments, since few commodities are imported in any quantity. Firms employing as few as ten workers frequently import raw materials on their own account direct from European wholesalers at prices which compare unfavorably with corresponding European price levels. In addition, industry tends to carry unusually large raw material stocks. The mission noted several instances where inventories were in excess of requirements for six months' production, thereby tying up capital resources which could be better employed for other purposes.

The mission has the impression that, by and large, and within the limits set by market opportunities and technical know-how, industry has adequately exploited the few domestic raw materials available. The tomato processing industry, for instance, developed as soon as increasing consumption made local manufacture economical. There is still room, however, for greater use of some local materials such as gypsum for housing (and, at a later stage, possibly silica sand for glass manufacture). More important, agricultural processing could well be extended in certain directions (see Annex IX). The development of Libyan agriculture depends in large measure on the availability of an adequate and efficient processing industry, just as industrial growth is promoted by the availability of agricultural surpluses. Programs for the cultivation, marketing and processing of agricultural raw materials should therefore be fully harmonized with each other in conception as well as in execution.

Power, Fuel and Water

Power. The postwar development of industries in Benghazi has been facilitated by the ample availability of public power at reasonable rates (15 milliemes per KWH) and nearly all industrial establishments requiring power are being supplied by the local power station. The position is quite different in Tripoli where, for years, industry has suffered from appreciable public power shortages. Current annual power requirements are estimated at 15 million KWH, out of which the Tripoli Power Station in 1958 supplied less than half or 7.2 million KWH. Few of the larger enterprises are connected with the public power station; indeed, so far as the mission could ascertain, the larger industries established since the war have almost invariably installed their own power generators. There is no evidence that the shortage of public power has prohibited the establishment of any new enterprise, but it has undoubtedly slowed down industrial progress, particularly in the case of small workshops, which would greatly benefit by making more use of power-driven tools and equipment. Further, industrial power rates charged by Tripoli Power are very high, amounting to between 23 milliemes and 25 milliemes (about 6 U.S. cents) per KWH. This is three times the power rate for agricultural undertakings (8 milliemes per unit) and compares most unfavorably with industrial power charges in other developed, as well as underdeveloped, countries. Calculations indicate that small-unit power generation provides industries with power at a cost, including depreciation and interest, of between 10 milliemes and 13 milliemes per KWH.

Apart from Tripoli and Benghazi, some 30 smaller towns and villages are operating public power stations, but many of these plants are not dependable, and they generally supply only a small part of the town. What little industry exists has therefore to operate its own generators. The mission heard complaints about considerable voltage fluctuations, the unreliability of the power supply and high rates, varying between 15 milliemes and 25 milliemes per KWH.

The need for more reliable and cheaper supplies of power for industry has been taken into account in our recommendations for developing electricity, which are set out in Chapter 11. The completion of the Tripoli Power expansion scheme should put an end to the shortage of electricity in and around Tripoli itself.

Fuel. The only sources of domestic fuel at present are brushwood and charcoal, both of which are extensively used by small industrial undertakings. The position is, however, likely to be radically changed as a result of the discovery of oil and natural gas. It is too early to say exactly what use can be made of oil and natural gas as industrial fuels, but appreciable savings in fuel costs should be possible since the larger enterprises (including Tripoli Power itself) now depend on imported coal and oil which are rather expensive.

The few olive oil refineries mostly depend for fuel on exhausted sansa which is the final residue of olive oil pressing. Sansa has a calorific value of only 3,000 calories per kilogram as compared with 9,000 calories per kilogram for anthracite and 12,000 for fuel oil. Prices of anthracite and fuel oil are, however, much higher than the price of sansa, which now largely runs to waste; thus for every 1,000 calories, the price of anthracite is currently 1.3 milliemes and for fuel oil 1.2 milliemes, against 0.23 milliemes for sansa.

Water. There is no shortage of water for industry, as the great majority of the industrial enterprises in Libya are light water consumers. Since the municipal waterworks in Tripoli has not always been able to meet industrial requirements, some of the larger enterprises have installed their own water supply by sinking wells; a similar practice is followed in rural industries. The salinity and the high calcium content of the water present more of a problem, especially for boiler water and for water used in the food processing industry. The beer factory, for example, has to condition the water for the manufacture of a quality product.

Entrepreneurship and Capital

In Tripolitania nearly all the 100-odd industrial enterprises which are organized along factory lines are under foreign control, whereas craftshops employing five workers or less are predominantly owned by Libyans. Most factories were established before the war when industrial entrepreneurship was exclusively supplied by the Italian population and a few foreigners of other nationalities. After Independence, and more particularly within the last few years, some Libyan capital has found its way into Tripolitanian industry. The picture is markedly different in Cyrenaica where the evacuation of the Italian population in 1942 created industrial investment opportunities which Libyan entrepreneurs were quick to take advantage of. It is because of this that, with only two exceptions, all the 50 or so manufacturing units in Cyrenaica are Libyan-owned; 30 units have been established since Independence alone.

Since Libyan industry consists largely of small undertakings, it is understandable that capital requirements are mainly supplied by the entrepreneur himself, eventually supported by relatives and a few friends; the few joint stock companies are largely family-owned. Industrial entrepreneurship is often interlocked with other interests, and many of the larger industrial entrepreneurs have interests in trade, real estate and occasionally agriculture as well. This makes it easier to get bank credit for industrial purposes, since banks are willing to extend sizeable credits to industrial undertakings if the borrower can show a satisfactory business record, which need not refer to industrial performance only. Bank credits, which bear not unreasonable rates of 7 percent to 10 percent, are not provided specifically for long-term investment, but long-term credit is in practice often obtained through successive renewals of overdrafts.

All things considered, industry is profitable, and industrial failures are few. A study of the balance sheets of twelve industrial undertakings in nine different trades disclosed that in 1953, 1956 and 1957 profits before tax[2] varied between 14 percent and 18 percent of total capital employed, and between 21 percent and 25 percent of share capital invested. The numbers of enterprises belonging to one single trade are too few to make it possible to draw reliable conclusions as to the relative profitability of specific industries. As in other countries, the quality of management is the most important factor in determining the financial success of any enterprise.

Although there is a marked investment preference for trade and real estate with their quick, high and safe earnings, the mission did not have the feeling that lack of capital as such had prohibited the establishment of any enterprise with satisfactory earning prospects. As a matter of fact, Libyan capital is not shy to participate in industrial ventures if and when their profitability have been demonstrated, as evidenced in the growth of Libyan-controlled industry in Cyrenaica. Most enterprises are plowing back part of their profits to modernize and extend plant and equipment, but industry is as a rule unwilling to tie up large amounts of capital in investments such as factory buildings, which do not yield a quick return. What has been holding back capital from investment in industry is the rather limited opportunities for the establishment of industrial undertakings, the lack of technical information needed to exploit the opportunities that exist, and the feeling that present-day industry is rather precariously based on a market which depends heavily on income generated by outside forces through foreign aid and foreign military expenditures. There are signs that investors are taking a more optimistic view of the possibilities of industrial expansion since the discovery of oil.

This is not to say that there is no place for improvement of the financial facilities available to industry. Marginal projects in which profitability would depend in some measure on government protection, or in which profitability has to be tested by actual operation (e.g., the leather tanning project), are unlikely to materialize without financial help from the government. Further, there is an urgent need to increase productivity through the introduction of a modern technology and the dissemination of better management techniques. It is against this background that the mission has suggested in Chapter 9 that measures be taken by the government to promote industrial growth through a mutually supporting scheme of financial and technical assistance.

[2] The present rate of company taxation is a flat 10 percent on profits.

Management and Technology

As a result of pre-war dependence on imported Italian labor and of postwar increases in labor costs, factory industry in Libya is quite highly mechanized. Rough estimates indicate that, as an average, one horsepower is installed for every worker employed, but this ratio is evidently appreciably higher in undertakings operating on a factory scale, which are usually well equipped, and where management is keen to replace obsolete and inefficient machinery if funds permit. Enterprises established since the war, such as pasta factories, flour mills and printing presses, have invariably installed up-to-date equipment which compares most favorably with similar industries in Europe. An exception is the fish processing industry which is operating with rudimentary equipment, partly because of operational conditions peculiar to the industry. The mission found little evidence of the existence of excess capacity as related to present and prospective market requirements. Exceptions were the flour milling industry and those industries established before the war which have suffered from a contraction of demand (e.g., the manufacture of ice and alcoholic beverages).

On the other hand, technological standards are desperately backward in the dwarf undertakings, where little or no use is made of power-driven tools and light equipment. This is particularly true of the textile industry in Tripoli, the development of which has been held back by the provincial government's policy of protecting hand-loom weaving.

Similar contrasts are to be observed in the quality of management. Some of the larger enterprises, especially those which are connected with companies in other countries, have excellent management records. Others are trying hard to keep themselves informed of postwar development in European management practices and to apply them in their plants. The majority of Libyan enterprises, however, are too small to afford specialized management, with the result that a limited staff (often confined to the owner-manager and one foreman) has to take care of a variety of functions.

Management in these plants is lopsided in the sense that important matters of internal and external organization are largely neglected. There is little understanding of the problem of working conditions as a factor in deciding efficiency, little systematic on-the-job training and insufficient appreciation of the human factor in industry. Few small plant managers are aware of the part played by plant layout, waste recovery, the organization of work flow, quality control and the selection of materials and supporting equipment in modern factory production. It is in these areas that much can be achieved, with little or no additional capital outlay, to raise productivity, decrease costs and improve quality. The mission was, for instance, struck by the excessive amount of material handling performed by hand in undertakings which are otherwise equipped with modern machinery. In one seasonal enterprise working on a round-the-clock basis 14 workers per shift were employed to feed a machine, whereas with the installation of a simple chute the job could have been done by two men. Similar situations were observed in many other factories, where costs could have been considerably reduced by economizing in materials and labor.

Labor and Productivity

Industry and handicrafts probably provide full-time employment for some 20,000 workers, nearly all men; an equal number of female workers may be engaged in home textile crafts as a part-time occupation. An estimated 6,000 workers are employed in undertakings organized along factory lines, of whom probably less than one percent are women. This exclusion of women from industry is unfortunate from the operational point of view since female workers are better suited for some jobs than men.

There is little recorded unemployment in most urban areas in Cyrenaica. In January 1959, for example, only 2.4 percent of the labor force in Benghazi was registered as being unemployed. In Tripolitania, on the other hand, there is a widespread belief that considerable unemployment exists in the province—a belief which finds expression in the employment policy of the public enterprises in Tripoli where appreciably larger numbers of workers are employed than required for efficient production. However, the rate of increase of industrial output since Independence (probably about 50 percent over 6 years) has largely outpaced population growth (1½ percent per annum), and it is evident that the growing demand for industrial labor has been met largely by an influx of rural labor into the towns.[3] One result is that agricultural expansion is being retarded by labor shortages notwithstanding the fact that rural wages have risen considerably in recent years. The Tripoli employment office had 2,140 unemployed on its register in

[3] A sample survey conducted by the Research Department of the National Bank of Libya in March and April 1959, covering 13 industrial enterprises of various sizes in Tripoli and Benghazi with a combined labor force of 793 Libyan workers, showed that 398 of the workers interviewed were born outside the city of present employment.

January 1959, about five percent of the economically active population in the city and its suburbs.

Most of these were unskilled workers. Considering that the figure is for a winter month when building activities are slowing down, and when many factories operating on a seasonal basis are only maintaining a small skeleton staff, the unemployment percentage is hardly very high.

Much can be done to improve the productivity of Libyan labor. Libya has hardly any crafts tradition, and most workers require time to adjust to industrial occupations. Moreover, the Libyan worker is operating against considerable odds. Only a minority is literate,[4] and very few have received any formal vocational training. Nor are present dietary standards and housing conditions conducive to creating a healthy laboring class. There is no regular inspection of factories, and working conditions in quite a number of plants are unsatisfactory from the point of view of health and morale. All these factors are reflected in the present low output levels of the Libyan worker. The few plants in which wage incentive schemes are applied show appreciably higher output rates, as was observed when the mission visited the factory of Government Tobacco Monopoly in Tripoli.

Labor-management relations are rather patriarchal and could be substantially improved. It is significant that the majority of industrial disputes refer to relations between workers and employers rather than to complaints about working conditions or payment of wages. Strikes are, however, virtually unknown; only one was registered in Tripolitania in 1958, and this lasted only one day. Apart from the handloom workers in Tripoli, who have so far been successful in inducing the administration to prevent the establishment of a competing factory, there is little apparent resistance to the introduction of labor-saving techniques.

Wage levels are comparatively low, but so is productivity. The government has established a minimum wage of 25 piasters per day, which appears to be generally enforced in urban areas. This regulation has undoubtedly contributed to the prevalent drift of the rural population to the towns. In practice, apart from young workers who are learning the trade under an informal system of apprenticeship training, unskilled male workers seldom receive less than 30 piasters per day. Skilled labor, which is scarce, receives appreciably higher wages, ranging between 50 piasters and £L 1 for Libyan workers and between 75 piasters and £L 1.50 for Italian personnel. Foremen, who are pre-

---

4 According to the returns of the sample survey mentioned earlier only 256 (32 percent) of the workers interviewed were able to read and write.

dominantly of Italian origin, earn £L 2 or more per day. The appreciable shortage of skilled workers is clearly demonstrated by the fact that wage rates for skilled labor have increased by 100 percent or more since Independence, against 50 percent for unskilled workers. The wages of the highest paid workers, mostly Italians, are now approaching the levels of some European industries. Actual earnings moreover are higher than the daily wage would suggest since the Libyan Labor Law requires employers to continue payment during public holidays, compulsory annual leave and the weekly rest day—the equivalent of a 20 percent increase in wages per working day.

From the mission's own observations, and from the opinion expressed by employers familiar with labor performance in Italian industry, it would appear that the productivity of the Libyan worker is approximately half that of his European counterpart working under similar factory conditions. The difference is further accentuated by the sharp decline in the productivity of Libyan labor during the month of Ramadan, when output is sometimes as much as 50 percent lower than during the rest of the year. In view of the fact that the majority of the undertakings are employing sizeable numbers of Italians, labor productivity in Libyan factory industry may be estimated at between 60 percent and 70 percent of productivity in Italian industry.

The mission has certain reservations about the present Labor Law. For example, during Ramadan nearly all enterprises under Libyan control (including government enterprises) reduce their hours of work fom 48 a week to 36 a week or less, since continuation of normal working hours would exert too great a strain on the workers. To make up for lost production, employers often want to arrange for overtime in the month following Ramadan, but if they do this, they have to pay overtime at the rate of time and a half. Again, the procedures laid down in the Labor Law for discharging workers seem to make it difficult to maintain a reasonable measure of discipline within the enterprise concerned. The mission therefore suggests that the Labor Law should be carefully reviewed by the government, together with representatives of labor and management, and if necessary in consultation with the International Labor Office, with a view to providing greater flexibility in its practical application in such respects as those mentioned above.

ANNEX XIII *REVIEW OF SELECTED INDUSTRIES*

Cold Storage

Present exports of perishable commodities are limited in range and value. Table A.15 gives details for 1957, the only year for which separate external trade statistics are available for Tripolitania and Cyrenaica.

TABLE A.15   Export of Perishable Products, 1957

(£L '000)

Commodity	Tripoli	Benghazi	Main Destination
Eggs	14	—	Malta
Fresh fish	24	—	Egypt
Prepared fish	152	—	Italy
Fruits	63	—	Malta
Vegetables	86	3	U. K.
Live animals	11	489	Egypt
Total	350	492	

Libya has to cope with many problems in exporting perishable products. Temperatures range between 0° and 50° C., and relative humidity may well rise from 6 percent to 90 percent within a few hours, thereby shortening the lifetime of fruits and vegetables. Exportable surpluses are limited, irregular in quantity and varied in quality, which makes shipping difficult since it is not easy to collect paying loads for export abroad. Specialized facilities for storage and handling, including refrigeration plants, are lacking, and the present decentralized organization of agriculture and trade is a handicap to exports. It is for these reasons that the government has in recent years paid considerable attention to the establishment of cold storage units to facilitate the accumulation of stocks for efficient shipping to the more

448

profitable markets in Europe and to promote domestic sales in off-season periods.

Proposals have been made to establish two perishable products terminals, including refrigeration units, as central collecting, grading, processing and marketing points for such products.[1] The proposed unit in Tripoli would mainly be used for the storage of winter agricultural produce, for meat and fish products during summer and for storage of imported food products. The Benghazi plant, on the other hand, would predominantly handle meat, mainly mutton and beef, and possibly fish as well. Since it is unlikely that a sizeable export of fruit and vegetables could be developed from Cyrenaica in the near future, the plant would confine its operations to the handling of summer products.

In Tripoli, a private ice factory is already operating a chilling unit with a refrigeration capacity of 3,000 cubic meters. The plant is used for the storage of imported food products, mainly for foreign troops, foreign residents and the oil companies. Plans are under consideration for the construction as a private undertaking of a cold storage plant with a capacity of 5,500 cubic meters, and if this scheme goes through, it should solve the refrigeration problem in Tripoli. However, no action has been taken on it in the year since the mission's visit.

Since no private initiative is forthcoming in Benghazi, the federal government is at present establishing a chilling unit as part of the proposed cold storage project. The total volume of refrigerated space is 950 cubic meters providing a storage capacity of 33 tons of meat, and requiring an investment of £L 100,000, including expenses to improve the adjoining abattoir. A further amount of £L 135,000 has been earmarked for the establishment of the cold storage plant with a combined space of 3,800 cubic meters and with a meat freezing capacity of 50 tons. The cost estimate for the cold storage plant was made a few years ago, and as building costs in Benghazi have since risen substantially, the actual investment costs may well exceed £L 200,000.

It is understood that the British military forces and the oil companies have both indicated an interest in using the new cold storage facilities when they become available, and this provides a good base on which to build up the project. It is not yet clear, however, what contribution the project will be able to make toward the development of agricultural and livestock production in the province.

[1] Dr. E. M. Rascovich, UN/FAO Mission to Libya, *Export of Agricultural Produce from Libya,* January 1956; Covell and Matthews F/Ariba Ampti, *Abattoirs and Export Terminal Buildings,* LPDSA, August 1956; R. Sbordoni, *Reports to the Government of Libya on Tripoli and Benghazi Cold Storage,* FAO, 1958.

Libya is the largest livestock exporting country in the Mediterranean area, and there is no doubt that, in principle, the provision of refrigeration facilities should have a favorable effect on the livestock economy of Cyrenaica. It would appear, however, that insufficient thought has been given to the problems involved in running the chilling and cold storage plants as a commercial venture. At the time of the mission's visit, no information was available on the estimated operation cost or on the organization of the undertaking (e.g., whether the plants would operate as servicing units for private meat merchants or would buy, process, store and sell cattle and meat on their own account). Nor had much thought been given to finding markets for the products. We understand that a preliminary survey for the marketing of meat abroad has been carried out by the government, with the help of an FAO expert, but this does not provide adequate evidence on which to base plans for developing exports.

Cyrenaican exports of perishable products are mainly live animals exported to Egypt overland, and a careful study should be made of this country as a potential market for the slaughtered and frozen product. An intensive study should also be made of possible markets for meat elsewhere in the Mediterranean area. The exploitation of these markets will call for a variety of measures of livestock improvement. In particular, there is urgent need for the enactment of a veterinary law in Libya and for the introduction of a proper system of meat inspection (see Chapter 8).

The second aspect of the project requiring immediate and expert study is the potential supply of meat for storage. Cyrenaican exports of cattle, sheep and goats vary from year to year, but have in recent years never exceeded 125,000 animals in total, which is the equivalent of approximately 10 tons of meat a day. The proposed plant capacity would greatly exceed currently available export surpluses of livestock. It may well be that the livestock development program will result in larger surpluses in future, but there is no sign of these materializing at present, and the rise in meat prices during the past year is indicative of shortage. Apart from operational expenses, depreciation and interest costs alone would amount to £L 1.40 for the daily storage of one ton of meat if the chilling and cold storage plants were to operate at full capacity; serious consideration should therefore be given to extending the project by providing facilities for the recovery of by-products so as to reduce meat processing costs.

Prospects for the storage of beef and mutton for local consumption in Benghazi should also be investigated. Present consumption is estimated at three tons a day. During the period 1956-58 the average mutton price at the Benghazi market varied between 20 piasters per kilo in spring and summer and 55 piasters per kilo in late winter. The seasonal price difference would provide room for the profitable storage of mutton, thereby leveling out prices in the interest of the consumers. But larger supplies would be needed to make efficient use of the plants, and the people in Benghazi should be encouraged to consume frozen instead of fresh mutton.

Date Processing

The date processing industry is at present confined to alcohol distilling and the preparation of table dates and paste for human consumption. There are two distilleries in the country, both located in Tripoli, which require together 500 tons of dates per year to produce 1,200 hectoliters of alcohol: their output covers all domestic requirements for medicinal alcohol and for the manufacture of liqueurs. Distilling costs are too high to enter the export trade, and since domestic consumption is limited, there is little prospect for an expansion of the industry. In recent years two date packing plants have been established, one by the government in Tripoli and the other in the Kufra oasis in Cyrenaica as a private enterprise; their combined yearly output is approximately 1,000 tons. Total date requirements for industrial purposes may thus be estimated at 1,500 tons or less than 5 percent of the annual date crop.

To improve nutritional standards, the government initiated in 1955 a school-feeding program under which processed dates are distributed free of charge to the school population. This was the reason for the setting-up of the date packing house in Tripoli where Fezzan dates, and to a very limited extent coastal Bikraari dates, are graded, fumigated, mechanically washed, dried and packed. The plant, managed by the Tripolitanian Government on behalf of the federal government, has a capacity of 1,200 tons to 1,800 tons per season depending on the type of date to be processed; £L 40,000 is invested in the enterprise. Actual output has been considerably less since the Ministry of Education, which administers the school-feeding program, has so far only contracted for yearly supplies of 500 tons to 700 tons; another 200 tons for the scheme is supplied by the Kufra plant. The date packing house has not been able to cover expenses, and during the period September 1957 to October 1958, when commercial accounting was first introduced, the plant suffered a loss of £L 7,000 inclusive of depreciation and interest charges. The price paid for the dates was, of course, an artificial one, but there is reason to believe that costs of production were excessive. Factors contributing to high costs include: underutilization of plant capacity; purchase of dates at prices above current market rates; and employment of more workers than required for efficient production.

Consumer taste has tended since the war to shift away from dates as a staple food in favor of cereals. While dates should continue to be bought for the school-feeding program, the quantities of dates required for distribution under the program are unlikely to grow rapidly in view of the fact that other more popular foods, such as wheat flour and milk powder, are being provided under U. S. relief schemes. With this prospect in view, and considering that civil domestic consumption of processed dates is very limited, the management of the date packing house has been trying to find export markets for its product. Experiments are also being made to manufacture date paste for the confectionery industry. So far not more than 100 tons of processed dates have found their way abroad, mainly to the United Kingdom and to continental Europe. Another possibility which deserves attention for utilizing the idle plant capacity would be the grading and processing for export of other fruits such as winter tomatoes.

A promising project to increase the industrial utilization of the Libyan date is the manufacture of date syrup. With the assistance of the FAO and the Netherlands Government, a small date syrup extraction plant has been installed in Tripoli. This pilot plant has a capacity of one ton of syrup of 75° Brix per 24 hours. Capital investment amounts to £L 20,000, and the plant would process 250 tons of dates annually for the manufacture of 200 tons of syrup. An advantage of the process is that the low-quality Bikraari date, which is unsuitable as a table fruit, can be successfully used as a raw material for syrup extraction. Further, the pollution of dates with sand, which increases the cost of processing for direct human consumption, does not present a major difficulty in syrup manufacture. It is proposed to utilize the plant to supply syrup under the school-feeding program, possibly to be mixed with milk, but at the time of the mission's visit no decision had been taken by the government as to the quantities to be supplied or the price to be charged. Calculations indicate that a small commercial plant with a capacity of 1,000 tons could produce syrup at a price of approximately £L 42 per ton, as compared with a sugar price of £L 38 per ton c.i.f. Tripoli; such a price would enable the plant to compete successfully with imported syrups. The domestic market is, however, too small to support a plant of such minimum economic size, and its establishment would thus depend on the development of an export trade.

To sum up, the mission recommends that the government should try to develop date processing on the following lines:

1. Measures should be taken to ensure that the government date packing house is operated as a commercial enterprise; it should economize on labor and purchase dates at current market rates; attention should also be paid to using the plant in the off-season for other processing activities.

2. There would appear to be little possibility of the Libyan date competing successfully as a table date on the European market with dates from other areas, particularly from Iraq and Tunisia. However, Libya enjoys a tariff preference in Italy, and in view of the importance of finding new outlets for dates the government should investigate the possibilities in this direction. If results are disappointing, the effort should be abandoned.

3. Vigorous action should be taken to start experiments with date syrup manufacture. Since the future of the project depends in large measure on the development of export markets, special attention should be paid to exploring the export opportunities for this product.

Curing, Tanning and Leather Manufacture

Curing. With an average export value during 1952-57 of approximately £L 200,000 per year, the curing of hides and skins is the only major domestic export industry apart from olive oil. Better flaying and curing practices would increase earnings and exports, and the development of the domestic tanning industry (which, in turn, largely determines the growth of leather manufacturing) depends on the supply of quality hides and skins. The government, with assistance from FAO,[2] has therefore since 1951 taken active steps, mainly in Tripolitania, to improve flaying and curing practices through demonstrations of improved techniques, the enactment of a Hides and Skins (Improvement) Law to raise the skills of the flayers through a system of flaying licenses, the distribution of denatured salt at concessional rates to the curers and

[2] R. Faraday Innes, *The Improvement of Flaying, Curing and Tanning of Hides and Skins,* FAO Report No. 216, Rome, 1953; C. F. Harding, *Improvement of Flaying and Curing of Hides and Skins,* FAO Report No. 441, Rome, 1956.

the training abroad of one Libyan official. These activities have undoubtedly helped to develop curing in the province as demonstrated by the increased salt consumption in the industry, which amounted to 119 tons in 1958 against 56 tons in 1954.

However, it would appear that, since the departure in 1958 of the last of the three FAO experts, this promotional activity has lost its momentum. The Tripolitanian Hides, Skins and Leather Committee, which made a very useful contribution by bringing together government officials, flayers, curers, tanners and exporters, is no longer meeting regularly. The main problem which faces the industry is not so much the dissemination of improved techniques as the promotion of a wider application of these techniques. This depends on the introduction of better marketing practices whereby, through a system of price differentials in the purchase of hides and skins, the flayers and curers can be induced to take better care of their product. The proposed establishment of technical rules for the export of hides and skins is being considered by the Tripolitanian Government and should undoubtedly improve the present defective marketing procedures.

So far, little has been achieved in Cyrenaica in improving the industry. The mission understands that the Law of Raw Skins, which contains similar provisions to those of the Tripolitanian Hides and Skins (Improvement) Law, is not being enforced, partly because of lack of competent personnel. Considering the importance of the livestock industry in the province, the mission strongly recommends that this law should be implemented without delay, initially in a limited geographical area which could be progressively expanded. Consideration should also be given to establishment of a coordinating and advisory committee along the lines of the one in Tripolitania, so as to support government promotional activity. In view of the absence of qualified personnel to guide and organize the development of the industry, the mission recommends that a qualified foreign flaying and curing specialist should be engaged for at least five years as a federal official to advise and assist the provincial governments. In addition, a systematic program for the training of Libyan personnel should be initiated. The cost of this program would amount to £L 20,000.

Tanning. With one exception, the tanning industry consists of a small number of primitively equipped and operated plants, producing low-quality leather which can satisfy only the demand of the poorer sections of the rural population. The leather required for the shoe industry is wholly imported, while the quality of artistic leather work is being kept down because of the supply of defective raw materials.

The yearly import value of leather has increased substantially from £L 32,000 in 1954 to approximately £L 58,000 in 1958, and should grow further if measures are taken to promote the domestic shoe industry. Further, there should be good opportunities to export tanned instead of cured skins so as to increase export earnings. There is thus ample room to improve and expand domestic leather production for local consumption and export. The development of the tanning industry has been the subject of an FAO study,[3] the findings of which the mission fully supports. In particular, the mission recommends the establishment of a pilot tannery production, demonstration and training center, preferably in Tripolitania where Misurata might be the best location. The main objective of this undertaking would be to demonstrate to local tanners the importance of modern processing techniques, to operate as an extension center for the existing plants and to train skilled personnel required to modernize the industry. The required capital would amount to £L 35,000, providing employment to some 20 workers. The center should be initially established by the government and should operate for a number of years as a public undertaking; after it has served its objective and has demonstrated its profitability, it should be sold to private interests. A foreign specialist should be employed for a period of five years for the management of the plant. At the same time two Libyans should be sent abroad for training in modern tanning techniques. The total cost of the program would amount to £L 60,000.

Leather Manufacture. The domestic manufacture of leather products is limited to footwear, harness gear and a variety of artistic products (mainly for the tourist trade). Although the consumption of footwear in Libya at 0.3 pairs of shoes per head a year is not quite the lowest in the world, it is still appreciably below that of other countries in the Mediterranean region. The domestic shoe industry is of recent origin. There are two plants in Benghazi and Tripoli respectively, of which one, being a subsidiary of an international footwear concern, is at present confined to assembling footwear out of imported parts. Handicrafts production is limited to cobblers who ply their trade in rural towns. The import of footwear has nearly doubled from £L 178,000 in 1954 to over £L 300,000 in 1958, but domestic output still accounts for only 10-15 percent of the yearly demand. The industry is supported through tariff concessions and import restrictions, but has difficulty in getting a larger share of the market, partly because of

[3] C. C. van Hoorn, *The Improvement of Hides, Skins, Leather and Leather Articles*, FAO Report No. 975, 1958.

consumers' preference for imported footwear. The fact that domestic leathers are less suitable for the manufacture of quality footwear and that all leather for footwear manufacture on a factory scale has to be imported adds to the difficulties of the industry. To place the industry on a better footing, the Benghazi factory requires assistance from a footwear manufacturing specialist so as to improve its operational practices; the cost of such assistance is included in the expenditure proposed for supporting an industrial extension service. The industry should receive preferential treatment in respect of government purchases as recommended in Chapter 9.

Flour Milling

The flour-milling industry consists of three large modern plants in Tripoli, a few small but fairly modern units in Benghazi and a number of very small grist mills (each with a capacity of approximately 0.3 tons of wheat or barley per hour) in the main coastal towns. Total milling capacity is estimated at 280 tons of wheat per 24 hours or approximately 84,000 tons per year. The largest plants mainly process domestic wheat of the hard and soft varieties into different types of flour for bread, pasta ("semola") and couscous ("semolene"); small quantities of imported wheat are also used. The small mills are processing domestic wheat and barley into a coarse type of flour. At the time of the mission's visit two of the modern mills in Tripoli had considerable idle capacity, estimated at 90 percent of the installed equipment (160 tons per 24 hours). The third mill (50 tons per 24 hours) had only recently been established and was assisted by the government in that it was being permitted to operate on duty-free imported wheat under facilities provided in accordance with the Law for the Promotion of National Industries. Milling cost varies, depending on capacity utilization, between £L 3 and £L 7 per ton. Since in recent years the price of imported wheat has been consistently higher than that of imported flour, and since the same duty (£L 7 per ton) is levied on both imported wheat and flour, it is difficult for local industry to process imported wheat, particularly as the domestic market for bran is restricted by the underdeveloped state of the dairy industry.

Elsewhere in the report (Chapter 8), the mission has recommended the adoption of a policy for promoting the cultivation of wheat in Libya and for substituting home-milled flour for imports. The present milling capacity in the country is very much underutilized, but if flour imports are largely eliminated, the present excess capacity will be

TABLE A.16   Average C.I.F. Values of Wheat Flour and Wheat Per Ton

(£L)

	Wheat flour	Wheat
1955	31.6	32.4
1956	32.2	40.3
1957	31.0	34.5
1958	26.0	n.a.[a]

[a] No wheat was imported commercially into Libya in 1958.

taken up, and some additional capacity will be required. On the basis of recent figures for imports and domestic production, total annual wheat requirements amount to about 100,000 tons, against a present milling capacity of 84,000 tons per year. Any further expansion of the milling industry should be directed toward the establishment of mills in the wheat-growing areas.

TABLE A.17   Wheat Consumption Estimates

	Tons
Average yearly domestic production of wheat (1956–58)	27,700
Average yearly import of wheat (1954–57)	19,100
Average yearly import of wheat flour (1954–57) converted into wheat	54,400
Total average yearly domestic wheat consumption	101,200

Fruit and Vegetable Processing

In recent years a growing demand has developed for a variety of canned agricultural products, including orange, grape and tomato juices, ketchups and sauces, jellies and concentrates. Imports have risen sharply from £L 152,000 in 1955 to £L 366,000 in 1957, but only one of these products, tomato paste, is being processed domestically. A factory was established in Tripoli in 1954, and a second plant, also in

Tripoli, was scheduled to start operations during the 1959 processing season.

The growth of domestic production and the still fairly high import volume indicate that the present consumption of tomato paste may amount to 2,500 tons annually. Domestic production may rise to approximately 2,000 tons when the second factory has come into operation, but as demand for this product is growing rapidly, there should be room for a third plant with a processing capacity of 800 tons per season. Such a plant may require a capital investment of about £L 90,000, including funds for the pre-financing of the tomato crop. Employment would amount to a few permanent and about 120 seasonal workers. Since only 15 kilograms of paste are processed out of every 100 kilograms of tomatoes, the plant should be located in a tomato-growing area, so as to economize on transport costs. The most profitable location for a third factory might be in Cyrenaica, possibly in the Jalo oasis, where tomatoes are already grown. Such a location would have the additional advantage of being able to recruit seasonal labor in the area. Moreover, the Cyrenaican market can be more cheaply supplied by local production than by import from Tripoli.

So far little progress has been made with the processing of other fruits and vegetables. The opportunities have been explored in an FAO report,[4] and the findings of this report by and large support the mission's view that efforts to develop such an industry are sound and economically justified. Instead, however, of establishing one large integrated processing plant, as proposed in the report, the mission suggests a more gradual approach either through the construction of a number of units or by extending existing plants. The tomato paste industry in particular could well add other products to its processing program, thereby making better use of its equipment which now stands idle during the greater part of the year.

Similarly, more might be done to process edible nuts. Groundnuts are exported in shells for direct human consumption, and have as such to be graded in size and appearance so as to meet the fairly high quality requirements of foreign buyers. In recent years, production and export have increased substantially, exports rising from 4,000 tons in 1952/53 to 10,500 tons in 1958/59. Consequently, the residue unsuitable for export has also increased and has reached a point where sufficient supplies should justify the local processing of this product. There should be opportunities for the manufacture of peanut butter and for the processing of canned, roasted and salted groundnuts and almonds for

[4] Gustave Roebben, *The Establishment of a Fruit and Vegetable Cannery*, FAO Report No. 613, 1957.

domestic consumption and possibly, at a later stage, for export as well.

Capital requirements for light agricultural processing industries are modest, processing techniques are simple, and the scale of operations could be kept small. The reason why so far no local production has developed is mainly to be found in the absence of sufficient information on processing techniques, particularly in relation to the limited size of the domestic market, and the fear that it will be difficult for local production to compete with well-known import brands.

Technical assistance for fruit and vegetable processing could be provided by the assignment of a processing specialist under the scheme which the mission suggests should be operated through an Industrial Credit Department of the National Bank. The proposed course in food technology at the Institute of Higher Technology will in time furnish a supply of young Libyan technicians for the industry. A slight increase in the customs tariff might be considered, and regulations should be enacted prescribing standards for the hygienic processing and packing of food products.

The two Italian laws regulating the manufacture of, and trade in, preserved vegetables and fish products, although never repealed, are not being enforced any more. This has the unfortunate result that western consumers in Libya are hesitant to buy the local product. The mission was also informed that the absence of properly enforced standards of hygiene largely excludes the Wheelus Base from purchasing locally-processed food products for its forces and their dependents.[5] The mission does not favor enforcing the Italian regulations, which are not geared to the requirements of Libyan industry. Instead, the government should enact a simple law empowering the Minister of Finance and Economics to issue rules for processing and packing of selected food products as and when necessary for raising standards to meet market requirements. The law might initially be applied to macaroni, refined olive oil, tomato paste and canned fish products and extended to other products in due course. The government laboratory in Tripoli could assist in the enforcement of the regulations.

Olive Oil

Olive oil processing, which is responsible for much the largest number of units of any industry in Libya, has expanded steadily in recent years. According to a census taken in 1953, a total of 715 units were

[5] Wheelus Base could provide a most attractive market for domestic food products since the purchasing power of the personnel stationed there cannot be much less than that of all the Libyans in the town of Tripoli.

in operation in Tripolitania that year, of which 135 were mechanical, 108 animal-driven and 472 hand-operated. Their combined capacity was probably about 6,000 quintals of olives in 10 hours. Since then, the number of units has been appreciably reduced, but total capacity has increased as the inefficient hand and animal presses have been, and are still being, progressively replaced by mechanical equipment. More recent estimates, admittedly highly uncertain, indicate that by early 1959 the number of mechanical presses had increased to 200, while numbers of animal-driven and hand-operated presses had been reduced to 80 and 200 respectively. As many as 10 mechanical presses are probably now being installed each year, a few of the simpler ones being manufactured in Tripoli. There are only a few mechanical presses in operation in Cyrenaica since most of the olive trees are still in the nonproductive stage. The total capital invested in the industry in Libya as a whole might well amount to £L 400,000, providing employment during the processing season for up to 2,500 workers, depending on the volume of the olive crop.

No industry in Libya presents such a wide variation in applied technology. The hand-operated presses, mainly located in the Tripolitanian Gebel, are simply stone, timber and rope contraptions probably dating back from Roman times. Their processing capacity is not more than one quintal each in 10 hours, whereas the larger plants using modern machinery have a capacity of 100 quintals to 300 quintals in 10 hours. Four modern refining plants, which are also equipped to recover oil from sansa, have been established along the coast under Italian ownership and management; exhausted sansa is being used as fuel, but 80 percent of this product still runs to waste.

The future development of the industry depends in large measure on the availability for export of greater quantities of oil of uniform quality and of grades accepted internationally. It is claimed that 40 percent of total oil production has an acidity content of less than 1½ percent, 40 percent between 1½ percent and 4 percent (so-called *lampante* oil, which requires refining), and 20 percent between 4 percent and 8 percent. The Italian and most of the Libyan olive farmers along the coast are producing oil of excellent quality. The position is much less favorable in the Tripolitanian Gebel, where most olive growers are small holders dispersed over a relatively large area, and where most of the hand-operated and animal-driven presses are located. The low output, high acidity and variable quality of the oil pressed in this area makes it unsuitable for export. However, the Tripolitanian Government, assisted by the foreign aid agencies and FAO, have taken commendable action to promote the modernization of this sector of the industry. Four small but highly productive mechanical pressing units, each with a capacity of 25 quintals in 10 hours, were installed in various places in the Gebel in 1957 at a unit cost of about £L 6,000. These units are at present operated by the Tripolitanian Nazirate of Agriculture, but it is intended to have them eventually organized into cooperatives of olive growers. These plants are serving a most useful purpose, not only for production, but also as demonstration units; more than 15 additional plants of the same type have been installed by private investors. The standardization of equipment has the considerable advantage of simplifying maintenance and repair services, including the stocking of spare parts and expendable materials such as filtering disks. The government should consider additional measures to accelerate the modernization of this part of the industry, for instance, by providing long-term credit for the installation of more modern equipment (through the medium of the proposed Industrial Credit Department).

Printing

Printing is one of the few industries in which Libyan entrepreneurship has shown an increasing interest. Before the war the industry was exclusively owned and operated by foreigners, but in recent years a number of Libyan enterprises have come into existence. Of the twelve private shops existing in the country, which are all located in Tripoli and Benghazi, five are owned, and in part operated, by Libyans. The provincial governments have set the pace by establishing printing undertakings in the three provincial capitals. These are mainly working for government, but the mission noted that an increasing amount of work was being done for private customers in competition with private industry. No commercial accounting system is applied in these undertakings, and this opens the door for unfair competition with private printing shops. Since it is the policy of the government to promote private rather than public enterprises, the public printing shops should refrain from accepting private work as long as the private sector is in a position to supply the demand for printed matter. Apart from this, it is advisable to introduce commercial accounting in the government undertakings as an incentive to efficient management.

The consumption of paper has increased steadily since 1954. The rapid extension of education will do much to stimulate the demand for printed matter, and the government should include the printing trade in its program for industrial development.

The Libyan sector of the industry is faced with a number of problems of which the most pressing is the lack of skilled personnel, including works supervisors and managerial staff. Although in the main the industry is well equipped with modern machinery, output levels are low, qualitatively as well as quantitatively. The mission gathered the impression that labor productivity may be only about one-quarter that of European workers operating under similar industrial conditions, and this impression was supported by managers of printing works in Libya with experience of the European printing industry. This low productivity is not surprising since printing is one of those trades which requires long and intensive training to create an efficient labor force. So far only a few Libyans have received any formal training in printing techniques; for example, one out of the 80 workers in the government printing press in Tripoli was trained in a printing school abroad. The great majority are learning the trade by "seeing and doing," and no formal system of apprenticeship training is applied in the industry. Since printing is relatively free from international competition, there is thus little incentive to increase output and reduce costs in the interest of the consumers. A first step to improve conditions is the supply of better skilled workers, and it is in this area that the government should step in.

The mission accordingly recommends that the government printing press in Tripoli should systematically develop an apprenticeship training program not only for its own personnel, but also to supply skilled printers for the two other government undertakings and for private firms. The Tripoli Press is the largest of the Libyan-owned enterprises and is rather well managed with the help of a specialist from abroad. Three skilled technicians capable of instructing workers should be employed, initially for a period of three years, to organize the proposed apprenticeship scheme, and the government might turn to ILO for expert advice. In addition, funds should be made available to send a number of young Libyan workers abroad to receive formal schooling in printing techniques so that a cadre of well-trained technicians can be built up. For this purpose we suggest that ten trainees should be selected from the three government presses over a period of five years. The total cost of apprentice training and overseas schooling might run to £L 40,000.

Salt

The production and sale of salt was a government monopoly in Italian times. Salterns based on solar evaporation of sea water were established in both coastal provinces, in Cyrenaica at Giuliana near Benghazi and in Tripolitania at Mellaha near Tripoli. The Giuliana works adjoining the Benghazi harbor had modern equipment, including an overhead transport system to facilitate the loading of salt for export. During the war the works were so thoroughly damaged that large-scale production came to an end, and the monopoly in Cyrenaica was subsequently abolished. Common unrefined salt is now being produced by a number of small hand-operated salterns located along the coast of the province. Their combined yearly output would amount to some 1,000 tons per year, which is sufficient to supply the provincial market. The very limited requirements of table salt are met by import from abroad. The position is similar in the Fezzan where no salt monopoly exists; the requirements of the province are met by import from Tripoli and to a limited extent by exploitation of a few marshland salt deposits.

In Tripolitania, on the other hand, the monopoly has continued to operate, and it at present supplies all the salt requirements in the province apart from the eastern province where marshland salt is available in sufficient quantities for local consumption; the eastern province is therefore excluded from the monopoly area. The Mellaha works, extending over an area of 11 hectares, is favorably located from a manufacturing point of view insofar as the salt pans are situated below sea level. The settling ponds are connected with the sea by an 800-meter long canal, and cost of pumping the brine into the crystallizing pans can therefore be kept to a minimum. The works, however, constitute an enclave within the U. S. Wheelus Base; storage space is limited and free movement of materials and labor is restricted, causing inconvenience for both the military and the monopoly. For this and other reasons the administration is considering relocation of the works at a more suitable site.

The works are equipped with a mechanical scooper and two salt crushers with a combined capacity of 20 tons per eight hours; two years ago a small salt refining and packing unit was added to manufacture table salt. The Mellaha salt is of excellent quality of more than 98 percent purity and free of magnesium. Since the price of table salt is less than that of the imported product, there is no need to continue import of table salt in Cyrenaica. Annual consumption in the area served by the monopoly is currently estimated at 4,500 tons, including some 2,000 tons of industrial salt sold at concessional rates to domestic industries such as fisheries, fish canning and curing of hides and skins. Since the salt consumption of the whole of Libya is estimated at 6,500 tons per year, the monopoly supplies about two-thirds of domestic requirements.

The monopoly's contribution to provincial revenues has been negligible. During the fiscal years 1953/54 to 1957/58 inclusive gross revenue amounted to £L 104,700 against a total expenditure of £L 105,500.[6] In 1958/59, when there were exceptional exports, revenue slightly exceeded profits. The figures are set out in Table A.18.

TABLE A.18   Operations of Tripolitania Salt Monopoly

	(In £L)		(In tons)		
Year	Expenditure	Gross Revenue	Production	Domestic Sales	Export Sales
1952/53	n.a.	n.a.	12,000	2,800	nil
1953/54	13,000	15,900	13,000	3,100	nil
1954/55	20,100	16,200	15,000	3,100	nil
1955/56	22,800	18,300	16,000	3,200	nil
1956/57	22,400	21,900	6,500	3,000	nil
1957/58	27,200	32,400	nil	4,300	380
1958/59	40,469	43,514	13,700	n.a.	31,000

Two main factors appear to be responsible for the disappointing performance of the salt monopoly. In the first place, the salt works in Cyrenaica and Tripolitania were originally established primarily with a view to exporting to Italy and Northern Europe; their combined output before the war was about 50,000 tons per year. After the war, however, shipping rates increased to such an extent that the monopoly was unable to sell its products abroad at competitive prices, and between 1949 and 1957 no salt was exported. Instead of adjusting production to the changed market conditions, the monopoly continued to produce salt in the hope of a resumption of the export trade. As a result, stocks began to accumulate until they amounted in 1957 to some 50,000 tons. Because of lack of storage space, 12,000 tons had to be destroyed in 1956 by dumping it back into the sea, and production had to be suspended in 1957. A drop in freight rates in 1958 made it possible to export 31,000 tons to Italy, at a price, however, which only covered manufacturing cost. Had the monopoly refrained from pursuing a

[6] A small part of this expenditure is attributable to the maintenance of a preventive force for the tobacco monopoly.

policy of producing salt in excess of domestic consumption, it would undoubtedly have earned a net revenue for the administration.

Secondly, it would appear that there is little desire by the management of the monopoly to run the salt works as a commercial undertaking by economizing on resources, including labor, and by taking measures to increase manufacturing efficiency. As a matter of fact, the monopoly is partly operated as an employment relief agency, since many more workers are being employed than are required for efficient production. Calculations indicate that at least one-third of the labor force is redundant since the average output is as low as 500 kilograms of salt per man/day. Even during 1957/58, when no salt was produced, the monopoly employed some 200 workers, since the decision to suspend production was taken only after preparatory work on the salterns had started. The mission understands that this employment policy was initiated during the early postwar years when widespread unemployment existed in the Tripoli area, but it has now lost its meaning in view of the changed conditions in the labor market. Further, the fact that the salt works are not a self-accounting unit and are operating as a government department instead of as a commercial undertaking does not help to promote efficient management.

Since the government still has hopes of resuming the salt export trade, it is relevant to refer to a UN study of the Mellaha works conducted in 1952/53.[7] The report arrives at the conclusion that there is hardly any opportunity for export to Asian markets, which can be better supplied by salt works located south of the Suez Canal. All Mediterranean countries produce their own marine salt, while, apart from Scandinavia, continental Europe is endowed with considerable salt deposits. Present freight rates to the Scandinavian market are prohibitive for export from Libya.

While recognizing that the Mellaha works are inconveniently located, the mission suggests that manufacture should continue there, since the facilities are sufficient to supply the domestic market for many years to come. If, however, a significant drop in shipping rates made it possible to resume exports on a continuous basis, a saltern should be established at an alternative site where loading costs can be kept to a minimum. (The cost of transport from Mellaha to Tripoli harbor is as much as the cost of production.) Consideration might then be given to rehabilitation of the Giuliana salt works, which is in the Benghazi harbor area and therefore well located to produce salt for export.

[7] W. H. Campbell, *Preliminary Report on Mellaha Salt Works in Tripolitania*, UN Mission in Libya, Report Series No. 16, 1953.

It is further recommended that the monopoly be reorganized in such a way that it will fulfill its original purpose of earning revenue for the administration. To this end the mission recommends that the monopoly enter into a contract with a private firm to manage the salt works on its behalf as a commercial enterprise. The experience of the tobacco monopoly in this respect has been satisfactory, and there is no reason why the salt monopoly could not be profitably operated along similar lines.

Soap

At the time of the mission's visit there were 16 small soap factories in Libya, of which 15 were located in Tripoli and one in Homs; their combined manufacturing capacity was estimated at 1,000 tons of hard washing soap per month. The plants are very primitively equipped and operated. Many plants have closed down since 1956, and those which are still operating have considerably reduced their output. According to an investigation made in July 1957 by the Tripolitanian Nazirate of Finance and Economics, the monthly output was then only 43 tons. Although no recent statistics are available, the mission understands that present output levels are even lower, and that 11 plants have closed down or suspended production since the investigation was made. On the other hand, imports of soap have substantially increased in recent years from 774 tons of laundry soap (value £L 57,000) in 1954 to approximately 1,400 tons (£L 150,000) in 1958; during the same period the import of toilet soap increased from 148 tons (£L 23,000) to approximately 300 tons (£L 50,000). The industry is based on sansa oil. The local product is generally of a fair quality, with a fatty acid content of 50 percent to 70 percent.

The decline in local soap manufacture is mainly due to the price increase of sansa oil in recent years which is finding a more profitable market overseas, in part as a result of the duty-free import quota into Italy. Further, the rise in living standards has contributed to increased consumption of detergents and powdered, flaked and liquid soap products.

To assist the industry, it has been proposed to switch the raw material basis from sansa oil to other vegetable oils such as coconut and palm oil. The import duty on such oils, at present £L 30 per ton, would have to be substantially reduced to make this possible;[8] similarly, the

[8] From 1954 to 1957 imports of vegetable oils averaged over 2,000 tons a year valued at £L 300,000.

import duty on caustic soda, at present 25 percent, should also be reduced, while the import duty of hard washing soap should be considerably increased. The olive oil refineries would benefit from increased soap production, since they could refine crude vegetable oils and secure better utilization of their plants, which are at present working for only a few months of the year.

In the mission's view such a policy would be justified only if at the same time measures are taken to modernize the industry by introducing improved techniques, permitting the manufacture of a good quality soap at reasonable prices. Total domestic soap consumption in Libya is still low, amounting to less than 2 kilograms per capita per year. A policy of promoting this local industry at the expense of the consumer cannot therefore be justified. Since the total consumption of hard washing soap may be estimated at about 2,000 tons per year, there should in principle be an opportunity to establish a small but modern plant, together with a glycerine recovery unit. We therefore suggest that the economic prospects for such an enterprise be carefully investigated.

Tobacco Products

The cultivation and import of tobacco, and the manufacture, import and sale of tobacco products, including requisites for processing, is a monopoly of the Tripolitanian Government under legislation promulgated by the former Italian Administration. For the management of the monopoly, the British Military Administration entered into a contract with a foreign company in 1946, and the provincial government took the contract over in 1952. Under the terms of the agreement, the company issues licenses to tobacco growers, wholesalers and retailers in the province, establishes prices for tobacco and tobacco products, and manages a tobacco factory in Tripoli which is the only enterprise of its kind in the country. These functions are discharged under the guidance and supervision of the provincial government. The monopoly is an important source of revenue, net profits accruing to the provincial government having increased from £L 370,000 in 1952/53 to £L 754,000 in 1958/59.

The legal basis for the monopoly in Cyrenaica is a proclamation of the former British Administration in 1947 which also designates the company as its managing agent. No licenses are being issued for tobacco cultivation, and the monopoly is therefore confined to the sale of tobacco products. Revenue accruing to the administration amounted to £L 277,000 in the fiscal year 1957/58. According to the proclamation, interprovincial trade in tobacco products is restricted and subject to customs duties.

In the Fezzan, the trade in tobacco products is in the hands of the government, but people are free to cultivate tobacco, which is done on a limited scale for household consumption. Since the Fezzan Administration has so far not used its prerogative under Article 38 of the Constitution to monopolize the industry, no legal basis exists for the present practice of using the tobacco sales as a source of revenue.

Previously in the report (Chapter 8) the mission has reviewed the present policy concerning tobacco cultivation and has recommended the progressive removal of restrictions on growing. This recommendation is designed not only to promote an orderly development of tobacco cultivation, but also to improve the operational practices in the factory in Tripoli. The factory would then be in a position to purchase domestic tobaccos of the required quantities and qualities at competitive prices, thereby increasing its earning capacity. We turn now to two other areas in which the monopoly operates, namely manufacture and selling.

The factory is a small, but modern, well-equipped and well-managed plant. It supplies approximately 90 percent of domestic consumption, at present estimated at some 700 million cigarettes per year. Since 1952 some £L 150,000 has been invested in new equipment, thereby nearly doubling capacity, which is currently 3.3 million cigarettes per eight hours. Cigarette consumption has increased steadily since 1952 at an average rate of 8 percent per year. Since current output is approximately 50 percent of rated capacity (based on a two-shift operation), there is room for some years to come to meet rising domestic demand without enlarging the enterprise.

The factory is employing more workers than justified by current production levels. Moreover, wages paid (at an average of £L 225 per worker per year) are considerably higher than elsewhere in private industry (£L 125 per worker per year), whereas working hours are shorter than in private industry. Restrictions are placed on the hiring and dismissal of workers, wage setting and the determination of conditions of work.

As the mission sees it, the principal objective of the monopoly is to earn revenue for the government, and to achieve this objective the factory should be left free to operate on sound business lines. The mission can see no justification for a policy under which a tiny fraction of the working population is placed in a privileged position solely by virtue of its employment in a public enterprise, thereby receiving at the expense of the taxpayers more favorable treatment than that accorded to workers in private industry. We would therefore strongly urge that in future the managing agent should be left free within the limits prescribed by legislation to operate the factory in a manner consistent with the objective of earning revenue for the government.

As stated earlier, the monopoly issues licenses to wholesalers and retailers in tobacco products. No restrictions are placed on the number of retailers appointed in any area, since it is considered to the advantage of the monopoly to have its products on sale at as many shops as possible. On the other hand, the number of appointed wholesalers for each district is limited according to the size of the population; the reasoning behind this is to ensure that only financially sound and otherwise adequately equipped wholesalers are handling this trade. The restrictions have naturally increased the earning capacity of the individual wholesalers, and a wholesaler's license is therefore in much demand. At the same time difficulties are being encountered by the monopoly in selecting and appointing wholesalers. The mission can see no justification for subjecting trade in this commodity to special regulations. It is unlikely that the licensing system has contributed significantly to increased sales volume and revenue earnings; on the other hand, it harbors the danger of abuse and patronage. The mission therefore recommends that the trade in tobacco products throughout the country should be free from any restriction apart from that of fixing wholesale and retail prices.

Weaving

The Libyan weaving industry consists of three sectors—self-subsistence weaving, handlooms and the powerloom industry. Approximately 20,000 women in rural areas are engaged part-time in producing from local wool such products as rugs and carpets, tent material and, to a limited extent, barracanes.[9] The looms in use have a low output; they generally consist of weaving frames of the horizontal or vertical type, in which the shuttle is thrown by hand. The industry is, however, well geared into the living habits and consumption patterns of the nomadic and semi-sedentary populations, and little or no competition is encountered from imports or from the two other domestic weaving sectors.

[9] The principal external clothing for both men and women.

The second category of weavers, of whom 1,000 to 1,500 are in Tripoli, use heavy hand-operated fly shuttle looms and produce wool, cotton and artificial silk barracanes out of imported yarn for sale in the market. It is claimed that 60 percent to 70 percent of the weavers are working for merchants under a contract system, whereby the looms and the yarn are supplied by the merchants, and operators earn about 30 piasters a day for manufacturing the woven product according to certain specifications as to design, quality and size. The craft can thus be considered as a form of decentralized factory industry.

Lastly, there are two power-loom weaving units, respectively in Benghazi and Tripoli. The Benghazi plant was established before the war under foreign ownership and management; it has installed 70 looms partly equipped with jaquard attachment and is manufacturing mostly ladies' barracanes and fabrics with the traditional designs peculiar to the country. In 1958 a small plant equipped with six modern looms started operations in Tripoli with Libyan capital, but under Italian management; the plant is manufacturing ladies' fabrics of the traditional type. Both plants are working exclusively with imported materials.

Apart from household weaving, rough estimates indicate that in 1958 domestic consumption was approximately 23 million square meters of various types of fabrics, of which 20 million were imported (87 percent), 2.3 million produced by the Tripoli handloom industry (10 percent) and 0.7 million manufactured in the two mechanized plants (3 percent).

The Tripolitanian Government has adopted a policy of protecting the urban handloom weavers from competition from factory-made barracanes, both of domestic and foreign origin. The import of barracanes is prohibited, and the Tripoli factory has been induced by the government not to manufacture such fabrics, so as to reserve this production for the handloom industry. It would seem that the handloom weavers are a well-organized group who are able to exert strong pressures on the administration.

The mission strongly recommends that this policy be reconsidered. Cost calculations indicate that the machine-made product would cost at least 30 percent less than handwoven fabrics, and lower cost levels could be reached if the industry were given free reign to expand. We realize that the livelihood of some 1,500 families is a matter of grave concern to the government, and that their interests should not be treated lightly. But we cannot agree that the interests of the Libyan consumer in general should be sacrificed to those of a small minority.

Moreover, experience in other countries with little unemployment (as distinct from rural under-employment) has shown conclusively that a policy of protecting workers operating with inferior tools and methods is self-defeating since it deprives such workers of the higher earnings and better working conditions which accompany the application of improved techniques. Lastly, the mission is convinced that, through the implementation of a careful plan for the gradual conversion of the handloom industry into power-loom manufacture, much of the accompanying social friction can be avoided or mitigated.

The mission therefore suggests that government should encourage expansion of the power-loom industry, not only for the manufacture of fabrics in competition with handlooms, but also for the production of cloth at present supplied through imports. Imports of all types of cloth have now reached a value of more than £L 1½ million a year, and the import of cotton cloth alone amounts to approximately £L 1 million a year. Arrangements should be made for the expanding power-loom industry to employ exclusively workers at present employed in the handloom sector, who could be easily retrained into machine operators. Further, deliberate efforts should be made to introduce in the handloom industry the manufacture of fancy fabrics for the tourist trade, possibly of a similar type to those being successfully manufactured in the small-scale industries center at Sebha. Technical and financial assistance would be required to induce the weavers (and perhaps even more so the controlling merchants) to adopt such new production lines, and marketing assistance could be provided by the proposed handicrafts emporia in Tripoli and Benghazi. A specialist should be engaged under the auspices of the proposed Industrial Credit Department to draw up a plan of operations.

Miscellaneous Industries

Beer. Consumption has increased from 20,800 hectoliters in 1954 to 30,000 hectoliters in 1958, but the share of this trade obtained by Libya's only beer factory, located in Tripoli, dropped from 66 percent to 52 percent during the same period. The factory, which manufactures a good product, is at present operating at only 43 percent of capacity. Local beer is subjected to an excise tax of £L 4.812 per hectoliter, which is rather high as compared with similar taxes in other countries. The import duty on beer varies according to the alcoholic content from £L 6 to £L 9 per hectoliter, but imported beer is free from excise tax. In many countries with a domestic beer industry imported beer is subjected to an excise tax in addition to import duty so as to provide domestic production with a reasonable measure of protection. We would recommend that the Libyan Government consider the adoption of a similar policy in the interest of local industry.

Bottle Caps. Total domestic consumption of bottle caps, mainly by soft-drink manufacturers, is estimated at 12 million annually; all bottle caps are imported from abroad. Since the soft-drink industry is steadily growing, it should be possible to establish a small plant for the manufacture of such bottle caps out of imported tin plate. Investment costs would be small and the manufacturing technique simple.

Household Utensils. Imports of household utensils have increased from £L 48,000 in 1955 to approximately £L 130,000 in 1958. The domestic market is now large enough to justify the establishment of a small mechanized plant for making household utensils out of imported aluminum sheet metal. The capital requirements for such a plant would be about £L 30,000, and it would provide employment for some 25 workers. To promote the establishment of such a plant, technical assistance might be provided by the proposed Industrial Credit Department. Further, the import duty on household utensils made of iron, steel and brass should be raised from 20 percent to 25 percent so as to equalize the duty with that on similar products made of aluminum. The Moslem Arts and Crafts School is experimenting with the manufacture of pressed utensils.

Metal Containers. The vegetable and fish canning factories are each equipped with small and primitive units for the manufacture of cans for their own use out of imported tin sheet. Since the enterprises are all working on a seasonal basis, this practice is wasteful and uneconomic. Investigations should be made as to the possibility of establishing a small but modern plant for the manufacture of flattened cans.

Ready-made Clothing. The import of ready-made clothing has increased sharply in the last few years from £L 509,450 in 1954 to approximately £L 1,000,000 in 1958, thereby reflecting the rise in living standards, as well as a shift in consumers' preference toward western dress. This rapid increase has favored domestic production, and a small ready-made clothing plant was established in Tripoli in 1958. Considering the relatively high labor costs, particularly for semi-skilled and skilled labor, the mechanization of the tailoring trade has considerable advantages. Preliminary comparative cost calculations indicate that for certain types of clothing savings of up to 50 percent can be achieved through mechanized production as compared with hand manufacture. Moreover, this is the only way in which domestic industry would be in a position to capture a share of the market in competition with imports. The mission therefore recommends investigation into the possibility of a further expansion of the industry, particularly in view of the clothing requirements of the armed forces.

Tire Retreading. A small but highly efficient tire retreading plant, affiliated with a reputable international concern, was established in Tripoli in 1952 and is at present retreading some 4,000 tires a year. This would seem to be a low figure, considering that there are about 30,000 motor vehicles in the country, requiring a yearly import of tires to the amount of £L 400,000. To stimulate the retreading of tires, the mission suggests a reduction in the import duty on rubber material (at present 10 percent) and possibly an increase in the duty on tires (at present 25 percent).

Vegetable Fiber Processing. Recently a small plant was established in Tripoli to manufacture fibers for stuffing and upholstery from date palm fronds. This industry is well established in Morocco, which exports appreciable quantities of such fibers (manufactured from the *doum* or dwarf palm), but it is the first of its kind in Libya. The government should give this enterprise every assistance possible since, if successful, it could become a most important rural industry in the areas where date palms grow.

ANNEX XIV *HANDICRAFTS IN THE DESERT OASES*

Sebha is the only desert oasis where there is sufficient purchasing power to support any organized industry. A few factories have in fact recently been established there, including a government printing press and a motor vehicle repair shop, and plans are under consideration for a soft drinks plant. A small date grading, washing and packing unit is operating in the Kufra oasis for export to coastal Cyrenaica. Apart from this, industry in the desert oases is confined to manual crafts, largely based on the few raw materials available locally, such as animal fibers for the manufacture of clothing, tents and furnishings and vegetable fibers derived from date palms or rushes which are used for basketry, matting and rope making. Clay is also used in a few cases to make coarse household pottery. Only in exceptional cases are hides and skins locally tanned, and the manufacture of footwear and harness equipment is based in part on material imported from Tripoli. Likewise, scrap imported from Cyrenaica is used for iron and copper work. These crafts are predominantly pursued by women as a part-time occupation, and production is mainly for local consumption.

The best prospects for industrial development in the desert oases thus appear to be in the promotion of handicrafts. A small-scale industries center was set up in 1958 with the assistance of the ILO and USOM, and about 80 young Fezzanese are at present being trained there in a variety of crafts. The products of the center are intended partly for sale in Tripoli to foreign buyers and partly to meet local needs; they include carpets, fancy handloom fabrics, rush matting, packing boxes and simple furniture. The mission was most favorably impressed with the operation of the center and especially with the evident keenness and ability of the trainees to master new skills in a comparatively short time.

Consideration is being given to the possibility of eventually organizing the center as a workers' cooperative society, with its trainees taking over its operation and management. While there are undoubted advantages in centralizing production facilities, this particular type of cooperative organization calls for marked changes in attitudes and relationships between workers, and such changes are not easily achieved. The mission thus has some doubts as to the likelihood of this form of cooperation succeeding in Libya. An alternative policy, which might be considered, would be to arrange for a physical concentration of production facilities which are owned and operated by independent craftsmen: in this manner a group of independent craftsmen could organize much in the manner of a cooperative society, working under the same roof, yet having surrendered only limited functions and rights to the cooperatives. Or, as another alternative, a development policy could be planned to move toward the establishment in the various oases of independent craft shops in which the trainees could put up their own business. Such shops, run by independent craftsmen, could eventually be grouped into cooperatives for the supply of raw materials, servicing and marketing operations. The center at Sebha could be retained for training and for giving technical assistance to craftsmen, and the proposed handicrafts emporia in Tripoli and Benghazi would provide convenient sales outlets.

For the manufacture of utilitarian products for local use, the mission suggests that the handicrafts center at Sebha should coordinate its activities closely with the fundamental education services organized by the provincial government with the assistance of UNESCO. These services are designed to bring the people in these isolated areas into closer touch with modern life through a number of community centers. These centers should provide a useful medium for disseminating the new skills imparted in the small industries center, particularly in respect of products based on the date palm, which grows in all the oases. Economical manufacture of date palm furniture, for example, requires that such furniture become standard equipment in the Fezzanese homes. This calls for changes in consumers' tastes as well as for the training of crafstmen in new skills. Social change and economic progress are in fact usually complementary, and of nowhere is this more true than the desert oases.

Various experiments are being carried out in Tripoli in processing dates for export and for the manufacture of syrup and in developing the use of date palm fronds for making upholstery and stuffing fibers. If these experiments are successful, consideration might be given to establishing manufacturing units in the Fezzan and in the Kufra oases. Again, if agriculture develops in the Fezzan, there might be room for simple local processing units—for instance, for the pressing of oil seeds.

ANNEX XV *SPONGE FISHING AND TUNNY FISHING*

Sponge Fishing

The Cyrenaican Government tried as early as 1952 to develop a national sponge industry by granting a concession to a private company established for the purpose, which was given the exclusive right to fish sponges in the territorial waters along the Cyrenaican coast. The concession is for ten years and obliges the company to pay the government an annual fee of £L 7,028. Under the terms of the concession, the company is obliged to train Libyan sponge divers and to process all sponges in the country so as to export a fully marketable product. The company started operations in 1954 when a number of Tunisian divers were employed as instructors to train Libyan personnel.

Earlier, in 1953, the company, with the approval of the provincial government, concluded an agreement with the Greek Government under which Greek sponge boats would be allowed to operate within the territorial waters along the Cyrenaican coast against the payment of an annual fee of £L 500 per craft. The company received an appreciable income from this source in the following years.

On the other hand, the experiment in developing sponge fishing operations failed. To begin with, negligible quantities of sponges were collected, while the Libyan workers under training found other, more congenial and remunerative employment, largely in diving for metal scrap. Since 1956, no sponges have been collected by the company at all.

Considering the peculiar and largely hereditary skills required for sponge fishing, and the distinct advantages which the Greek sponge industry has over any newcomer in this field, the mission suggests that no attempt should be made to develop a domestic sponge industry until substantial progress has been made in the development of the surface fishing industry. A law to regulate the activities of foreign sponge fishing boats is understood to be in an advanced stage of preparation.

476

Tunny Fishing

The mission was informed that conclusive evidence, based on the returns of catches over thirty years, shows that an increase in the number of tunny traps, at present thirteen, would not result in a proportional increase in the total catch, and that it is unlikely that the industry could expand further. Promotional efforts should therefore be directed toward a rationalization and modernization of the tunny canning industry, which consists of eight plants located at various places along the Tripolitanian coast from Misurata to Zuara. Concessions for the operation of tunny traps are at present granted on an annual renewable basis. This practice discourages entrepreneurs from investing substantial capital in their enterprises, and we recommend that the government should grant long-term concessions and provide the industry with financial and technical assistance to promote the concentration of the various small processing plants into two large modern canning factories. These might be located in Zanzur and Homs, respectively west and east of Tripoli. Such reorganization would assist in the development of surface fishing by providing better processing facilities, including facilities for converting waste products into fishmeal for use as a fertilizer. Furthermore, we suggest that facilities be provided for the freezing and storing of the local catch so that the canneries could operate over a longer period than the fishing season proper. Technical and financial assistance might be provided by the proposed Industrial Credit Department of the National Bank.

ANNEX XVI *ELECTRIC POWER*

Installed Capacity

The installed capacity and power generated by public utilities as at the beginning of 1959 are shown in Table A.19.

TABLE A.19   Installed Capacity and Power Generated

Location	Installed capacity (kilowatts)	Peak load to date	Power generated (in thousands of kilowatt/hours)			
			1955[c]	1956[c]	1957[c]	1958[c]
Tripoli	18,150[a]	9,400	44,609	47,395	50,688	54,300
Benghazi	6,150	4,020	10,214	12,457	14,977	16,840
Beida (old)	730	—	—	—	—	551
Small stations:						
Cyrenaica	3,112	—	—	—	—	6,679
Tripolitania	1,425		Figures not available			—
Fezzan[b]	376		Figures not available			—

[a] Limit set by steam capacity.
[b] Installed capacity small.
[c] Calendar years for Tripoli and years ending March 31 for other stations.

Tripoli Power

There are two stations belonging to this undertaking, the Marconi steam station (14,900 KW installed, firm capacity 12,700 KW) and the Miani diesel station (5,850 KW installed, firm capacity 5,450 KW). Some of the plant at Marconi is old, and for the purposes of projecting future supply it has been assumed that by 1967 the firm capacity of the now existing plant in the Marconi and Miani stations together will be only about 11,000 KW. Two new units, each of 10,000 KW capacity, have been purchased for the Marconi station and should be installed by 1961. The present steam units are run on coal, but oil will be used for those supplying the two new turbo-generators.

478

The annual increase in consumption of power generated by this undertaking, which had averaged more than 20 percent a year in the early 1940's, fell to 9 percent in the period 1951-58 (as shown in Table A.20).

TABLE A.20   Units Sold by the Tripoli Power Undertaking

(In thousands of kilowatt/hours)

Year	Lighting	Domestic power	Industrial power	Agricultural power (pumping)[a]	Totals[b]
1943	2,250 (21.43%)[a]		4,058 (38.64%)	4,193 (39.93%)	10,501 (100%)
1951	6,067 (26.5%)	182 (0.8%)	5,556 (24.3%)	11,090 (48.4%)	22,895 (100%)
1952	6,978	246	5,316	11,190	23,729
1953	7,830	256	5,530	11,631	25,247
1954	8,667	263	5,463	14,112	28,506
1955	11,021	300	5,969	15,854	33,145
1956	12,979	373	6,140	15,820	35,311
1957	15,972	503	6,899	15,612	38,985
1958	17,850 (42.49%)	598 (1.42%)	7,201 (17.14%)	16,363 (38.95%)	42,012 (100%)

[a] All figures in this column, except the first, include power used in pumping water for municipal and other purposes in addition to pumping water for agriculture.
[b] Difference in totals and percentages due to rounding.

Expenditure by the undertaking on capital equipment amounted to £L 265,863 in the calendar year 1957 and to £L 172,571 in the calendar year 1958. The financial results for these years are shown in Table A.21.

Other Power Stations in Tripolitania

Power stations in the towns of Misurata and Homs are under the control of the Tripoli undertaking. The local people are complaining of bad service, and the profit and loss accounts of Tripoli Power show that these stations had worked at a loss of £L 13,515 in the period February 1, 1956 to March 31, 1958. The bad service and loss of profits are

TABLE A.21   Financial Results of Tripoli Power, 1957 and 1958

(£L)

			1957	1958
Expenditure				
Operation costs including management			656,000	644,493
Capital charges (interest, depreciation, etc.)			200,000	143,455
Total			856,000	787,948
Income	*Units Sold*	*Rate (mills.[a])*		
Irrigation	12,922,133	8.291[b]	107,142	111,524
Municipal waterworks	2,689,573	13.4	36,308	15,970
Street lighting	689,759	21/27	13,085	—
Industrial	6,899,023	23/25	182,209	229,363
Domestic	15,784,830	27/29/31/33	435,198	484,924[e]
Miscellaneous (meter rents, etc.)			50,999	91,420
Rounding			2	
Total			824,943	933,201
Surplus or deficit of income over expenditures			−31,057	+145,253

[a] Rates variable due to minimum charges and variations in and out of Tripoli.
[b] Power for irrigation was sold at less than the cost of production and distribution.
[e] Includes street lighting.

undoubtedly due to the difficulties the undertaking has been experiencing in recent years, and once new generating units are installed at Tripoli and the new electricity corporation takes charge, the stations at Misurata andHoms should be better managed.

Table A.22 below sets out information that the mission was able to obtain from official sources and personal visits about these and other power stations in Tripolitania. The mission experienced considerable difficulty in obtaining official statistics in the province.

Power Stations in Cyrenaica and the Fezzan

Details of installed capacity and sales of power stations in Cyrenaica are set out in Table A.23. All these stations are owned and operated by the provincial government.

TABLE A.22   Other Power Stations (Tripolitania)

Location	Installed capacity (in KW)	Remarks
Misurata	256	7 units, mostly old.
Garian	150	Distribution poor.
Giado	130	112 KW unit good. Distribution poor. Requires additional 120 KW capacity.
Jefren[a]	46 } 168	{ Two 84 KW units new. Old plant at Rumia.
Sabratha	48 } 150	{ 150 KW military plant used for pumping only. Old sets transferred from Garian.
Zuara	135	Five old units. Needs additional 120 KW capacity and improvements to distribution system.
Cussabat	91	Units new.
Ten small stations	251	Some of these need enlargement, e.g., Sirte requires 60 KW additional; Tarhuna, 250 KW additional; Zliten, 150 KW additional.

[a] At the main power station at Jefren it was noticed that one of the new 84 KW units had been out of action for more than two months, and that the second unit worked for 12 hours a day only, although the new local hospital depends entirely on the station and takes most of its power. On enquiry locally and at Tripoli it was learned that ownership of the plant was vested in the Department of State Property, while repairs were carried out by the Nazirate of Public Works. The State Property Department found it difficult to obtain funds (£L 200) for the repairs, and these were consequently delayed, although it appeared that they could have been carried out cheaply and quickly in the well-equipped workshops of Tripoli Power.

It will be seen that many of the smaller stations are to be equipped with plant removed from the bigger stations when they are enlarged, as was done in the past. A plan is being considered to supply some of the smaller towns by high tension lines from the bigger stations, and action on these lines is recommended when feasible. A feature of the Beida scheme is that provision is made in it for transmission lines at 6,600 volts and 11,000 volts to Cyrene, Susa and Lubrok, and some pumping stations.

About 50 percent of the power supplied in Cyrenaica is consumed by domestic users, mainly for house lighting (see Table A.24). This

TABLE A.23 Capacity and Sales of Power Stations in Cyrenaica

Location	Serviceable installed capacity in KW	1957/58 output in millions KWH	Remarks
Benghazi	6,150	16.840	See Chapter 11.
Derna	928	2.428)	Plant mostly from the old
Barce	830	1.717)	station at Benghazi.
Tobruk	600	1.551	Old units (1944/45).
Beida			
(old system)	730	0.551	Plant to be transferred to Tobruk Agedabia
(new system)	1,650	—	Susa, etc. Completed June 1959.
Susa	80	0.551	Current largely supplied from Beida.
El Abiar	50	0.067	New power station under erection.
Agedabia	264	0.099	Units recently installed.
Un Saad	140	0.036	Units recently installed.
El Gubba	100	0.030	Units recently installed.
Battisti	20	0.014	Units recently installed.
Solluk	100	0.022	New building, new plant.
Cyrene	nil	0.121	There are now no units at Cyrene or Messa.
Messa	nil	0.043	Current supplied from Beida.

results in heavy concentration of demand at peak periods, especially as government departments draw most of their supplies at the same time.

No information was available from official sources on power generating capacity in the Fezzan. The new (1958) power station at Sebha has a capacity of about 326 KW and the station at Hon about 50 KW. No other generating plant was seen by the mission.

Management of Electric Supply Undertakings

The mission has suggested in Chapter 11 that the new electricity corporation should in due course take over the management of all public electric supply undertakings in Tripolitania and ultimately throughout Libya. At present most of the undertakings in Tripolitania are under the management of municipalities and are heavily subsidized.

TABLE A.24 Breakdown of Output by Users (Cyrenaica)

(As projected for 1959)

	Industrial		Street lighting		Water pumping		Government and military		Domestic	
	KWH mn.	Revenue in £L	KWH mn.	Revenue in £L	KWH mn.	Revenue in £L	KWH mn.	Revenue in £L	KWH mn.	Revenue in £L
Benghazi	2.330	34,950	0.600	6,000	2.000	30,000	1.460	36,500	6.020	150,550
Barce	0.885	1,702	0.064	639	0.172	3,448	0.400	12,000	0.240	7,211
Derna	0.148	2,965	0.168	1,683	0.104	2,076	0.200	6,000	0.876	26,276
Tobruk	0.012	231	0.115	1,150	0.075	1,500	0.167	5,000	1.071	32,119
Beida	0.035	706	0.135	1,350	0.098	1,966	0.133	4,000	0.283	8,478
Grid and small stations	—	—	0.053	530	0.020	400	0.130	3,861	0.148	4,129
Total	3.410	40,554	1.135	11,352	2.469	39,390	2.490	67,361	8.638	228,763

If the corporation takes charge, it will be put to the expense of employing staff to visit small installations, holding stocks or spare parts, carrying out repairs in its central workshops (or such regional workshops as may be set up) and collecting revenue. However, expenditure on all these heads is already being incurred at public expense, and if the corporation suffers any loss on account of the widespread duties it will be called upon to undertake, it could be reimbursed by the government.

The mission is confident that its recommendations will make for considerable savings on the upkeep of public utilities and will result in their longer life and more efficient service. Commercial management should avoid most of the limitations of governmental or municipal management, such as insufficient delegation of power to inspecting staff, delays in obtaining funds and (most important) employment of poorly qualified technical staff and mechanics because of the low rates of pay offered by government.

Statistics of Traffic and Equipment

The **Tripolitanian Railway** consists of 178 kilometers of trackage, and some ancient rolling stock as shown in Table A.25. Goods traffic is very light but fluctuates considerably from year to year. Passenger traffic has remained at a fairly constant figure since 1952 owing probably to low fares charged.

TABLE A.25   Rolling Stock of the Tripolitanian Railway

Year Built	Locomotives		Rail Cars	Passenger Coaches	Freight Wagons		
	Steam	Diesel			Covered	Open	Special
1890	7	—	—	—	—	—	—
1912	—	—	—	—	40	130	71
1920	—	—	—	12	—	—	—
1924	—	—	1	—	—	—	—
1939 or earlier	—	5	1	3ᵃ	—	—	—
Total	7	5	2	15	40	130	71

ᵃ 1st and 2nd class coaches.

Because of road competition, the railway has been running at a loss averaging £L 30,773 a year during the four years up to 1957/58 when the goods freight carried averaged only about 27,500 tons a year. The loss in 1958/59 was about £L 50,000. It has been found, for example, that dressed stone from the Aziza quarries, 25 miles from Tripoli, all now goes by road in spite of the fact that railway sidings run into the quarries. The cost of road transport is some 25 percent higher than rail transport to the rail depot in Tripoli, but the difference is more than offset by the cost of reloading and transport to the job sites in Tripoli from the depot and the quickness and convenience of road transport.

Passenger traffic is fairly high in areas not well served by road, and fares are low. Besides taking steps to bolster passenger revenue the government has sporadically tried to support rail revenue by, for example, transporting salt for shipment from the salt pans by rail and by other measures. In future it has been decided locally to transport salt by road in spite of the fact that there is direct rail communication between the salt pans and the port.

The Cyrenaica Railway consists of 164 kilometers of trackage and much ancient rolling stock as shown in Table A.26. Goods traffic is exceptionally light and decreasing in volume (only 9,058 tons moved in 1957/58), but passenger traffic has remained very steady over the last several years.

TABLE A.26 Rolling Stock of the Cyrenaica Railway

Year Built	Locomotives		Rail Cars	Passenger Coaches	Freight Wagons		
	Steam	Diesel			Covered	Open	Special
1929 & earlier	—	—	—	4	—	194	10
1939 & earlier	—	2[a]	—	—	—	—	—
1952	—	1	1	—	—	—	—
Total[b]		3	1	4	—	194	10

[a] One diesel locomotive out of service.
[b] No steam locomotives in service.

This railway has also been running at a loss averaging nearly £L 24,700 a year over the last 6 years, largely because of road competition. Passenger and parcel revenue exceeds goods revenue by more than 50 percent on an average, but even so this total revenue is relatively insignificant (£L 9,933 in 1957/58).

Possibilities of Extending the Railways

For the reasons explained in Chapter 12, the mission came to the conclusion that the existing, short-length railways cannot hope to compete with motor transport. It was suggested to us that long-haul freight by rail would be in a better competitive position and we considered whether there was sufficient traffic potential between Tripoli and Benghazi or between Tripoli and Tunis to the west, or Benghazi and Egypt to the east to justify joining the railways or extending them to the east or west. We found that, since the existing railways are about 1,000 kilometers apart and most of the intervening land is desert which cannot produce much traffic, the cost of joining the railways would have to be justified by the traffic operating between the settled areas of Tripolitania and Cyrenaica. At present the normal channel of trade in Libya is from the interior to the coast and vice versa and it seems fairly certain that such east-west trade as might arise in the future, between Tripolitania and Cyrenaica or between these provinces and Tunis to the west of Egypt to the east, could more cheaply be handled by coastal shipping or by road transport.

We examined in the same way the feasibility of developing the railways so that they would extend continuously from the Tunisian to the Egyptian border. The Italians appear to have once had some project in mind, and traces of railway embankments, including fully built railway stations, can be seen west of Zuara and east of Barce. But that was before the days of development of motor transport. The project would entail the construction of long lengths of railway line across deserts or "marginal" country which would provide few goods for export. The capital cost of construction (an estimated £L 3.0 million to join the railways, £L 3.7 million for an extension to the Egyptian border, £L 0.43 million for an extension to the Tunisian border) would be extremely high and could be only justified economically if potential traffic movements between the termini were also high (since there are few intermediate traffic possibilities).

There is no great traffic potential between Egypt or Tunisia and Libya since all three countries produce the same type of products. Similarly there is little exchange of trade between the provinces of Tripolitania and Cyrenaica, and what trade exists or may be expected could, in the future, be carried more economically by coastal shipping or by road. The mission therefore does not recommend any extensions of the existing railways. In making this recommendation the mission has been influenced by the fact that there is already a good road connection between Egypt and Tunisia, and that trade by a direct sea route could be developed, if sufficient traffic offered, without heavy capital expenditure.

Disposal of Railway Assets

If our proposal to close down the railways is accepted, it will still be necessary to retain certain sections of permanent way in the ports of Tripoli and Benghazi, and certain sidings used by the ports. The line between Benghazi and nearby quarries might be retained until the proposed harbor works are completed and, both at Tripoli and Benghazi, the right of way between ports and nearby quarries should be retained indefinitely. Railway operation in this very limited area could be managed by the port authorities, as is done at present beyond the exchange sidings.

The fixed assets (land and buildings) of the existing railways are considerable. In Tripoli the railway station, yards and workshops occupy more than 390,000 sq. meters of valuable land and would provide an excellent site for a developing industry. The residential buildings, sheds, etc., have a high letting value because of their central location. If the railways close down, all fixed railway assets could be valued and sold or leased to very great advantage. The same remarks apply to the fixed assets of the Cyrenaica railway, though these are much less valuable. The surplus moveable assets of the railways (rolling stock, machinery, plant, etc.) are of little value and could be auctioned.

ANNEX XVIII ROADS AND ROAD TRANSPORT

Road Expenditures

The types of roads and their lengths in Libya are shown in the following table:

TABLE A.27   Lengths of Roads in Libya[a]

(kilometers)

Administration	Black-top	Macadam	Tracks	Total
Tripolitania	860	342	1,349	2,551
Cyrenaica	482	—	1,921	2,403
Fezzan	10[b]	—	1,433	1,443
Federal Government	1,951	—	1,252[c]	3,203

[a] Does not include roads within major cities and towns.
[b] Approximate figure which includes roads in or near oases.
[c] About 600 kms. of track are now being converted to a black-top road.

The expenditure on these roads during the last year is shown in the following table:

TABLE A.28   Expenditure on Libyan Roads

(£L '000)

Administration	1954/55	1955/56	1956/57	1957/58	1958/59[a]
Tripolitania	233	170	182	140	184
Cyrenaica[a]	35	45	40	78	54
Fezzan[b]	6	4	4	3	3
Federal Government	201	205	169	157	166
Aid agencies	8	191	895	805	495
Total	483	615	1,290	1,183	902[b]

[a] Estimated.
[b] Excluding expenditure on the Fezzan road to Sebha.

489

No clear distinction has been made in the government accounts between expenditure on new construction and on maintenance. But there is no doubt that the bulk of the expenditure recorded in Table A.28 (including that financed by the development agencies) is attributable to maintenance, much of it deferred maintenance, and to restoration of war damage.

Road Maintenance

The provision to be made for road maintenance depends very largely on the "life" of the road surface under the prevailing soil, climate and traffic conditions of the localities through which it runs. Experience elsewhere, based on a study of past expenditures on maintenance, indicates that the life may be anything from 5 to 14 years or more. In Libya no help can be obtained from the accounts, since maintenance expenditure is not shown separately from capital expenditure. But from technical considerations it appears the surfaces should have a fairly long life as most conditions are favorable, viz., good soil for bases, low rainfall (or none) in most areas, and light traffic (but not too little). Adverse factors are generally fairly long leads for the best quality of local road stone (which is of itself of not very good quality), difficulty due to drifting sand in some areas, unsuitable soil for berms (verges), and high cost of maintaining road gangs in desert regions.

The mission has assumed, on the evidence available, a road surface life of 10 years. Surface dressing would cost about £L 1,000 per kilometer for a 5 meter wide surface, and the ten-year average annual maintenance allowance for this would be £L 100 per kilometer. To this is to be added the cost of patch repairs; maintenance of berms (verges), removal of sand drifts in many sections; maintenance of road signs, kilometers and boundary stones, etc., ditches, and masonry structures (very few in Libya); repairs to occasional flood damage; upkeep of cantoneria; and other miscellaneous maintenance work. The cost of this would not be less than £L 25 per kilometer. A seal coat will also be necessary once in 10 years after surface dressing has been done (£L 75 per kilometer). Total cost will therefore be £L 200 per kilometer a year for a five-meter wide surfaced road.

For greater or less surfaced width the allowance should be increased or decreased by £L 35 a year for each meter of difference in width, the allowance for a three-meter surfaced road being £L 130. A maintenance allowance of £L 25 per kilometer might be sufficient, but the allowance would best be fixed by trial and error after a proper system of accounting is adopted as mentioned below.

On the basis of these recommendations, the cost of such maintenance will be roughly as follows:

	(£L)
Tripolitania	219,700
Cyrenaica	129,500
Fezzan (ignoring 900 kms. not now maintained)	12,800
Federal Roads	421,300
Total	783,300
Fezzan Road (after 1965)	120,000

To these figures should be added 5 percent for repairs and carriage of ordinary small tools and plant and 10 percent for the purchase, repairs and carriage of heavy plant (boilers, sprayers, scrapers, graders, etc.,) and contingent expenditures—making a total budget provision of about £L 900,000 a year up to 1965. This provision should not be reduced if the existing valuable road assets are to be preserved.

Road maintenance allotments are best fixed by taking into account past expenditures on maintenance, which include increases in expenditure incurred from time to time over a period of years to cope with wear from increased traffic. If only to facilitate budgeting, therefore, it is desirable that Libya should follow the normal rule, i.e., classify as "capital" expenditure in the road accounts only that portion of the cost of work done which represents the increased value of the road as an asset, the rest of the cost being chargeable to "repairs and maintenance." If the road is restored to its original condition when new, all the expenditure incurred is chargeable to "repairs and maintenance."

The Fezzan Federal Road

It came to the notice of the mission that a "rate contract" had been let for the construction of about 600 kms. of black-top road to follow roughly the alignment of the desert track from a point on the coastal road 120 kilometers south of Misurata to Sebha in the Fezzan. The contract was not based on any instrument survey of the alignment from which a bill of quantities of the various kinds of work to be done could be prepared. In these circumstances a rate contract based on guessed-at quantities is little more than a gamble. If, moreover, the tendered rates depart widely from the normal rates (which was actually the case in the tender documents seen), a contract let in this manner is open to serious objection.

For example, the mission found that one of the rates accepted for bituminous surfacing was much less than the cost of the specified quantity of bitumen alone, excluding the cost of stone, rolling and labor. The mission also observed that, if the actual quantities of some of the items of work done differed appreciably from those shown in the notice inviting tenders, the successful contractor would stand to gain or lose a considerable sum of money. This gain or loss might conceivably amount to more than £L 300,000 because of the abnormal rates for ordinary types of work written into the contract.

It is obvious that it is bad in principle for government to enter into a contract of this nature. It is not clear why no technical representative of one of the development agencies was on the board when tenders were considered. The mission hopes that, in the interests of Libya, the final bill for the contract work will be kept within reasonable limits; it is already clear that it will greatly exceed the tendered amount of £L 1,896,000.

The mission was not able to appreciate the reason for letting the contract before the road was surveyed as the work will take three years to complete in any case and a few months delay for a survey would not have made much difference.

Road Administration

As discussed in Chapter 12, the mission considers that the Federal Roads Department should not in future execute its own road works. On the other hand, the mission suggests that the Ministry of Transport and Communications should retain over-all responsibility for federal roads and for all other road works toward which federal contributions of funds have been made. The Director General of the Federal Roads Department would be a member of the standing committee of directors envisaged by the mission, and this committee would determine road and road traffic standards, cost account codes, codes of practice and so forth for common adoption.

It is mentioned in Chapter 12 that, in the mission's opinion, provincial and federal road projects may not always be adjusted at the technical level to mutual advantage. The mission saw several examples of such apparent lack of coordination. This and other such problems relating to other provinces could be discussed by the director's committee, and the Director General, Federal Roads, could comment on provincial proposals, enabling the committee to make recommendations to the general advantage of Libya as a whole.

Consequent on the proposals mentioned above, the Director General, in consultation with the provincial directors, would *approve* all estimates for road projects financed or partly financed by the federal government. He would also be responsible himself for *sanctioning* all estimates prepared by the provincial directors for federal road works, and have power to decide on the agency for their execution. This agency might be the roads department of the provincial Nazirate of Public Works, or if that department is not considered technically competent, the Director General should be free to propose other arrangements for carrying out surveys, preparing estimates and executing some or all federal road works financed in whole or part from federal grants.

The Director General will, under this proposal, require adequate technical and office staff both to deal with business of the standing committee and to inspect federal works during execution, examine estimates and check expenditures. His staff will have to do all the initial work in preparing draft standards for the consideration of the director's committee and in bringing the standards (binding over the whole of Libya) to their final form.

TABLE A.29   Privately Owned Motor Vehicles in Circulation, 1955–59

Type	1955/56	1956/57	1957/58	1958–59[a]
Private cars, taxis etc.	9,751	11,785	10,233	13,214
Trucks	3,851	5,542	7,077	9,021
Trucks with trailers	1,071	1,211	1,934	1,639
Tankers, water and fuel	59	121	206	341
Buses	134	150	253	307
Motor cycles	2,631	3,714	4,075	4,828

[a] Estimated.

Note: Full information was not available for Cyrenaica, and some of the figures included in the table are based on estimates obtained from other than official sources, but tax revenue suggests that there is no serious error in the figures.

Road Transport Statistics

Table A.29 has been compiled from the limited figures available showing motor vehicles (other than government owned vehicles) in circulation.

The number of government owned vehicles could not be ascertained with any exactitude. An indication of the growth in the use of motor vehicles can be obtained from the fuel consumption statistics, but allowance must be made for the fact that not all this fuel is consumed by motor vehicles.

TABLE A.30   Fuel Consumption in Libya (Commercial)

(long tons)

Type of fuel	1955	1956	1957	1958
Motor spirit	13,150	15,986	21,407	26,280
Diesel fuel	895	1,259	1,451	1,841

No statistics were seen on sizes of vehicles, although the system of registration and licensing adopted in Tripolitania is very elaborate (too elaborate for practical use) and it should have been possible to extract such statistics from the records. It is recommended that throughout Libya a common system of registration and licensing be adopted, based on the British or some other system which is not too elaborate, and that the statistical information tabulated should (as in the British system) indicate sizes or tonnage of trucks so that a true picture of the tonnage in circulation can be obtained. Motor registrations and licensing should be transferred to the police department.

A traffic census should also be taken periodically by the road authorities, with estimates of tonnage, as such information can be a useful guide in determining road improvement needs. Such traffic counts as were seen by the mission gave no clear picture of the road use as they were not related to types of vehicles, or to seasonal movements of goods, and were in the nature of random individual samples of unclassified vehicles taken on one day of the year only at each checking point.

Bus fares are low on the whole, as indicated in Table A.31, and the general condition of the buses, except for some old stock still operating indicates good maintenance.

TABLE A.31 Bus Fares

Service	Kilometers	Fare (£L)
Tripoli-Misurata	210	0.450
Tripoli-Cussabat	130	0.310
Tripoli-Zuara	110	0.270
Tripoli-Benghazi	1,050	2.250
Tripoli-Town (inside city walls)	—	0.010
Tripoli-Town (suburbs)	—	0.020

ANNEX XIX *BENGHAZI HARBOR*

There was a port at Benghazi in ancient Greek and Roman times, but it is believed that the Turks were the first in modern times to build a small harbor for the protection of shipping. The Italians later built a mole (shown as the Italian Mole in the plan facing page 242 of the Main Report) as an extension of the mole protecting the Turkish Harbor. Later, in an endeavor to provide a deep harbor fit to take naval vessels, they built in sequence the Outer Mole (1929-34), the Giuliana Mole on a reef to the East and the Central Mole (1937). The Outer Mole was not well designed and began to show signs of weakness during, or shortly after, construction. The naval port never functioned satisfactorily, and its further development was not pursued by the Italians.

War damage, storms and defects in the original design all contributed to the failure now observed in the Outer and Central Moles. The main defect was the absence of suitable breakwaters along the Outer Mole (except for the first 800 feet which are undamaged), and the present position is that very little of the last 2,300 feet of this mole remains above sea level. With the failure of the Outer Mole, the sea began to attack the Central Mole (built to an even lighter design).

Investigations have shown that disintegration was *not* due to any settlement of the foundations, but to the pounding action of storms which attacked the wall at its main joint near sea level, pushed or sucked the upper parts out of position and ultimately tumbled them into the sea. At the same time the sea forced its way into the continuous joints in the substructure in the form of high velocity jets, and these jets, together with the imprisoned air, set up bursting effects which caused progressive deterioration. The same bursting effect of imprisoned air may be seen in action today on the Central Mole; this was reported to be in fairly good repair in 1947, but the western 700 feet are now in imminent danger of collapse.

The British Admiralty spent considerable sums during and after the war in an attempt to save part of the Outer Mole, but their efforts were unavailing. In 1955 a firm of consulting engineers was appointed "to advise on the reconstruction of the port," and they submitted in

1956 a scheme estimated to cost £L 5.63 million. This scheme provided for abandoning the Outer Mole and consequently the outer harbor (the Italian naval port). The scheme was not accepted by the provincial government who asked for a revised scheme which would not "reduce the size of the harbor," together with some other modifications. The consulting engineers then submitted a scheme (June 1957) which included the outer harbor, but the estimated cost went up to £L 7.03 million. They pointed out that they had been instructed to provide a port reconstruction and not a port development scheme and expressed doubts on the necessity for a large port to serve the small hinterland behind Benghazi.

The problem of financing a project that would cost more than £L 7 million presented considerable difficulties. In the meantime nothing has been done to save the Central Mole which is rapidly disintegrating at its outer end. This mole will have to be repaired before any major new construction is taken in hand. The development scheme proposed by the mission and illustrated in Chapter 12 is tentatively estimated to cost about £L 1½ million. It involves the dredging and reconstruction of the middle harbor which is in use today.

Under this scheme, and included in the cost, some work can be done toward improving the amenities of the sea front by providing a sandy beach between the Cathedral Mole and the cathedral itself. No provision has been made for sheltering tourists ships, as accommodation for these has been suggested at Ras el Hilal. If the port is developed as now proposed, the mission considers it will be able to handle more than three times the present cargoes. There would also be room for further development, as indicated in the outline plan, which would provide for a much greater volume of cargo.

ANNEX XX *MINOR PORTS AND COASTAL SHIPPING*

Minor Ports

There are about a dozen minor ports along the coast of Libya, most of which have existed since early Greek and Roman times. Only two of these ports (Derna and Tobruk) have harbors of any size for sheltering ships: in all other cases, ocean-going ships of even moderate size *always* had to discharge from open anchorages. It is necessary to emphasize this because the Italians used the minor ports along the coast quite extensively in the days of their occupation, when they found it unsafe to use the roads in the interior for military supplies. Local opinion now mistakenly assumes that there were harbors at most of these ports.

Following are notes (with main emphasis on the harbor) relating to ports visited by members of the mission:

> *Zuara.* Small vessels of 9 to 12 feet draft could use the harbor until it was damaged. In 1951 a gap was noticed near the root of the Northern Mole as a result of which the quay has lost its usefulness. Silting at the quay prevents the approach of ships and only the smallest types of boats can use it.
>
> *Homs.* A mole shelters small craft which secure to a small wooden pier.
>
> *Zliten.* No harbor. Small vessels with local knowledge can shelter from east and north-west winds inside a reef parallel with the coast.
>
> *Misurata.* A pier sheltered by some reefs was rebuilt a few years ago, but is already beginning to fail from lack of maintenance and use. There are many uninhabited Italian military buildings in the port area five kilometers from the town of Misurata. No one appears to live in the area.
>
> *Buerat el Hsun.* Wooden pier (damaged since 1946), which is sheltered by some reefs, can take vessels from 6 to 10 feet draft.
>
> *Sirte.* Remains of moles of ancient port (Aspis) can be seen. Harbor silted, but there is evidence that it never was of great depth.
>
> *Tolmeta.* There was a jetty (sheltered by a reef) in 1947, but it has since disappeared. Small vessels (draft up to 8 feet) can approach

to 150 feet of the shore. Small boats with local knowledge can land on the beach.

Susa. There is an old harbor behind a small promontory and a little jetty. This can be used only by small boats and could never take ships of any size.

Ras el Hilal. A damaged concrete pier extends about 600 feet southeast from the head of the bay. The Ras shelters ships from northerly winds, and large ships can come in close to the shore.

Derna. The harbor lies between two moles and was formerly accessible to vessels drawing 16 feet, but it has always been subject to silting, probably from the nearby Wadi Derna. Appreciable expenditure has been incurred in recent years in repairing the moles and dredging (£L 64,000), but the silting difficulty remains and could probably only be permanently solved by directing attention to the Wadi. The cargo handled in the period 1952-57 averaged 4,203 tons a year, of which about 20 percent was military cargo. The number of animals shipped from the port annually in the same period varied from 28,437 head to 521 head.

Tobruk. A fine natural harbor three miles long and well sheltered from all winds except from the east near the entrance. There are seven jetties (mostly in need of repair) with a maximum depth alongside of 17 feet, but vessels of any size can be worked in the harbor by lighters. The cargo handled averaged 49,551 tons a year in the period 1953-57, but 34,179 tons of this was military cargo. The hinterland is very poor and practically all the trade concerns Tobruk itself.

To restore Zuara, Homs, and Susa would cost £L 103,000, as ascertained after an engineering survey in 1956. The mission recommends that only Zuara should be restored, but the essential maintenance of all the minor ports should be undertaken regularly every year as explained in Chapter 12.

Coastal Shipping

The use made by the Italians of the minor ports, mainly for military purposes, encouraged the development of some coastal trade and this trade continued after the last war. It is on record that in 1947 there were regular steamer calls at Misurata, Sirte, Tolmeta, Susa and Derna on the Tripoli-Benghazi-Tobruk run, and occasional calls at Buerat el Hsun. By 1951 most of this trade had ceased, *not* apparently because of deterioration in the facilities provided by the ports (as there was no very great deterioration between 1947 and 1951), but because the coastal road had captured the traffic.

Enquiries made by the mission at Tripoli and Benghazi revealed that, although transport by road was more expensive in the first cost, it was so much quicker, more convenient and reliable (with fewer breakages), and less subject to the nuisance of filling out forms and customs vexations, that most consignors were prepared to pay the extra cost. For example, one trader said he sent a consignment of goods from Tripoli to Benghazi by ship. The cost was £L 136, on which he got 15 percent rebate as he was a shipping agent. Net cost therefore was £L 115.6. The cost of sending the same consignment by road was £L 125, but sending by ship involved so many delays, breakages and so much form filling that he decided to send no more consignments by sea. The main difficulty, however, is that generally very small quantities of cargo are offered, and it is not worth while for coasters to put in at the ports for this.

Idris and Benina Airports

Idris airport, situated about 28 kilometers from Tripoli by a good road, has a main runway more than 7,000 feet long which has recently been improved. Runways, taxiways and aprons will take the largest modern piston-engined planes and some jet-powered planes, although not the largest. The terminal apron will have to be extended if there is appreciable growth in traffic. Regular services connect Idris with Rome, London, Amsterdam, Brussels, Paris, Tunis, Malta, Cairo and West Africa.

Monthly aircraft movements handled by Idris airport average about 3,650 in the summer and some 200 less during the winter. Most of these movements arise from United States instrument flights from the nearby Wheelus Air Base (1,300) and Royal Air Force flights from Idris itself (800). The equipment for the airport includes full lighting to ICAO specifications, war-time high frequency point-to-point transmitters (being gradually replaced) and a stand-by 150 KW diesel power-generating plant. Air traffic control is assisted by the loan of staff for radar control and the contribution of radio equipment from the U.S. Air Force at Wheelus Base. The R.A.F. have also lent radio equipment, so that at present there is satisfactory control of all movements.

It is difficult to forecast the growth of civilian air traffic. Both Idris and Benina have been important refueling stops on intercontinental routes, but this traffic is likely to fall off with the general adoption of long-range aircraft. Terminal and stage-route traffic is linked with the economic development of Libya, oil operations and the growth of tourist traffic. The number of passengers carried at Idris has grown from 22,900 in 1955 to an estimated 80,000 in 1959, and if this growth is maintained, an expenditure of £L 150,000 on improvements to the apron and hard standings will be necessary by 1961/62.

Training flights at the Wheelus Base and the activities of the R.A.F. at Idris are both expected to increase, and with a prospective increase in civilian air services as well the airport will need additional equipment, including the following items:

501

	Estimated Cost in £L
Purchase of channel recorders and VHF equipment	13,000
Purchase of airfield radar equipment	60,000
Replacement of existing (obsolescent) HF transmitters	30,000

Since the need for some of this equipment arises largely from the growth of traffic which was not contemplated when the existing agreements between Libya, the U. S. and the U.K. were entered into, we have assumed that its installation will be largely financed by direct foreign grants.

The main runway at *Benina* has been built to a lighter specification (L.C. No. 30) than that at Idris, but at present aircraft up to the weight of 44 tons are being accepted. Passenger traffic has increased from 7,000 in 1954/55 to 10,300 in 1958/59, but apart from expenditure on maintenance and air control (let on contract to a private firm) only minor expenditures of about £L 23, 000 are indicated over the next five years on improving passenger handling, servicing and control facilities.

Neither Idris nor Benina require cross-wind runways at present.

Rules and Regulations

The Libyan Civil Aviation Law was enacted in 1956 and has led to increased efficiency in the implementation of international air regulations and the management of the airports by the provincial administrations. A great deal of work has also been done in the drafting of rules and regulations to implement the standards and recommendations of the International Civil Aviation Organization (ICAO). This has been particularly necessary in order to control the large number of internal flights (600 a month or so) of aircraft employed by the oil exploration companies in areas in which air to air firing, rocket firing, or guided missile firing may take place, or where training flights of the U.S.A.F. or practice bombing flights of the R.A.F. may occur.

ANNEX XXII IMPROVEMENTS IN HOSPITAL SERVICES

Cyrenaica

The Benghazi general hospital has accommodation for 453 patients and has facilities for the treatment of eye, E.N.T., V.D. and children's diseases apart from wards for medical, surgical and obstetrical and gynecological patients and a TB wing. The surgical block has recently been rehabilitated and equipped by LAJS, but the whole hospital is in urgent need of repairs, improvements and some special equipment and hospital furniture.

The Barce general hospital (100 beds) is located in an old Italian hotel building and needs some alterations and additions and a compound wall to make it suitable as a hospital unit. The alternative of building a new hospital on another site would be an expensive proposition (estimated cost £L 50,000) and is not immediately necessary.

The Messa general hospital (125 beds) is housed in buildings of the old Italian community center, and although not ideal as a hospital unit, is quite a satisfactory institution. If a hosptial is later constructed at Beida, it would be advisable to reduce the number of beds at Messa, and to enlarge Beida hospital by another 100 beds for general patients.

Derna has a large hospital of 246 beds which needs improvements to the existing buildings, some additions to ward accommodation for female patients, children and eye wards, new laundry and kitchen units, and some hospital equipment to modernize the X-ray department, the operation theater, and the surgical block. The separate TB wing also needs improvement and a compound wall.

The general hospital at Tobruk (159 beds) is at present located in an old garrison building, but is being shifted in the near future to a well-planned new hospital building nearing completion under the LAJS medical services rehabilitation program. The plan of this new hospital (120 beds) includes a water desalinization plant, a laundry and a modern kitchen unit.

The hospital at Agedabia (50 beds) needs much improvement, additional ward accommodation, a laundry, more surgical equipment with a shadowless operating-theater light and a small X-ray unit.

The town of el Abiar and the Kufra oasis each have small hospital units of 20-25 beds. It is difficult to find medical officers willing to serve at these isolated places despite special financial inducements. At present, one medical officer from Benghazi visits el Abiar two or three times weekly, and one doctor is posted at Kufra.

The TB hospital at Barce is located in a converted old farm. Some improvements have been carried out recently, but it needs a lot more rehabilitation. It should not be expanded if a new TB hospital is to be opened at Shahat. The mental hospital at Barce is very unsatisfactory both as regards buildings and equipment and staff. It needs a good deal of remodeling, additions and alterations to make it an acceptable mental hospital and it should be properly equipped and should be in medical charge of a trained Arabic-speaking psychiatrist. The present institution is hardly more than a detention place for mental patients.

TABLE A.32 Proposed Hospital Capital Expenditures, Cyrenaica,[a] 1960/61 to 1964/65

(£L '000)

Benghazi general	80
Barce general	25
Derna general	65
Agedabia	20
el Abiar	10
Kufra	10
Barce TB	5
Barce mental	20
Benghazi TB clinic	25
Benghazi isolation	50
Total	310

[a] See Chapter 14 for details on some expenditures listed here.

Tripolitania

The Tripoli government hospital has one director for the hospital group but there are separate buildings for the emergency surgery and traumatic department and chronic diseases wards. The main hospital has the following departments: medical, surgical, obstetric and gynecological, pediatric, ophthalmic, E.N.T., urological, infectious diseases, dermatology and leprosy, tuberculosis and casualty. A good E.N.T. block has recently been constructed, and poliomyelitis and blood transfusion departments organized. There is a well-equipped radiology department with two powerful X-ray units and two X-ray therapy units —for deep and superficial therapy. There is also a dental department with two chairs. The dermatological and pediatric departments need rehabilitation and more equipment.

The tuberculosis hospital in the suburb of Busetta has 166 beds and is well equipped. The building, which now houses the British Military Hospital at Tripoli, is expected to be handed over to the government of Tripolitania at some future date and this could well accommodate 200 tuberculosis patients as there is need for more TB beds in the country. Its conversion to a TB sanatorium would not entail large expenditure and it is located in ideal surroundings with a compound wall.

The general hospital at Misurata (172 beds), originally established during the Italian occupation, is the second largest hospital in Tripolitania and it is an excellent building and well equipped. A new kitchen unit and a new laundry have been installed by LAJS, which has also supplied some hospital equipment and furniture and is currently installing a new X-ray unit and air-conditioning plants for the operation theater and labor room, with 24 hours electrical supply. There were 3,042 admissions to this hospital during 1959, and a total of 474 operations were carried out. It is always full and needs some expansion. The Misurata hospital is a model of what a district hospital should be, although qualified nursing service is still lacking.

TABLE A.33   Proposed Hospital Capital Expenditures, Tripolitania,[a] 1960/61 to 1964/65

(£L '000)

Tripoli general, dermatology section	15
Gargaresh mental	100
Leprosarium	20
Busetta TB	50
Zawia	50
Gadames	15
Tripoli isolation	50
Total	300

[a] See Chapter 14 for details on some expenditures listed here.

The hospital at Zawia (80 beds) was originally established in 1944 by the Islamic Benevolent Association and was taken over by the government in 1955. Since then improvements have been carried out and more equipment provided. It still needs a good deal of rehabilitation and expansion by another 70 beds to make it a 150-bed hospital. It affords hospital coverage to the whole of the western province up to the borders of Tunisia but, because of lack of proper facilities and staff, a large number of patients have to be sent to Tripoli.

The hospital at Jefren (100 beds) has been recently constructed and equipped, financed by the LPDSA (cost £L 100,000). This is an excellently planned and equipped hospital, but like all other district hospitals suffers from inadequacy of doctors and nursing personnel, only two doctors being posted to each district hospital. The total admissions during 1958 were 1,511, and 181 operations were performed. The hospital serves the south Gebel areas.

The Fezzan

The central hospital at Sebha (88 beds) has been comparatively recently developed and was first opened up with 40 beds in 1953. It was remodeled and enlarged to 88 beds and provided with new equipment by LAJS at a cost of £L 28,000 during 1957/58. Considering the population of the Sebha area and the widely scattered areas of population in the province, no further increase in the number of beds appears to be necessary, but it does need some further improvements and the provision of a hospital laundry. The compound wall should also be

TABLE A.34   Proposed Hospital Capital Expenditures, Fezzan, 1960/61 to 1964/65

(£L '000)

Sebha central (including TB wing)	40
Brak	10
Gat	10
Hon	10
Murzuk	20
Total	90

raised and completed. There is a separate building for the tuberculosis or contagious diseases hospital (20 beds) which has been designed as two wings of 20 beds each but at present only one wing has been completed by the LPDSA (cost, £L 12,500). This should be completed and equipped and a compound wall, five feet high, should be provided.

The small hospitals at Brak (20 beds), Gat (18 beds) and Hon (20 beds) all need rehabilitation of buildings and equipment while at Murzuk a new hospital is necessary as the present one with 15 beds is totally unsuitable. A 20-bed hospital with facilities for emergency surgery would be sufficient.

Existing Facilities

Table A.35 shows the existing domestic water supply facilities in Tripolitania and Cyrenaica.

TABLE A.35   Pumped Domestic Water in Tripolitania and Cyrenaica

(In cubic meters)

Location	Maximum daily demand 1958/59	Average daily demand 1958/59	Reservoir capacity
Tripoli	37,000	20,000	6,800
Benghazi	9,090	8,181	10,909
40 small towns and villages in Tripolitania	7,970	—	n.a.
9 small towns and villages in Cyrenaica	—	3,616	6,469
Tobruk	—	454	978
Ain Debussia	1,818[a]	—	—

[a]Total capacity of existing plant.

Tobruk Water Supply

Drinking water for the garrison at Tobruk is brought by tanker ships from Bardia or Cyprus at great cost because the locally pumped water is saline. Water is also brought by truck from Marassas. Much infructuous exploratory work has been done in the neighborhood to find a source of potable water, and a scheme costing £L 1 million was at one time under consideration to bring water from Derna, 190 kilometers away. However, such heavy expenditure was clearly out of line with the benefits to be gained, and the development agencies have

508

recently been experimenting with devices to obtain potable water by treatment of the existing local saline source. The LARC is planning to install a demineralizer which will deliver about 22 cubic meters a day to the new hospital, and LPDSA has already installed a pilot plant which has successfully "desalted" the local water by a process of electrodialysis. The LPDSA is now installing an additional plant so that there would be enough capacity to supply the present needs of the community for water for all purposes.

The Ain Debussia springs have been developed to supply 1,818 cubic meters a day for the new administrative center at Beida. The spring has a yield which varies from 18,200 to 11,400 cubic meters a day, but the lift is high (1,700 feet) and the pumping and distribution charges are heavy. Under this scheme, use has been made of the partially completed Italian pipeline originally laid from a nearby source (Ain Mara) to the Barce Plain 160 kilometers away. By the middle of 1959, the Ain Debussia project was supplying 60,000 gallons of water a day to Beida, this being the total requirement at the present stage of the town's development. The cost of pumping that amount, not including amortization of the investment, is about 450 milliemes per 1,000 gallons. At full capacity of about 10 times the present amount, the cost would fall to about 200 milliemes per 1,000 gallons.

Tripoli Water Supply

The first and most urgent need in Tripoli is to sink new wells. The municipal proposal is apparently to sink these at the Bu Meliana source. No drop in water level at this source (or at any of the other municipal sources) has been recorded since the first well now in use was sunk in 1927, but there has been a marked increase in the salt content of the water, as shown by the following figures.

Source	Wells	Year	$CaCO_3$[a]	NaCl
Bu Meliana	3	1926	14.0	0.114
		1957	23.5	0.170
Porta Fornaci	6	1938	22.0	0.131
		1957	29.0	0.189

[a] $CaCO_3$ is shown in French degrees.

The mission has suggested in Chapter 7 that no increase in the pumping of water should be permitted in the neighborhood of Tripoli because of the observed fall in the water table and increase in salinity observed. It is recommended therefore that the municipality should consult the proposed federal Department of Geology and Hydrology before proceeding with its proposals, and that the federal government should finance the scheme that emerges on a part-loan, part-grant basis. Additional reservoir capacity also seems to be indicated. A provision of £L 300,000 has been included in the mission's five-year capital budget for urban water supplies in Tripolitania as a whole, and of this total amount £L 200,000 should be devoted to the above needs in Tripoli itself.

In order to keep a closer watch over the increase in salinity of the existing wells, the municipality should be required to make periodical tests in a "sentinel" well located between each of its three sources and the sea. If no abandoned well is available, a new well north of each source should be sunk as a "sentinel" and should go down to the second water table. It should be cased to five meters below ground level, but not to the bottom. If the "sentinel" well of any source shows a marked chloride increase, pumping from that source should be reduced. A similar scheme has been adopted by several towns in Florida, U.S.A., and has proved successful.